George Craig of Galashiels

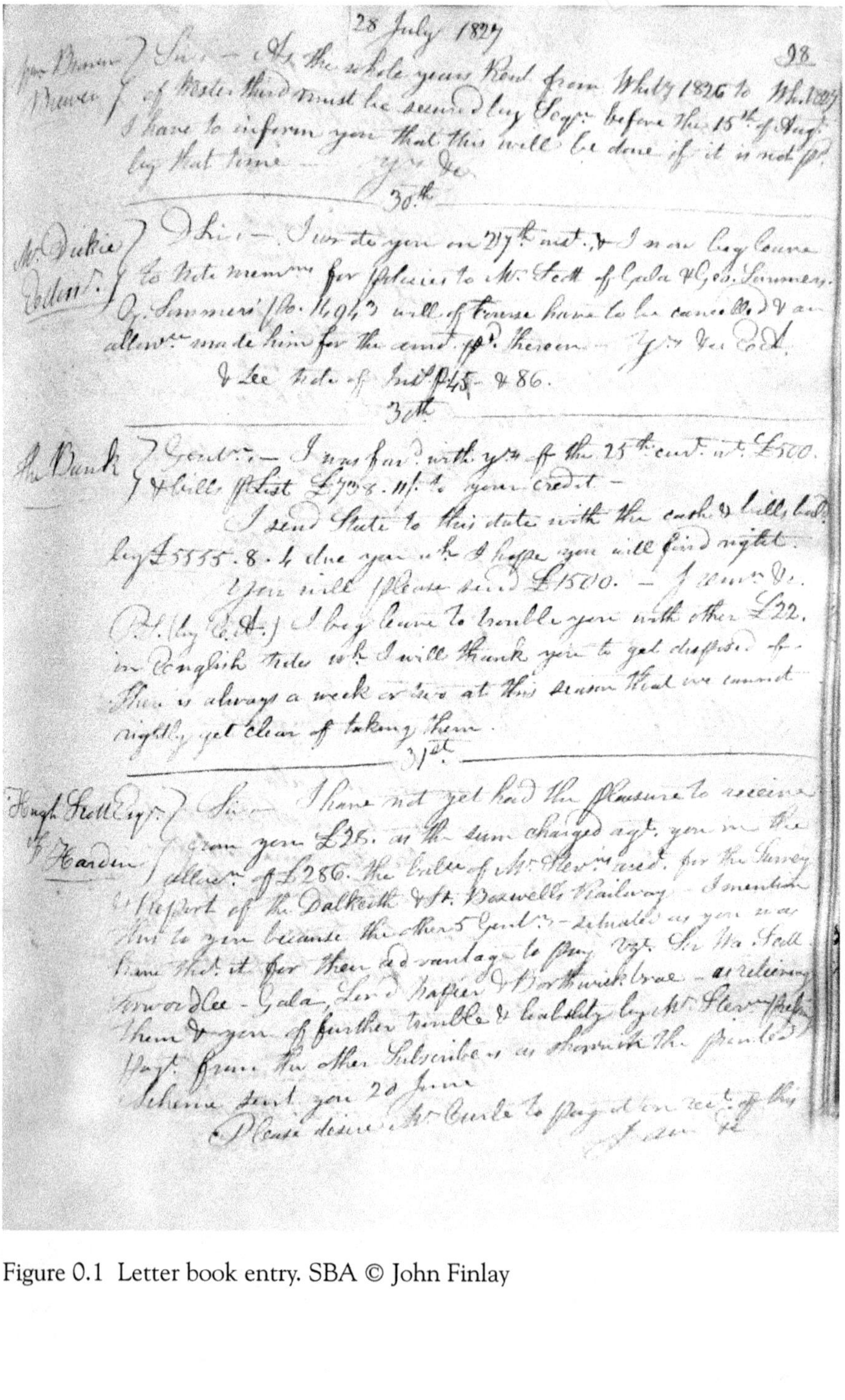
28 July 1827

98

[Brown] Sir — As the whole years Rent from Whit 1826 to Whit 1827 of Wester Third must be secured by Sequ. before the 15th of Augt. I have to inform you that this will be done if it is not pd. by that time — Yr &c

30th

Mr Dickie Edinr. — D Sir — I wrote you on 27th inst. & I now beg leave to note mem. for policies to Mr Scott of Gala & Geo. Summers. Geo. Summers' pol. 1494 will of course have to be cancelled & an allowce. made him for the amt. pd. thereon — Yr &c E.A.

& see note of Int. p 45 & 86.

30th

The Bank — Gentn. — I was favd. with yrs of the 25th curt. wt. £500. & bills p list £738. 11/- to your credit —

I send State to this date with the cash & bills bal. by £5555. 8. 4 due you wh. I hope you will find right.

You will please send £1500. — I am &c

P.S. (by E.A.) I beg leave to trouble you with other £22. in English notes wh. I will thank you to get disposed of — There is always a week or two at this season that we cannot rightly get clear of taking them.

31st

Hugh Scott Esqr. of Harden — Sir — I have not yet had the pleasure to receive from you £28. as the sum charged agt. you in the allowce. of £286. the value of Mr Stevn.'s acct. for the Survey & Report of the Dalkeith & St. Boswells Railway. I mention this to you because the other 5 Gentn. situated as you are have thot. it for their advantage to pay viz. Sir Wa. Scott as relieving Torwoodlee – Gala, Lord Napier & Borthwickbrae — as relieving them & you of further trouble & liability by Mr Stevn. [illegible] Wagt. from the other Subscribers as shown in the printed Scheme sent you 20 June

Please desire Mr Curle to pay it on rect. of this

I am &c

Figure 0.1 Letter book entry. SBA © John Finlay

George Craig of Galashiels

The Life and Work of a Nineteenth-Century Lawyer

John Finlay

EDINBURGH
University Press

Edinburgh University Press is one of the leading university presses in the UK. We publish academic books and journals in our selected subject areas across the humanities and social sciences, combining cutting-edge scholarship with high editorial and production values to produce academic works of lasting importance. For more information visit our website: edinburghuniversitypress.com

Grateful acknowledgement is made to the sources listed in the List of Illustrations for permission to reproduce material previously published elsewhere. Every effort has been made to trace the copyright holders, but if any have been inadvertently overlooked, the publisher will be pleased to make the necessary arrangements at the first opportunity.

Edinburgh University Press Ltd
13 Infirmary Street,
Edinburgh, EH1 1LT

First published in hardback by Edinburgh University Press 2023

Typeset in 10/12 Goudy Old Style by
IDSUK (DataConnection) Ltd

A CIP record for this book is available from the British Library

ISBN 978 1 3995 1483 5 (hardback)
ISBN 978 1 3995 1 484 2 (paperback)
ISBN 978 1 3995 1485 9 (webready PDF)
ISBN 978 1 3995 1486 6 (epub)

Contents

Figures

Acknowledgments

The world revealed by the letters of George Craig (1783–1843) is largely that of Sir Walter Scott who lived about two miles away: the Scottish Borders of the 1820s and 1830s. This was a rural society keenly developing its industrial base and Craig himself was at the heart of it. His correspondence has proved to be a rich resource. Living through the Industrial Revolution, Craig saw himself living in 'an age of adventure', yet some of the things he was ambitious to bring to Galashiels, such as the railway, remained just beyond his grasp.

Craig is a hugely interesting character but what particularly appeals about his story is that it is shared with people of every description, from weavers, shepherds and gamekeepers, to lairds, soldiers, bankers and insurance company managers. From his home in Galashiels, he ventured across miles of countryside as he spoke to landowners and tenants, attended fairs and made a substantial mark on the landscape through the works he instructed and the infrastructure developments he influenced.

For alerting me to what turned out to be Craig's letter books, I thank Greig McDonell, formerly of Iain Smith & Partners and now of Cullen Kilshaw. I am also grateful to James Pringle, 14th and present laird of Torwoodlee and Buckholm, for access to material in his possession and to the National Register of Archives (Scotland) for arranging this. The staff of the Scottish Borders Archive in Hawick have been extremely helpful, particularly Kathy Hobkirk and Amy Thomson, as have those in the National Records of Scotland and the National Library of Scotland. I am also grateful to Angela Schofield of the Advocates Library, Stephen Fairholme, Waveney Jenkins, John and Val Gray and John Ballantyne. My thanks to the editorial and production staff at the Edinburgh University Press who have been very helpful, efficient and accommodating.

I have been fortunate to have sole access to Craig's correspondence whilst preparing this book and it is pleasing that the volumes are now deposited in the Scottish Borders Archive. Their cataloguing was assisted by an ESRC Impact Acceleration Account for which I am grateful. Too many similar volumes, kept in solicitors' offices across Scotland, have sadly been lost over previous generations and the losses continue. If there is one thing that comes from this book, it is the plea that solicitors value their archives and do what they can to preserve them and place them in the public domain.

This book is dedicated to Greig McDonell who has been a friend for over thirty years.

Note on sources

This work is largely based on Craig's correspondence. Eight volumes of correspondence were found in the offices of Iain Smith & Partners, a firm which traced its roots back to nineteenth-century Galashiels before, in 2021, it was incorporated into the firm of Cullen Kilshaw. Sadly, the first volume has since been lost, an example of the fragility of historical sources when kept outside of archives.

The volumes were retained in the possession of William Rutherford (1805–1891), who became Craig's partner in 1836.[1] Alongside the letter books there was a cash ledger for the firm of Craig & Rutherford.[2] Rutherford was appointed senior magistrate when Galashiels became a police burgh in 1850, being re-elected in 1853 before retiring in 1856 and going on to continue his career in law and banking.[3] He had two sons, Frank (1832–1885) and Alexander (1830–1901), who became notaries and writers and founded the partnership of W.A. & F. Rutherford.[4] Alexander Rutherford also had two sons who became lawyers, William (1865–1949) and Frank (1875–1930).[5] The firm was still operating under the same name into the 1950s from premises in Channel Street in Galashiels. At some point subsequently the firm's papers came into the possession of Iain Smith & Partners. They now reside in the Scottish Borders Archive.

The volumes of correspondence cover the following periods:

Table 0.1

	Period	Folios	Archival reference
I	20 Oct 1819–23 Mar. 1821	375*	SBA/1303/1
II	26 Mar. 1821–19 Jun. 1822	253	SBA/1303/2

* Only photographs of a few folios survive.

[1] A copy of the first edition of Sir James Dalrymple of Stair, *Institutions of the Law of Scotland* (Edinburgh: Andrew Anderson, 1681), bears Rutherford's signature, dated 5 Jan. 1836.

[2] Scottish Borders Archive, SBA/1303/9. The ledger, extending beyond Craig's lifetime, bears to cover the period 1 Jan. 1836–14 Nov. 1856, although the entries only run to 1843. Earlier and later ledgers are referred to but apparently have not survived.

[3] R. Hall, *History of Galashiels* (Galashiels, 1898), 127.

[4] J. Finlay, ed., *Admissions Register of Notaries Public in Scotland 1800–1899* (Edinburgh: Scottish Record Society, 2018), no. 2873 (Frank Rutherford).

[5] Ibid., no. 4097 (William Rutherford) and no. 4544 (Frank Rutherford).

III	19 Jun. 1822–13 Mar. 1824	323	SBA/1303/3
IV	16 Mar. 1824–12 Jan. 1827	524	SBA/1303/4
V	13 Jan. 1827–24 Dec. 1829	495	SBA/1303/5
VI	25 Dec. 1829–28 Jul. 1834	500	SBA/1303/6
VII	28 Jul. 1834–21 Jul. 1837	509	SBA/1303/7
VIII	21 Jul. 1837–11 Feb. 1840	710**	SBA/1303/8

** There are three additional folios containing an excerpt from the *Edinburgh Courant* of 15 Mar. 1838 entitled 'Endowment of Scotch Church Question'.

Throughout this work, I have used the simple archival reference when citing Craig's letters. The letter books, written in more than one hand, were paginated and indexed during Craig's lifetime. That is not the case with some other examples of letter books from the period. Craig & Rutherfurd's Cash Book (SBA/1303/9) also survives for the latter period of Craig's life.

The letter books are not the only source for Craig's career. Some original letters survive beyond the copies in the letter books. There are also letters prior to 1819 which provide some details of Craig's earlier career. An outline of Craig's importance in Galashiels is given in Robert Hall's *History of Galashiels*.[6] Hall appears to have had good primary sources, despite his own comments that for the early part of the nineteenth century 'little of an authentic nature is to be found'.[7] This included the 'Unpublished Annals of the Parish' by Henry Sanderson (one of Craig's clients), a source which has sadly not been traced for the present study.

Quotations
Contractions are commonly used in the letter books. As a general rule, in any quotations from letters given in the text, these contractions have silently been lengthened to aid clarity.

[6] R. Hall, *History of Galashiels* (Galashiels, 1898).
[7] Ibid.

Abbreviations

ARNP	Admissions Register of Notaries Public, ed. J. Finlay
C&R	Craig & Rutherford
GCA	Glasgow City Archives, Mitchell Library
GUL	Glasgow University Library
HC	House of Commons
JP	Justice of the peace
LBC	Leith Banking Company
NLS	National Library of Scotland, Edinburgh
NRS	National Records of Scotland, Edinburgh
NSA	New Statistical Account of Scotland (1834–1845)
OSA	Old Statistical Account of Scotland (1791–1799)
RPCB	Rodger & Paterson Cash Book, Scottish Borders Archive
RPLB	Rodger & Paterson Letter Book, Scottish Borders Archive
RPS	Records of the Parliament of Scotland, ed. K. Brown
SBA	Scottish Borders Archive, Hawick
SSC	Solicitor(s) to the Supreme Courts of Scotland
TAB	Torwoodlee Account Book (held privately)
TNA	The National Archives, Kew
WS	Writer(s) to the Signet

Chapter 1

Introducing George Craig

> ... I have the counsel & backing of an admirable judge George Craig, writer, Galashiels, for whose judgment, sagacity, and even for whose taste I have much respect.
>
> Sir Walter Scott[1]

George Craig (1783–1843) was baron bailie of Galashiels in the Scottish Borders but is today paradoxically best known for being unknown despite having a bridge named after him. Who, then, was George Craig? That we now have a much better answer to that question is due to the discovery of Craig's letter books not long after the George Craig Bridge was opened in 2010. This book draws on this resource to reveal Borders life and legal practice in the period between 1821 and 1840.

Craig was a banker, a law agent and many things besides. This chapter will sketch out his life and working environment and highlight some of the major clients whose affairs feature prominently in his correspondence. Characteristic of Craig's life was his interaction with everyone, from the duke of Buccleuch and prominent landowners to weavers, shepherds and the parish poor. What has been left to us, in the papers of the firm Craig & Rutherford, illustrates an important era in the development of Galashiels but, as we shall see, Craig's reach went far beyond one small town.

FAMILY AND BACKGROUND

In 1717 William Craig and his wife, Margaret Donaldson, had a son, George (d. 1781).[2] George married Mary (or Marion) Paterson in Galashiels in December 1747.[3] He was given a ninety-nine-year lease of property by John Scott (1732–1785), sixth laird of Gala in 1778, at an annual rent of six shillings.[4] George, who became a member of the merchant community, had three sons: George jr (b. 1751),

---

[1] H. J. C. Grierson, ed., *Letters of Sir Walter Scott* (9 vols, London, 1932–1937), IX, 169, Sir Walter Scott/John Richardson, 4 Jul. 1825.

[2] NRS, Galashiels register of baptisms, CH2/1255/1/45. George was born on 29 Nov. and baptised on 1 Dec. 1717. He died on 4 Jun. 1781: Old parish registers, Deaths, Galashiels, Registration district 775/10, p. 314, digital image from NRS www.scotlandspeople.gov.uk.

[3] They married on 19 Dec. 1747: Old parish registers, Marriages, Galashiels, Registration district 775/10, p. 235.

[4] NRS, Court of Session, unextracted processes, CS235/K/6/4, Tack betwixt John Scott of Gala and George Craig, 1778.

William (1753–1803) and James (b. 1755). A court case in 1800, concerning the lease to this house, provides further hints as to the family background.[5] George jr, who had moved to Calcutta, claimed the lease, as heir to his father, with the support of his brother William. This was contested by their mother and brother James whose claim was based on a will made in 1781, in favour of the mother, which appears to have been invalid. George prevailed and it was William, probably as his assignee, who obtained the lease in 1801, although fraternal ill feeling seems to have subsisted on the part of James.

William married Jean Hall (b. 1753) in Stow in December 1781 and they were the parents of the George, born on 14 June 1783, who was their eldest child and is the subject of this book.[6] William was a law agent but also the agent for the earliest bank in Galashiels, a branch of the Leith Banking Company.[7] According to Robert Hall, the nineteenth-century historian of Galashiels, William, who became a notary public in 1779, was the first law agent in the village and highly regarded for his integrity and ability to settle local differences equitably.[8] Correspondence shows him active (with a Selkirk writer, George Rodger) in Court of Session litigation in 1795 and he is documented as receiving payment for notarial services in the 1780s.[9]

Both William and George had a close relationship with James Pringle (1759–1840), the ninth laird of Torwoodlee. Pringle inherited the estate from his uncle and built 'a handsome modern mansion', Torwoodlee House, having abandoned an intention to follow a career at the Scots bar.[10] Pringle's father, also James (d. 1776), was a writer to the signet (WS) who had been one of the principal clerks in the Court of Session (the same office Sir Walter Scott was later to hold).[11] Having succeeded to the estate in 1780, the young James devoted himself to improving his lands and to local affairs. He eventually became convenor of the county of Selkirk and, from 1827 to 1830, vice-lieutenant of the county. He was clearly a skilled agricultural improver. The judge Henry Cockburn (1779–1854)

---

[5] Scottish Borders Archive, Craig Letter Books, SBA/1303/5/233, Craig/Gala, 5 Apr. 1828; NRS, CS235/K/6/4. The letter books will be cited hereafter simply according to their archival reference.

[6] J. Finlay, ed., *Admission Register of Notaries Public, 1800–1899* [*ARNP 1800–1899*] (Scottish Record Society, 2018), no. 199. Craig had a sister, Alison (b. 1785) and a brother John (b. 1787) although nothing is known of them. There is no indication when his mother Jean, who was related to the Taits of Pirn, died. The writer R. G. Thomson in Melrose refers to a sum paid on account of 'the late Mrs William Craig' and 'the late Mrs Craig senior', by the sheriff clerk of Roxburgh from the Writers' Widows Fund (on which see infra): SBA/1303/5/400, Elliot Anderson/Robert G. Thomson, 10 & 12 Jul. 1833.

[7] R. Hall, *History of Galashiels* (Galashiels, 1898), 481.

[8] Ibid.; J. Finlay, ed., *Admission Register of Notaries Public, 1700–1799* [*ARNP 1700–1799*] (2 vols, Scottish Record Society, 2012), II, no. 2190.

[9] SBA, D/45/12/32, William Craig/Rodger, 15 Sep. 1795; ibid., Rodger Cash Book, D/44/1/5 (2 Dec. 1783).

[10] R. Chambers, *The Picture of Scotland* (Edinburgh, 1827), 139.

[11] Alexander Pringle, *The Records of the Pringles or Hoppringills of the Scottish Border* (Edinburgh, 1933), 222–3. 'WS' signifies 'writer to the signet' a member of the Society of Writers to the Signet based in Edinburgh.

later commended the development of the Torwoodlee estate, noting that the laird having 'planted judiciously, proved very successful'.[12]

William, a kirk session elder, was close to another important local figure, Reverend Dr Robert Douglas, minister of Galashiels.[13] In 1791, following the death of the session clerk John Graham, it was discovered that he had failed to make entries into the kirk session minute book and that the register of baptisms, marriages and burials was very incomplete from 1780. The minister, new session clerk and William Craig, undertook to procure 'certain intelligence of the Birth of such Children, whose parents had paid for Registrating them, also for prevailing upon all others to Registrate their Children who may have hitherto neglected it'.[14] Without these efforts, George's year of birth may have remained unknown.

The burgh's modest status is evident in the minute recording the creation of the Galashiels Friendly Society in 1802.[15] In the list of subscribers, George Craig's name as a member appears second only to that of the Rev. Douglas who was aged fifty-five at the time. Douglas was a man of considerable means and his promotion of the Friendly Society was typical of his concern for his parishioners. Its purpose was to build up a fund, through entry money and voluntary contributions, which could be used to relieve the circumstances of members in distress who had a reasonable prospect of being able to return to work and self-sufficiency. Craig's early association with Douglas, in this and other ventures, reflected his local status.

It was not uncommon in the legal profession for sons to follow in their father's footsteps and, at the age of twenty, this is what Craig did, taking over the business when his father died in 1803. In 1829, in writing a reference for David Thomson from Galashiels who had moved to Alnwick, he referred to having been 'in business habits with him both as land agent and banker for upwards of twenty-six years'.[16] There are unfortunately no details of his apprenticeship, but it would not have been unusual for him to have apprenticed as a writer to his father which seems likely since he also took over his father's bank agency. In Edinburgh, Glasgow or Aberdeen the indentures of apprenticeship would have been recorded with a local society of writers, such as the Royal Faculty of Procurators in Glasgow or the Society of Advocates in Aberdeen. In Galashiels, there was no equivalent society that had developed the same level of organisation or control over the profession. There is, however, a contract from the early 1770s in which the 'The Practitioners of the Law Belonging to the Shires of Roxburgh, Selkirk, Peebles, and Berwick' came together to create a widows' fund.[17] This organisation's records

[12] *Circuit Journeys by the late Lord Cockburn* (2nd edn, Edinburgh, 1889), 51.
[13] He became an elder prior to November 1791: NRS, CH2/1255/2/157 (20 Nov. 1791). The minute book is incomplete and the date of appointment not recorded.
[14] NRS, CH2/1255/2/158.
[15] R. Hall, *History of Galashiels*, 81.
[16] National Library of Scotland [NLS], Letters to Scott, MS 3910, fo. 252r, George Craig/Richard Robson, Alnwick Castle, 10 Oct. 1829.
[17] See J. Finlay, '"Tax the attornies!" Stamp duty and the Scottish legal profession in the eighteenth century' 34 (2014) *Journal of Scottish Historical Studies*, 141 at 147.

do not survive, but Craig regularly contributed to the 'Writers Widows Fund' via the sheriff clerk of Roxburghshire in Jedburgh, indicating the continuance of an insurance fund for widows and dependents.[18] There was also an annual meeting and Craig refers in 1825 to 'the Writers meeting at Kelso'.[19] Members had to pay entry money which Craig was happy to see increased in 1824 if it would protect the value of the fund.[20] He even suggested that the majority of the capital fund be invested in 'Bank of England or Government Stock of such description as an eminent Broker or Banker might advise'.

Craig would have served a three-year apprenticeship. After his father's death, he might have looked to experienced local practitioners for guidance. One candidate for such a role would have been Walter Scott's 'good and tried friend' Charles Erskine (1770–1825), in Melrose.[21] Erskine was sheriff substitute of Selkirkshire (and holder of other local offices), apprentice-master of the Melrose writers David Spence (1789–1846) and James Curle (1789–1861), and law agent of Sir Walter Scott.[22] Following his death, Craig referred to his friend Erskine as a man 'who will long be remembered amongst us as a pattern of public & private worth'.[23] This, however, is speculation. Little information survives about Craig's formative years as a writer, although he appears to have been well established locally by the time he became a notary, on 30 May 1805, when he adopted his late father's motto, *veritas* (truth).[24]

On Boxing Day 1806, he married Dorothea Laidlaw (b. 1785), daughter of Robert Laidlaw in Philiphaugh (although the family had moved there from Drumelzier in Peeblesshire).[25] So far as is known, the couple had no children. Dorothea's younger sister, Elizabeth (Betsy), is mentioned as a visitor to Galashiels in 1826.[26] Her brother, Robert, a law agent in Edinburgh, is more often referred to in Craig's correspondence and also recorded as a visitor.[27]

---

[18] E.g. SBA/1303/3/194, Craig/William Reid, writer, Jedburgh, 19 Jun. 1823. Had Craig been a procurator, the impact of professional organisation is likely to have been more evident on his practice.
[19] SBA/1303/4/198, Craig/Andrew Lang, Selkirk, 3 Jun. 1825.
[20] SBA/1303/4/41, Craig/William Rutherford, sheriff clerk, Jedburgh, 4 Jun. 1824.
[21] Grierson ed., *Letters of Sir Walter Scott*, IX, 5.
[22] Erskine was also clerk to the statute labour trustees of Selkirkshire and the turnpike trustees: SBA/1303/4/152, Craig/Robert Bruce, Kelso, 7 Feb. 1825; see also J. Chisholm, *Sir Walter Scott as a Judge* (Edinburgh, 1918), 8; Catherine Helen Spence, *Tenacious of the Past: The Recollections of Helen Brodie*, ed. J. King & G. Tulloch (Adelaide, 1994), 36–7.
[23] SBA/1303/4/151, 2 Feb. 1825, Craig/Tait & Bruce WS. Erskine died on 24 Jan.: Chisholm, *Sir Walter Scott as a Judge*, 8.
[24] Finlay, ed., *ARNP 1800–1899*, no. 199.
[25] *The Scots Magazine*, vol. lxix, Jan. 1807, p. 76. Robert Laidlaw and Dorothia [sic] Turnbull had nine children.
[26] SBA/1303/4/355, Craig/Mrs Lawson, 26 Mar. 1826.
[27] He is designed 'Solicitor No. 11 Duncan Street, Edinburgh': SBA/1303/7/28, Craig/Alexander Monro, 7 Nov. 1834. Laidlaw was listed in the *Edinburgh Post Office Directory* in 1833–4 (p. 119) as a member of the SSC Society but does not appear in the list provided in J. B. Barclay, *The S.S.C. Story* (Edinburgh, 1984). His parents, Robert Laidlaw and Dorothia Turnbull, had three sons called Robert, the first of whom died in 1782. Robert the law agent was born either in 1790 or 1800.

Craig appears in the 1841 census, living with his nineteen-year-old housekeeper, Sophia Wright. His accounts mention five guineas as 'Sophy's half year wage' in the period to Martinmas 1841, probably her first full year of employment.[28] Evidently Craig by then was a widower, although there is no record of Dorothea's death. 'Mrs Craig' appears regularly in the accounts but the last recorded payment to her was on 4 July 1840 when she received £1 in silver, presumably for housekeeping.[29] This suggests that she died in the late summer or autumn of 1840. After that, Sophy regularly appears in receipt of money for household expenses.[30] Craig continued to pay into the writers' widows' fund, however, perhaps in case he remarried.[31]

Craig's portrait (Figure 1.1), probably the one given to him by the community in 1826, reflects Hall's description of him as tall and thin with dark hair.[32] Walter Scott mentioned an accident in which Craig (a member of the Abbotsford Hunt) was kicked on the leg by a horse. Craig's reluctance to have his boots removed was because, in Scott's words, his legs had 'an unhappy resemblance to a pair of tongs'.[33] The wound, however, was not serious. Other anecdotes about Craig, not always reliable, circulated for generations after his death.[34]

Galashiels

When Craig was born Galashiels was, in the words of the later MP for Selkirkshire, Alexander Pringle of Whytbank, 'a mere village'.[35] Surrounding areas, such as Longhaugh, Buckholmside, Langlee, Hemphaugh and Darling's Haugh, were not part of Galashiels proper when Craig was at school. According to the burgh's historian, Robert Hall, it was under Craig's management that the village became 'a budding town'.[36] Already in 1803, Dorothy Wordsworth had experienced the 'townish bustle' which manufacturing was bringing to the place.[37] Henry Cockburn, Craig's near contemporary, noted the transformation of Galashiels. When he knew it first it was simply 'a rural hamlet' but, as he observed as he travelled through the town in 1839 to attend the criminal circuit court at Jedburgh, 'Galashiels has become the Glasgow of Selkirkshire'.[38] He may have meant this more in tribute

[28] SBA/1303/9/593, C&R Cash Book, entry dated 29 Nov. 1841.
[29] SBA/1303/9/410.
[30] E.g. SBA/1303/9/451 (11 Nov. 1840); SBA/1303/9/526 (1 Jul. 1841); SBA/1303/9/637 (7 and 19 Apr. 1842).
[31] SBA/1303/9/526 (24 Jun. 1841).
[32] *Caledonian Mercury*, 7. Jan 1826; Hall, *History of Galashiels*, 83.
[33] Grierson, ed., *Letters of Sir Walter Scott*, VI, 295, Scott/Charles Scott, 14 Nov. 1820.
[34] Cf. G. Reavely, *A Medley, History, Directory and Discovery of Galashiels* (Galashiels, 1875), 73–6, 78, 127, 132–3. I am grateful to John Ballantyne for directing me to this source.
[35] Ibid.; NRS, Scott of Gala papers, GD477/464/9/1, Alexander Pringle/Gala, 20 Jun. 1836.
[36] Hall, *History of Galashiels*, 99.
[37] D. Wordsworth, *Recollection of a Tour in Scotland made in 1803 AD*, ed. J. C. Shairp (3rd edn, Edinburgh, 1875), 255.
[38] [Cockburn], *Circuit Journeys*, 51.

Figure 1.1 George Craig (1783–1843). Creative Commons/Hall, History of Galashiels

to its greenery than its industry, but the town had certainly expanded due to the woollen trade.

The transformation in Galashiels is generally attributed to Dr Robert Douglas, parish minister there between 1770 and 1820. According to the minister of Yarrow, James Russell, Douglas used his substantial private wealth to support the small-scale manufacturers who eked out a living by making 'Galashiels grey', a coarse woollen cloth.[39] The main commercial success of Galashiels, however, and the strongest growth in its commerce, came about under the stewardship of Craig and this will be explored in later chapters.

---

[39] William Veitch, ed., *James Russell, Reminiscences of Yarrow by the Late James Russell D.D., Minister of Yarrow* (Selkirk, 1894), 45.

Douglas and Craig, along with three others including George Bruce of Langlee, became partners in a new venture in 1804, the Low Buckholmside Brewery.[40] This was an attempt to manufacture the popular dark beer, 'London porter', a project Hall thought 'both foolish and extravagant'.[41] The business failed and was wound up in 1809. Some of the correspondence from this process survives. Craig, on behalf of the partners, employed the Selkirk firm of Rodger & Paterson to pursue the brewery's debtors.[42] These lawyers, located near the sheriff court, had been previously employed by Craig in his general business affairs as well as on behalf of the brewery.[43] The brewery premises were sold to the builders Sanderson & Paterson, with whom Craig was to have an enduring relationship as Galashiels expanded.

Galashiels was unusual in that it consisted of three legally distinct areas spread over the two counties of Selkirkshire and Roxburghshire. The town itself was in Selkirkshire and property there was held under ninety-nine-year leases.[44] According to Douglas, Galashiels houses enjoyed 'striking superiority, both in outward appearance and in workmanship', to most of the more superficial properties constructed for labourers and shepherds elsewhere in the county.[45] An area outside the town, situated in Roxburghshire, consisted of properties held of the laird of Gala, under feu tenure. The third part, the village of Buckholmside where the brewery had been built, was also held in feu but of a different superior, James Pringle of Torwoodlee. The royal commissioners who examined municipal corporations in Scotland in 1835 reported that Galashiels was, aside from Hawick, the most important manufacturing town in the south of Scotland despite its small but growing population of 2,100 people.[46]

Craig referred to the geographical complications of Galashiels when writing to Robert Roy WS in 1827. He had just been in his office with the sheriff depute, Sir Walter Scott, discussing an action of declarator. Scott had to delay a hearing due to the abundance of 'books and papers' from the defender's witnesses. Craig advised Roy to ensure that the next step of the process was addressed to the sheriff of Selkirk 'generally' because several of the parties lived in Roxburghshire, 'the town being situate in two counties'.[47]

---

[40] Hall, *Galashiels*, 88.
[41] Ibid.
[42] E.g. Scottish Borders Archive, Hawick (SBA), D/47/80/15, Craig/Rodger & Paterson, writers, Selkirk, 2 Apr. 1810; D/45/13/11, Rodger & Paterson/Craig, 18 Apr. 1810; D/47/80/17, Craig/Rodger & Paterson, 19 Jun. 1810.
[43] E.g., Ibid., D/45/13/7, Account of Business for Buckholmside Brewery Company, Mr George Craig/Rodger & Paterson, 12 Apr. 1810; D/45/13/8, Account of Business, George Craig/Rodger & Paterson, 13 Apr. 1810.
[44] NRS, Scott of Gala papers, GD477/464/9/1.
[45] R. Douglas, *General View of the Agriculture in the counties of Roxburgh and Selkirk with Observations on the Means of their Improvement* (Edinburgh, 1798), 248.
[46] *Municipal corporations (Scotland). Appendix to the General Report of the Commissioners* 615, H.C. (1836) (547) XXIII.547 [Henceforth, HC, *Report on Municipal Corporations, Appendix*].
[47] SBA/1303/5/3, Craig/Robert Roy WS, 15 Jan. 1827. Scott detoured to Gala on his way to Edinburgh: W. E. K. Anderson, ed., *Journal of Sir Walter Scott* (Edinburgh, 1998), 300.

Roxburghshire had by far the busier sheriff court. In the period 1828–1835, the total number of actions brought into court in Selkirk was only 135 compared to 1,189 in Roxburghshire.[48] In the period 1826–1833, Roxburgh had ten times the number of small debt claims that Selkirk had.[49] As Mark Pringle MP told the duke of Buccleuch in 1799, when the office of sheriff was vacant in Selkirk, 'the [court] business is in fact so completely little & trifling that it requires nothing more in our Sheriff than to fear God & honor the King'.[50]

CLIENTS AND PROFESSIONAL RELATIONSHIPS

John Scott, Eighth Laird of Gala

Of Craig's clients the most significant to him was John Scott (1790–1840), the eighth laird of Gala (Figure 1.2) and son of Colonel Hugh Scott (d. 1795) from whom he inherited Gala House. His mother was Isabella Monro, daughter of Dr Alexander Monro *secundus* of the family of Monro of Auchinbowie, famous for producing three successive professors of anatomy at the University of Edinburgh. Dr Alexander Monro *tertius* (1773–1859), of Craiglockhart and Cockburn, was Gala's uncle and, during his minority, one of his curators and a trustee on his late father's estate. Craig references another uncle, the advocate David Monro Binning (1776–1843), describing him in 1832 as 'a capital hand' at advising on parliamentary bills.[51] Gala accompanied Sir Walter Scott on his trip to the continent in 1815, alongside the future MP Alexander Pringle of Whytbank (1791–1857), and the advocate (and future sheriff of Argyll) Robert Bruce (1790–1851), all three of Scott's companions being clients or closely connected to clients of Craig.[52] Gala's memoir of the trip was published posthumously in 1842.[53] As the others detoured, Scott and Gala returned on their own, lunching with Byron on the way, and Scott later described Gala as 'one of the kindest and best informd [sic] men whom I know'.[54]

For Craig, Gala was largely an absentee, leaving him to see to the leasing of Gala House and estate, for which he retained possession of the Gala rental book unless it was required by Gala's Edinburgh agents, Tod & Romanes WS.[55] When

[48] House of Commons, *First Report from His Majesty's Law Commissioners Scotland*, App., p. 312, H.C. (1834) (295), XXVI.179. Berwickshire had 1,302 cases.
[49] Ibid., p. 316.
[50] NRS, Buccleuch papers, GD224/663/6/8, Pringle/Buccleuch, 23 Nov. 1799.
[51] SBA/1303/6/292, Craig/Adam Paterson WS, 22 May 1832.
[52] Bruce was the younger brother of Thomas Bruce of Langlee WS (1785–1850): SBA/1303/7/441, Craig & Rutherford (C&R)/Editor of *The Courant*, 13 May 1837. He was (unsuccessfully) recommended to the lord advocate for appointment as advocate depute by the duke of Buccleuch in 1816: NRS, Buccleuch papers, GD224/655/7. On Scott's trip, see Iain G. Brown, *Frolics in the Face of Europe* (Stroud, 2021).
[53] John Scott, *Journal of a Tour to Waterloo and Paris, in company with Sir Walter Scott in 1815* (London, 1842).
[54] Anderson, ed., *Journal of Sir Walter Scott*, 53, 478.
[55] NRS, Scott of Gala papers, GD477/105/10, Tod & Romanes/George Craig, 21 Jan. 1820.

Figure 1.2 John Scott, laird of Gala (1790–1840). © The Hunterian, University of Glasgow

the family was in residence, Craig's tasks included ensuring that the wine cellar was properly stocked.[56] He was asked to organise redecoration of the house in 1818, a matter on which Gala had determined views.[57] When it came to one room, he wanted gold moulding round the cornices and in the corners but not around the doors, windows or chimney piece. If the decorator objected that this was out of style, he noted, 'that is of no consequence to any body but me and I am prepared to abide by it'.[58] During Gala's comings and goings to the house in his younger days, Craig was on hand to smooth any problems in the family's arrangements. An example is the loss of a portmanteau containing silver which may have

[56] SBA/1303/4/9, Craig/Mr Brougham, Wine merchant, Parliament Square, Edinburgh, 3 Apr. 1824.
[57] NRS, Scott of Gala papers, GD477/105/6, Scott, New Club, Edinburgh/Craig, 11 Sep. 1818.
[58] Ibid., GD477/464/4. Gala/Craig, 25 Apr. 1819.

been left on the Galashiels chaise.[59] In 1818, when at Auchinbowie with his uncle David Monro Binning, Gala anxiously sought a bulletin from Craig because 'the poor weather here & the accounts of the best methods of digging sheep out of the snow one hears of being practised in the highlands rather alarm me'.[60] He wanted to know how the wheat was and whether the sheep had begun to lamb and also about plans for a new inn of which he had heard.

Gala suffered 'a severe accident' which required him to leave Galashiels in September 1824 to recover his health in the south of England where he generally remained each winter thereafter.[61] Craig wrote to him in Hastings a few months later.[62] In 1826 he mentions his having 'not been so well again', at a point when the advocate Thomas Tod was about to begin a two-year lease of Gala House.[63] The same year, he remarked to Gala's Edinburgh agents that Mrs Scott (Magdalen Hope) had assured him, when the family left for England, 'that they would never winter at the house again on account of Mr Scott's health'.[64] Gala still visited Scotland regularly; Walter Scott saw him in Edinburgh in May 1830, for example.[65] In 1831 he was in Leamington in Warwickshire.[66] In 1836 he was in Edinburgh but then moved to Jersey.[67] He was again in Edinburgh the year after but in 1838 he was in Cheltenham and, the following year, Craig wrote to him in Exeter.[68] Travel arrangements were often made by Mrs Scott in conjunction with Craig. For example, Craig enquired for her about the quality of the road to Newcastle.[69] In 1827, when the family decided to move from England to Edinburgh at short notice, Craig contacted a firm in Leith on Mrs Scott's behalf informing them that they 'have taken the liberty to address their luggage consisting of 10 packages to your care' until they arrived.[70]

Despite his travels, Gala remained keenly interested in his estate and in the burgh. Like Craig, he was much concerned with the development of local industry and the road network both of which feature heavily Craig's correspondence. In 1831, for instance, Gala shared with his feuars the cost of 'bringing in water to the

---

[59] Ibid., GD477/464/5, idem, 10 Jun. 1815.

[60] Ibid., GD477/105/5, idem, 14 Apr. 1818.

[61] SBA/1303/4/225, Craig/James Wilson, solicitor of taxes, Edinburgh, 8 Aug. 1825. Hall, *History of Galashiels*, 98, apparently dates this to 1813, but that is not correct.

[62] SBA/1303/4/123, Craig/Gala, All Saints Cottage, Hastings, Sussex, 26 Nov. 1824; SBA/1303/4/331, idem, Northlands, Sussex, 18 Feb. 1826; SBA/1303/4/522, idem, Post Office, Hastings, 10 Jan. 1827.

[63] SBA/1303/4/355, Craig/Mrs Lawson, Kilmarnock, 26 Mar. 1826.

[64] SBA/1303/4/481, Craig/Tod and Romanes, 4 Nov. 1826.

[65] Anderson, ed., *Journal of Sir Walter Scott*, 664.

[66] SBA/1303/6/240, Craig/Gala, Leamington, Warwickshire, 6 Nov. 1831.

[67] SBA/1303/7/209, Craig/Gala, 26 Abercrombie [sic] Place, Edinburgh, 6 May 1836; SBA/1303/7/223, idem, Darnaway Street, Edinburgh, 2 Jun. 1836; SBA/1303/8/47, Craig/John McGowan, collector of taxes, Peebles, 25 Sep. 1837.

[68] SBA/1303/8/23, Craig/Gala, Edinburgh, 22 Aug. 1837; SBA/1303/8/164, Craig/Gala, Cheltenham, 24 Feb. 1838; SBA/1303/8/412, idem, 42 Southernhay, Exeter, 18 Jan. 1839.

[69] SBA/1303/8/36, Craig/Mrs Laing, Jedburgh, 6 Sep. 1837.

[70] SBA/1303/5/77, Craig/Wauchope & McAdie, Leith, 20 Jun. 1827.

upper part' of Galashiels.[71] Craig was also involved in domestic matters on Gala's behalf. A letter from Gala, dismissing his servant, John Innes, from his service in 1835 for failing to perform his duties is recorded amongst Craig's letters. It ends with the instruction that Craig pay Innes his wages to the date of dismissal.[72]

James Pringle, Ninth Laird of Torwoodlee

The laird of Torwoodlee's correspondence with his Edinburgh agents – initially Archibald Tod of Drygrange WS (1758–1816) and later Archibald Gibson WS (1782–1845) – shows that as a young man he relied heavily on Craig's father whom he described as 'my friend Willie Craig'.[73] William Craig, probably from the date the laird took over the estate, and certainly from 1782, can be found collecting the rents.[74] In September 1795, for example, Torwoodlee wrote to Gibson noting that, as 'Willie Craig sent you all my money at this time', he needed some of it back to pay those working for him during what was proving to be a particularly successful harvest.[75] Later that year, in a letter to Gibson which he dictated to Craig because of a hand injury, Torwoodlee instructed him to deal with a summons from the Rev. Robert Dawson, minister of Stow.[76] Craig added his own postscript noting that Dawson owed him money.

George Craig succeeded to the role of the laird's factor. As the laird had raised the Selkirkshire Corps of Yeomanry Cavalry, Craig naturally served as a lieutenant and participated in a well-known episode in January 1804 known as the 'false alarm' where the Borders beacons, warning of French invasion, were mistakenly set alight. Mustering in Selkirk, the laird's force moved to Dalkeith followed by its baggage train. Craig, at the head of his local company, headed north directly from Galashiels.[77]

For his work for Torwoodlee, Craig received a salary of £40 per year and he kept the estate account book in which these payments are recorded in a neat hand. The figures for each calendar year of account appear under the title of 'Account Current Betwixt James Pringle Esq of Torwoodlee and G. Craig'.

71 SBA/1303/6/163, Craig/H. D. Dickie, 25 Mar. 1831.
72 SBA/1303/7/69, Gala/John Innes, Gala, 19 May 1835.
73 NRAS, TD2017/14/Box 11, Bundle 2, James Pringle of Torwoodlee/Archibald Gibson WS, 8 Dec. 1795. I am grateful to James Pringle, 14th and present Laird of Torwoodlee, for access to this material and to the Torwoodlee Account Book [TAB]. The ninth laird was related by marriage to Archibald Tod having, in 1782, married Elizabeth, daughter of the late Charles Tod of Drygrange: Pringle, *Records of the Pringles*, 223. Archibald Gibson WS began as a sole practitioner but, by 1806, was in partnership with Charles Oliphant WS with a third partner, David Cleghorn WS, added by 1809. Gibson acquired the estate of Ladhope in Galashiels in 1813: Hall, *History of Galashiels*, 20.
74 NRAS, TD2017/14/Box 11, Bundle 2, Fitted accompt betwixt James Pringle and Archibald Tod WS dated 24 Dec. 1782 and 20 Jan. 1783.
75 NRAS, TD2017/14/Box 11, Bundle 2, James Pringle of Torwoodlee/Archibald Gibson WS, 1 Sep. 1795.
76 Ibid., idem, 8 Dec. 1795.
77 Hall, *History of Galashiels*, 85–6; cf. Reavely, *Discovery of Galashiels*, 74.

Craig's own cash book from the period of the Torwoodlee account book unfortunately does not survive, but there are references to it in the latter. For example, in 1824 there is reference to £15 paid to the laird's eldest son, Captain James Pringle, which was 'paid at Gal[ashiel]s p[e]r Rec[eip]t in G.C.'s C/B'.[78] In 1821, an entry records payment by Craig of the laird's one guinea subscription to the Selkirk Bible Society.[79]

There are many references to the Pringles in Craig's letter books. One entry, also in 1821, notes the family's attendance at the funeral of Violet Pringle, daughter of the judge, John Pringle, Lord Haining (d. 1754) and sister of Lord Alemoor (d. 1776):

> Torwoodlee & the Captain are at Clifton Park today burying old Miss V. Pringle who has at length left this world & all its enjoyments after a large share of them for 96 years I think she was.[80]

James Pringle was a JP, a fact which Craig once made use of by offering to accompany a client's wife to Torwoodlee to swear an oath before him relating to the inventory of her late father's estate.[81]

After the laird's death on 2 August 1840, Craig worked for the new laird, Captain (later Vice-Admiral) James Pringle. He is found, for example, administering the payment of an annuity to Miss Pringle (probably the laird's sister, Frances) in December 1840.[82]

George Fairholme of Greenknowe (1789–1846)

In 1800 George Fairholme inherited the estate of Greenknowe, near Gordon in Berwickshire, from his uncle who was an eminent and wealthy banker and art collector.[83] Fairholme is noted for his writings on geology in which he attempted to accommodate science to scripture, an approach for which he was subject to criticism.[84] In 1818 Fairholme married Caroline Forbes, daughter of Lord Forbes and granddaughter of the earl of Atholl. In the late 1820s, they lived abroad for a time in Switzerland and Brussels, before moving to Ramsgate in Kent towards the end of 1830.[85]

Fairholme's peregrinations, from Rome to Milan, Brussels to Thoun (near Berne) and London to Ramsgate, can be traced through Craig's correspondence

[78] TAB, 9 Feb. 1824. 'C/B' stands for Cash Book.
[79] Ibid., 27 Jun. 1821.
[80] SBA/1303/2/30, Craig/George Fairholme, Goury [Gowrie?] Cottage, Perth, 27 Apr. 1821; Pringle, *Records of the Pringles*, 174. According to the latter source, she was ninety-five. Clifton Park is near the village of Morebattle, south-east of Kelso.
[81] SBA/1303/7/457, Craig/James Dun, dyker, Stow, 29 May 1837.
[82] SBA/1303/9/506 (4 Dec. 1840).
[83] John Kay, *A Series of Original Portraits and Caricature Etchings* (2 vols, Edinburgh, 1842), I, 413.
[84] Terry Mortenson, *The Great Turning Point* (Arkansas, 2004), 115.
[85] SBA/1303/6/113, Craig/G. Fairholme, 9 Nov. 1830. This was addressed to the Post Office in Ramsgate.

and presented him with challenges, not least in ensuring lines of credit. In 1828 this came unstuck, as Craig discovered through a letter from Fairholme in Geneva. The managers of the Leith Bank had neglected to arrange a renewal of credit for Fairholme with their London banker, Barnetts Hoare & Company, as a result of which a bill of exchange drawn for £25 was not paid.[86] The Leith Bank wrote to London but, according to Craig, the bill 'had galloped back faster than it could be overtaken & now it would appear had reached Berne, which is a great pity & a very disagreeable circumstance'.[87] In 1831 the Leith Bank extended Fairholme's credit with their London correspondent.[88]

Prior to moving to Ramsgate (which Craig facilitated by sending books and furniture south in 1832), Fairholme considered moving back to the Borders. Craig wrote to him in Brussels in January 1830 describing potential houses for rent in the area, including 'Old Melrose' which had about thirty acres for pasture.[89] Fairholme's own property was let to tenants but his return to the area was contemplated and Craig was told not to let other property beyond a year without direct instructions.

When, in 1838, a Kelso law agent enquired about a five-year lease, Craig replied that the policy of annual leases would continue 'till recalled by Mr F. which we apprehend is not likely'.[90] The same year, Craig described Fairholme to the Leith Bank as 'one of the most moderate living men of my acquaintance', living a life of retirement in Ramsgate 'on the rents of his estates in Berwickshire of £1200 a year, free of debt' with no personal debt worth mentioning.[91]

Fairholme's residence in Kent did not preclude him making the occasional visit to Galashiels. In October 1831 he and two sons visited Craig's office.[92] Fairholme took the opportunity to sign a new letter of security to his servant, Jean Anderson, in regard to a deposit receipt. Evidently, he had mistakenly destroyed a previous version of the document and took the opportunity of his visit to complete this routine business.

Craig also acted for George's brother Adam Fairholme of Chapel. In 1826, he assisted them both in an attempt recover some outstanding debts following the sale of the effects of another brother, the late Thomas Fairholme at the village of Bolton in Northumberland.[93] Craig refers in one letter to having, in 1816, spent an

<hr/>

86 Craig refers to 'Barnetts' rather than Barnett and I have retained this throughout.
87 SBA/1303/5/282, Craig/G. Fairholme, Bellevue, Thoun, Switzerland, via Paris, 24 Jul. 1828.
88 SBA/1303/6/210, Elliot Anderson/Fairholme, 11 Aug. 1831.
89 SBA/1303/6/10, Craig/G. Fairholme, Ramsgate, 20 Jan. 1830; SBA/1303/6/277, Craig/G. Fairholme, 14 Apr. 1832.
90 SBA/1303/8/357, Craig/Robert Swan, writer, Kelso, 16 Oct. 1838.
91 SBA/1303/8/248, Craig/LBC, 14 May 1838.
92 SBA/1303/8/231, Craig/LBC, 17 Oct. 1831. Fairholme had four sons: G. Fairholm, 'Notes on the Family of Greenknow [sic]'. I am grateful to Mrs Waveney Jenkins for a copy of this document. I have adopted the spellings Fairholme and Greenknowe since they are the ones used by Craig in his correspondence.
93 SBA/1303/4/353, Craig/Clement Pattison, solicitor, 20 Mar. 1826.

hour with the estate manager at Alnwick Castle, Richard Robson, in the company of Thomas Fairholme of Bolton.[94]

Alexander Monro Tertius *of Craiglockhart and Cockburn*

Alexander Monro tertius (Figure 1.3) was one of his most active correspondents from 1825 onwards and Craig visited his estate at Cockburn in Berwickshire regularly. His job as a land agent was to identify tenant farmers who would be potential assets rather than liabilities and it was in his letters to Monro that Craig was at his most didactive on agricultural matters, expressing strong ideas on crop rotation and animal husbandry.

Figure 1.3　Professor Alexander Monro tertius (1773–1859). © Edinburgh University

---

[94]　NLS, Letters to Scott, MS 3910, fo. 252r, George Craig/Richard Robson, Alnwick Castle, 10 Oct. 1829.

As a university professor, Monro is often regarded as undistinguished, certainly when compared to his father and grandfather.[95] He demonstrated 'mere competence, rather than brilliance', although he enjoyed a good income.[96] His property at Cockburn was quite distant from Craig.[97] Their relationship was therefore conducted largely through letters, although Craig occasionally visited Monro at Craiglockhart and Monro also visited Galashiels.[98] Trips to Cockburn allowed Craig to improve his knowledge of nearby Duns which was useful to him professionally, just as he learned from neighbouring burghs such as Kelso, Melrose and Selkirk. As with Gala, there was a 'Cockburn Book' detailing rent and other payments which passed between Craig and his client.[99]

Monro entered Craig's network through the Scott of Gala connection and, in turn, benefited from Craig's wider network of clients. An example of the ease with which Craig was able to link clients to their mutual advantage arose in 1830. Craig, on Monro's behalf, wrote to Rev. Dr Colvin in Johnston near Moffat, in connection with Monro's wish to find a good school for a young member of his family (he had twelve children with his first wife). He described Colvin to Monro as 'a well informed & very active person . . . [who] has got great merit in his pupils the Hopes & Hope Johnstones &c'.[100] Colvin was distant from Galashiels but was connected to Craig through his brother, Dr William Colvin, a naval surgeon. While the latter long resided in the south of England, his ownership of Torquhan near Stow made him a client and correspondent of Craig.[101]

Sir Walter Scott

Sir Walter Scott, whose home at Abbotsford is near Galashiels, was not a major client of Craig.[102] Nor did Craig practise as a procurator in the sheriff court where Scott occasionally presided (the regular courts were held by his sheriff-substitute).[103] Scott's business affairs, however, did enter Craig's orbit because he held a deposit account with the Leith Bank, although they were not his main bankers, and it was through Craig that Sir Walter 'transacted all his local

---

[95] I. Macintyre, 'Alexander Monro tertius (1773–1859)' 43 (2012) *Journal of the Royal College of Physicians of Edinburgh*, 282.

[96] L. Rosner, 'Monro, Alexander, tertius (1773–1859), *Oxford Dictionary of National Biography*, 23 Sep. 2004 (accessed 1 Mar. 2021).

[97] The bounds of Cockburn were set out by Craig in 1839: SBA/1303/8/491, Craig/Patrick Hume, writer, Duns, 11 May 1839.

[98] E.g. SBA/1303/6/213, Craig/G. Turnbull WS, 16 Aug. 1831 ('Dr Monro was here yesterday').

[99] E.g. SBA/1303/8/551, Craig/Dr Monro, 12 Aug. 1839.

[100] SBA/1303/6/56, Craig/Dr Monro, 19 May, 1830.

[101] SBA/1303/6/234, Craig/Rev. Dr Colvin, Johnstone, 27 Oct. 1831.

[102] Scott's local legal affairs were handled by Charles Erskine and, later, the firm of Erskine & Curle: NLS, Acc. 9430.

[103] See Chisholm, *Sir Walter Scott as a Judge*, 4.

banking business'.[104] For example, Craig was heavily involved in the relationship between Scott and the local building firm, Sanderson & Paterson, who worked on the construction of Abbotsford.[105]

There was also a personal side to their relationship. In 1821, Craig commiserated with Scott on the death of the publisher John Ballantyne (1774–1821) 'who I had known above 20 years & always found him a pleasant kind hearted man'.[106] He was glad to hear Scott was going to the coronation of George IV, wishing him 'all manner of happiness & pleasure in the occasion'. Most of the dealings between Craig and Scott, however, concerned banking matters and this extended, on one occasion, to providing cash on request to one of Scott's daughters.[107]

In April 1827, Craig wrote to Scott, at the height of his financial troubles after the collapse of his publisher, Constable & Co. the year before. Referring to him as 'you who should not be troubled with any thing', he was obliged to enclose a letter from the engineer Robert Stevenson seeking to resolve his bill for a survey into a potential railway between St Boswells and Dalkeith which Scott had strongly promoted.[108] He also had to inform Scott that a draft on the Leith Bank for £20 had been rejected because his account was overdrawn by £8 3s 2d, leading Scott to note in his diary the 'incivility' from the bank 'which I despise with my heels'.[109]

Craig's relationship with Scott can be traced through his letters, Scott's correspondence, and Scott's *Journal,* although the latter source mainly mentions Craig in connection with Scott's book-keeping. An 1826 letter in which Craig explains how Scott had gone wrong in calculating his personal accounts, is not in Craig's letter book.[110] In terms of the collapse of Constable & Co., Scott's factor, William Laidlaw, updated Craig on Scott's financial affairs in the immediate aftermath.[111] Craig's bank had a claim in respect of two bills, due in February and March 1826, one for £600 and the other for £700.[112] Both had been returned to Craig with charges. Craig, having overpaid Scott's deposit account by £300, described these additional debts as 'a serious business'.[113] Scott explained to Craig, in January 1826, the private trust arrangement made by his agent, John Gibson WS. He expressed sorrow for what had happened, in the 'most unexpected' collapse of Constable, but also optimism.[114]

---

[104] W. Rutherford, *Galashiels in History* (Galashiels, 1930), 31 *The Scotsman*, 7 Nov. 1894, p. 9.
[105] E.g. NLS, Scott Letters, MS 1750, fo. 163; Acc. 9430, fo. 48; NRS, Scott of Gala papers, GD47/433, Walter Scott/Craig, Feb. 1817.
[106] SBA/1303/2/76, Craig/Sir Walter Scott, 9 Jul. 1821. Ballantyne had been born in Kelso.
[107] SBA/1303/5/63, Craig/Miss Scott, Abbotsford, 15 May 1827.
[108] SBA/1303/5/46, Craig/Sir Walter Scott, 7 Apr. 1827. On the railway project see Chapter 7.
[109] Anderson, ed., *Journal of Sir Walter Scott,* 334. The quote paraphrases *Much Ado about Nothing*.
[110] Ibid., 213. Scott refers to a note from Craig but nothing of this date is in the letter book.
[111] SBA/1303/4/307, Craig/LBC, 23 Jan. 1826.
[112] SBA/1303/5/121, Craig/Gibson & Murray WS, 2 Sep. 1827.
[113] NLS, Letters to Scott, MS 3902, fo. 117, Craig/Sir Walter Scott, 18 Mar. 1826.
[114] SBA, SC/S/5/2, Scott/Craig, 28 Jan. 1826.

Craig and Scott were on friendly terms. Scott invited Craig to share a Christmas goose with him in 1817, dropping off the invitation personally on his way from Edinburgh to Abbotsford.[115] He invited Craig to his annual coursing party in October 1824 and dinner afterwards.[116] In 1825, not for the first time, Scott asked Craig to inquire into the possibility of purchasing the estate of his neighbour, Nicol Milne of Faldonside. Craig met Milne and got him to agree to a meeting with him and Scott in Edinburgh. He noted of the meeting that

> Mr Milne I observed to be less anxious to sell than last time we spoke of it, both because he says he knows of no other place to buy, & that farm produce & land itself are in [sic] the rise.[117]

No such sale ever took place, although Scott, forlornly, still had hope of it shortly before his death.[118]

Scott's money problems placed a wedge between him and Craig. In March 1826 Craig frankly owned that Scott's deposit account with the Leith Bank 'being overpaid by me to you is an awkward business', hoping for £150 in part repayment.[119] A rather difficult episode occurred a few months later when Scott had no ready cash except for £20 which was in Craig's hands.[120] He called upon Craig only to find that he was out. When Craig wrote to him, he had only bad news, a reminder of Robert Stevenson's demands. He added a postscript:

> I was sorry to miss the honour of your call the other evening & I would have taken the opportunity to ask if you knew when a payment would be made towards the two bills in the Bank so long over which the Bank sometimes enquire about.[121]

The bank, through John Gibson as trustee for Scott's creditors, eventually received a dividend of six pence in the pound which Craig directed to be paid in Leith.[122] Ultimately, Craig was a banker and Scott was a client. Their general relationship, however, was cordial and professional and Craig, who held Scott in great respect, was invited to his funeral in 1832.[123]

[115] NLS, Scott Letters (copies), MS 1750, fo. 155, idem, 23 Dec. 1817.
[116] NLS, Scott Letters, MS 1846, fo. 25.
[117] SBA/1303/4/157, Craig/Gala, 21 Feb. 1825.
[118] Anderson, ed., *Journal of Sir Walter Scott*, 785. Milne died, aged eighty-two, in Dec. 1837 and Craig was involved in the executry of his estate: SBA/1303/8/233, Craig/John Bisset S.S.C, 27 Apr. 1838.
[119] SBA/1303/4/347, Craig/Gala, 13 Mar. 1826.
[120] Anderson, ed., *Journal of Sir Walter Scott*, 184, refers to the cash.
[121] SBA/1303/4/409, Craig/Scott, 26 Jun. 1826.
[122] SBA/1303/5/174, Craig/John Gibson jr WS, 24 Dec. 1827.
[123] NLS, Acc. 9430, fo. 103.

CRAIG'S OFFICE

Until forming a partnership with William Rutherford (1805–1891) (Figure 1.4) in 1836, Craig was a sole practitioner engaged in the business of law agent, banker and insurance agent.[124] He did not, however, work alone. In 1825 there is a reference to his 'late clerk 'Mr D.F.''[125] This was the writer Daniel Ferguson (c.1791–1836).[126] An attorney certificate had formerly been ordered for Ferguson but 'not taken out' since

Figure 1.4 William Rutherford (1805–1891). © SBA

[124] The partnership appears to have taken effect in Feb. 1836 when letters cease to be signed 'I am &c' and become 'We are &c': SBA/1303/7/157, C&R/John Karrasch, Temple Chamber, London, 5 Feb. 1836. The following week, 'our Mr Rutherford' is mentioned: SBA/1303/7/163, C&R/Andrew Lang, Selkirk, 13 Feb. 1836. No copy of the partnership agreement seems to survive but Craig was undoubtedly the senior partner. On Rutherford, see Finlay, ed., *ARNP 1800–1899*, no. 1862.
[125] SBA/1303/4/191, 10 May 1825.
[126] SBA/1303/4/191, 10 May 1825.

he 'left this some time ago'.[127] Ferguson left Galashiels parish prior to June 1820 when he married Ann Sanderson, daughter of the builder, Henry Sanderson.[128] He appears to have practised in Selkirk sheriff court before, having 'passed his examinations' to do so, commencing practice in 'the Leith courts before the sheriff' in 1833.[129] Craig helped Sanderson arrange credit for Ferguson with the Leith Bank, now that he 'had begun business for himself'. He noted that 'both Mr S[anderson] & I are most anxious to see him do well from the very favourable accounts we have heard of him for these 2 or 3 years past, as well as in his family's account'.

There is a fleeting reference to David Wyness as Craig's secretary in 1828 but nothing else is known about him.[130] Craig certainly kept an eye on entries made to his letter book by others. He indicated his disapproval when a letter had been summarised rather than copied by writing underneath the entry 'I dont [sic] wish Letters to be copied in this way'.[131]

Many letters are subscribed 'E.A.' which stood for Elliot Anderson (c.1799–1857).[132] Anderson was proficient in conveyancing and trusted to undertake work for Craig in the fields of banking and insurance. He was also highly knowledgeable about the history and traditions of Galashiels, being an authority for the Peebles-born author Robert Chambers (1802–1871).[133] According to Hall's source, the *Unpublished Annals of the Parish*, Craig had 'a most trustworthy assistant' with whose services he was compelled to dispense due to political differences.[134] That assistant had become heavily involved in Whig politics locally, prior to the passing of the Reform Bill, and may have been Anderson. The last letter bearing the signature 'E.A.' in the letter books appears in December 1835.

Anderson set up independently as a writer and banker in Galashiels, and later letters to him from Craig & Rutherford were businesslike, indicating a purely professional relationship. In January 1837, for instance, a man named William Hoy turned up at Craig's door intimating that Anderson had agreed to engage him at ten shillings per week until Whitsunday but was now refusing to employ him. Craig politely wrote to Anderson asking why.[135] The following year Anderson was asked to send documents in his possession to Bruce of Langlee in connection

---

[127] SBA/1303/4/204, Craig/William Turnbull, Peebles, 16 Jun. 1825; SBA/1303/3/46, Anderson/Tait & Bruce WS 12 Sep. 1822.

[128] Scotlandspeople.gov.uk, Old Parish Registers, Marriages, Melrose, 799/50/287.

[129] SBA/1303/4/491, Craig/James Hunter, Wellfield, Duns, 16 Nov. 1826; SBA/1303/6/352, Craig/Mr Sutherland, Leith Bank, 2 Jan. 1833.

[130] SBA/1303/5/254, Craig/Gibson & Hector WS, 26 May 1828.

[131] SBA/1303/6/485, 2 Jun. 1834.

[132] In 1840 Craig refers unambiguously to Anderson as his former 'bank clerk': SBA/1303/8/589, Craig/John Bisset SSC, 17 Jan. 1840. There is clear evidence in SBA, WM/17/58, Craig/Peter Rodger, 17 Sep. 1833.

[133] Chambers, *Picture of Scotland*, 133. NRS, GD477/463/7 is a copy of a text sent to Chambers, presumably by Anderson. The author (at fol. 8) describes himself as a friend of Adam Paterson WS.

[134] Hall, *History of Galashiels*, 482; Reavely, *Discovery of Galashiels*, 78.

[135] SBA/1303/7/340, Craig/Anderson, 17 Jan. 1837.

with a case against the Leith Bank.[136] Anderson and local writer Robert Haldane were both sent a similar letter in 1839 asking them to exhibit papers in a bid to end protracted family litigation in another case.[137] In 1840 another letter was addressed to Anderson designing him 'banker'.[138] Not long after, Anderson's business ran into trouble and he was sequestrated in a process that began in 1841 and lasted four years.[139] He ended his days as a clerk in Edinburgh.

According to a source cited by Hall, in 1836 Craig dismissed his next clerk for spending too much time in the public houses of Galashiels.[140] In 1837 John Cranston appears in a deed as Craig & Rutherford's clerk, and William Ireland is described as Craig's servant.[141] A few months earlier there is a note indicating that a letter to the writer John Welsh in Peebles had not been copied. It was added in, along with a warning that 'should Mr Cranston make a similar omission he must leave the office'.[142] He possibly did so since he is not recorded in the firm's cash book as being in receipt of wages. He does appear in a printed notice, dated 29 March 1839, as secretary of the Galashiels Savings Bank (with Craig as treasurer), although his name as secretary was struck out and replaced by that of George Thomson.[143] Ireland, on the other hand, was regularly given wages although he was no office worker, being also paid for ploughing, composting and other fieldwork tasks.[144] He may also have worked about the house. There is a reference to him having placed a rug (which later went missing) in Robert Laidlaw's gig when he visited his sister and her husband.[145] John Brown was another man regularly paid wages by Craig for his labour.[146] As for George Thomson, he is referred to in the cash book as receiving £5 in 1841 'for attending to Bank business previous to expiry of his apprenticeship as agreed upon'.[147] He continued as a salaried employee.[148]

Craig's home and office were, at least for part of the period of the correspondence, in the same building. This was common, even for bank agents. His house, which was called The Green, is in the Old Town on John Wood's 1824 plan and

---

[136] SBA/1303/8/214, C&R/Anderson, 5 Apr. 1838.
[137] SBA/1303/8/449, idem, 28 Feb. 1839.
[138] SBA/1303/8/676, C&R/Anderson, 4 Jan. 1840.
[139] NRS, Court of Session, Bill Chamber, Concluded sequestrations, 1845, CS280/7/1.
[140] Hall, *History of Galashiels*, 482.
[141] SBA/1303/7/499-500, C&R/Robert Anderson, writer, Hawick, 12 Jul. 1837; also, SBA/1303/7/504, Craig/Robert Laidlaw SSC, 17 Jul. 1837.
[142] SBA/1303/7/365, 16 Feb. 1837. Cf. a note by Craig on 2 Jun. 1834 relating to a summary of a letter added to the book ['Wrote him regarding . . .'], that 'I do not wish letters to be copied this way': SBA/1303/6/485. On Cranston, cf. Reavely, *Discovery of Galashiels*, 73.
[143] The notice is inserted in SBA/1303/8/468. On the Savings Bank, see Chapter 5.
[144] SBA/1303/9/381 (20 Apr, paid 'for work'); (11 and 25 May 1839, paid 'per account'); SBA/1303/9/385 (14 Oct. 1839, paid 'for labour').
[145] SBA/1303/7/432, C&R/Robert Laidlaw SSC, Edinburgh, 3 May 1837.
[146] E.g. SBA/1303/9/387 (7 Dec. 1839).
[147] SBA/1303/9/524 (3 May 1841, paid 'for working on hay').
[148] E.g. SBA/1303/9/592 (19 Oct. 1841); SBA/1303/9/595 (20 Dec. 1841); SBA/1303/9/637 (11 Apr. 1842).

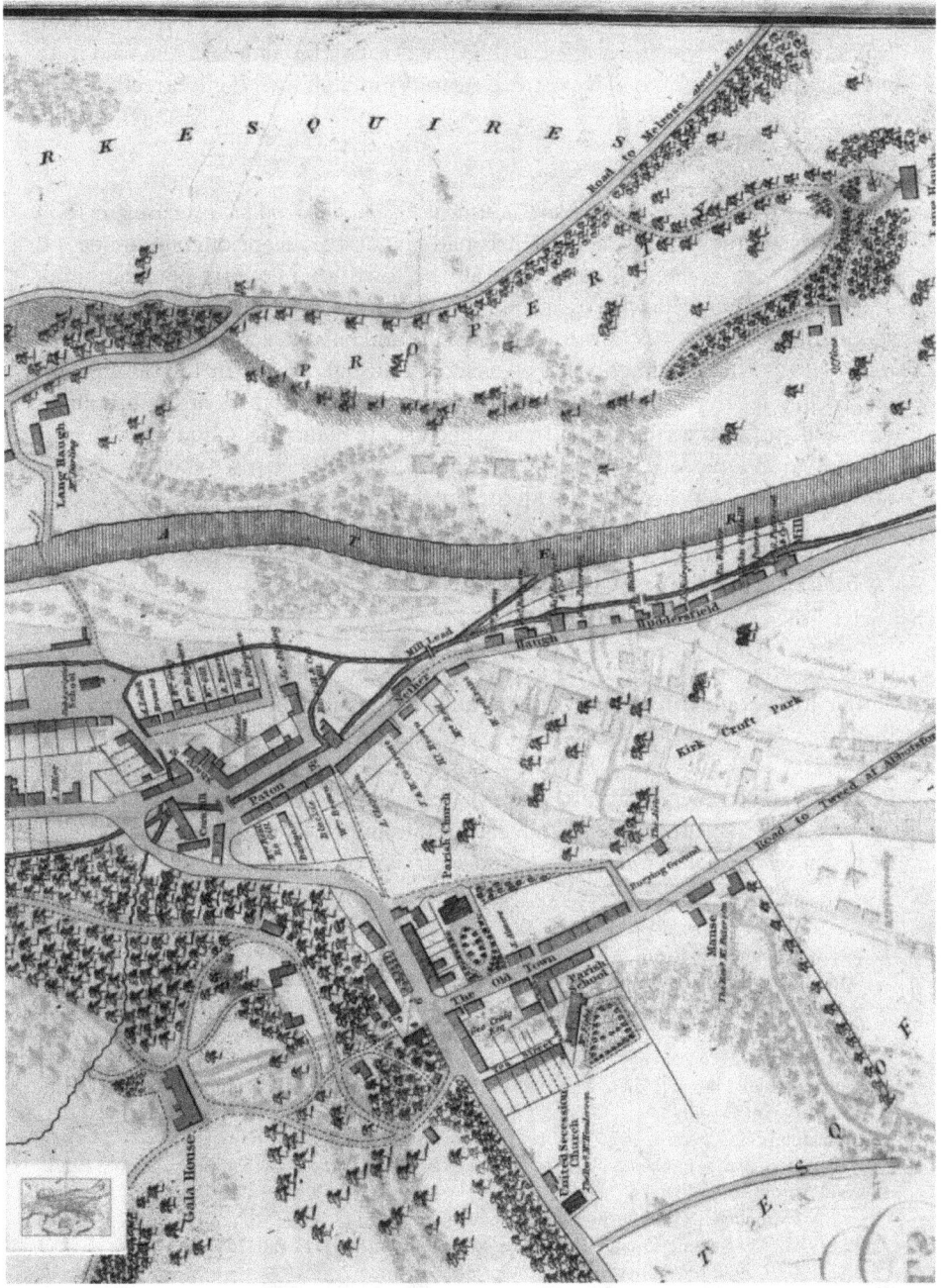

Figure 1.5 Detail of John Wood's Plan of Galashiels, 1824. © NLS

he was still there in the 1841 census (Figure 1.5).[149] This put him aside the parish school and the house of the schoolmaster, Robert Fyshe; near Rev. Paterson's famous manse garden, and close to Gala House.[150] In 1849 Craig's former partner, Rutherford, took over the agency of the City of Glasgow Bank and removed it 'to premises at the foot of the High Street, near its junction with Bank Street'.[151]

Craig's Correspondence

According to the entry in the *New Statistical Account of Scotland* prepared in 1833 by Rev. Nathaniel Paterson, Galashiels had favourable means of communication and there were 'numerous carriers to all the towns and country places around, and the roads are every where excellent.'[152] As well as letters, Craig sent his correspondents deeds, such as instruments of sasine and bills of exchange, petitions, tax returns and other documents as well as more unusual objects. In 1837, for example, he had received by mail from Dublin a pointer dog from George Fairholme's son, William, who was in Ireland with the 71st Highland Light Infantry.[153] Craig, as per instructions, sent it on to the forester Thomas Robertson to be looked after until Fairholme appeared. Craig offered the following advice:

> You will take good care of it by giving it moderate quantities of porridge and milk, bannocks &c & exercise once a day – should it get itchy Dr Gibson will give you some medicine to give it – more inwardly than outwardly.[154]

Craig would generally send and receive cash to the Leith Bank by means of the carrier John Young or his son William and there is regular mention of Young in his letters as a trusted carrier.[155] It was a challenging job and, in the worst of the winter weather, Young might be 'stormstaid' and prevented from reaching Edinburgh.[156] In 1823, the road was only passable by horses with difficulty, precluding Young setting out with his cart. Craig informed the Leith Bank that if he began to run out of money, he would send him on horseback.[157]

---

[149] *The Scotsman*, 7 Nov. 1894, p. 9; Wood's Plan may be seen via maps.nls.uk. Digital image of the census, reference Census 775/1/1, from NRS www.scotlandspeople.gov.uk. On the 1858 OS Town Plan of Galashiels, his house would be on the corner of Church Street and Elm Row. This can be seen online here: https://maps.nls.uk/view/74415824 (accessed 22 May 2021). Paterson was a keen horticulturist: N. Paterson, *The Manse Garden* (Glasgow, 1836).

[150] The site, on the corner of Church St and Elm Row, now bears a plaque stating that Sir Walter Scott transacted business there with the Leith Banking Company [LBC] from 1812 to 1832, with no mention of Craig.

[151] Hall, *History of Galashiels*, 487, 489. See the Note on Sources.

[152] N. Paterson, 'Parish of Galashiels', *New Statistical Account of Scotland* (15 vols, Edinburgh: Blackwood & Sons, 1845), III, 24.

[153] George Fairholme, 'Notes on the Family of Greenknow [sic]'.

[154] SBA/1303/7/355, Craig/Thomas Robertson, wood forrester [sic], 17 Feb. 1837.

[155] SBA/1303/3/59, Elliot Anderson/LBC, 9 Oct. 1822.

[156] SBA/1303/5/34, Craig/LBC, 10 Mar. 1827.

[157] SBA/1303/3/122, Craig/LBC, 10 Feb. 1823.

An alternative carrier, Thomas Richardson, was employed in Young's absence in 1824. This was the 'next best' option but in sending a parcel to the bank Elliot Anderson thought that Richardson 'will be careful in delivering it safe'.[158] Surprisingly, Young and Richardson departed for Edinburgh on the same days of the week, Tuesdays and Thursdays, returning on Wednesdays and Fridays.[159] Sometimes, Craig took the opportunity of acquaintances travelling to Edinburgh to make deliveries for him. To send a large sum to the bank at short notice, he made use 'of Mr G. Douglas by the Sir Walter Scott Coach this evening'.[160] Like-wise, he sent money to the bank by his partner, Rutherford, when he was going to Edinburgh anyway.[161]

Less important documents might be transported more casually, for instance by means of the Blucher guard, the Blucher being a coach which made its way from Edinburgh to Jedburgh, via Melrose, three times per week.[162] It was rare for things to go awry in transit but there are some examples. For instance, a box expected by a Mrs Cockburn in Edinburgh 'had been taken to Machell the Carlisle Carriers . . . in place of Richardson's who both put up at the same quar-ters' in Edinburgh, leading to confusion.[163]

CRAIG AND POLITICS

Craig was active in politics in the Tory interest, as were a number of his cor-respondents, including George Rodger (d. 1834) and James Curle who became Sir Walter Scott's man of business after the death of Charles Erskine.[164] His only local rival in Galashiels for banking and insurance, the writer Robert Haldane, agent for Norwich Union and the National Bank, was a Whig (as, later, was his firm Haldane & Lees) although political rivalry did not get in the way of busi-ness.[165] Local contacts, understanding of voter qualification, and knowledge of conveyancing, qualified all these agents to execute electoral strategy by influenc-ing the voters' roll.[166] Craig acted before the electoral registration court in 1832

---

[158] SBA/1303/4/21, Anderson/LBC, 28 Apr. 1824.
[159] *Pigot & Co.'s New Commercial Directory of Scotland for 1825–6* (London, 1825), 122.
[160] SBA/1303/3/223, Craig/LBC, 7 Aug. 1823.
[161] SBA/1303/7/294, Craig/LBC, 17 Nov. 1836.
[162] E.g. SBA/1303/5/448, Craig/Dr Monro, 21 Sep. 1829; Anderson, ed., *Journal of Sir Walter Scott*, 143, n.3.
[163] SBA/1303/8/55, Craig/Mrs Cockburn, 131 Princes St, Edinburgh, 30 Oct. 1837. Richardson lodged at Watson's on Candlemaker Row: *Pigot's Commercial Directory 1825–6*, 122.
[164] E.g., NLS, Acc. 9430, fo. 85, Scott/Curle, 6 Jul. 1825; V. G. Childe, 'James Curle' 78 (1943–4) *Proc Soc Antiq Scot*, 145; J. N. G. Ritchie, 'James Curle (1862–1944) and Alexander Ormiston Curle (1866–1955): pillars of the establishment' 132 (2002) *Proc Soc Antiq Scot*, 19, 20.
[165] SBA/1303/5/178, Anderson/Mr Haldane, National Bank, Galashiels, 27 Dec. 1827; *Pigot's Commercial Directory 1825–6*, 657; *Kelso Mail*, no. 4109, 25 Aug. 1836. Haldane's partner was Hugh Lees: Finlay, ed., *ARNP 1800–1899*, no. 1842.
[166] Cf. V. R. Parrot, 'Pettyfogging to respectability: A history of the development of the profession of solicitor in the Manchester area 1800–1914' (PhD thesis, University of Salford, 1992), 114–118.

when Alexander Pringle of Whytbank lost the Selkirkshire election and he over-saw the 'canvass & election' accounts of Lord John Montagu-Douglas-Scott who lost Roxburghshire the same year.[167]

Craig actively advised on and created entitlements to vote under the rules brought in by the Scottish Reform Act, legislation which, in the words of William Ferguson, 'ushered in a new era of faggot votes in the counties of Scotland'.[168] Lord John, Craig's candidate in 1832, complained of the 'arts and deception' used on behalf of the successful candidate, Captain George Elliot, but allegations of vote manufacturing bedevilled his own side.[169] The evidence before a parliamen-tary select committee investigating fictitious votes in 1837 suggested that some local practices were intended to subvert the aims of the legislation.[170]

Prior to 1832, under legislation drafted in 1681, voter qualification depended on infeftment in land, as proprietor (holder of the *dominium utile*) or feudal supe-rior, worth at least £400 in valued rent.[171] Provided they had interest in a sufficient value of land, wadsetters, liferenters and fiars might also qualify.[172] Given that houses in the Selkirkshire part of Galashiels were held on ninety-nine-year leases from Gala, and were not held as indefeasible right, as Craig told Lord Napier in 1831 'there will not be one voter in the town'.[173]

That changed the following year, although the 1832 Act was drafted poorly and opened the way to new types of malpractice to replace the old.[174] Robert Haldane elucidated before the parliamentary committee the potential difficulties of votes being given to joint proprietors, joint liferenters and joint tenants. In particular, he was concerned that individuals with no connection to the coun-try were obtaining votes, noting that liferenters in Selkirkshire were 'nearly alto-gether non-resident'.[175] The Tory political agent, Donald Horne WS, before the same committee, noted that of the 280 voters in Selkirkshire in 1832, ninety-one were non-resident.[176] It was freely acknowledged, by Peter Rodger in Selkirk and a number of other witnesses, that votes were being created for political purposes and this was a practice in which Craig was fully engaged.[177]

---

[167] SBA/1303/6/355, Craig/John Gibson jr WS, 9 Feb. 1833. Scott was a son of the duke of Buccleuch.

[168] W. Ferguson, 'The Reform Act (Scotland) of 1832: intention and effect' 45 (1966) *Scottish Historical Review*, 105, 109.

[169] SBA, The Conservatives, Part II, SBA/183/28, Samuel Wood, writer, Jedburgh/John Smith, writer, Kelso, Dec. 1832.

[170] House of Commons, *First Report from the Select Committee on Fictitious Votes (Scotland) with the Minutes of Evidence and Appendix*, p. 2, H.C. (1837–1838) (14), XIV.1 [HC, *Report on Fictitious Votes*], pp. iiii–iv.

[171] W. Ferguson, 'Electoral law and Procedure in Eighteenth and Early Nineteenth Century Scotland' (PhD, University of Glasgow, 1957), 16.

[172] Ibid., 17.

[173] SBA/1303/6/168, Craig/Lord Napier, 1 Apr. 1831.

[174] Ferguson, 'The Reform Act', 108–9, 111.

[175] HC, *Report on Fictitious Votes*, 87.

[176] Ibid., 205 (per D. Horne, 10 Mar. 1837).

[177] Ibid., 114 (per P. Rodger, 1 Mar. 1837); ibid., 71 (per R. Haldane, 24 Feb. 1837).

Horne elucidated the five classes of tenant who might, under the 1832 Act, qualify to vote, depending on the nature and duration of their tenancy or the value of their rent.[178] At the election court in Jedburgh, the sheriff determined that waygoing tenants (tenants at or near the expiry of their lease) had no right to vote unless they were actually in possession of land 'worth £50 a year of rent'.[179] A tenant for life, or a tenant with a lease for at least fifty-seven years, obtained a vote if their interest in the land was not less than £10 (such voters were known as 'tenpounders'). Craig and Horne, in light of the new legislation, became embroiled in a race with the opposition to purchase property and grant joint liferents or leases in order to ensure friendly votes.[180]

In the 1832 election, five of Craig's friends (including the future New Zealand politician Sir David Monro), claimed votes based on liferents granted by him in properties which he held on ninety-nine-year leases.[181] Their claims were rejected by the registration court. They had claimed as tenants for life whereas what Craig had assigned to them was tenancy during the unexpired period of their respective leases. They should have claimed, as Sir Walter Scott successfully did in similar circumstances, simply as a tenant under a long lease.[182] The difference was a subtle one. A 'tenant for life' was a misdescription because such a person could theoretically survive beyond the duration of a long lease, at which point his right would expire and he would no longer be a tenant. Craig, who argued for the claims in court, had erred: it was legally impossible for him, as holder of a ninety-nine-year lease, to grant anyone a tenancy 'for life'.[183]

Craig's efforts to increase or preserve the Tory vote were generally within the law and extended well beyond the momentous election of 1832. An example is a letter to Alexander Pringle of Whytbank about William Brown, an old shepherd. Brown had always been a voter in Roxburghshire but, having sold part of his property, was no longer on the voters' roll. All that would require his return to the roll was the addition of £15 or £20 of property, such as a small stable. Craig asked Pringle to persuade Brown to make such an investment as it was 'a pity to lose a voter for such a trifle'.[184] This was a stratagem, but elsewhere Craig made his boundaries clear. For example, in 1838 he noted that what the English newspapers

[178] HC, *Report on Fictitious Votes*, 298; Ferguson, 'Electoral Law and Procedure', 111; Scottish Reform Act, 1832, s. 9.
[179] SBA, The Conservatives, part II, SBA/183/28, John Gibson jr WS/John Smith, writer, Kelso, 21 Sep. 1832.
[180] HC, *Report on Fictitious Votes*, 204–5.
[181] Ibid., 213–4. The five were David and William Monro, Archibald Gibson WS of Ladhope, John David Hope (Gala's brother-in-law), and William Clark. Gibson is mentioned in 1827 as having paid £90 for his vote a decade before: SBA/1303/5/28: Craig/John Gibson WS, 1 Mar. 1827. That letter indicates that the price of the assignation varied with the life expectancy of the assignee. See also SBA/1303/5/23.
[182] HC, *Report on Fictitious Votes*, 67, 258.
[183] Ibid. (per R. Haldane, 24 Feb. 1837), p. 67.
[184] SBA/1303/8/661, Craig/Alexander Pringle, 17 Dec. 1839.

and Commons committees referred to as 'overleasing of property' produced 'the most fictitious sort of vote' and declined to engage in it.[185]

The political tensions around reform in 1832 surrounded Craig, even in his own office, and his letters refer to making votes, the purchase of votes, and finding objections to votes made on behalf of others.[186] He was associated with those Tories – particularly Whytbank and Torwoodlee – who urged Sir Walter Scott, against his inclination, to intervene against the First Reform Bill.[187] In November 1832, Craig was called to a Court of Review in Melrose 'as one of Lord John Scott's agents' while his own clerk, Elliot Anderson, was 'summoned there by Captain Elliot's'.[188] District electoral registration courts brought their own tensions as, no doubt, did the Registration Appeal Court for the counties of Berwick, Peebles, Roxburgh and Selkirk sitting in Jedburgh in 1836. On that occasion, with the four local sheriffs-depute presiding, an array of legal talent was present, including the advocate John Inglis who used feudal law to argue successfully for his own claim to a vote in Darlingshaugh.[189] The judges sat for a week hearing legal argument and more than seventy other cases were settled 'by agents and counsel' without a hearing.[190]

Craig's business partner, William Rutherford, was in sympathy with his political views. Rutherford became secretary of a Conservative Reading Room that was set up in Galashiels in a room hired from Adam Purdie, probably in the autumn of 1835, just before he entered into partnership with Craig.[191] The membership of the reading room may be gleaned from the firm's accounts and it included Craig and a number of his clients and connections, such as Torwoodlee, Scott of Gala, Thomas Bruce of Langlee, Donald Horne and the schoolmaster Robert Fyshe.[192] Publications in the reading room included a range of newspapers such as the *Berwick Warder*, *Kelso Mail*, *Edinburgh Observer*, *Edinburgh Advertiser*, *Edinburgh Courant* and the *Leeds Mercury*. In 1839 reference is made to a 'Parliamentary Guide', which was to lie in the reading room alongside other publications.[193] *Thomson's Gazetteer* was mentioned in 1842.[194] Craig and Rutherford received the subscriptions of members and also ensured that newspaper subscriptions were paid.

---

[185] SBA/1303/8/195, Craig/WS Walker, Bowland, 19 Mar. 1838.

[186] E.g. SBA/1303/5/23, Craig/Adam Fairholme of Chapel, 22 Feb., 1827; SBA/1303/7/322, Craig/William Lorraine-Ker, Musselburgh, 2 Jan. 1837; SBA/1303/8/26, Craig/Horne, 26 Aug. 1837.

[187] Anderson, ed., *Journal of Sir Walter Scott*, 714–15 (5 Mar. 1831). He drafted, but did not give or publish, an address. The Third Reform Bill received royal assent on 17 Jul. 1832.

[188] SBA/1303/6/331, Craig/LBC, 9 Nov. 1832.

[189] *Kelso Mail*, no. 4119, 29 Sep. 1836.

[190] Ibid., nos 4118, 4121.

[191] SBA/1303/8/78, Rutherford/editors of the *Carlisle Patriot*, 8 Nov. 1837.

[192] SBA/1303/9/29 (26 Oct. 1836).

[193] SBA/1303/9/238 (23 Mar. 1839).

[194] SBA/1303/9/611 (13 May 1842).

CONCLUSION

In the course of his working life, Craig encountered characters of every description and his letters highlight the everyday concerns of people in Galashiels in intricate detail, leaving us a valuable and unique testimony of time and place. Anyone meeting Craig in real life would have been struck by his strong Borders accent, something which very rarely comes across in his correspondence but is suggested from other sources.[195] He made his living, as lawyer, banker and land agent, through judging the character and credit of others and he was a sagacious commentator on life in general. By the time his letter books commence, he was highly experienced and this comes across in the efficient way in which, as a rule, he conducted business.

Craig worked hard to protect and improve his community. Aspects of his character readily emerge despite the dry and repetitive nature of much of his business correspondence. He had a social conscience, not only demonstrable in some of his dealings with the parish poor but also in the fact that he was treasurer of the Galashiels Savings Bank. He can also be found contributing to the 'distressed operatives in Paisley' in 1841; making a contribution to the unfortunate weavers in a town that, at that moment, was suffering 'socially horrific' levels of unemployment and poverty.[196] This may have been done as a token, from the bailie of one (by then successful) centre of textiles to one that was in economic decline. Craig was certainly no social radical: his principal concerns lay with the landowning classes, those whom they employed, and those whom they allowed to tenant their lands.

He was a shrewd business adviser who, paradoxically, near the end of his life found himself sequestrated due to the failure of the Leith Bank in which he had become a partner. He was a complex figure and is not someone about whom easy judgments can be made. Whether he merits a bridge bearing his name is firmly for the reader to decide. The chapters that follow may help to inform that opinion.

---

[195] E.g. G. Hughes, ed., *The Collected Letters of James Hogg* (Edinburgh, 2004–8), III, 142, James Hogg/John Wilson, 16 Mar. 1833.

[196] SBA/1303/9/593 (17 Dec. 1841); A. Leitch, 'Radicalism in Paisley 1830–1848 and its economic, political, cultural background' (M.Litt Thesis, University of Glasgow, 1993), 23.

Chapter 2

Parish Life in the Borders

The heritors, the substantial landowners of the parish, enjoyed social prominence and local influence. A landowner such as James Pringle of Torwoodlee supported the parish financially. Under 'public burdens' in the Torwoodlee accounts may be found payments in respect of the poors' rates and schoolmasters' salaries in Stow and Melrose; statute labour assessments for Melrose and Selkirkshire; county rogue money; a share in the payment of the ministers' stipends in Stow and Melrose and in the assessment on heritors for the upkeep of the manse in Stow.[1] Torwoodlee was also called upon to make occasional extraordinary contributions, as during the cholera epidemic in 1831–1833.[2]

Craig linked the wealthy and the poor within the parish. For all his contact with tenants, weavers and the parish poor, he could write of having the lairds of Gala and Torwoodlee visit his home or of conversing with the laird at church.[3] He shared his subscription to the *Literary Gazette* with Rev. Nathaniel Paterson (1787–1871) and Rev. James Henderson (1797–1874).[4] His social reach was such that he could write to the duke of Buccleuch, or Sir Walter Scott, as readily as to a gamekeeper, dry-stone dyker, or errant son failing to support his poor mother.

As law agent for heritors in Galashiels, Stow, Duns and other parishes, he had wide experience of heritors' meetings and knowledge of those who served as clerk. Professionally, this gave him useful understanding of affairs across at least three counties and allowed him the opportunity to be involved in projects of social or economic benefit. An example was a proposal in 1827 to extend the parish church in Galashiels. The builders Sanderson & Paterson planned an extra 300 seats at a cost of £450.[5] Craig, however, wrote to Gala with a revised proposition of his own which would extend the church by 100 seats for about £160. The builders were prepared to cover the cost in return for the rents of the additional seats until their outlay was repaid, plus about 7 per cent interest.

---

[1] NRA(S), TD2020/2/vol. 11, Torwoodlee Account Book, volume 11. Rogue money was a sum collected by the commissioners of supply and JPs from which payment might be made for manhunts when alleged criminals absconded.

[2] SBA/1303/6/430, Craig/Alexander Pringle of Whytbank, Edinburgh, 6 Nov. 1833.

[3] SBA/1303/3/305, Craig/Andrew Lang, Selkirk, 8 Feb. 1824; SBA/1303/5/245, Craig/Gala, 4 May 1828.

[4] SBA/1303/5/4, Craig/Rev. James Henderson, 16 Jan. 1827; SBA/1303/5/79, Craig/Rev. Nathaniel Paterson, 27 Jun. 1827. Both ministers became moderator of the Free Church.

[5] SBA/1303/5/65, Craig/Gala, 16 May 1827.

Craig thought this 'a very safe speculation' because the return was entirely at the builders' risk, and 'at the end of 15 or 16 years the property will become the heritors' & the people sit free'.[6]

The focus of this chapter will particularly fall on two aspects of parish life which are often connected: education and care for the poor. The connection lies in the role of the heritors, the parish schoolmaster and, to a great extent, Craig himself as adviser and law agent.

SCHOOLMASTERS

One of the most important decisions heritors had to take was selecting the local schoolmaster, since the appointee became intimately connected with shaping the parish. As well as being engaged to teach, some teachers were also charged with acting as clerk to the heritors or local kirk session. Such status gave them influence over the administration of poor relief and other matters, including control of the parish register of births and deaths. The schoolmaster David Wilson in Gordon, for example, was asked by Craig in 1826 to add to the register the birth of George Fairholme's daughter, Elizabeth Margery, who was born on 19 November at Châtelaine in Geneva.[7] By legislation dating back to 1696, the heritors and local ministers in each parish had a duty to pay the schoolmaster's salary and to provide him with suitable accommodation.[8] When a vacancy arose, Craig was closely involved in finding a replacement schoolmaster and framing a newspaper advertisement if necessary.[9]

The experienced schoolmaster in Galashiels, Robert Fyshe, was highly regarded and the parish school, located near Craig's house, was thriving in the 1820s.[10] Hall describes a visitation by the Presbytery in 1819, in which Craig was involved, which underlined how successful Fyshe was as a teacher, attracting pupils from Edinburgh.[11] In fact, a parent presented Fyshe with a coat as a gift following the public examination of the School, having been 'particularly pleased with the conspicuous figure his son made on that occasion'.[12] A former pupil later described Fyshe as 'dapper in figure, with a clean-shaven fresh coloured

---

[6] Craig was assuming that the seats did not accede to the church when they were built.

[7] SBA/1303/5/514, Craig/David Wilson, 22 Dec. 1826. At this time the hall used for heritors' meetings, owned by the heritors, was disponed to the feuars, with Wilson and his successors in office named in the deed.

[8] Ewen A. Cameron, 'Education in rural Scotland, 1696–1872' in R. Anderson *et al.*, ed., *The Edinburgh History of Education in Scotland* (Edinburgh, 2015), 154.

[9] SBA/1303/8/156, Craig/William Walker WS, 18 Feb. 1838.

[10] *The Scotsman*, 24 Apr. 1824, p. 263; 18 Apr. 1826, p. 296. Fyshe became schoolmaster in 1810: NRS, Scott of Gala papers, GD477/143/2; Helen E. Ross, ed., *Letters from Rupert's Land 1826–1840: James Hargrave of the Hudson's Bay Company* (Montreal, 2009), 12.

[11] Hall, *History of Galashiels*, 454. Hall indicates that Fyshe had a number of teaching assistants: ibid., 458. Visitations of this kind were reported in the press. In 1833, for instance, Mr Wanless was noted as Fyshe's assistant: *Caledonian Mercury*, no. 17438, 2 May 1833, p.1.

[12] SBA/1303/3/195, Craig/J. S. Mack, Edinburgh, 22 Feb. 1822.

face, shaggy eyebrows, and a firm and determined looking mouth . . . He spoke the vernacular in all its purity, and . . . his whole appearance, though undersized, appeared to his pupils almost awe-inspiring'.[13]

When Fyshe's salary came under review in 1829, his employer, John Scott of Gala, remarked favourably on the state of education in the parish. As he wrote to Craig:

> Keeping in mind of course that altho' the chief part of his emolument is derived from the boarders (& which circumstance undoubtedly enables him to afford better assistants than he would otherwise be able to engage) still that without the aid of the parish & the many advantages in the way of encouragement from the heritors, the convenience of the premises, & other circumstances connected with his situation as a parish schoolmaster, he could not in all likelihood have carried on the school on so large a scale – of this however I have no doubt Mr Fyshe will be quite sensible.[14]

A £30 salary, he thought, was the highest that might be justified.[15] As Fyshe charged each child boarding with him 30 guineas per year, his salary was only a modest element in his income.[16] When George Haldane of Whitebanklee sought a discount in 1829 because his son visited and ate with him on Sundays, and threatened to refer the matter to an arbiter, Craig thought him wrong to ask and considered that Fyshe would be equally wrong in making any such allowance.[17] Even so, Fyshe deducted £5 10s charged for the boy's laundry. He could well afford to do so, since in the same year Craig described him as 'a person of considerable property & in independent circumstances'.[18]

Craig was directly responsible for paying Fyshe's salary.[19] He also aided Fyshe in recovering fees, as when he wrote to his London solicitors Richardson & Connell seeking money from a parent. He enclosed a letter from the parent, a Mr Poole, indicating his satisfaction with the account furnished for his son's 'board & education'.[20]

Fyshe was the secretary of the Galashiels Bible Society of which Craig was the treasurer.[21] Despite being clerk to the kirk session, somewhat unusually for

---

[13] Hall, *History of Galashiels*, 455. A likeness of Fyshe appears at p. 454.

[14] NRS, Scott of Gala papers, GD477/138/20, Gala/Craig, 9 Mar. 1829. Punctuation added.

[15] The salary in 1792 was £6 7s 2d: Douglas, *OSA*, 314. It was raised to £30 in 1825, according to Hall, *History of Galashiels*, 454. The salary appears unaltered in 1845 at £30: Patterson, *NSA*, 25.

[16] Hall, *History of Galashiels*, 454.

[17] SBA/1303/5/383, Craig/Haldane, 11 Apr. 1829.

[18] SBA/1303/5/460, Craig/J. Willoughby, Esq., Berwick, 17 Oct. 1829. In 1823 Fyshe, then engaged in litigation, is described as needing money due to several recent disappointments: SBA/1303/3/112, Craig/John Younger, Haddington, 21 Jan. 1823.

[19] In a rare error, Craig even mistakenly paid Fyshe his salary twice in 1842: SBA/1303/9/579 (31 Dec. 1842). The share of the half-year salary paid by Scott was £8 14s 10½d.

[20] SBA/1303/6/145, Craig/Richardson & Connell, Fludyer Street, Westminster, 19 Feb. 1831.

[21] SBA/1303/6/174, Craig/Messrs George Paxton and N. Macdonald, Secretaries to the Bible Society, Edinburgh, 26 Apr. 1831.

a teacher he declined being precentor at church services.[22] He was, however, involved in the appointment of a substitute in the role and in 1834 presented Craig with a 'subscription paper' for a precentor's gown. As Craig confessed to the Edinburgh merchant James Paterson, they were both ignorant of the cost of such things. Characteristically, however, Craig knew what he wanted:

> The *quality* of course must not be so fine as the Minister's – It is *not* to have a velvet collar – in short to be a plain Gown of tolerably good stuff – at an expense as we suppose of 2 or £3. If we are pretty near in this – the sooner it is sent out the better, & as you & Adam are Galashiels Heritors you may each give us your half crown along with your neighbours.[23]

Fyshe could afford to forgo the fee of acting as precentor and was well enough off to invest in property which he let out.[24] Craig acted for him when he sought rent from the Galashiels house painter, Edward Gray and, later, Fyshe was landlord to Robert Brunton.[25] Craig also handled other business for Fyshe, including paying his subscription to the Edinburgh Association for the Promotion of the Fine Arts.[26] There was a strong relationship of trust between the two men. Craig's accounts even indicate Fyshe informally acting as Craig's agent in receiving rent for him from a woman named Betty Dobby.[27] Craig also took the opportunity of Fyshe going to Edinburgh to have him deliver a sealed parcel to the Leith Bank head office containing several hundred pounds in cash.[28]

    In 1838 Craig wrote to the Melrose schoolmaster, Thomas Murray, indicating Torwoodlee's agreement to him having the 'maximum salary'.[29] Craig added that he did not suppose 'any other of our clients will object', referring to his clients amongst the remaining heritors. Torwoodlee's bi-annual contribution to Murray's salary had hitherto been 15s 2d, as appears in his accounts and also in Craig's.[30] This contrasts with James Paris in Stow, whose salary, significantly less than that of Robert Fyshe, was insufficient to keep him free from money problems.[31] In 1821,

[22] Hall, *History of Galashiels*, 209. Rev. Russell recollected that his own teacher at Yarrow school, James Scott, acted as precentor: Russell, *Reminiscences of Yarrow*, 127. The offices of session clerk & precentor were normally held together, e.g. CH2/12/55/2/155 (16 Dec. 1781).
[23] SBA/1303/7/37, Craig/James Paterson, merchant, Edinburgh, 24 Dec. 1834. Craig was a regular correspondent of Adam Paterson WS of Whitelee (1799–1875). He and his brother James, both native to Galashiels, were sons of the Galashiels merchant Adam Paterson.
[24] SBA/1303/3/80, Craig/Mrs Peron, Edinburgh, 23 Nov. 1822; SBA/1303/3/83, Craig/H. D. Dickie, 29 Nov. 1822.
[25] SBA/1303/7/450, Craig/Gray, 23 May 1837; SBA/1303/9/42 (12 Jan. 1841); SBA/1303/9/43 (26 May 1841). Gray went out of business in 1838: SBA/1303/8/233, C&R/John Young, carrier, 23 Apr. 1838.
[26] SBA/1303/9/42 (20 Feb. 1838); see also SBA/1303/9/129. For some reason it was refunded on 14 May 1838. Craig himself also subscribed to Fine Arts (SBA/1303/9/296).
[27] SBA/1303/9/297 (14 May 1838).
[28] SBA/1303/3 fo. 240, Craig/LBC, 8 Sep. 1823.
[29] SBA/1303/8/130, Craig/Murray, 23 May 1837.
[30] E.g. Torwoodlee Account book, 26 May 1832; SBA/1303/7/235, Craig/Murray, 28 Jun. 1836.
[31] General Alexander Walker of Bowland contributed £1 0 5½d to his half-year salary in 1827 but the total salary is unknown: NLS, MS13965, fo. 9.

for instance, having already received his salary in advance, he was unable to pay his rent.[32] By then, he had been the schoolmaster for over twenty years (he had conducted the first census in Stow in 1801), teaching both local children and boarders.[33] As well as clerk to the heritors, Paris was clerk to the local kirk session (as was Fyshe in relation to Galashiels).[34]

When trying to arrange his retirement in 1827, Paris sought Craig's advice. He hoped for an 'assistant and successor' to be recruited from whose salary he might receive an annuity.[35] Craig, however, advised him that such a subvention was impossible, for any such individual 'must have the salary, school fees, house & garden with all the emoluments'. Any putative annuity for Paris would have to be paid as a gift from the heritors, unless the successor in question agreed to pay an annual sum in return for obtaining the situation. Were that the case, according to Craig, 'suppose the successor [agreed] to pay £10 & the heritors £15 – you would be better than with £20 from the heritors', although this was something for negotiation with the principal heritors, Gilbert Innes and John Borthwick of Crookston.

After Paris died aged sixty-three in 1830, his wife and family decided to emigrate to America and Craig was left to clear up the financial details, made more complicated by the death of Gilbert Innes of Stow in February 1832. Craig therefore had to work with Innes' Edinburgh agent, Hugh Watson WS.[36] The Paris family wished to dispose of the house and garden which they had bought in 1798 from James Frier, but they had no title, only Frier's missive of sale. Innes would not grant them a disposition of this property, as feudal superior, until any debts he held against Paris had been discharged. Given that the new schoolmaster, James Jackson, and his wife were keen to take the house at a rent of £3, Craig wanted to arrange this while allowing Innes' estate to draw the rent in satisfaction of any debts. The Paris family left Scotland about 1836 and settled in Canada. Paris' daughter, Margaret, had married George Lee and their sons, who grew up in Canada, were prolific inventors. James Paris Lee (1831–1904) developed munitions, famously including the Lee-Enfield Rifle used by the British Army.[37]

Craig took an interest in schools. When there was a vacancy at the parish school in Earlston in 1828, he wrote a recommendation to Lord Napier on behalf of Fyshe's assistant, William Tait, whom he had known for over two years. Tait, aged twenty-five with no pretensions to the church, was of excellent character,

---

[32] NRS, Papers of the Innes family of Stow, GD113/5/27b/17, James Paris/Gilbert Innes of Stow, 11 Apr. 1821.

[33] E.g. NRS, Papers of the Innes family of Stow, GD113/5/447/47, 24 Nov. 1798, idem; GD113/5/448/103, idem, 23 Apr. 1799. On the census, see NRS, GD113/1/470.

[34] Ibid., GD113/5/363/23, n.d.; e.g. NRS, Galashiels kirk session, CH2/1255/3/1, 4 Oct. 1835; Torwoodlee Account Book, 21 Oct. 1835, payment of £1 10s to Fyshe for 'Gala church rent'.

[35] SBA/1303/5/94, Craig/Paris, 21 Jul. 1827.

[36] SBA/1303/6/271, Craig/Hugh Watson WS, 13 Mar. 1832.

[37] A. M. Redpath, 'James and John Lee: the Hawick born brothers who changed the course of wars' *The Hawick Paper*, 30 Dec. 2016.

had prior experience of teaching in Peebles, and was 'an excellent Teacher of all the branches of Education now taught at Grammar Schools'.[38]

Craig made a point of speaking to schoolmasters as he traversed the country on clients' business since they were a key local point of reference. In 1825, having just taken on Dr Alexander Monro as a client, he visited Cockburn to make enquiries in the parish and called at the schoolmaster's house, writing to him later, with another visit in mind, hoping to make it coincide with the next heritors' meeting.[39] Another such visit, this time to Gordon in 1837, yielded a practical result by facilitating an extension to the school playground which the local tenants and feuars had recently repaired. Noticing that the walls of two thatched houses at the kirk-style (the entrance to the churchyard) were giving way, he had suggested to the schoolmaster David Wilson that if he asked the heritors for £20 for the land on which the houses stood, Craig would ask George Fairholme, who owned the land, to accept it.[40] Fairholme, as Craig predicted, readily agreed to allow the playground to be increased 'for the scholars' (with the additional benefit of improving access to the churchyard).[41] A few months later Wilson enquired about the purchase of two 'coo houses' and gardens at the kirk-style.[42] This time Fairholme refused to sell the gardens or grant Wilson any right to extract peat from Gordon Moss.[43] A lease of the gardens was possible but Wilson would have to negotiate with the local feuars for a share of the peat moss.[44] Craig advised him that the feuars had 'ten times more moss than they can work' so that he might be able to purchase cart loads from them or be allocated a corner to extract his own peat in return for payment. He knew the peat moss at Gordon well because he himself enjoyed the annual right to 120 horse loads of peat.[45]

In Bowden, the teacher John Scott was in charge of three children, George, William and Robert Bonnington, who benefited from a trust set up by their late father (also Robert) which Craig administered as one of the trustees.[46] Expenses for the children were always paid in Craig's office.[47] In 1829, Craig questioned items Scott charged in his quarterly account since they were significantly higher than those in Galashiels.[48] The quarterly fees in Galashiels were 2s 6d for English, 3s for English and Writing, and 3s 6d for English, Writing and Accounts.[49] Scott,

[38] SBA/1303/5/203, Craig/Lord Napier, 30 Jun. 1828.
[39] SBA/1303/4/257, Craig/Mr Nairne, schoolmaster, Duns, 21 Oct. 1825.
[40] SBA/1303/8/18, Craig/G. Fairholme, 16 Aug. 1837.
[41] SBA/1303/8/30, Craig/D. Wilson, 31 Aug. 1837.
[42] SBA/1303/8/150, Craig/G. Fairholme, 10 Feb. 1838.
[43] SBA/1303/8/173, Craig/D. Wilson, 1 Mar. 1838.
[44] What remains of Gordon Moss is today a Site of Special Scientific Interest.
[45] SBA/1303/8/191, Craig/T. Robertson, forester, Gordon, 15 Mar. 1838. On Gordon Moss, see Chapter 7.
[46] There is a reference to Bonnington's trust estate in 1823 when it was valued at £311: SBA/1303/3/250, Craig/W. Turnbull, Peebles, 22 Sep. 1823; SBA/1303/3/241, Craig/William Ramsay, Stamp Office, Edinburgh, 8 Sep. 1823.
[47] SBA/1303/4/197, Elliot Anderson/John Scott, 1 May 1825.
[48] SBA/1303/5/420, Craig/Mr Scott, Bowden, 10 Jul. 1829.
[49] Paterson, *NSA* (1845), 26.

however, charged 3s for all of these in respect of George, but 5s for William who received the same classes and the same for Robert who was taught only writing and accounts. Scott charged also for copy and accounting books, and what he charged for 'statutory ware' was out of comparison with Galashiels charges. Craig therefore returned his account 'to be made up anew consistent with regular parish rates'. In 1825, with trust income declining, Craig asked Scott to provide the boys with shirts and stockings 'in as economical a way as you can'.[50] On another occasion, he relied on Scott to purchase seed and plant some potatoes for Mrs Bonnington.[51]

Craig's relationship with Robert Bonnington can be traced in his correspondence. He admonished him for his conduct in 1828, noting that he was 'just at the age to commence your ruin both of yourself and your Brothers' and advising him that the quicker he took up an apprenticeship in some trade the better, otherwise those helping him on his late father's account would cease to do so.[52] In 1835, after Robert had been established as a wright near Edinburgh, he sent Craig a letter which the latter thought 'sensibly written', however the spelling needed improvement.[53] This Craig advised could be done easily 'by noticing accurately the words as you read slowly along for some time either books or newspapers'.[54] After Bonnington inherited land as heir to his grandfather, William, Craig collected the rent on his behalf.[55] In 1839 he endeavoured to put him on the voters' roll, seeking a precept of *clare constat* from the duke of Roxburghe.[56] He also approved of his brother, George, becoming apprentice to a Galashiels tailor in 1833.[57]

ADMINISTRATION OF THE POOR LAW

In rural communities, responsibility for administering the poor law (which was introduced in 1574) lay jointly with the kirk session and the heritors.[58] The Berwickshire judge, Lord Kames, who opposed a perpetual tax for poor relief but regarded charity as a natural duty, thought that the system in Scotland was less subversive of morals than any other. The parish landowners oversaw the poor fund

[50] SBA/1303/4/253, Craig/Scott, 13 Oct. 1825. Craig noted interest in a one-year lease of Bonnington's land in 1823: SBA/1303/3/270, Craig/John Dun, Bowden, 18 Mar. 1823.

[51] SBA/1303/4/179, Elliot Anderson/Scott, 13 Apr. 1825.

[52] SBA/1303/5/192, Craig/R. Bonnington, Bowden, 17 Jan. 1828. There is reference in 1823 to land held by the widow Bonnington: SBA/1303/3/108, Craig/John Thomson, Bowden, 16 Jan. 1823.

[53] Craig also established William Bonnington in an apprenticeship with a wright at Lessudden (St Boswells): SBA/1303/6 fo. 346, Craig/James Thomson, 3 Jan. 1832.

[54] SBA/1303/7/73, Craig/R. Bonnington, 2 Jun. 1835.

[55] Ibid., Craig/Robert Bonnington, Newcastle upon Tyne, 17 Jul. 1839; Craig/Archibald Donaldson, farmer, Bowden, 13 Jan. 1840.

[56] SBA/1303/8/451, Craig/Mackenzie & Innes WS, 15 Mar. 1839; SBA/1303/8/478, Craig/John Smith, Kelso, 18 Apr. 1839. On such precepts, see Chapter 6.

[57] SBA/1303/6/350, Craig/Thomas Walker, tailor, Galashiels, 17 Jun. 1833.

[58] RPS, 1575/3/5; on the background, see R. Mitchison, *The Old Poor Law in Scotland* (Edinburgh, 2000), chapter 1.

while, as Kames put it, 'leaving the objects of their charity, and the measure, to their own humanity and discretion'.[59]

The mechanism for poor relief came in the twin forms of legal assessments (taxation) and voluntary contributions (such as church collections).[60] Various legislative acts specified those groups deserving of relief and required parishes to place a stent (tax) upon the heritors and other inhabitants. The stent was upon the valued rent although, in some places, it had begun to be assessed on the real rent.[61] The difference between the two was noted by Rev. Douglas in the *Old Statistical Account*. The valued rent of the heritors in Galashiels in 1792 was just over £8,225 Scots, whereas the real value of the rent was £16,000 sterling.[62] In 1672 it was enacted that the heritors bore 'the burden of the maintenance of the poor persons of each parish', and the local kirk session, while it might act independently, was accountable to the heritors; neither body could meet without first informing the other.[63] Moreover, support had to be given according to 'where these idle persons were born, or have most haunted the last three years'.[64] Evidence of three-years' residence within a parish therefore attached liability for support to the local heritors and kirk session.

Craig had definite ideas about the poor's roll, as he explained to Alexander Monro in 1838 in connection with a report he had seen of the system in Berwickshire. He disapproved of applicants for poor relief having to answer queries in writing about their circumstances. He preferred

> that in every case when they can appear at a quarterly or half yearly Heritor's Meeting that they do so personally and give an account of their situation and if admitted on the Roll that they make an assignment of their effects before leaving the Meeting of which the Clerk to the heritors will next day take an Inventory.[65]

Handing out pre-printed schedules to applicants, he thought, was simply an invitation for them to be put on the roll. On the relationship between the kirk session and the heritors, he made this observation:

> I am against applications being made in the first place to the Kirk Session for a supply from the Church collection which I would invariably keep distinct from the assessments and entirely at the disposal of the Kirk Session.[66]

Craig's advice was that Duns parish employ someone to look out for those likely to come onto the poor's roll to see whether work might be found for them, even

---

[59]   Henry Home [Lord Kames], *Sketches of the History of Man* (Edinburgh, 1778), 540.

[60]   R. A. Cage, *The Scottish Poor Law 1745–1845* (Edinburgh, 1981), 7.

[61]   Mitchison, *Old Poor Law*, 127; Cage, *Scottish Poor Law*, 8–9.

[62]   Douglas, *OSA*, 314.

[63]   RPS, 1672/6/52; Cage, *Scottish Poor Law*, 7.

[64]   RPS, 1672/6/52.

[65]   SBA/1303/8/259, Craig/Alexander Monro, 4 Jun. 1838.

[66]   SBA/1303/8/259–260.

in the short-term, so that temporary financial support (from the kirk session or the heritors) might be given rather than have them fully admitted to the roll. He mentioned his disapproval of poorhouses being built anywhere in the county, although he did not provide reasons (Galashiels had no poorhouse until 1859).[67]

Poor relief was aimed at those unable to work or provide for their own mainte-nance, such as the sick, elderly, orphans or other poor children. The able-bodied who could work but were unemployed gained no relief from assessed funds, but might be provided for out of voluntary contributions.[68] As Mitchison noted, all assessment had an element of voluntariness about it, since heritors might try to avoid paying the assessed rate.[69] Besides, philosophically, the preference was for voluntary contributions which the poor would receive with gratitude, rather than funds from compulsory taxation which they might come to demand as of right and which might therefore 'debase the morals of the lower classes'.[70] The idea that funds from the kirk session were seen as a benefaction, whereas funds from the heritors were considered as a right, was echoed by Rev. George Thomson when commenting on the situation in Melrose in 1834.[71]

In Selkirk, the arrangements concerning the method of assessing burgh inhab-itants for poor relief were determined in 1765, following a legal opinion from the advocate Alexander Lockhart which required the heritors to contribute in confor-mity with the value of their rents. The bailies and heritors were to meet and agree

> in making up a list of the whole poor in the parish and to assess the town proportionally to its valuation alongst with the heritors, and in case of their refusal . . . to require the heritors to do it under form of instruments.[72]

The council reverted to Lockhart, via their Edinburgh agent Cornelius Elliot WS, for further advice on how to force heritors to provide for the town's poor as well as those 'in the country part of the parish'.[73] The need to sue heritors for pay-ment cannot have been unusual. There is an example from Selkirk in 1783 when John Shortreed of Greenhead was successfully pursued in the Court of Session for payment of his contribution by the clerk of the poor rates.[74] Craig, however, seems not to have been placed in the position of having to go to court.

The level of allowance to the poor was reviewed at heritors' meetings which took place bi-annually, normally in November and April or May, although extraordinary

---

[67] Hall, *History of Galashiels*, 578.
[68] Cage, *Scottish Poor Law*, 10–11; see the opinion of Lord Craigie in *Landward Heritors v Magistrates of Dunbar* (1833) S.C. 886.
[69] Mitchison, *Old Poor Law*, 125.
[70] Cage, *Scottish Poor Law*, 85.
[71] Thomson, *NSA*, 73.
[72] SBA, Selkirk TCM, BS/1/1/8, 13 Feb. 1765.
[73] On eighteenth-century burgh agents, see J. Finlay, *Legal Practice in Eighteenth-Century Scotland* (Leiden, 2015), chapter 9.
[74] SBA, Selkirk TCM, BS1/1/1/9, 25 Jan. 1783, 11 Apr. 1783, 8 Apr. 1784, 27 Sep. 1786. Thomas Cockburn WS was then the burgh's agent; the advocate George Currie appeared for the clerk.

meetings were called if necessary. In 1836, Craig authorised John Wilson jr in Cockburn to attend a heritors' meeting in Duns on his behalf since, as Monro's agent, he held a proxy vote. The meeting was to discuss whether to alter 'the mode of assessing for the poor rates by taking the actual in place of the valued rents as the Rule'.[75] Craig took the view, following a recent Court of Session decision, that Duns should use the actual value of land.[76] In the relevant judgment, *Cochrane v Manson*, the court had decided that in a rural parish the entire personal property of a heritor should be subject to assessment, rather than simply the value of property which he owned within the parish. This remained a major topic of discussion in Duns, prompting 'many a long meeting', as Craig noted in 1838.[77]

The plan adopted was to assess the parish according to the real value of the rents, with the town of Duns itself being valued at £300 Sterling. There had been delays in facilitating this, however, due to some land not being valued in the cess books and some having been split in the old valuation books. The parish in general was valued at £1,200 and the assessment rate was 1s 2d per £1 (a rate of 5.83 per cent). The revision meant a reduction in liability for Craig's client Monro at Cockburn, although for others the reverse was true.

Craig was given access to the records by the heritors' clerk, William Waite. As he told Monro,

> I was glad to observe on looking over the books for some years back that the number of paupers was rather decreasing than increasing. Mr Waite has a laborious task of it, though pretty well paid with a salary of £50 per annum.[78]

Payments of poor rates made by the Galashiels heritors to Robert Fyshe came through Craig & Rutherford's accounts and can be found in their surviving account book. Mr Plummer of Lindean, for example, paid £6 10s 5d in September 1843 covering what he was due for the half year between Whitsunday and Martinmas.[79] Craig also collated contributions from elsewhere. An example is the poor rate receipts left with him by the Melrose schoolmaster Thomas Murray, for which Craig provided a letter of credit in March 1837.[80]

Craig himself was liable to contribute to the poor's rates.[81] He also had to see to the appropriate division of valued rent when part of a property was sold, as when James Pringle sold part of the land of Crosslee in 1822. To the buyer, Colonel Walker, was attributed £155 of the total valued rent of £233 Scots, with Pringle's share given the remainder. As this also affected the stipend of Mr Cormack, the local minister, Craig asked James Paris to inform him.[82]

[75] SBA/1303/7/291-2, Craig/John Wilson jr, 15 Nov. 1836.
[76] *Cochrane v Manson* (1823) S.C. 134.
[77] SBA/1303/8/368, Craig/Dr Monro, 5 Nov. 1838.
[78] Ibid.
[79] SBA/1303/9/690 (22 Sep. 1843).
[80] SBA/1303/7/383, Craig/Murray, 9 Mar. 1837. See also, SBA/1303/8/559, idem, 29 Aug. 1839.
[81] SBA/1303/9/296 (3 Mar. 1838); SBA/1303/9/380 (25 Feb. 1839).
[82] SBA/1303/2/84-5, Craig/James Paris, 3 Dec. 1822.

The Parish Poor

In 1833 the Galashiels minister, Nathaniel Paterson, noted that in the parish the average number of poor enrolled was nineteen, with a further six persons receiving interim supply.[83] There were church collections from which those not enrolled, but suffering hardship due to temporary sickness, would receive support.

Throughout Craig's correspondence, poor people are mentioned in a range of different circumstances. William Douglas and his wife, Margaret Watson, provide an example. In 1825 Douglas was aged eighty-four and his wife was over fifty.[84] They had two young children: one, aged thirteen and in service; the other, aged nine, living at home. Stow parish was liable to aliment them due to historical residence, even though they now lived in Galashiels, where their children had been educated liberally. Craig insisted that they be added to the regular poor's roll at Stow, since Stow and Galashiels had both been providing them with interim supply but this was proving inadequate. The following year, the Stow heritors increased their allowance 'in consequence of old age and increased infirmities', despite their children now being 'almost all' off their hands.[85] According to Craig, the parents were still fit for summer work and, all things considered, 'might shift pretty well' given their circumstances. He sought repayment from Stow, however, of money advanced to them by Galashiels.

Parish relief in such cases, in line with Craig's general philosophy, was provided only if there was no alternative. When Marion Phin sought aid from Galashiels in 1825, Craig wrote to her brother, a church minister in Wick, asking him to support her in order to free the parish of the burden.[86] This, Craig, ventured, was no more than performing a duty to his sister befitting one of his rank in society. Similarly, in 1831, faced with 'the utmost destitution' in which Joseph Thorpe, his pregnant wife, and their four children, found themselves, he wrote to the deputy overseer in Thorpe's previous parish, Uppingham in the County of Rutland.[87] Thorpe had failed to find work in Gala but had a brother, Charles, a shoemaker in Uppingham, and Craig sought immediate funds from him or from the parish, noting that Thorpe's wife was ill and had been attended by a surgeon.

The Wandering Poor

The 'wandering poor' were unpredictable and therefore regarded as a nuisance, particularly as by definition they had no strong parish connection. Part of Craig's job was to avoid unnecessary additional costs and, while responsibility for the long-settled local poor had to be borne, every parish was keen to wash its hands

---

[83] Paterson, *OSA*, p. 26.
[84] SBA/1303/4/171, Craig/Rev. John Cormack, Stow, 14 Mar. 1825.
[85] SBA/1303/4/308, Craig/Alexander Pringle, Yair, 24 Jan. 1826.
[86] SBA/1303/4/261, Craig/Robert Phin, minister of Wick, 27 Oct. 1825. Craig described himself as writer and praeses of the heritors.
[87] SBA/1303/6/230, Craig/Mr Wortley, 13 Oct. 1831.

of the wandering poor if it could. No clearer example of this can be found than the case of James Wight in 1831. Melrose parish, which had been alimenting him, claimed he belonged to Stow, but Craig (on behalf of the Stow heritors) was keen to disprove this. According to Craig's own records, Wight left Bankhouse, in Stow parish, at Whitsunday 1822, but Craig did not know whether he had remained elsewhere in the parish the following year long enough to qualify him for parochial support. Elliot Anderson therefore instructed Stow schoolmaster James Jackson to make enquiries.[88] Craig refused to acquiesce in the claim because Wight 'might live for 20 years & so cost the parish £100 or more'.[89] He was surprised to hear that an Edinburgh solicitor-at-law, Joseph Brown, was threatening to raise a summons on behalf of Melrose, particularly as he knew that James Curle, agent for many of the heritors of that parish, had thought it better to come to some mutual arrangement than enter an expensive lawsuit.[90] Pragmatically, while confident that Melrose could not demonstrate that Wight had resided for the required period of three years in Stow, Craig was content to let the heritors reach a compromise.

In another case, he took the opposite approach. This involved Helen (Nelly) Scott whom he described as 'a young woman totally unfit ever to do anything for herself'.[91] Galashiels regarded the case as important because of the potential cost. The dispute lay with the parish of Crailing in Roxburghshire whose new minister, Andrew Milroy, had proposed referring the matter to an advocate for arbitration. Craig, certain that Crailing was liable, refused and, within a month, raised a sheriff court action and, when Crailing backed off, insisted on obtaining expenses for the action raised.[92] Unfortunately, confusion then reigned. While Craig sought expenses plus recompense for the money Galashiels had expended on Nelly, Milroy was apparently unaware that the matter had been settled. Following a desperate visit from Nelly's sister, Craig urged Crailing's agent to act because 'the poor woman is almost in a state of starvation'.[93] While the matter was resolved, and Craig's account submitted in October 1837, the money had still not been paid by the following January.[94]

In 1839, in the case of a former Edinburgh merchant, James Kilgour, Craig again showed a robust attitude to avoid Melrose parish getting 'into a scrape'.[95] He was alerted by the procurator fiscal to the fact that Kilgour had been certified

[88] SBA/1303/6/203, Anderson/Jackson, 21 Jul. 1831. Craig himself visited Bankhouse in Dec. 1831, SBA/1303/6/252.

[89] SBA/1303/6/209, Craig/Mr Jackson, Stow, 5 Aug. 1831.

[90] SBA/1303/6/402, Craig/Joseph Brown, 22 Jul. 1833.

[91] SBA/1303/7/264, Craig/Rev. Andrew Milroy, Crailing, 21 Sep. 1836. Milroy (b. 1801) became the local minister in 1829: A. W. Milroy, *Memorials of a Quiet Ministry, Being the Life and Letters of Rev. Andrew Milroy* (London, 1876), 10.

[92] SBA/1303/7/313, Craig/Simon Scott, writer, Jedburgh, 16 Dec. 1836.

[93] SBA/1303/7/331, idem, 10 Jan. 1837.

[94] SBA/1303/8/60, Craig/clerk of Crailing parish, 10 Oct. 1837; SBA/1303/8/133, Craig/Rev. Andrew Milroy, 22 Jan. 1838.

[95] SBA/1303/8/506, Craig/Thomas Murray, 11 Jun. 1839.

insane. The fiscal, Robert Gillon Thomson, was at a loss how to provide support, but Craig was quite certain: the answer was to return Kilgour to the parish to which he belonged. He advised the local schoolmaster to identify the clerk of the parish containing the Tron Kirk in Edinburgh because Kilgour would have

> either an alimentary allowance from that Parish, or from the Merchant Company of Edinburgh; he will become a serious burden on Melrose parish in all probability if his case is not speedily and well looked into.[96]

Speed was necessary because Kilgour's period of residence in the neighbourhood of Buckholmside was almost sufficient for Melrose to acquire liability for parochial poor relief.

As adjacent parishes, occasional tension between Galashiels and Melrose was to be expected. Robert Fyshe wrote to Thomas Murray, his Melrose counterpart, in November 1834 threatening a lawsuit because Galashiels had directed a pauper to Melrose only to see him sent returned over the parish boundary the next day.[97] Fyshe castigated Melrose's 'stupid' legal adviser for resisting 'the common opera-tion of the law' and committing 'an absurdity' by promoting the idea that paupers should be supported in the parish in which they were found, rather than by the parish to which they properly belonged. Unless Melrose sent for the pauper imme-diately, he threatened, 'legal steps will be resorted to, to compel you to relieve Galashiels parish of the burden in the usual manner & to relieve it also of the heavy expenses already incurred'. It is unlikely that this letter was sent without Craig's advice and approval.

Thomas Brydon of Stagehall

One of the longest-running claims which Craig had to deal with as agent to the heritors of Stow was by Thomas Brydon of Stagehall. It related to those who constituted perhaps the clearest example of the wandering poor. Brydon, 'a most respectable farmer & a man of talents', was collector of the assessments and distributor of money to the ordinary poor of Stow parish.[98] As directed by the War Office, the heritors and kirk session were, as Elliot Anderson later explained it,

> in the habit of making certain payments to the wives & children of soldiers who might be passing towards England which advances were repaid by the Collector of Excise from time to time, on the receipts being presented accompanied by certain certificates of the payments.[99]

The heritors had made Brydon responsible for making such payments to eligible dependents passing by on the Edinburgh to Carlisle road. There was no national

---

[96] Ibid.
[97] SBA/1303/7/27, Fyshe/Mr Murray, Melrose, 4 Nov. 1834.
[98] SBA/1303/5/270, Craig/William Walker WS, 25 Jun. 1828.
[99] SBA/1303/6/309, Anderson/schoolmaster of Selkirk, 3 Jun. 1832.

system of payments to support military families, despite attempts to incentivise recruitment into the armed forces, and local provision was seen as an extension of poor relief.[100]

Brydon, according to Craig, was the most suitable person to be employed by the heritors 'in paying the soldiers wives & children their allowances according to the certificates & passes which they bore'.[101] On at least one occasion, he was directly ordered to do so when several soldiers' wives appeared during a heritors' meeting. He was then told, probably on Craig's advice, that in continuing to make such payments he bore less risk than his counterparts at Middleton, to the north, or Selkirk, to the south, since he could always follow their example in deciding whether to advance any funds. Brydon's claim amounted to £90 15s 9, of which he received £28 11s from the Excise Office in Edinburgh, leaving £52 1s 9d outstanding. An investigation in 1817 by the commissioners of excise, however, had rejected Brydon's claim for relief on the basis that in many cases he had been misled by 'misrepresentations & fraudulent certificates' into making payments that were not due. Craig disagreed with their conclusion, citing the evidence of the collectors' books from Selkirk and Middleton which demonstrated that they had been reimbursed for advances to the same parties.

Brydon's case was managed by William Walker WS in Edinburgh and, following a heritors' meeting at the Torsonce Inn on 27 October 1823, Craig wrote to Walker asking what had been done to advance his claim against the commissioners of excise.[102] Brydon's loss was by then around £70 (including interest) and if the Commissioners would not make this good he looked to the heritors to do so. The collector of excise at Kelso, William Gillespie, informed Brydon in May 1824 that according to the Commissioners no investigation had, in fact, been undertaken at the Excise Office when these claims 'were recent & admitted of being checked and examined' and that his receipts were now too old to be allowed. Unhappy with this, the heritors decided that a memorial should be drafted, either by Walker or Gilbert Innes, to be approved by the other heritors and sent to the Treasury Board in London.[103] The matter, however, rumbled on. It was the first item on the agenda of a heritors' meeting at Stow on 30 October 1826.[104] At that juncture, Craig was content for the heritors to pay Brydon because Gilbert Innes, by far the wealthiest amongst them, had long held on to the papers in the case,

---

[100] For England the relevant legislation, from 1803, was 43 Geo. III, c. 61, *An Act for the Relief of Soldiers, Sailors, and Marines, and of the wives of Soldiers, in the cases therein mentioned, so far as relates to England*; cf. J. Hurl-Eamon, 'Did Soldiers Really Enlist to Desert Their Wives? Revisiting the Martial Character of Marital Desertion in Eighteenth-Century London' (2014) 53 *Journal of British Studies*, 356, 367–8.

[101] SBA/1303/5/270, Craig/William Walker WS, 25 Jun. 1828.

[102] SBA/1303/3/269, Craig/Walker, 7 Nov. 1823. Craig mistakenly dates the advances to 1816–1818 in his letter, but there was only one claim and it was in respect of £52 1s 9d laid out between 1813 and 1816. To this sum, interest was added and the debt therefore increased over time.

[103] SBA/1303/4/41-2, idem, 5 Jun. 1824.

[104] SBA/1303/4/472, idem, 24 Oct. 1826.

including the petition and appeal to the Treasury, and deserved to be saddled with the expenses unless they were lodged quickly.[105] Eventually the matter was brought, by the commissioners of excise in London, to the attention of the Secretary for War, Lord Palmerston, who noted that proper evidence was required that Brydon was duly authorised to make the payments for which he claimed.[106]

In 1830, Craig wrote to his own London agents, Richardson & Connell, sending them copies of previous correspondence. Brydon, whose claim now exceeded £93, still sought payment directly from the heritors. In turn, they pressed a demand for payment against the War Office with Craig noting that the latter 'do not resist it altogether, but the matter never comes to a settlement'.[107] Offering to furnish any further details necessary, Craig asked Richardson & Connell to enquire at the War Office and, if necessary, prepare a fresh memorial on the subject. Two years later, Elliot Anderson wrote to the schoolmasters in Selkirk and Middleton, asking them whether any documentary evidence survived mentioning the names or circumstances of the individuals to whom similar advances had been made.[108] By now, fifteen years had passed since the payments were made but Selkirk provided a certified list of eighty-two wives which Craig sent to William Walker in December 1832. Middleton could not produce a list, but the parish schoolmaster there at the time had moved to Borthwick and a letter was sent to him.[109] How the matter was finally resolved, if it was, does not appear.

AFFILIATION AND ALIMENT

The Galashiels kirk session minute book bears testimony to numerous instances of 'antenuptial fornication' and Craig's correspondence occasionally mentions unwed mothers who had been abandoned by the alleged fathers of their children, a common issue for parishes across the country.[110] Any claim brought by women in such circumstances required proof, and, without evidence, the sheriff would not allow the pursuer to rely on her oath of verity naming the defender as father.[111] All that could be done was a reference to the defender's oath and this was precarious, although admissions of paternity were by no means unusual.[112] Whenever paternity was straightforwardly acknowledged, Craig's task was to ensure that the father paid, and found someone to act as guarantor for, financial maintenance for the child and the 'inlying expenses' connected with the birth. For example,

[105] SBA/1303/4/476, Craig/James Paris, 28 Oct. 1826.
[106] SBA/1303/5/270, idem, 25 Jun. 1828.
[107] SBA/1303/6/110, Craig/Richardson & Connell, 29 Oct. 1830.
[108] SBA/1303/6/309, Anderson/schoolmaster of Selkirk, 3 Jun. 1832.
[109] SBA/1303/6/337, Craig/William Walker, 1 Dec. 1832.
[110] SBA, CH2/1255/2, Galashiels Kirk Session, Minutes, 1715–1835.
[111] SBA/1303/7/414-5, Craig/James Turnbull, Musselburgh, 12 Apr. 1837.
[112] R. Mitchison and L. Leneman, *Girls in Trouble: Sexuality and Social Control in Rural Scotland 1660–1780* (Edinburgh, 1998), 107–8, indicated in their data a variable percentage of men admitting paternity within one month of being named, but the national sample suggested a figure of 65 per cent.

Alison Brown, despite being in 'a destitute situation', employed Craig to ensure that she received maintenance from William Scott, a dyer in Hawick, who had acknowledged paternity of the child she was carrying.[113] Elliot Anderson wrote to Scott seeking pecuniary assistance and asking whom he proposed to co-sign a bond of obligation as guarantor to ensure ongoing maintenance. In another case, John Aitken, a writer in Dalkeith, was employed to raise letters of supplement or a summons on behalf of Elizabeth Howden against William Fairgrieve of Kilcoulter near Heriot.[114] Pressure was brought to bear by means of an arrestment against Fairgrieve's relatives with whom, according to Elizabeth's father, he had 'deposited his trunk & effects & also any money he had'.[115] The result was a proposal to Stow kirk session from Fairgrieve that he pay £17 10s, a sum Craig authorised Aitken to accept.[116]

In an earlier case, also with a Dalkeith connection, Craig acted for Christian Brown who had been in service there, between Whitsunday and Martinmas 1822, during which time she conceived a child.[117] Craig having 'reason to know & believe' that the alleged father, John Williams, had acknowledged paternity, instructed a local agent, described only as 'the successor of William Roberton', to bring the matter to the JP court because Williams had failed to respond to requests for money.[118] He was to be libelled 'for the usual allowances granted by the Justices in your district', reflecting the fact that awards tended to become standardised.[119] The 'successor to Roberton' was the firm of Bell & Gardner who promptly replied but seem to have done little else. Both mother and baby became ill and this, joined with her poverty and 'the decreasing kindness of her friends so common in such cases', prompted Anderson to write expressing the hope that the agents had obtained an order for payment and would do whatever they could to compel its enforcement.[120] Unfortunately, months passed without payment.[121] The accumulation of arrears of aliment, and the need to threaten or bring law suits, was, of course, a perennial issue even after initial court action. An example is a letter sent to a Selkirk man giving only two days' notice to pay arrears owed to Eliza Thomson in Galashiels, which failing an action would be raised.[122]

The absence of paternal acknowledgement and support could have unpleasant consequences, including even child abandonment. In one such case, where

[113] SBA/1303/2/98, Elliot Anderson/William Scott, 9 Aug. 1821.
[114] SBA/1303/6/485, John Cranston[?]/Aitken, 2 Jun. 1834. Letters of supplement were granted by the Court of Session to authorise a party domiciled in one jurisdiction to be cited before the inferior judge in another, in this case presumably the JP court in Dalkeith. Heriot was then situated in Midlothian.
[115] SBA/1303/7/18, idem, 10 Oct. 1834.
[116] SBA/1303/7/43, Craig/Aitken, 8 Jan. 1835.
[117] Cf. SBA, CH2/1255/2/191, Galashiels Kirk Session, Minutes, 1 Jun. 1823.
[118] SBA/1303/3/171, Craig/the successor of William Robertson, Dalkeith, 14 May 1823.
[119] As noted by Mitchison and Leneman, *Girls in Trouble*, 80.
[120] SBA/1303/3/216-7, Elliot Anderson/Bell & Gardner, 29 Jul. 1823.
[121] SBA/1303/3/258, idem, 15 Oct. 1823.
[122] E.g. SBA/1303/8/193, Craig/Gilbert Aitken, 19 Mar. 1838.

an infant had been left exposed at the door of George Haldane's inn at Galashiels, the procurator fiscal at Selkirk informed Craig when the suspected mother was granted bail.[123] Craig's interest lay in the fact that it had fallen to his parish to maintain the child.

If fathers could not be found, additional strain was put upon the parish poor's roll. To avoid this, heritors were willing to go to substantial lengths to see that responsibilities were met. Craig recommended his London agents, Richardson & Connell, to Robert Fyshe who wrote to them in 1833 as clerk to the Galashiels heritors 'with a small piece of business' of an urgent nature.[124] The matter related to George Brown, servant to Archibald Gibson of Ladhope. Both were visiting Gibson's son, James, a lieutenant in the Royal Navy residing in Epping Forest. Brown, it was understood, was to accompany James on a voyage to Upper Canada where he intended to settle. Unfortunately, he was the reputed father of an illegitimate child by a fellow servant at Ladhope, Janet Rutherford, and had made no provision for the child. It was only after Brown had left the neighbourhood that Rutherford publicly named him, otherwise the parish would have acted sooner. As it was, Richardson & Connell were asked to find some means of forcing him to find security for the payment of £4 per annum until the child, presently sixteen months old, reached the age of seven. The heritors were 'disposed to go any length' against him and sought to detain him pending the provision of adequate security for payment. He escaped them, however, and at the end of 1834 Craig reported that Brown was 'now in America'.[125] As Rutherford was residing in Galashiels, she required interim aliment until her proper parish could be established. Craig, therefore, having reason to believe that she belonged to West Kirk parish in Edinburgh, wrote to Adam Paterson WS instructing him to make enquiries and 'find out the proper way of getting at that'.[126]

Craig also took great trouble to trace absent fathers. In 1827 he wrote to a London millwright hoping to trace a journeyman, William Smith, who had left Galashiels two years earlier and deserted his wife and six children. Smith had sent only a few shillings the year before and, if he persisted in such 'cruel treatment', Craig warned that the parish would bring proceedings against him.[127] He was keen to discover Smith's salary, offering to put off litigation if a proportion of his wages would be sent for the support of his family.

A more complicated case had arisen in 1821. Tods & Romanes WS wrote to Scott of Gala in relation to Margaret Cairns, a pauper who had been deserted by her husband and forced to rely upon parish support. Liability for her was disputed between Galashiels and Melrose given that she had lived in both parishes. Tods & Romanes counselled that Galashiels should advance funds under protest that

[123] SBA, Rodger & Paterson Letter book [RPLB], D/45/35/2, fos 511–12, George Rodger/George Craig, 1 May 1820.
[124] SBA/1303/6/394, Robert Fyshe/Richardson & Connell, London, 28 Jun. 1833.
[125] SBA/1303/7/36, Craig/Phin and Pitcairn WS, 13 Dec. 1834.
[126] SBA/1303/6/450, Craig/Adam Paterson WS, 20 Jan. 1834.
[127] SBA/1303/5/106, Craig/Robert Morton, millwright, 327 Strand, London, 15 Aug. 1827.

doing so neither implied liability nor prevented seeking recovery of the money from Melrose should they ultimately be found liable. Having done so, the way was clear to bring an action before the sheriff of Roxburghshire. They further advised Gala to form a committee from both parishes and seek the opinion 'of one or more respectable counsel thereon by which they should be guided'.[128] An offer to arbitrate, however, fell through in September 1822.[129] The case was ongoing in 1823, when Craig discussed it with the Selkirk writer and sheriff clerk, Andrew Lang (1784–1842). Craig was confident that a memorial drafted for Melrose posed no threat. He advised Lang to insist on Melrose reimbursing payments already made by Galashiels parish and, if they agreed to do so, then he would agree to expenses being borne equally by each party. If not, then 'we must push for both the repayment & expenses & allow the case to go on after the Memorials'.[130]

In concluding the discussion of aliment, it is important to remember that there were two sides to every story. In 1839 Craig acted for one of Torwoodlee's servants, James Drahill, who had acknowledged being the father of Elizabeth Dickson's child. Drahill had nothing but his wages and was unable to pay anything until he received them at Whitsunday, when he engaged to pay £5 and a similar amount each half-year term thereafter.[131] Craig asked the mother's agent, Thomas Scott, to accept this, and refrain from bringing a summons, since 'that may affect his present situation'. Predictably, the agent asked for security for payment and also arrested Drahill's wages.[132] Security was something Drahill could not provide since his friends were as poor as he was. Craig himself, however, undertook to become bound for £5 the following Whitsunday and £3 half yearly thereafter 'so long as Drahill remains at Torwoodlee as Servant'.[133] Drahill was not employed at Torwoodlee in or before 1835 and does not appear in the accounts. However, James Pringle confirmed that he was to receive £9 at Whitsunday from which he had to furnish himself with clothes.[134] Craig, evidently, had met his match in Thomas Scott, who insisted on £7 at Whitsunday, although in the end £5 was agreed. It was, however, not paid immediately and Craig had to send a letter of credit on Drahill's behalf in June because Drahill had not given him the money.[135]

CONCLUSION

Craig was much involved in the lives of the vulnerable in the parishes where he had influence through his relationship to the heritors. For many he would have been the public face of the heritors, providing a channel of communication to the great and the good with the power to influence their lives and the welfare of

[128] NRS, Scott of Gala papers, GD477/105, Tods & Romanes/Gala, 8 Jun. 1821.
[129] SBA/1303/2/44, Craig/Andrew Lang, 6 Sep. 1822.
[130] SBA/1303/3/120, Craig/Lang, 5 Feb. 1823.
[131] SBA/1303/8/454, Craig/Thomas Scott, Gattonside, 18 Mar. 1839.
[132] SBA/1303/8/456, Craig/Drahill, 20 Mar. 1839.
[133] SBA/1303/8/463, Craig/Thomas Scott, 25 Mar. 1839.
[134] SBA/1303/8/476, idem, 15 Apr. 1839.
[135] SBA/1303/8/513, idem, 18 Jun. 1839.

their children. If it was his job to protect the interests of the heritors above all, particularly in competition with other parishes, he still had opportunities to assist those in great need. If he tended to insist on following the rules, and repatriating a pauper to another parish, the consequence would generally be to protect parish funds and enable better conditions for the poor of his own district.

Poverty was fairly widespread, sometimes the consequence of economic change or familial dislocation, sometimes the result of the early death of breadwinners. There was considerable mobility of labour in the Borders and the north of England and that also led to Craig taking on responsibility for the highly vulnerable, as when a three-year-old orphan, whose parents had both died, was left with a grandmother in Galashiels who lived in poverty. The father was a millwright from Corbridge and the mother was from Hexham, both in Northumberland, and Craig hoped for financial support from the parish of Corbridge.[136]

Early in the eighteenth century, fornication had ceased to be prosecuted as a crime.[137] In rural communities, kirk sessions continued to exert considerable social control and the condemnation and punishment of individuals for sexual relations outside of marriage continued unabated up to Craig's day. Craig, however, reflects a less moral and more practical perspective in his correspondence: how to deal with the consequences of children born in relations that did not result in marriage where there was financial need. This was a matter of public concern for the parish and, particularly, the main funders of social support and it was therefore the perspective from which he became personally involved.

Craig's wider contribution to his own parish, as we shall see in the next chapter, affected areas of life well beyond education and poor relief and the boundaries between his multifarious roles – as law agent, baron bailie and factor – are by no means neatly drawn in his correspondence. An example of where there was some degree of crossover arose in 1833 in the case of a mentally ill woman who was living in Selkirk but belonged to the parish of Galashiels. As he reported to Andrew Lang, Galashiels were happy to take her 'under our protection & keeping by providing her with lodging & a person to take care of her'.[138] In return for this significant commitment, however, there was a quid pro quo in the shape of a woman of Selkirk parish, Julian Coates, who resided in Galashiels in 'extreme poverty & helplessness'. Coates wished to return to Selkirk, but the surgeon certified that she was unable to be moved and Craig wanted Lang to agree to take her as soon as it was safe to do so. Here was a practical arrangement, a deal to be worked out between near neighbours, of a kind that clearly appealed to Craig's sense of propriety: for every problem, Craig saw a solution.

---

[136] SBA/1303/6/304, Craig/[blank] Hexham, 16 Jun. 1832.

[137] B. P. Levack, 'The prosecution of sexual crimes in early eighteenth-century Scotland' 89 (2010) *Scottish Historical Review*, 172 at 173.

[138] SBA/1303/6/364, Craig/Lang, 11 Mar. 1833. A case of 'mental derangement' in 1818 is reported in SBA, RPLB, fo. 28, Rodger/Rev. Dr Douglas, 2 Apr. 1818. The sufferer, Adam Tait, was 'lodged as a 'boarder' in Selkirk jail until he died. Galashiels parish was pursued for the balance of his upkeep and funeral expenses.

Chapter 3

Baron Bailie and Factor

This chapter considers aspects of Craig's formal, and informal, authority in his home town of Galashiels. Regardless of the offices he held, including in his youth that of lieutenant in the local yeomanry, he was a formidable character whose professional standing and relationships with local landowners ensured that he was often the first port of call when trouble arose.[1]

BARON BAILIE

Craig was not only Gala's factor but held at his pleasure the office of baron bailie of Galashiels, having succeeded Thomas Paterson.[2] Paterson drafted and witnessed Craig's grandfather's lease in 1778 for the sixth laird.[3] He sometimes worked with Craig's father, William, who drafted a lease for the laird in 1781 which Paterson signed as factor.[4] This proclaimed the laird's intention to encourage house building in Galashiels and leases and rentals, drafted or subscribed by Paterson, provide evidence of his success in feuing properties locally.[5] Paterson and William Craig were the two biggest subscribers to the repair of the well at Galashiels Cross in 1802.[6]

Paterson managed the Gala estate when the seventh laird, Col. Hugh Scott (1764–1795), went to America in 1791 and, after the laird's death on active military service, continued to do so during the minority of his son.[7] Before Paterson died in 1813, Craig had taken over 'as factor or doer for John Scott Esq of Gala' due to Paterson's ill health and it was Craig who subscribed the rental of the estates of Gala and Torwoodlee in July 1813.[8] Paterson had worked in conjunction with the Edinburgh lawyers, Tod & Romanes WS, a firm with strong Borders connections, and they continued as Gala's Edinburgh agents in Craig's time.[9] As well

---

[1] Hall, *History of Galashiels*, 85.

[2] Ibid., 98. It is possible that Craig was related to Paterson on his father's side, his paternal grandmother being one Marion Paterson.

[3] NRS, Court of Session, unextracted processes, CS235/K/6/4.

[4] NRS, Scott of Gala papers, GD477/122/17.

[5] E.g. ibid., GD477/463/22 (tack, 1788, written by Paterson, witnessed by Archibald Tod WS); GD477/463/27 (lease, 1782, signed by Paterson); GD477/463/10 (rentals, 1802, signed by Paterson).

[6] Ibid., GD477/463/13 (7 Feb. 1802).

[7] Ibid., GD477/463/12, Hugh Scott to Gilbert Thomson, 20 Mar. 1791.

[8] Ibid., GD477/463/20 (17 Aug. 1812); GD477/122/23; ibid., GD477/143/2, Discharge of Baillie Paterson's account or rental (entries 15 Feb. 1810, 2 Aug. 1810).

[9] The firm consisted of John, Archibald and Thomas Tod (all sons of Thomas Tod WS of Drygrange) and John Romanes. A five-year partnership agreement survives, to run from 31 Dec. 1809 to 31 Dec. 1814: NRS, Records of Tods, Murray and Jamieson WS, GD237/20/43.

as correspondence, Craig sent them his 'annual book of account' with the receipts evidencing his transactions.[10]

Paterson relied for advice on Archibald Tod WS who, along with others including Dr Alexander Monro, was appointed curator for the laird in 1805 when he reached his minority.[11] Despite Paterson's generally high standard of record keeping, Craig sometimes struggled to locate deeds which Paterson had sent to Tod. An example occurred in 1822 when he attempted to find a feu contract which had been granted by Scott's tutors in 1808 in favour of the Galashiels baker, William Ovens. It was one of the documents drafted in Edinburgh 'after the Bailie could no longer write them'.[12] Craig suspected it was amongst the Gala estate papers held by Tod at Drygrange, near Earlston. No system of organisation was proof against documents going missing, although Craig usually had a good idea of who might possess them and why.[13]

According to the historian Elizabeth Sanderson, Gala gave Craig a free hand to modernise decaying houses in Galashiels and to develop streets 'to connect with the buildings growing up around the mills'.[14] He saw to the construction of stone and slate-roofed houses in the vicinity of Bank Street and Bridge Street in the years after 1813, although his later surviving correspondence says very little about this.

Jurisdiction

The bailie was nominated by the feudal superior since Galashiels only had a town council from 1868 when it became a parliamentary burgh.[15] Tradesmen and merchants therefore enjoyed no privileged status, although deacons of trades were appointed annually.[16] The bailie's powers as a magistrate, stemming from the original burgh charter in 1599 and recognised in 1633 by legislation in favour of James Scott of Galashiels, had been extensive but were largely stripped away by

[10] E.g., SBA/1303/4/144, Craig/Tod & Romanes WS, 18 Jan. 1825.
[11] NRS, Scott of Gala papers, GD477/143/7. There is a cash-book entry, dated 22 Feb. 1813, referring to payment of £50 as half-year salary to Baillie Paterson 'being the first on the new arrangement': Ibid., GD477/765. The next payment of £50, on 27 Aug., was simply paid to the bailie with no name mentioned. Paterson's annual salary as factor in 1809/10 was £70: ibid., GD477/143/2.
[12] SBA/1303/2/227, Craig/C. Erskine, Melrose, 20 Apr. 1822. Paterson was still active in 1807: NRS, Scott of Gala papers, GD477/464/8, Archibald Tod/Bailie Paterson, 12 Sep. 1807. Tod of Drygrange is mentioned in the Gala estate cash book.
[13] E.g. SBA/1303/2/192, Craig/John Scott, writer, Lauder, 11 Feb. 1822.
[14] SBA, SBA/83/9, Elizabeth M. C. Sanderson, 'Old Galashiels 1793–1884: Its transition from village to industrial town' (1980), 10–11.
[15] Representation of the People (Scotland) Act, 1868, s. 10, Sched. A. When this Act came into force Galashiels was to be treated for electoral purposes as if wholly in Selkirkshire (ibid., s. 45). As a parliamentary burgh, it had fifteen councillors including a provost and four bailies in the traditional sense.
[16] *General Report of the Commissioners appointed to inquire into the state of Municipal Corporations in Scotland*, 88 H.C. (1835) (29), XXIX.1, part I; *Pigot's Commercial Directory 1825–6*, 656–7.

statute in 1747.[17] The terms of the legislation are reflected in Hall's description of the office in Craig's time:

> This functionary, within the bounds of his jurisdiction, could enforce the payment of rents, and decide in disputes regarding money affairs up to a certain amount. In the event of the goods arrested being of less value than the sum sued for, he could sentence the debtor to imprisonment for a term not exceeding one month. For small offences he had power to impose a fine to the amount of twenty shillings, and, as an alternative, could sentence delinquents to be put in the stocks during the daytime for the space of three hours.[18]

In practice, however, even some of this may have atrophied. According to one writer (probably Elliot Anderson) in 1826, the penal regulations which had distinguished the barony from neighbouring towns had not been observed for the previous forty years.[19] Craig's correspondence does not refer to him holding courts of any description, and Galashiels had neither a courthouse nor jail.[20] He remained, nonetheless, chief magistrate.[21]

In 1819, the inhabitants of Galashiels, Darlingshaugh and Buckholmside petitioned the justices of the peace for the counties of Selkirk and Roxburgh to appoint a local procurator fiscal to take cognisance of minor crimes. According to the petition, rapid population growth had seen these areas effectively become one town and had caused greater frequency of 'petty crimes and misdemeanors [sic], breaches of the peace and deviations from just weights and measures much to the inconvenience and loss of the Inhabitants'.[22] Transgressions included driving carts carelessly; obstructing the road; allowing horses to run free; breaking into gardens, and stealing fruit. The petition, which Craig conspicuously did not sign, was unsuccessful.

As a result, Galashiels continued to fall within the purview of the two county prosecutors. Whatever attenuated criminal jurisdiction the bailie enjoyed was not considered sufficient. Nor was the geographical extent of it clear. In the parts of Galashiels beyond the barony, Craig acknowledged that as bailie 'he has no regular or formal authority; but . . . his recommendations as magistrate are ordinarily obeyed by the inhabitants'.[23] Even so, Hall stressed the limits on his power.[24] Craig's correspondence does not show him acting judicially, deciding disputes

---

[17] Heritable Jurisdictions (S) Act, 1747, s. 17; RPS, 1633/3/161; the bailie's heyday is described by Chambers, *Picture of Scotland*, 136–8.

[18] Hall, *History of Galashiels*, 98.

[19] NRS, Scott of Gala papers, GD477/463/7, 'Traditions of Galashiels written for Chambers' Traditions of Scotland', fo. 12. The reference is to Chambers, *Picture of Scotland*.

[20] HC, *Report on Municipal Corporations, Appendix*, 615.

[21] R. M. Urquhart, *The Burghs of Scotland and The Burgh Police (Scotland) Act 1833* (Motherwell, 1989), 47.

[22] NRS, Scott of Gala papers, GD477/463/14, Copy petition to the justices of the peace, 16 Mar. 1819.

[23] HC, *Report on Municipal Corporations, Appendix*, 615.

[24] Hall, *History of Galashiels*, 117.

over money or issuing fines.[25] He certainly enforced payment of rent, but did so by regular legal means. The baron bailie of Melrose, appointed by the duke of Buccleuch, was seemingly in a similar position.[26]

In contrast, the bailie of Kelso (also, from 1634, a burgh of barony) held a court, established regulations in relation to criminal prosecutions and matters of police (which were revised in 1827) and in civil cases (revised in 1813), and employed court officers.[27] In a letter to the duke of Roxburgh in 1814, William Smith, having been relieved of the office of bailie having held it for fifteen years at an annual salary of only £25, defended his conduct and described some of the challenges he had faced. His jurisdiction included the 5,000 or so inhabitants of Kelso 'besides disorderly people, vagrants, and thieves, resorting to a Borders District, and the numerous disputes and disturbances which take place at the markets and fairs'.[28] These had caused him both expense and trouble and, as he informed Roxburgh, 'my situation has been such as often to subject me to responsibility without power, and always to labour without emolument'.

Craig, however, had to deal with challenges of his own. As noted in Chapter 1, Galashiels was highly unusual in traversing two counties.[29] Part of the town was located in Selkirkshire and another part, lands that had been feued by Gala, were in Roxburghshire as was Buckholmside, the superiority of which was held by the laird of Torwoodlee. According to Craig, nearly two-thirds of Galashiels' population was situated in Roxburghshire.[30] Due to the complexity of living in a burgh that straddled two discrete counties, each with their own separate jurisdictions and courts, Craig, in corresponding with the prosecutors for the respective counties, always had to delineate carefully where crimes or disturbances had taken place and identify the domicile of those to be summoned to be sure that he had identified the correct court. He remarked how easy it was, due to the situation of Galashiels, for an alleged offender to move from one jurisdiction to another.[31]

In 1832 he suggested that Melrose had 500 inhabitants and Galashiels five times that number.[32] Other data suggests that this grossly exaggerated the

[25] Cf. Hall, *History of Galashiels*, 98, where Craig's successor was apparently given authority in 1849 to determine complaints in the grain and meal market.
[26] HC, *Report on Municipal Corporations, Appendix*, 679. The Pringle barony of Stichill, on the other hand, seems to have long retained its court: C. B. Gunn, ed., *Records of the Baron Court of Stitchill* [sic] *1655–1807* (Edinburgh, 1905).
[27] SBA, SBA/183/27, George Main, Kelso/praeses of the Town Council, 20 Apr. 1830. On Kelso as a burgh of barony, see A. Moffat, *Kelsae: A History of Kelso from Earliest Times* (Edinburgh, 2006), 106.
[28] SBA, Papers of William Smith, SBA/183/10, Smith/Roxburgh, 29 Nov. 1814.
[29] HC, *Report on Municipal Corporations, Appendix*, 615.
[30] SBA/1303/6/433, Craig/William Oliver, sheriff of Roxburghshire, 15 Nov. 1833.
[31] Hall, *History of Galashiels*, 117. Craig provided a declaration to the commissioners on municipal corporations which has not been traced, although Hall apparently refers to it.
[32] SBA/1303/6/292, Craig/Adam Paterson WS, 22 May 1832.

difference in population.[33] An official calculation of the population, which was accepted by a parliamentary committee in 1835, put it at a much more modest 2,100.[34] This appears to be a more reliable figure. Craig's perception was perhaps influenced by the fact that many Melrose residents worked in Galashiels, but that seems unlikely. His population estimate, made in the context of the police bill (discussed below), may have been an attempt to make a political point about the relative importance of his burgh.

CRAIG'S AUTHORITY

While being bailie clothed Craig with some authority, his correspondence rarely makes explicit the basis on which he acted in any given situation and, if he recorded his activities as bailie in a separate act book, it is now lost. This makes it difficult to distinguish between his roles as bailie and factor and, in practice, there may have been little significant distinction. Certainly, in letters there is often ambiguity as to whether he was acting as bailie, Gala's factor or, indeed, as agent for another local heritor. For example, he collected the Ettrick Forest feu duties on behalf of Archibald Gibson of Ladhope, deputy to the forest chamberlain, Alexander Pringle of Whytbank.[35] This he probably did as Gibson's agent, rather than as baron bailie.

In matters of public hygiene, Craig would have acted as bailie, although he lacked any general power to impose a tax to keep the streets clean.[36] He did intervene, on public health grounds, following complaints about a sow which the spinner John Clapperton kept behind his house, near the public well.[37] Similarly, when the weaver, Charles Dobson, intended to place his cow in the kirk croft for a season, Craig threatened that the cow would be turned out and Dobson prosecuted for 'causing trouble and unnecessary expense'.[38] On the other hand, employing a man to hunt and kill an owl which had 'infested the Pigeon house' on Gala's estate fell within his role as factor.[39]

---

[33] NSA, Melrose, 62–3. Rev. Thomson, citing the 1831 census, gives the figure of 4,339 inhabitants in Melrose, compared to 1,534 for Galashiels. Rev. Paterson, quoting in 1834 a population of 2,209 for Galashiels, noted that 1,079 of these lived in the parish of Melrose. According to the answers given under the Population Acts, Melrose had a population of 3,467 in 1821, 4,339 in 1831 and, in the Census, 5,331 in 1841; Galashiels had a population of 1,358 in 1821, 1,364 in 1831 and 3,014 in 1841. Selkirk's population was generally between the two: 2,696 (1821), 2,883 (1831) and 4,347 (1841). See J. S. Duncan, 'The Royal Burgh of Peebles in the nineteenth century: the impact of a locally organised railway on a moribund Scottish county town' (PhD thesis, The Open University, 2005), 30.

[34] HC, *Report on Municipal Corporations*, Appendix, 615. Chambers, *Picture of Scotland*, 130, suggested 2,000 inhabitants.

[35] SBA/1303/5/126, Craig/Capt. Cunningham, Coldstream, 16 Oct. 1827. Ettrick Forest was crown land and the chamberlain of Ettrick Forest was a salaried officer, the salary (and that of the depute) taken from the rents which were submitted to the Exchequer.

[36] Hall, *History of Galashiels*, 117.

[37] SBA/1303/8/395, Craig/John Clapperton, spinner, 24 Dec. 1838.

[38] SBA/1303/5/54, Craig/Charles Dobson, 21 Apr. 1827.

[39] NRS, GD477/765, Scott of Gala papers, cash book, entry 16 Jun. 1813.

In 1818 Craig sought to prosecute a labourer for cutting wood in Gala's plantations. He wrote to the Selkirkshire procurator fiscal naming the witnesses and retained as evidence the four young trees that were cut down.[40] A decade later, he reflected local concern by complaining about changes to the Blucher coach service. The Edinburgh contractors had to recognise 'that the two horse coach without a Guard is totally insufficient' and ensure 'that it will soon be supplied with 4 horses & a guard as before'.[41] A further decade on, he wrote to the fiscal of the JP court about the theft of apples to which Peter Brown, a brewer's servant, had confessed in front of witnesses. As there had been a spate of 'fruit stealers', he expected a prosecution.[42] In none of these cases is his basis for acting made clear, giving a sense that it did not greatly matter.

In one important task, however, the presentation of Nathaniel Paterson as minister of Galashiels in 1821, following the death of Dr Robert Douglas, Craig was certainly acting as factor. Paterson, at the time, was a tutor in Northumberland and Craig wrote in April 1821 informing him that his formal presentation had to be given in to the moderator of the presbytery either by Gala, as patron of the church, or his agent. Craig himself attended the presbytery meeting and submitted Paterson's presentation, sending on an extract of the sederunt.[43] Since he had 'the pleasure to take charge of Mr Scotts [sic] affairs here', Craig, at the meeting, had arranged 'the cropping of the Glebe for this season' but had done nothing in regard to the garden because Mrs Douglas had made no mention of it.[44] As Hall notes, Paterson was initially not a popular choice with the congregation, ostensibly because Scott had appointed him on the advice of his uncle – and Paterson's former employer – Monro Binning, giving him the appearance of being a discarded tutor.[45] When Paterson himself later moved to Glasgow, the presentation of his successor, James Veitch, was signed by Gala and again passed through Craig's hands before being sent on to Tod & Romanes WS.[46]

Maintaining Order

On the night of 22 December 1822, a man on horseback appeared at Craig's door. He had ridden from Edinburgh, searching for the robbers 'of the bodies lately traced in a Gig from Dalkeith'.[47] Technically, this was not robbery but the crime of violation of sepulchres, the practice of resurrecting cadavers with a view to

---

[40] SBA, D/47/84/1, Craig/Rodger & Paterson, writers, Selkirk, 18 Mar. 1818.

[41] SBA/1303/5/250, Craig/Mr Scott, Messrs Scott & Co., Star Hotel, Princes Street, Edinburgh, 17 May 1828.

[42] SBA/1303/8/579, C&R/R. G. Thomson, JP Fiscal, Melrose, 25 Sep. 1839.

[43] The meeting was on 3 Apr. 1821: SBA/1303/2/6, Craig/Adam Fairholme of Chapel, 30 Mar. 1821.

[44] SBA/1303/2/10, Craig/Rev. Nathaniel Paterson, Lilburn Tower, Belford, 6 Apr. 1821.

[45] Hall, *History of Galashiels*, 212; D. P. Thomson, *Those Ministers of Galashiels!* (Galashiels, n.d.), 12.

[46] SBA/1303/6/475, Craig/Tod & Romanes WS, 26 Apr. 1834.

[47] SBA/1303/3/96, Craig/the Superintendent of Police, Edinburgh, 23 Dec. 1822.

selling them to Edinburgh medical students.[48] The bodies had been taken but whence was not known. Craig sent the man on to Melrose but, next day, having received a description of two suspects from local men who had encountered them on Bowden Moor, he wrote to the police superintendent in Edinburgh. He speculated that the bodies 'must either have been lifted at Bowden about 2 miles, or at Lilliesleaf about 4 miles from where the parties met', judging that the suspects could not have reached Minto or Hawick.[49] One man was already in custody and this was probably George Cameron, a mason from Edinburgh, who was tried in March 1823 for violating the sepulchres of two women, Agnes Carse and Margaret Thorburn, whose bodies were taken from Bowden and Earlston churchyards respectively.[50]

Only Craig's informal authority explains the knock on his door in 1822: he was recognised as the appropriate person to deal with emergencies, petty crime and disturbers of the peace in the vicinity. Another example of it was the reaction to the robbery of the mail carrier which occurred, in January 1822, near Clovenfords and was apparently reported to him by the victim.[51] Craig raised a number of locals and organised a search for the assailant who was captured by Robert Howden.[52] Some of those involved in the search later claimed payment of expenses from George Rodger, the procurator fiscal, to whom Craig passed on their claims.[53] According to Craig, few claimants expected any result. They thought they would try their luck, given that the two or three of the most active searchers 'had heard that they ought or were to have something', presumably from the county rogue money.[54] Craig invited Rodger to his office to discuss the claims and 'dispose of them conscientiously'.

As well as taking responsibility for mobilising the community, Craig was not slow in telling people off for unacceptable behaviour. An example is a warning letter he wrote in 1823 to a comedian called Cameron, after a complaint that he had struck a boy for tearing down one of his playbills. Craig acknowledged that the boy was at fault, but more so was Cameron who was warned that if Craig heard of 'any other instance of the kind' Cameron's party would be required to leave Galashiels.[55]

Craig's authority as bailie, while much less extensive, is reminiscent of the general neighbourhood authority that Walter Scott enjoyed as sheriff depute of Selkirkshire. In 1807 Scott reported to the Selkirk fiscal a 'lunatic person' named

---

[48] This was not an isolated local example. See, e.g. SBA, Walter Mason Archive, WM/10/5, Archibald Scott, Edinburgh/procurator fiscal, Selkirk, describing body snatchers, 23 Mar. 1829.

[49] SBA/1303/3/96.

[50] NRS, Precognition against George Cameron, JC26/448; ibid, Trial papers, JC26/1823/174.

[51] Hall, *History of Galashiels*, 516. Hall dates this to '30 February 1822', an obvious misprint. The actual date must be 30 Jan. 1822.

[52] Ibid.

[53] SBA/1303/2/195, Craig/George Rodger, Selkirk, 20 Feb. 1822.

[54] Ibid., idem, 8 Mar. 1822. Rogue money was collected by the commissioners of supply and JPs and it could fund manhunts when alleged criminals absconded.

[55] SBA/1303/3/272, Craig/Mr Cameron, 13 Nov. 1823. Comedians are referred to in Galashiels kirk session minutes: NRS, CH2/1255/2/205, 13 Aug. 1827; cf. also SBA/1303/7/526, Craig/Mr Watson, comedian, Selkirk, 5 Jul. 1839.

John Gray who had passed by his house at Ashiestiel, noting that if a constable had been near he would have sent him back to Selkirk. He asked him to make out a warrant for confining the man until his friends could 'give bail on promise to have him properly looked after'.[56] In 1829 Craig encountered a similar case and, like Scott, wrote to the fiscal, this time in Jedburgh. The man in question, Samuel Brown, was the son of a London greengrocer. Aged about twenty and 'seemingly insane', Brown was taken to a lodging house where two men had to take charge of him.[57] He escaped them, however, and attempted to drown himself in the Gala Water from where he was taken to John Moffat's hayloft near the Commercial Inn. As this was in the parish of Melrose, Craig and James Curle, baron bailie depute of Melrose, both dealt with the matter, writing to Brown's father as well as Sir Richard Birnie, the Scots-born Chief Magistrate of Police in London. Birnie replied, through the clerk of police in Bow Street, declining to give advice other than that the case be dealt with 'under the poor laws'.[58] Brown's identity, however, was confirmed: he had been an apprentice to a ship's carpenter at Deptford from where he had run away.

Craig was unsure how to proceed. Brown was not eating properly, was in a weak state and was draining parish resources. He told James Stevenson, the Roxburghshire fiscal, that

> in England they send down paupers to Scotland at the expense of the parishes thro which they pass, setting out with some document which carried them in, & I should hope that the same course can be taken by Scotland against England, & when the lad can be moved with safety that he should be sent to the parish of Paddington near London.[59]

He urged Stevenson to write to Brown's father to obtain his consent to execute this plan, lest he later deny liability should any parish, through which his son passed on his journey south, claim repayment of the expense of supporting him. Craig visited Brown twice but the latter would not speak: 'he appeared stout & healthy tho' evidently deranged' and Craig thought it odd that his father, obviously in good circumstances, 'should be so hard hearted' towards him.[60] Two months later, with Brown still in Melrose, he expressed the fear that if Brown was 'set adrift' he might simply return '& plague us more, unless he were landed somewhere at a distance, say Carlisle, from whence he last came'.[61] Financial matters were settled with the fiscal soon after Craig informed him that 'the people have been asking after their

---

[56] SBA, SC/S/12/19/1/6, Scott/George Rodger, 15 Aug. 1807.
[57] This may have been 'constables Thomson and Howden', whose expenses amounted to 18 shillings: SBA/1303/5/469, Craig/Thomas Bruce of Langlee, 3 Nov. 1829.
[58] SBA/1303/5/447, Craig/James Stevenson, Jedburgh, 18 Sep. 1829.
[59] SBA/1303/5/454, Craig/James Stevenson, Melrose, 2 Oct. 1829. For Stevenson, see Finlay, *ARNP* 1800–1899, no. 1829.
[60] SBA/1303/5/469, Craig/Thomas Bruce of Langlee, 3 Nov. 1829.
[61] SBA/1303/5/484, Craig/Stevenson, Melrose, 30 Nov. 1829.

money', and he sent a bill to cover the local expenses of dealing with Brown.[62] Craig, who received a guinea for his efforts, hoped that they should have 'no more such troublesome visitors'.[63]

Craig was well-placed to hear of discontent. When the stocking-maker John Oliver was subjected to abuse by two characters well-known to Peter Rodger (1804–1888), the procurator fiscal in Selkirk, Craig urged Rodger to take Oliver's statement in writing and show it to the sheriff, Sir Walter Scott. His parting comment is particularly interesting:

> I am anxious & so is Gala that not the least instance of violence & abuse should pass unnoticed at present as the only remedy to cheque that too much freedom of thought & action operating among the lower classes.[64]

This was the year of the Scottish Reform Bill and tensions were running high. There was an attack on the carriage of Thomas Bruce of Langlee (of Tait & Bruce WS), a prominent Tory, as he left a dinner party at Gala House in 1832, indicative of popular resentment against conservative interests.[65] Behind the scenes, in 1831, Craig was dealing with the circulation of anonymous letters, political in nature, which he described as 'breathing an infernal spirit'.[66] He sought a meeting in Galashiels of the authorities in both counties to investigate the matter, so that the 'bad nest in this place be destroyed'. He told the Selkirk fiscal:

> Reform is a mere pretext & has nothing to do with what has been going on among some of the young lads for some time; a subversion of order & authority is their aim. The heads of families of the whole town are determined to turn out & support the legal authorities.[67]

Craig represented hierarchy, Tory tradition and legal authority. The 'subversion of order' would have been his greatest fear although, sadly, whatever discussions took place and whatever action followed is not revealed from his letter books. Another incident in 1831, related to the election of a delegate to represent Lauder town council in the county election, saw the temporary kidnapping of a Tory supporter. There was widespread sympathy for the kidnappers. This led to mobbing and rioting in Lauder, with seven men charged in the High Court for the offence.[68] It also caused trouble for Craig's officer, Robert Howden, who was apparently

---

[62] SBA/1303/6/15, Craig/Stevenson, 28 Dec. 1829.
[63] SBA/1303/6/16, Craig/Stevenson, 2 Jan. 1830.
[64] SBA/1303/6/199, Craig/Peter Rodger, 1 Jul. 1831.
[65] Hall, *History of Galashiels*, 112. For another such incident, see SBA, WM/17/58, Craig/Peter Rodger, 17 Sep. 1833.
[66] SBA/1303/6/184, Craig/Peter Rodger, procurator fiscal, Selkirk, 18 May 1831.
[67] Ibid.
[68] R. Romanes, *Lauder* (privately printed, 1903), 55–7; NRS, Crown Office precognitions, AD14/31/379, Precognition against Alexander Clapperton, Samuel McLachlan, William Badger, George Murray, Robert Brown, John Henderson, Thomas Turnbull for the crime of mobbing and rioting at Lauder, 1831; also JC26/1831/552.

forced to present his gun to an unruly mob.[69] Craig's correspondence sheds little light on any of this, but he does refer in passing to 'a Galashiels lad who had been assisting at Stewart's riotous election' in Lauder.[70]

Craig's experience of conflict within Galashiels would only have added to his misgivings and some of the activities of the 'young lads' mentioned are reflected in his correspondence. In 1819, Walter Scott expressed no fear 'of the reforming mania' then becoming apparent in the west of Scotland and regarded the Galashiels weavers as 'contented and happy', but a decade later things were different.[71] In 1829, Craig instructed the Melrose procurator Robert Thomson to obtain summonses in respect of an alleged assault on the manufacturer James Sime.[72] The five accused comprised three journeymen dyers, an apprentice shoemaker and the son of a spinner. Later the same year, the clothiers Robert Gill & Son employed two weavers, Cairns and Mowat, on a broadloom who were able to produce cheaper cloth than those weavers operating narrow looms. The latter gathered together one evening 'in a tumultuous manner & erected an effigy or effigies of Cairns & Mowat which they carried in triumph thro the town'.[73] They burst into Cairns' house with a burning effigy, although it was soon extinguished.

This episode indicates the fine margins which had come to threaten the livelihoods of local weavers and spinners. The year 1829 was particularly difficult in that industry, although the depression of that year prompted local industry to adapt to tartan and tweed products which became lucrative.[74] It was not new, however, for disputes to turn to violence. In 1823, six young men, including a piecer, a dyer and an apprentice weaver, engaged in 'a most violent attack' with stones on the house of Robert Miller, a spinner with the manufacturers W. & D. Thomson.[75] One of the assailants, William Thorkel, a piecer with the same firm, seems to have taken a lead. A witness, Andrew Dobson, alleged that 'Jock Lindsay spinner told Thorkel to drive a stone at Millars door'.[76] Lindsay was not one of the accused, but Thorkel and another, James Leith, were from Melrose parish and Craig asked James Curle there to bring them before the Roxburghshire JP court in Melrose. The other four were to be taken before the justices at Selkirk. In 1835 there was another riot and Craig wrote to Peter Rodger about the 'renewal of disorderly scenes' involving a 'parade through the town' and damage to a house being built by the innkeeper Adam Purdie.[77] Rob Howden and others being able

[69]   The incident is described by Hall, *History of Galashiels*, 109.
[70]   SBA/1303/6/179, Craig/John Wilson jr, Preston, 11 May 1831.
[71]   Grierson, ed., *Letters of Scott*, V, 509–10.
[72]   SBA/1303/5/419, Craig/R. G. Thomson, 9 Jul. 1829.
[73]   SBA/1303/5/489, Craig/James Stevenson, 9 Dec. 1829.
[74]   F. J. Groome, *Ordnance Gazetteer of Scotland* (6 vols, Edinburgh, 1882–1884), III, 68.
[75]   'Piecer' was the hardest job in a woollen factory, necessarily done by children. It involved leaning over the spinning machines to tie up broken ends of yarn.
[76]   SBA/1303/3/274, Craig/James Curle, Melrose, 15 Nov. 1823.
[77]   SBA, WM/17/59, Craig/Rodger, 12 Feb. 1835.

to identify the ringleaders, Craig expected Rodger, with the sheriff and Andrew Lang, to take witness statements in a precognition.

If weavers could be prone to threatening behaviour, their wives also engaged in direct action. In 1828 Archibald Gibson of Ladhope wanted three women, all wives of Galashiels weavers, brought before the Melrose JP court for trespassing on his land and 'breaking down & carrying off his paling from his plantations at Ladhope'.[78] The reason for this behaviour is unknown, however Craig again wrote to Curle in Melrose, naming the witnesses (this time all from Roxburghshire) and instructing him to bring the case.

Craig's willingness to investigate crimes is revealed in a letter to the victim of an assault in Buckholm Wood.[79] He advised him to write to the Roxburgh county fiscal to enquire what a proper reward might be for information about the two men who had attacked him, so that a newspaper advertisement might be drafted. The burgh of Galashiels and the county of Selkirk each offered £10 towards the reward. Moreover, Craig wanted a description of the men, adding

> every house in Galashiels shall be searched in order to find out who were absent, as I have now too much reason to suspect that the two delinquents are amongst ourselves from the former instances of attack at the same place.

For Craig to claim that he could organise the search of every house in Galashiels, purportedly without a warrant, is remarkable. It is unlikely that the residual powers he had as bailie sufficed to make this lawful, nor was the sheriff depute likely to grant so extensive a warrant. Yet while the householders could close their doors to Craig as bailie, it is at least possible that they might be opened to him as the landlord's agent. If so, his power was immense.

Craig was also involved in evidence gathering following a break-in at the mansion house at Torwoodlee in 1821. One of the two suspects, Peter Steele, was well-known in Galashiels and could be easily identified. Craig, having spoken to Torwoodlee's gardener and another witness, had no doubt that Steele and his neighbour were responsible. He described Steele as the bigger and older of the two, someone who had 'constantly engaged in vice & quarrels', 'pock pitted', slender, black-haired, five foot seven or eight, forty or fifty years old, and having an Irish accent.[80] He notified the sheriff substitute, Charles Erskine, in Melrose that Torwoodlee thought he and the fiscal should be arranging to find these men 'either in Scotland or Ireland or both' without delay. Craig himself wrote to the Superintendent of Police at Glasgow with his description of the 'two Irish lads', believed to be heading his way or to Edinburgh.[81] He offered a reward. Elliot

---

[78] SBA/1303/5/240, idem, 25 Apr. 1828.

[79] SBA/1303/5/159, Craig/Mr Ingram, Copland, 6 Dec. 1827.

[80] SBA/1303/2/127, Craig/Charles Erskine, 11 Oct. 1821; the original of this letter may be found at NRS, Transcripts and photocopies of miscellaneous papers, RH1/2/658. On Irish workers in the Borders, see Anon. [Alexander Somerville], *The Autobiography of a Working Man* (London, 1848), 71.

[81] SBA/1303/2/129, Craig/the Superintendent of Police, Glasgow, 28 Sep. 1821. Other superintendents were also written to. The material taken included a pound note of the Leith Bank.

Anderson followed this up by writing to the procurator fiscal in Jedburgh to see whether persons he had in custody might be connected to the crime, describing the articles stolen which included a crown piece from the reign of William and Mary.[82] The most significant crime in the area referenced in Craig's letter books was a double murder at Fans Farm, near Earlston, in 1822 committed by a local man, the gamekeeper Robert Scott. The murderer was to be executed at the scene of his crime on 29 October between 2pm and 4pm and Craig imagined that 'there will be such a gathering in that neighbourhood as never was before'.[83] There were six such crime-scene executions for murder in Scotland in the 1820s, aimed at deterrence and reflecting a desire to impress judicial revulsion upon the locals.[84] Thousands attended and it clearly had an effect on Craig who mentioned it to a London correspondent. Scott's body was sent to Dr Monro in Edinburgh for dissection.[85] Despite Craig's own brush with the trade in cadavers, and his close acquaintanceship with the anatomist, Monro's dissection of the murderer William Burke in 1829 is not mentioned in Craig's correspondence.

Constables

While Craig could rely on community action, he could not deal with matters of law and order on his own. Constables had been introduced in Scotland in the seventeenth century, acting as the parish representatives of justices of the peace.[86] The office was not highly regarded, with constables effectively functionaries of the county JP courts, rather than keepers of the peace. By the early nineteenth century, heritors were even exhibiting reluctance to fund their salaries.[87] There is evidence in Craig's correspondence of efforts to put in place parish constables. Craig, along with Torwoodlee – justice of the peace and vice-lieutenant of the county – and William Scott, sheriff substitute of Selkirkshire, nominated ten 'fit persons' to be sworn in as parish constables in December 1829. He wrote to Andrew Lang, asking him to inform the nominees. In Berwickshire, he added 'they get each a baton along with a printed paper of directions &c explaining the

---

82 SBA/1303/2/141, Anderson/the fiscal, Jedburgh, 18 Oct. 1821. For another letter by Anderson on Craig's behalf, this time to Peter Rodger as fiscal of Selkirkshire asking him to 'come over *immediately* & take a precognition' following a stone-throwing incident, see SBA, WM/17/59, 17 Sep. 1833.

83 SBA/1303/3/251, Craig/Adam Scott, 3 Great St. Helens Street, Bishopsgate, London, 23 Sep. 1823. On the murders, see NRS, High Court of Justiciary processes, JC26/1823/242; also AD14/23/148; *The Scotsman*, 5 Jul. 1823.

84 R. Bennett, 'An awful and impressive spectacle; crime scene execution in Scotland' 21 (2017) *Crime, History and Societies*, 101, 105, 107.

85 *The Scotsman*, 1 Nov. 1823; there is an account of the execution in a broadside entitled 'execution', NLS, F.3.a.13(109). Characteristically for the time, Scott was subjected to an amateur phrenologist: *The Scotsman*, 27 Sep. 1823.

86 Ann E. Whetstone, *Scottish County Government in the Eighteenth and Nineteenth Centuries* (Edinburgh, 1981), 33.

87 Ibid., 35.

nature of their office – I suppose they will get the same from you'.[88] Further 'special constables' were nominated in 1831.[89] They swore to keep the peace and 'at every Quarter Session and meeting of Justices give true and due information of any breach which hath been made of His Majesty's peace within the bounds of my commandment'.[90]

Craig did not find the system satisfactory. When he read about a parliamentary bill in 1832 intended to enable certain burghs of regality and barony to establish a system of police, he encouraged Adam Paterson WS to 'use some influence' to ensure it covered Galashiels.[91] The fact that the new road from Carlisle to Edinburgh was passing through the town, filling the place 'at all times with every description of people', in his view necessitated greater protection either by general legislation or a special Act covering Galashiels. The bill was enacted in 1833 and permitted burghs to establish a general system of police.[92] The provisions were adopted in the barony of Kelso in September 1838, but not in Melrose.[93] In 1848, an attempt was made in Galashiels to adopt them but, due to its peculiar situation across two sheriffdoms, the Court of Session found that the legislation could not apply.[94] It was not until 1850 that Galashiels used legislation to introduce a more modern style of police.[95]

While the Royal Commission reported in 1835 that there was no regular police service in Galashiels, Craig's correspondence sheds light on the system which was then operating.[96] This involved a 'watching constable', paid for by the county, who by 1835 had been in place for more than a year.[97] In 1833, Craig had written, on the heritors' behalf, to William Oliver, sheriff of Roxburgh, seeking authority to replace the only acting constable for the Roxburghshire part of Galashiels who had just resigned.[98] At that time the Selkirkshire part of the town also only had a single 'watching constable'. Craig pointed out that Selkirk had no objection to continuing this constable and paying one half of the expense, provided Roxburghshire paid the other half, so that he would thereafter act as 'a

[88] SBA/1303/5/493, Craig/Andrew Lang, 15 Dec. 1829.
[89] Hall, *History of Galashiels*, 111. In 1831 Craig had a list of fourteen names for blank citations for ordinary and special constables with other proposed constables mentioned: SBA/1303/6/129, Craig/Andrew Lang, 3 Jan. 1831.
[90] Ibid.; SBA/1303/5/493, Craig/Andrew Lang, 15 Dec. 1829.
[91] SBA/1303/6/292, Craig/Paterson, 22 May 1832.
[92] Royal Burghs (Scotland) Act, 1833 (3&4 William IV, c. 76); J. D. Marwick, 'The Municipal institutions of Scotland: A historical Survey (Concluded)' 1 (1904) *Scottish Historical Review*, 274, 282.
[93] S. C. Oliver, 'The administration of urban society in Scotland 1800–50, with reference to the Growth of Civil Government in Glasgow and its suburbs' (unpublished PhD, thesis, University of Glasgow, 1995), 221; see also D. G. Barrie, *Police in the Age of Improvement* (Abingdon, 2012), 176.
[94] *Mather v Stalker* (1850) 12 D. 476; Urquhart, *The Burghs of Scotland*, 55–6.
[95] Oliver, 'Administration of urban society', 223; Police of Towns (Scotland) Act, 1850 (13&14 Vict., c. 33).
[96] HC, *Report on Municipal Corporations, Appendix*, 615.
[97] Ibid.
[98] SBA/1303/6/433, Craig/William Oliver, sheriff of Roxburghshire, 15 Nov. 1833.

watching & permanent constable for the whole town in both counties'. Replacing the part-time special constables, this would have been a desirable improvement, yet Roxburghshire demurred.

The following July, Torwoodlee for the heritors wrote to George Scott, clerk to the commissioners of supply at Jedburgh, mentioning that Robert Howden, a former weaver, was acting as 'special constable' for Galashiels in both counties. His role was to suppress crime and Torwoodlee had expected there to be an arrangement to share the expense.[99] Unless Roxburghshire was willing to do so, Selkirk had resolved to discontinue the constable's service altogether. To show that Selkirk was not asking for a favour, Torwoodlee noted that the areas within Roxburgh, such as Darlingshaugh and Bemersyde,

> contain above 1200 inhabitants whereas Galashiels in Selkirk contains little more than 1000; & this circumstance alone only requires to be made known to the Roxburghshire Gentlemen either to see the propriety of paying the half, or like Selkirkshire take their choice in having no Constable at all.[100]

Howden is probably the person to whom Craig supplied a wheelbarrow in 1833 for the purpose 'of keeping the streets of Galashiels free of loose stones & other missiles'.[101] He is also noted, as mentioned earlier, as being 'the Baron Bailie's man' in 1831.[102] The expense of the wheelbarrow Craig thought properly chargeable to the Selkirkshire Road Trustees, but he urged the town clerk, Andrew Lang, to obtain it if necessary from 'Bridge & Rogue money'. The word 'missiles' suggests the purpose was crime prevention, rather than clearing the road.

In the background to all this was uncertainty over the boundaries between Roxburghshire and Selkirkshire. Torwoodlee asked Craig to produce a plan of the marches in Darlingshaugh and Weirhaugh in Galashiels and Craig entrusted the task to the schoolmaster in Heriot. The plan, according to Craig,

> was found necessary in the execution of Diligences & in the apprehending of vagrants & will be of great use in this point of view & perhaps ought to be signed by the sheriffs or other legal officers of each County.[103]

Boundaries clearly mattered, not only in questions of jurisdiction but also in regard to policing.

The work of special constables can be traced in Craig's correspondence. In 1826, for instance, Inglis, the then constable, brought before Craig a man called Logan. Craig described him as an 'incorrigible vagabond' whom the Selkirk councillors

---

[99] SBA, SBA/1063, Andrew Lang/Scott of Gala, 25 Nov. 1834. For Howden as a weaver, SBA/1303/5/493, Craig/Andrew Lang, 15 Dec. 1829.
[100] SBA/1303/6/496, James Pringle of Torwoodlee/George Scott, 11 Jul. 1834.
[101] SBA/1303/6/412, Craig/Andrew Lang, 23 Apr. 1833.
[102] Hall, *History of Galashiels*, 109.
[103] SBA/1303/7/15, Craig/Robert Henderson, clerk to the commissioners of supply, Selkirk, 25 Sep. 1834.

were likely not to punish but to do what they could to get rid of him.[104] Craig opposed his coming to Galashiels as an apprentice and saw no option 'but sending him on board some ship', apparently having in mind penal transportation.[105]

The story of police in Galashiels contrasts with Kelso. In 1828, when appointed bailie there, George Main asked the council for funds for a town officer. While reluctant to increase the local tax (the stent), he noted that 'a more necessary and legitimate cause of Stent, than the keeping up a respectable Police, for the protection and peace of the Inhabitants, cannot well exist' and asked for two officers in addition to the existing town officer.[106] While this seemingly received a cool response, on grounds of expense, the burgh, as noted, did adopt the Burgh Police (Scotland) Act 1833 with such initial success that by May 1840 the county JPs had decided to create a police establishment for the whole of Roxburgh.[107] This involved police districts, a superintendent in Jedburgh, and a number of salaried constables, in districts and parishes across the county, who were to adhere to defined police regulations.[108] Even so, policing remained inefficient and under resourced; as late as 1858, Kelso and Galashiels had only three police officers each which meant, in the case of Galashiels, one for about every 2,000 inhabitants.[109]

Poaching

A key concern for Craig, as bailie and land agent, was infringement of the game laws. These were fortified by legislation in 1828 (concerning night poaching) and 1832 (trespassing by day), although prior to the latter Act the solicitor-general regarded the country as being 'in a most lawless state' on the subject.[110] Craig worked closely with tenants and gamekeepers to ensure proper enforcement. With Gala, George Fairholme and Alexander Monro largely absentee landlords, their estates were leased out, with the rental including the right to shoot. This might also be sublet by a tenant. Fairholme was reluctant to spend money preserving the game at Greenknowe 'seeing he never takes a bird from his estate'.[111] He had no objection to it being let to his neighbours at a 'very low' rent, but was not disposed to contribute when a gamekeeper was appointed at Gordon.[112]

When it came to poachers, Craig had a list of usual suspects. Shooting without a game licence could be prosecuted at the instance of the Stamp Office, potentially

---

[104] An officer was appointed to expel vagabonds from the barony as early as 1698: Hall, *History of Galashiels*, 52. An interesting Galashiels case of men who harboured vagabonds in 1817 is given in Chisholm, *Scott as a Judge*, 98.

[105] SBA/1303/4/362, Craig/Torwoodlee, 6 Apr. 1826.

[106] SBA, SBA/183/27, George Main/Henry Swan, praeses of Kelso town council, 15 Jan. 1828.

[107] Ibid., George Main, Kelso/praeses of the Town Council, 20 Apr. 1830.

[108] Ibid., Police Establishment of the County of Roxburgh, 1840.

[109] Barrie, *Police in the Age of Improvement*, 185.

[110] E. J. Cowan, 'The "Despotism of Law" in an Agricultural Community' (1980) *Juridical Review*, 47, 58; [H. Cockburn], *Letters Chiefly Connected with the Affairs of Scotland* (London, 1874), 381.

[111] SBA/1303/8/339, Craig/Robert Swan, Kelso, 19 Sep. 1838.

[112] SBA/1303/8/353-4, idem, 13 Oct. 1838.

giving Craig, as a sub-distributor of stamps, another basis upon which to demand action. In 1830 he asked Robert Henderson in Selkirk, county surveyor of taxes and procurator fiscal, to prosecute the 'notorious poacher' Robert Melrose. Melrose had been sighted by various witnesses shooting partridge, hare and other game. He also had a well-known associate:

> One Adam Beattie in Galashiels goes along with him & is also a celebrated poacher & altho' Gala has employed a man since December to watch the two, he has not been able to detect them though they have been seen by others on the grounds between this & Lindean . . . It is almost impossible to get direct cases, but I hope I have stated as much as will answer for a prosecution . . .[113]

Poaching apparently ran in Beattie's family. In 1839 John Beattie, described as 'a determined poacher', was observed setting gin traps in hare runs on Netherbarns farm by James Burns, one of Gala's gamekeepers.[114] As Craig mentioned to the procurator fiscal, the tenant was anxious to obtain a conviction and if Beattie was put to his oath 'he would say he had taken 50 hares lately'.[115]

As well as prosecution, given the challenges of catching culprits in flagrante, more subtle means could be used to disrupt their activities. Craig reported the 'professed poacher' and Galashiels stocking-maker, William Wintrop, to John McGowan, the surveyor of taxes in Peebles, for having three terriers two of which he had failed to notify to either McGowan or his counterpart in Selkirk.[116] One of the terriers, Wintrop claimed, was owned by one of the duke of Buccleuch's gamekeepers at Bowhill and another by a woman in Galashiels. Craig asked McGowan to send his local officer, McLeod, a notice to serve on Wintrop so that he might not pretend ignorance of the charge.[117]

In 1836 had Craig discussed with George Bruce at Greenknowe how to protect the game on that estate. He advised that 'you had better employ the constable once a week or so to watch and give in the names of transgressors that they may be prosecuted', adding that Bruce should record what he paid the constable for doing so.[118] The mere threat of prosecution could achieve results while reinforcing Craig's authority. Two poachers caught on George Fairholme's land in Gordon, for example, were sent to Craig by the forester, George Robertson. Craig brandished the threat of prosecution which Fairholme then agreed to remove if the poachers immediately sold their dogs and guns, and paid half a guinea to the parish

---

[113] SBA/1303/6/29, Craig/Robert Henderson, 6 Mar. 1830.

[114] A John Beattie was born in Ettrick parish in Feb. 1821 to Adam Beattie (presumably the poacher) and his wife Elisabeth Sword.

[115] SBA/1303/8/666, C&R/Peter Rodger, 21 Dec. 1839.

[116] SBA/1303/8/39, Craig/John McGowan, 15 Sep. 1837. Notification was a duty because the dogs were taxable (see *infra*).

[117] McLeod was involved in other poaching cases. In the prosecution of Ormiston and Aitchison (below, n. 124), he was sent with a letter to provide information to the fiscal about the timing of the offence.

[118] SBA/1303/7/286, Craig/George Bruce, 5 Nov. 1836.

poor.[119] Another form of direct action was attempted, as a last resort, against the Galashiels labourer John Scott who was given a final warning in 1840 that if his dog was found in any of Gala's fields or plantations it would be destroyed.[120]

As well as local poachers, there was an instance of an organised poaching trip which gave rise to 'a most serious complaint' from one of Gilbert Innes of Stow's tenants. He came across four young men, pretending to be in a shooting party at Caddonhead, who passed along the Blackhaugh sheepwalks which he tenanted.[121] When challenged, they claimed to have Innes' leave to shoot there. Two others, spotted the day before, reappeared but then ran off and all six were part of the same group. These 'birkies', as Craig described them to James Miller, the Edinburgh insurance agent who had leased the shooting rights at Caddonhead, had even told the tenant that 'the shepherds at Caddonhead were so busy with their meadow hay that they could not get away to point out the marches'.[122] If Miller confirmed they had no permission to shoot, Craig wanted to trace the parties using notices in the newspapers.

There is also reference to active prosecutions. The approaching trial of 'Graham the Poacher' at Selkirk in 1837 was notified by Craig to the gamekeeper at Torwoodlee, Robert Anderson.[123] As a witness, Anderson was to wait upon Peter Roger, the fiscal, at Selkirk at between eleven and twelve since the court was to sit a noon. On a later occasion, Craig told Rodger that he should proceed against two individuals, Ormiston and Aitchison, without delay 'as Gala and Mr Fraser mean to prosecute in every case of poaching', John Fraser being the then tenant of Gala House who enjoyed the shooting rights.[124] Craig's clerk had precognosed Fraser's servant in the case, but it was not possible to prove by witnesses that the accused had game in their possession.[125] He pointed out to Rodger that under the legislation it was competent to determine the case by reference to the oath of the accused and was optimistic that 'they will prove the case against themselves'.

TAX MATTERS

An important element of domestic management Craig undertook for his major clients was their tax affairs. These reflected the operation of the tax regime established when William Pitt was chancellor of the exchequer.[126] The Treasury had

[119] SBA/1303/8/48, Craig/Thomas Robertson, 27 Sep. 1837.

[120] SBA/1303/8/682, C&R/John Scott, Galashiels, 8 Jan. 1840.

[121] Caddonhead was on the Torwoodlee estate where an entry for the advertisement for the game there in the *Edinburgh & Leith Advertiser* appears in 1826: TAB, 2 Nov. 1826.

[122] SBA/1303/6/97, Craig/James Miller, 28 Aug. 1830. A 'birkie' was a conceited fellow. Miller sublet the rights to a local brewer, in 1831, for two years, at a slightly lower rent than his own: SBA/1303/6/177, idem, 10 May 1831.

[123] SBA/1303/7/356, Craig/Robert Anderson, 1 Feb. 1837.

[124] SBA/1303/8/45, Craig/Peter Rodger, 23 Sep. 1837. Fraser himself had no interest in shooting: NRS, Scott of Gala papers, GD477/143/23, Fraser/Craig, 23 Aug. 1830.

[125] SBA/1303/8/48-9, unsigned/Peter Rodger, 27 Sep. 1837. A precognition is a preliminary witness examination.

[126] See John Jeffrey-Cook, 'William Pitt and his taxes' (2010) *British Tax Review*, 376–391.

four departments which collected tax: customs, excise, stamps and taxes. Craig was, as a sub-distributor, concerned primarily with stamps but he also dealt with the Tax Office.[127] Stamps concerned deeds which by law had to be written on stamped paper, including instruments of sasine, bills of exchange, certificates of fire insurance and, from 1785, attorney certificates.[128] The Tax Office dealt with both land tax and 'assessed taxes'. The assessed taxes formed a group of disparate taxes on inhabited houses; windows; carriages; servants; horses; dogs; armorial bearings and hair powder.[129] They were collected by the commissioners of supply in Scotland who had statutory powers to act as Commissioners for the Assessed Taxes and were appointed from time to time in every county.[130]

In Scotland, the tax year ran from Whitsunday, at which point the local collector would send out a return to each individual taxpayer. The number of taxpayers was, of course, very limited. Government taxation policy traditionally avoided charges on income (until Pitt's income tax was introduced in 1798) in favour of taxing luxuries and only used direct taxation when it came to land.[131] Income tax does not feature in Craig's letters because it was repealed in 1816 and not reintroduced until 1841.

Given the position of the estates he dealt with, Craig interacted with collectors of taxes in Roxburghshire, Selkirkshire, Berwickshire and, less often, Midlothian (the latter for his clients William Walker of Bowland and Dr Colvin of Torquhan).[132] He seems to have been on particularly good terms with Charles Robson in Jedburgh who collected the taxes for Roxburghshire. Robson had gained the office in 1821 in competition with William Scott of Maxpoffle (1773–1855) and had unsuccessfully sought Craig's support. While Craig wished him success, he declined to interfere for either candidate 'as Maxpoffle is my old friend and acquaintance'.[133] This has been described as a 'bitter contest', with Craig informing George Fairholme that the two candidates were having 'as hard a run for the collectorship . . . as ever was in the county', and Robson emerging victor by forty-seven votes to forty-one.[134] This disappointed Sir Walter Scott who, alongside Gala and Torwoodlee, had backed his cousin Maxpoffle.

[127] On the stamp office, see Chapter 6.
[128] See Finlay, '"Tax the attornies!"', 141, 143.
[129] P. D. Allfrey, 'Arms and the (tax)man: the use and taxation of armorial bearings in Britain, 1798–1944' (Unpublished DPhil., University of Dundee, 2016), p. 14. The taxes on horses, carriages and servants were excise taxes until 1785: Jeffrey-Cook, 'William Pitt and his taxes', 382.
[130] Allfrey, 'Arms and the (tax)man', 16.
[131] Jeffrey-Cook, 'William Pitt and his taxes', 381.
[132] Craig first contacted the collector for Midlothian in 1837 and did not even know his name: SBA/1303/7/440, Craig/collector of taxes for Midlothian, 60 New Building, Edinburgh, 10 May 1837.
[133] SBA/1303/2/13, Craig/Robson, Black Bull Hotel, Edinburgh 10 Apr. 1821. Maxpoffle was Sir Walter Scott's cousin.
[134] SBA/1303/2/30, Craig/G. Fairholme, 27 Apr. 1821; D. R. Fisher, ed., *The House of Commons 1820–1832* (7 vols, Cambridge: Cambridge University Press, 2009), III, 550.

Craig described Robson to his employers at the Leith Bank as follows:

> Charles Robson is proprietor of Samieston, a considerable property in Roxburghshire & is well connected in that County. He is also collector of Land & assessed taxes for that County & resides & farms at Lundenlaw under the Duke of Roxburgh. His brother John is an opulent stone farmer in the same County & also respectably connected.[135]

There was no inconsistency in Robson simultaneously farming and collecting tax. While his office may have been lucrative, it was not full-time and much of the work could be done by a clerk. Indeed, Robson's deputy in the Jedburgh tax office (known also as the 'cess office'), George Scott, was also one of Craig's correspondents.[136]

Craig also dealt with William Molle WS (1765–1840), collector for Berwickshire, through the tax office at Duns. George Fairholme had his lands in that county (he also lived for a time in Bemersyde), therefore his returns should have been sent to Molle but, in 1823, Elliot Anderson mistakenly sent them to George Scott in Jedburgh.[137] When the error came to light, Craig asked Scott to send his payment to Molle (who lived in Edinburgh) and explained that Fairholme had no property in Roxburghshire whereas his brother, Adam Fairholme of Chapel, did (including Bluecairn near Blainslie).[138] Craig acted for both brothers and made it clear that he was happy for Scott to draw on him when any county rates (land taxes) were payable by Adam.

Craig's working library appears to have been a good one, although he seldom referred to it. However, he did occasionally rely on Erskine & Curle in Melrose for tax-related material. In 1821 he sent them a query about the property tax (which had been ended in 1816), the question being whether, when that tax operated, a widow whose only income was an annuity was liable to it. He could have worked this out for himself, but the Melrose firm had the legislation to hand and Craig did not.[139] That year Elliot Anderson also obtained, from the same firm, a copy of the Roxburghshire land valuation book.[140]

The county surveyor of taxes for Selkirk was Robert Henderson, erstwhile local procurator fiscal, clerk to the commissioners of supply for Selkirkshire, and agent for the Scottish Union Insurance Company. Henderson was also clerk to the statute labour trustees, responsible for making and repairing the county's roads. By private legislation, the requirement to provide labour had been converted to money (a proportion of the valued rent in the natural possession of landowners

---

[135] SBA/1303/3/200, Craig/LBC, 20 Jun. 1823. Some punctuation added and contractions extended. A stone farmer, presumably, is the owner of a quarry. Samieston lies in the parish of Eckford.

[136] E.g., SBA/1303/3/14, Craig/George Scott, Tax Office, Jedburgh, 12 Jul. 1822.

[137] SBA/1303/2/133, Craig/George Scott, 10 Mar. 1823. In the late 1830s, Fairholme was also being assessed for county rates at Greenlaw, e.g. SBA/1303/8/274, Craig/Robert Knox, 22 Jun. 1838; SBA/1303/8/536, idem, 15 Jul. 1839.

[138] Molle was to send his receipt to the Leith Bank for transmission to Craig: SBA/1303/2/138, Anderson/Molle, 17 Mar. 1823.

[139] SBA/1303/2/19, Craig/Erskine & Curle, Melrose, 14 Apr. 1821.

[140] SBA/1303/2/81, Anderson/Erskine & Curle, 14 Jun. 1821.

and their tenants).[141] There are references to him in this capacity, including in the
Torwoodle Account Book where, for example, he was paid just over £9 for 'road
& rogue money for Selkirkshire' recorded under the public burdens which the
laird had to pay.[142]

It was to Henderson that most of Craig's clients made tax returns, using a
pro-forma to detail the number of horses, servants (house servants or occasional
servants), and dogs they had as well as any armorial bearings.[143] Thus Archibald
Gibson of Ladhope in 1822, having received his tax schedule from Craig, informed
Henderson that the only addition to his taxes was a pony under thirteen hands.[144]
He pointed out that he had already made a return in Edinburgh for his house
servant, pointer dog and armorial bearings. In 1826, a Mrs Clark argued that she
should not be charged as per the schedule for armorial bearings because she only
used them on a small ring on one of her fingers.[145] An armorial device was not pre-
cisely defined in the legislation, but examples in Craig's correspondence of where
it was thought chargeable included those on seals, plates and carriages.[146] Anyone
who used or wore, or caused to be used or worn, any armorial bearing or ensign
was liable to the tax, therefore conceivably a finger ring might qualify, although
the Board of Taxes and the judges could differ in their interpretations of the
statute.[147] The rate varied, not according to use but according to the taxpayer's
circumstances, and there were three rates. The owner of a carriage, for example,
would pay at the highest rate which was set, in 1808, at £2 8s per annum.[148]

In 1835, Elliot Anderson made returns to Henderson for Gala, James Pringle of
Torwoodlee and George Pringle, and also his own employer, George Craig.[149] Gala
returned one house servant (Mark Haymans), a groom who was also employed as
a gamekeeper, Daniel Stewart, and one gardener, John Robertson. The house servant was liveried and the gamekeeper, for whom a stamped licence was obtained,
occasionally assisted in the house unliveried.[150] He had two four-wheeled carriages
(a phaeton and a carriage); one carriage horse; one riding horse; a pointer dog and

[141] 53 & 54 Geo. III, cap. 39, *An Act for amending an Act passed in the 41st year of His present Majesty, respecting the High Roads in the County of Selkirk* (this was a local and personal Act); NRS, GD477/464/6, Robert Henderson/Scott of Gala, 19 Jun. 1827; see also GD477/464/6, Andrew Henderson/Scott of Gala, 1 May 1813, which is in similar terms.

[142] TAB, 1821, Branch 7, Public burdens, 27 Mar. 1821.

[143] An example of the Roxburghshire pro-forma can be seen in SBA/183/10, subscribed by George Scott as evidence of payment received.

[144] SBA/1303/2/37, Gibson/Henderson, 28 Aug. 1822.

[145] SBA/1303/4/324, Craig/Henderson, 9 Jan. 1826.

[146] SBA/1303/8/70, Craig/J. Caird, St Leonards, Edinburgh, 24 Oct. 1837. Initially a stamp duty, the tax on armorial bearings was an assessed tax between 1801 and 1869: Allfrey, 'Arms and the (tax) man', p. 2.

[147] 41 Geo III c. 69 s. 4; Allfrey, 'Arms and the (tax)man', 15, 23, 39. As Allfrey notes, the wearer of a ring was found liable to the tax in *Milligan v Cowan* (1896) 23 R. 731.

[148] 48 Geo III c. 55, Sched. K; Allfrey, 'Arms and the (tax)man', 16.

[149] SBA/1303/7/96, Anderson/Henderson, 2 Sep. 1835.

[150] SBA/1303/7/14, Craig/Henderson, 2 Sep. 1834.

a terrier. He also paid the armorial bearings tax.[151] The phaeton (a lighter, open carriage) is noteworthy, since in 1837 it was mentioned that 'Mr Scott never kept horses of any kind for his four wheel'd carriage, always using post Horses, and when the Pheaton [sic] was used, it was drawn by a work horse'.[152]

Gala's migrations across the country caused complications as did the question of whether Craig had the status of his bailie or factor.[153] In 1828, for example, when Scott made an appeal to the tax commissioners, Craig informed him that he would have to state what he had in Edinburgh and what he had in Selkirkshire so that he could pay the appropriate tax in each office.[154] In the year to Whitsunday 1832, Scott was resident in England and had only one man servant and one carriage.[155] In October 1836, he broke up his establishment in Scotland altogether and moved briefly to Jersey.[156] Craig presumed he would pay his assessed taxes in England in respect of the carriage and male servant who still remained locally and this seems to have been the case.[157] Another absent client, Dr William Colvin who lived in Kent, likewise sent up his own return in respect of his property at Torquhan, with Craig only dealing with queries.[158]

As with insurance (see Chapter 8), much of the tax correspondence related to the correction of errors. The quickest and easiest mode of returning taxes was simply to compare the present year with the past year. In 1823, for instance, Pringle of Torwoodlee had '1 dog fewer' than the year before.[159] In 1833 both Torwoodlee and Gala had no changes at all to report from the previous year.[160] This was unusual. Torwoodlee's schedule had to be altered in 1834 because he only had three horses, not the four specified, and Craig noted, in case it made any difference, that the two carriage horses were sometimes used in agricultural labour.[161] On the other hand, Craig's own return was generally the same every year. He seems to have disliked the system of identifying changes by reference to the return made in the previous year. As he complained to the Peebles tax collector John McGowan, '[w]hen a return is made every year in July I cannot see the use of referring back to it in reference to any future establishment as each year will come to answer for itself'.[162] He also chastised McGowan in 1839, when Gala

[151] Torwoodlee's establishment in 1835 was similar, except he had two carriage horses and a coachman rather than a groom (and Torwoodlee's phaeton lacked armorial bearings): SBA/1303/7/14, Craig/Henderson, 20 Sep. 1834.
[152] SBA/1303/8/55, Craig/John McGown, collector of taxes, Peebles, 2 Oct. 1837. This was in respect of the tax year from 26 May 1836 to 26 May 1837 (a year and a day).
[153] SBA/1303/5/233, Craig/Gala, 5 Apr. 1828.
[154] Ibid.
[155] SBA/1303/6/323, Craig/Henderson, 26 Sep. 1832.
[156] SBA/1303/7/47, Craig/John McGowan, collector of taxes, Peebles, 25 Sep. 1837.
[157] SBA/1303/7/287, Craig/Henderson, 2 Nov. 1836.
[158] SBA/1303/8/70, Craig/J. Caird, Edinburgh, 24 Oct. 1837.
[159] SBA/1303/3/279, idem, 27 Nov. 1823.
[160] SBA/1303/6/418, Anderson/James Murray, tax office, Selkirk, 16 Sep. 1833.
[161] SBA/1303/7/27, Craig/Henderson, 4 Nov. 1834.
[162] SBA/1303/7/47, Craig/John McGowan, 25 Sep. 1837.

was wrongly charged for a carriage he had not had for some years, since McGowan had often been 'advised as to this'.[163] After the death of his dog in April 1838, he left it up to McGowan whether to charge him for a new dog which he acquired in May 1839 just before the end of the tax year.[164]

Of course, Craig was not simply there to pay and explain tax bills: part of his role was to raise queries and minimise liability. For instance, Elliot Anderson asked McGowan whether William Colvin would be liable in assessed taxes for Mitchelston farmhouse, where he used to live and which he now leased out, 'were he to remove part of the furniture from Torquhan house to be kept *shut up*' there.[165] Craig consulted George Rodger in 1825 regarding Gala House, taking the view that it was 'hard' on the laird to face house duty and assessed taxes when he was absent from home 'not from choice but necessity, on account of his health'.[166] He asked Rodger if he could think of any additional grounds of objection and then wrote to Francis Wilson, the solicitor of taxes, concerning Gala's assessment for the preceding year. He argued for a reduction on the basis that

> Mr Scott having met a severe accident, was forced to leave Gala on 8th September last, for the South of England for the recovery of his health, when instantly 14 windows out of the 48 were shut up, and the beds, bed clothes, carpet &c were tied up in bundles and lodged in the upper apartments in which state the house will remain till August 1826 at which time the family return.[167]

All Scott had left to declare to the local tax collector in Selkirk was a gardener and a watchdog (although he still had to pay an annual licence for Craig as his factor).[168] Craig, having received a seemingly non-committal reply, wrote to Henderson in Selkirk to enquire whether Gala might be freed from the taxes and house duty if the servants left and shut up the house altogether. As Gala had only maintained an establishment at Gala House until 8 September 1824, Craig thought he should not continue to be charged for it until Whitsunday 1825 and made it clear that he was ready to petition the commissioners of taxes.[169] Seeking an exemption for the house, he described the reduction in Scott's establishment compared to the previous year, noting that one of the ponies was so small it was not worth charging and 'the old deaf dog Sancho was dying every day'.[170]

After Gala moved to Northlands, near Chichester, Craig again described his establishment to Henderson in July 1826, but regarded any tax as exclusively

---

[163] SBA/1303/8/648, idem, 5 Dec. 1839.
[164] SBA/1303/8/587, idem, 28 Sep. 1839.
[165] SBA/1303/6/381, Anderson/McGowan, 11 May 1833.
[166] SBA/1303/4/218, Craig/George Rodger, Selkirk, 28 Jul. 1825.
[167] SBA/1303/4/225, Craig/Francis Wilson, solicitor of taxes, Edinburgh, 6 Aug. 1825.
[168] SBA/1303/4/226, Craig/Robert Henderson, 6 Aug. 1825; SBA/1303/5/179, Elliot Anderson/Robert Henderson, Selkirk, 26 Dec. 1827.
[169] SBA/1303/4/241-242, Craig/Robert Henderson, Selkirk, 12 Sep. 1825.
[170] SBA/1303/4/246, Craig/Robert Henderson, Selkirk, 21 Sep. 1825.

payable in England.[171] There was some confusion as to whether both Craig and Andrew Lang of Selkirk were factors to Gala in respect of different properties. Lang was factor to Robert Pringle of Clifton who, it seems, had been charged for having two factors but had petitioned successfully to be free of the tax for one of them (presumably Craig).[172] Craig obtained a copy of the petition from Lang and used it to ensure Gala was also charged for only one factor. Gala's taxes lay unresolved in December 1826, with Gala disputing a charge for a chaise he was using in England because the diameter of the wheels was below thirty inches. He also claimed that he had no dog, either in England or Scotland, and that he was giving his entire tax return in England that year.[173]

When Mrs Fraser, the widow of the tenant at Gala House, moved out Craig checked that she would not be obliged to pay tax in both Selkirkshire and Roxburghshire as a result of moving from one county to another.[174] The taxes involved in the lease of residential property, as Elliot Anderson explained to another client, Mrs Douglas, were the window tax (which varied according to the number of windows) and 'inhabited house duty'.[175] In her case, with a rental value of £45, Craig estimated taxes at about £10 to £15.

Revisions and disputes about taxes were fairly common. One such dispute saw Craig communicate with Allan Purves of the tax office in Duns in 1828.[176] This involved a game certificate that was taken out for John Brodie, a coachman for whom Alexander Monro paid tax. Purves, following investigation with the Inspector of Taxes, discovered that Monro had made no return in respect of Brodie in the county of Edinburgh and therefore decided to charge him in Duns. Monro, however, could supply a certificate from the collector of taxes confirming that he had paid for Brodie as an assessed servant. Purves had initially raised the matter at Cockburn, with Monro's tenant, John Wilson, but Monro sent all the paperwork to Craig to have it settled. Tax returns, it must have seemed to Craig, were never ending.

CONCLUSION

As factor, Craig enjoyed significant autonomy. He had the freedom, for instance, to agree rents with tenants.[177] Drafting leases and maintaining rentals (registers of tenants) within Galashiels, keeping the streets free of nuisance and generally superintending the environment were part of the role. Craig was ready to maintain order with more than his pen. Hearing the report of a gun in 1829 he

[171] SBA/1303/4/426, Craig/Henderson, 29 Jul. 1826.
[172] SBA/1303/4/398, Craig/Andrew Lang, 5 Jun. 1826.
[173] SBA/1303/4/509, Craig/Henderson, 16 Dec. 1826.
[174] SBA/1303/8/311, Craig/John McGowan, Peebles, 7 Nov. 1838.
[175] SBA/1303/2/23, Anderson/Mrs Douglas, Eskmount, Brechin, 21 Apr. 1821.
[176] SBA/1303/5/184, Craig/Allan Purves, tax office, Duns, 3 Jan. 1828.
[177] E.g. SBA/1303/7/538, C&R to Scott of Gala, 19 Jul. 1839; NRS, Scott of Gala papers, GD477/143/25.

physically went off in search of the culprits only to find two 'young lads' in the park, including a son of Thomas Clapperton the Galashiels clothier.[178] Craig naturally wanted them prosecuted in Selkirkshire where the offence was committed, rather than Roxburghshire where they lived, and wrote yet another missive to the fiscal. A decade later, in a case involving muirburn (setting on fire of heath and, in this case, young trees in Buckholmside belonging to Torwoodlee), this was so regular an occurrence Craig demanded that 'an example should be made' of the' idle fellows' responsible (including another Clapperton, Alexander, who was a weaver).[179] As the land this time lay in Roxburghshire, the appropriate fiscal was in Jedburgh. Craig, who had the culprits' names from the local sheriff's officer, expected prosecutions. Cases like this, brought with impeccable local knowledge, reinforced his position as an authority figure.

In the years leading up to the controversial Scottish Reform Act, there were tensions in Galashiels. These reflected increasingly difficult economic times (Craig refers to 'the numerous failures' amongst Galashiels businesses which took place in 1829).[180] At his disposal, Craig had the local special constables. His was the directing mind, maintaining order and, when necessary, mobilising the aid of sheriffs-substitute and justices of the peace.

Craig's Tory politics placed him firmly on one side of a social and political divide. When invited to do so by the royal commissioners in 1835, he declined to give an opinion on whether there should be a 'popularly-elected magistracy', but noted that if there was then the qualification to vote should be '£15 of yearly rent in property'.[181] This pointedly excluded the tenantry, 'a large and important body of the inhabitants', whom the commissioners favoured including by setting a lower qualification.[182] While Craig recognised a need for changes in governance, he was certainly no radical.

As an agent, Craig sought to insulate and protect his clients from the intrusions made into their lives by the tax authorities. He dealt with tax collectors with characteristic robustness and his correspondence with them permits a glimpse into the day-to-day households of some clients who, with their servants and carriages, lived in very different circumstances from the ordinary worker in Galashiels. Here again we see Craig as the conduit between two worlds: that of the local lairds in their mansion houses and that of the poacher or young apprentice dyer. As factor he dealt with tenants, overseers and landlords in great things and small, taking care of the detail of private matters. When Torwoodlee wanted to advertise his 'best bred forest stock' for private sale for example, it was Craig, not John Tillie the estate overseer, who arranged the newspaper advertisement.[183]

---

[178] SBA/1303/5/392, Craig/C. Rodger, Selkirk, 8 May 1829. The son was George Clapperton.
[179] SBA/1303/8/479. C&R/James Stevenson, Jedburgh, 23 Apr. 1839.
[180] SBA/1303/6/279, Craig/Adam Paterson WS, 19 Apr. 1832.
[181] HC, *Report on Municipal Corporations, Appendix*, 616.
[182] Ibid.
[183] SBA/1303/2/47, Craig/A. Ballantyne, Kelso Mail Office, 28 May 1821.

In an important sense Craig also had a residuary role within the burgh: if something needed done in the community, it was Craig who would normally be consulted or instructed to do it. It was Craig who disposed of the 'old town bell of Galashiels' on Gala's instructions by sending it to Edinburgh to have it sold to braziers.[184] John Young carried it and Craig was happy to take the first offer of £6. A small enough item of business, yet who but him would have done it? In recognition of his ubiquity and resourcefulness, the community, at a dinner held at Thornton's Inn in 1836, presented Craig with a silver salver and jug as a sign of gratitude to 'their worthy Bailie and respected townsman'.[185] It was noted that 'all classes' had contributed, 'manufacturers, artizans and farmers in the neighbourhood'.[186]

In the next chapter, the focus will be the Borders landscape and Craig's role in developing it. The changes wrought in the period 1820–1840, the enclosure of land, and the building of roads, mills and dykes, still mark the environment today.

---

[184] SBA/1303/8/306, Craig/Mr Moffat, Harrow Inn, Edinburgh, 3 Aug. 1838.
[185] Hall, *History of Galashiels*, 482.
[186] Robert Fyshe received a similar presentation in 1839 from his old pupils: SBA, SBA/83/9, Sanderson, 'Old Galashiels', 13–14.

Chapter 4

Craig and the Landscape

In 1825 Craig acquired from George Fairholme the long lease of land near the village of Gordon (about sixteen miles east of Galashiels), close to the Eden Water. This did not quite make him the 'Gordon laird' he jested of becoming but he was keen to develop a plantation that would add to the 'value & beauty of the muir'.[1] He later told James Laidlaw that he had 'sunk' all his money 'about Gordon and here' (meaning Galashiels).[2] References occur in his correspondence to 'Mr Craig's plantations' and stones on the land suitable for use in building dyke walls.[3] He also insured his twenty-six acres in Gordon with his own Caledonian Insurance Office.[4]

Craig stocked and farmed the land. Having bought lambs at St Boswells Fair in 1827, he sold them complaining that they 'had eaten as much grass as I could have paid £8 for'.[5] A decade later he was employing the labourer William Kirkwood to look after the property. His duties included killing moles and repairing dykes.[6] In 1838, he ordered Kirkwood to discover who had stolen some young trees from the plantation, instructing him to 'get Mr Wilson [the local schoolteacher] to write out the advertisements & offer a reward of half a guinea'.[7]

Personal experience of the concerns of the smallholder helped Craig as he exerted influence on the landscape far beyond Gordon. This chapter will focus on how Craig made a difference in this context, in Galashiels and on the estates for which he had responsibility as factor, including Cockburn and Torquhan. Part of being a good agent was finding able tenants and identifying competent farmers, shepherds, millers, spinners, weavers, gamekeepers and dykers. Craig seems to have gone out of his way to meet people and talk to them on his travels and his letters reflect only a fraction of the intelligence he gathered about land and people.

A letter to Alexander Monro illustrates his observational skills. Having been informed that his tenant, George Logan, had acquired a pair of lurchers, Monro was concerned about the threat to local game. Craig reported seeing

[1] SBA/1303/4/207, Craig/George Fairholme, Holy Island, Bedford, 28 Jun. 1825; SBA/1303/4/211, Craig/John Wilson, feuar, Gordon, 6 Jul. 1825.
[2] SBA/1303/5/139, Craig/James Laidlaw, Messrs Grieve & Scott, Edinburgh, 14 Nov. 1827.
[3] SBA/1303/5/193, Elliot Anderson/G. Baillie, Mellerstain, 18 Jun. 1828.
[4] SBA/1303/6/295, Craig/Dickie, 30 May 1832.
[5] Ibid.; SBA/1303/5/140, Craig/George Bruce of Greenknowe, 17 Nov. 1827.
[6] CRCB, SBA/1303/9/133 (9 Feb. 1836).
[7] SBA/1303/8/194, Craig/William Kirkwood, Gordon, 19 Mar. 1838.

only a black collie and a black terrier and that he had conversed with Logan's sons about the local game on his last visit. He had carefully noted that hares, grey fowl and partridges appeared to be in plentiful supply. He then went on, presumably in response to another observation by Monro, to discuss one of the farm workers:

> James Fleming the hedger appears to be from 45 to 50 is married & has a family and has been nine years if I remember right either as Grieve to Mr Logan or in his present situation of hedger & dyker and from his way of talking, I rather had a good idea of him. I tried him with a hedge bill and he seemed to be master of it.[8]

Paying such close attention to local affairs allowed Craig instantly to counter any misinformation or concerns he might hear from his client. Any effort to acquaint himself with useful people like Fleming he would not reckon time wasted.

GALA HOUSE AND OTHER PROPERTIES

At different times Craig had prominent houses in his care, including Gala House and houses at Torquhan (for Dr William Colvin) and Bemersyde (where George Fairholme lived for a time).[9] He took care that Gala House was properly insured for fire.[10] In 1825 Scott of Gala formally intimated that he wanted the property advertised for lease and the rental estimate reached was £150 per annum, including the wages of the gardener and the three or four acres of grassland around the house.[11] The matter had been contemplated for some time. Craig had informed David Monro Binning the year before that it would not be let that year but, if the family decided to remain longer in England where they presently were, then 'the saving would be considerable' if the property was let.[12] Two months later, Mrs Scott asked him to look for a tenant and Craig fully described the property to Tod & Romanes WS. He professed himself unable to determine a rental value, noting that for a property of that type 'I am really no judge'.[13] The £150 estimate was reached with the help of Scott's cousin, Binning, but Craig thought that John Tod WS would be the best judge.[14] He mentioned that Ogilvie younger of Chesters, when passing through, had told him that Colonel Napier's house in East Lothian had just been let 'to a Yorkshire Gentleman at no less than £200 with not more advantages'.[15]

---

[8] SBA/1303/4/299, Craig/Dr Monro, 10 Jan. 1826.
[9] SBA/1303/2/7, Craig/John Spence, Earlston, 31 Mar. 1821 (Bemersyde).
[10] SBA/1303/2/196, Craig/Tod & Romanes, 23 Feb. 1822.
[11] SBA/1303/4/189, idem, 11 May 1825.
[12] SBA/1303/4/134, Craig/Monro Binning, 22 Dec. 1824.
[13] SBA/1303/4/159, Craig/Tod & Romanes, 25 Feb. 1825.
[14] SBA/1303/4/189, idem, 11 May 1825; SBA/1303/4/164, Craig/William Ogilvy, Ettrickbank, 28 Feb. 1825.
[15] SBA/1303/4/159, Craig/Tod & Romanes, 25 Feb. 1825. The reference is to William Ogilvie (1785–1876).

Responding to an inquiry prompted by an advertisement, Craig described Gala House, specifying that that the rent would vary according to the number of acres let along with the house, garden and offices.

> The estate consists of 4038 acres of arable & pasture & woodland, lying compactly together, & there is none like it in the neighbourhood for abundance of game tho little of it is moorfowl, as there is little heath . . . The house is fully furnished except in napery & plate.[16]

When it came to working out what the rental value of property should be, as Craig informed the sheriff substitute of Selkirk, William Scott of Maxpoffle, there was a local rule that was in use: 'in this place for a number of years 7½ per cent has been the rule for return'.[17] In other words, the annual rent was that percentage of the property value.

In describing properties, or when compiling the inventory of goods included in the rental, detail was everything. Craig checked the state of premises during and after any lease. He confirmed to Dr Colvin in Woolwich that a recent tenant had left his house 'in the best order, and every thing in the Inventory in its place in excellent condition except some crockery & glass, which he [the tenant] took patterns of to Edinburgh to get matched'.[18]

The first tenant of Gala House was Thomas Tod, possibly a relative of John Tod WS. At the end of his lease, in May 1828, an inventory was taken and Craig recorded missing items in his letter book. Of these, Mrs Craig wanted replaced 'according to pattern' (i.e. identical to the lost items) eight large tumblers, two green finger glasses, seven ale glasses, a dozen wine glasses, three rummers [Roemers] and two bedroom looking glasses.[19] Tod decided to stay on longer, but those showing interest in renting the property included Sir Sidney Beckwith (soon after Commander in Chief of the Bombay Army).[20]

The next tenant was W. John Fraser who had offered £80 for the lease in August 1830, to commence from 15 September.[21] This sum was considerably less than 'what has been use to have been paid', but Gala was willing to negotiate and a deal was struck.[22] Craig, the following year, agreed to give him a one-year lease of certain fruit and vegetables from the Gala estate garden for £12.[23] In 1832, a lease of £100 was agreed for the year.[24] It is not entirely clear whether Fraser remained at Gala House continuously until his death in 1838. He may have lived for a time

---

[16] SBA/1303/4/324-5, Craig/William Douglas WS, Edinburgh, 10 Jan. 1826.
[17] SBA/1303/4/154, Craig/William Scott of Maxpoffle, 14 Feb. 1825.
[18] SBA/1303/6/480, Craig/Dr Colvin, 25 May 1834.
[19] SBA/1303/6/255, Craig/Thomas Tod, Coates Crescent, Edinburgh, 27 May 1828; see also NRS, Scott of Gala papers, GD477/463/28, inventory taken by Mrs Robertson and George Craig.
[20] SBA/1303/5/159, Craig/Lady Beckwith, Ancrum House, Jedburgh, 7 Dec. 1827.
[21] NRS, Scott of Gala papers, GD477/143/23, Fraser/Craig, 23 Aug. 1830.
[22] SBA/1303/6/92, Craig/Fraser, Old Meldrum, 24 Aug. 1830.
[23] NRS, Scott of Gala papers, GD477/143/24.
[24] Ibid., GD477/143/25.

at Allerby House in Gattonside, the property of Sir David Brewster.[25] There is later reference to 'a sort of Pass Book' that went between him and Craig, together with vouchers (receipts) which provided an accurate account of expenditure.[26] Prior to Fraser's tenancy, the house was enlarged and, amongst other changes, a stable was turned into a kitchen.[27] This necessitated an increase in the insurance premium.[28]

Craig seems to have had a good relationship with the tenants of Gala House with the exception of Richard Dennistoun WS (1806–1848), the son of a Glasgow merchant, who entered in 1838 after extensive negotiations.[29] Dennistoun considered turning the library into a dining room and wanted Gala to paint, paper and re-carpet the drawing room at considerable expense.[30] Gala agreed to the new wallpaper and repainting. Craig, no stranger to redecorating Gala House, said of the drawing room:

> Fairbairn the painter has measured it and finds it will need 11 pieces of paper, he will be set to the painting & sizing immediately. The old silk bottomed chairs to have gymp or gimp when newly covered of the same shade as the worsted damask and no brass nails to be put on them the wood to be well cleaned and varnished with polish the four old chairs already done to be cleaned much better and also varnished.[31]

When Dennistoun was dissatisfied with the water supply, however, he said so in terms which Craig thought went too far. Craig opposed leading a pipe from the 'uppertown cistern' used by the feuars because the supply was too small and, in a favoured phrase of his, this risked 'bringing them [the feuars] about our ears'.[32] Dennistoun would have to continue 'to use a water cart from the burn' as the lairds and their tenants had done. Given that an expensive washing house had been fitted up 'exclusively for your accommodation', Craig was not prepared to 'move one inch' on the matter until Gala himself appeared and expressed himself willing to enlarge the cistern.

Craig advertised houses and farm lettings in the press and wrote to the editors of newspapers, such as the *Kelso Mail*, the *Edinburgh and Leith Advertiser* and the *Caledonian Mercury*. He knew his market and was aware, for instance, that the *Edinburgh Weekly Journal* was 'much read among farmers'.[33] Sometimes

---

[25] Cf. SBA/1303/7/248, Craig/Mr Fraser, 6 Aug. 1836 and NRS, Scott of Gala papers, GD477/123/27, Sir David Brewster/Gala (containing Craig's notational reference to his own letter book).
[26] SBA/1303/8/413, Craig/Fotheringham & Lindsay WS, Edinburgh, 22 Jan. 1839. This was said to commence in May 1831 and run until 1838.
[27] SBA/1303/7/223, Craig/John Scott, Edinburgh, 2 Jun. 1836.
[28] SBA/1303/7/321, Craig/John Moinet, 30 Dec. 1836.
[29] SBA/1303/8/587, Craig/John McGowan, Peebles, 28 Sep. 1839.
[30] SBA/1303/8/185, Craig/Richard Dennistoun, 13 Mar. 1838; SBA/1303/8/210-11, idem, 4 Apr. 1838.
[31] SBA/1303/8/353, idem, 12 Oct. 1838.
[32] SBA/1303/8/471, Craig/R. Dennistoun, 8 Apr. 1839.
[33] SBA/1303/5/381, Craig/Robert Hogg, Checklaw, Duns, 8 Apr. 1829.

the draft of an advertisement appears in his letters. An example concerns regarding Colonel John Pringle's mansion house at Symington. Pringle had intended to advertise it locally to 'gentlemen or respectable farmers', but Craig thought the advert should be recast and put in the Edinburgh newspapers which would 'more readily' attract the right kind of client.[34] He also suggested that Pringle separate 'the sheep land from the parks and occupy it either as a hoggage or wedder gang & advertise it accordingly'.[35] James Hogg of Nethershiels had already offered to lease the 'sheep ground' which perhaps prompted the idea.[36] In the end the Symington mansion house, 'pleasantly situated on the banks of the Gala', was advertised as suitable to accommodate a 'genteel family' along with its sheep pen. Craig stressed the easy communication with Edinburgh, with enquiries (typical for such advertisements) to go to Pringle, his Edinburgh agent Hugh Watson WS of Torsonce, or Craig himself.

When it came to finding a tenant for Gala House in 1828, handbills were printed and distributed for display in local lawyers' offices in Peebles, Lauder, Kelso, Melrose, Jedburgh, Hawick and also in Craig's office, though he also recommended advertising in the *Kelso Mail*. Knowing that Scott intended to remove some furniture, he wrote to him for details because this affected the level of rent.[37]

GALA WATER

Craig was preoccupied with flood prevention, particularly protecting Galashiels from the Gala Water. Much of this work occurred prior to the surviving letter books, but flood defence works and adjustments to the flow of water through the town are nonetheless referred to frequently. One context for this were issues arising between Scott of Gala and the builders Sanderson & Paterson, his feuars in Bemersyde, from the construction of a £2,000 machinery house which began in 1825. This involved works in the Gala Water below Galashiels, lengthening a dam, increasing the fall of water and making a cut or a 'new run for the Gala a little to the north of the present course'.[38]

The lawyer Thomas Bruce of Langlee and the naval officer William Clark of Longhaugh, as neighbouring proprietors, both complained about these operations, although Craig thought neither worse off than they had been in the days when the water was 'running closer in upon their marches than the Cut will make it'. He later had to revise his view, however, when the operations did expose Bruce's land to a greater pressure of water and he sought damages for flooding to his field. As Craig informed Scott's Edinburgh lawyers, 'we must either do something towards

[34] SBA/1303/3/312, Craig/Lt Col. Pringle, Symington, 19 Feb. 1824.
[35] A 'wedder gang' was a pasturage for wethers (castrated male sheep); a hoggage was the same for hogs (young sheep of either sex).
[36] SBA/1303/3/306, idem, 10 Feb. 1821.
[37] SBA/1303/5/211, Craig/Gala, 11 Feb. 1828.
[38] SBA/1303/4/206, Craig/John Tod WS, 28 Jun. 1825; also NRS, Scott of Gala papers, GD477/105/17, Tod & Romanes/Craig, 23 May 1826; SBA/1303/4/391, Craig/Tod & Romanes WS, 24 May 1826.

deepening the bed of the water & lengthening the flood dyke in the north side, or run the risk of a law suit'.[39] The threat, he noted, could be lessened with the removal of gravel and by allowing Galashiels masons 'to take stones out of the bottom of the Cut so as to deepen it'. This appears to have been achieved successfully and 'at very little expense' to Scott.[40]

A wider dispute with Sanderson & Paterson continued regarding their right to remove stone from the bed of the water for use in their business. In Craig's view, the builders mistook the boundaries of their land, on the north side of the Gala Water at Buckholmside, due to the old road being removed by floods which caused a permanent change to the course of the water.[41] The southern movement of the water placed Scott's land to the north between the builders' property and the river. As a result, Scott sought to interdict them from encroaching on his land and taking stone from the river.[42] The case threatened to escalate from the sheriff court to the Court of Session and, in 1830, Tod & Romanes asked Craig to prepare a sketch, 'shewing the old run of the water, – the road at that time, – with the alterations that have since been made', to help them draft a case for the opinion of counsel.[43] In 1833, Craig was still negotiating with the builders about the removal of cartloads of stone from the river.[44]

Craig elsewhere explained how successful his operations had been in defending Galashiels from persistent flooding through caulding (creating a weir across the river to disrupt and control its flow) and building embankments:

> The system of caulding & embanking seems to be well understood in this part of the Country now & in no instance has the method adopted by us 15 years ago failed either on Tweed or Gala.[45]

This places these improvements two years before Gala reached his majority in 1814 when it is known a local improvement works were carried out, including the foundation of a new bridge over the Gala Water.[46] Gala's tenants were expected to make an annual financial contribution to the caul and dam and it was a condition in their leases that they render assistance to repair the caul.[47]

A crisis caused by a flood in 1829, however, showed that Craig's optimism was misplaced. While the Tweed did little damage, the Gala Water 'was fully as large as in September 1807 when the bridge was run away'.[48] The caul was swept

[39] SBA/1303/4/365, Craig/Tod & Romanes, 10 Apr. 1826.
[40] SBA/1303/4/391, idem, 24 May 1826.
[41] SBA/1303/5/469, Tod & Romanes/Sanderson & Paterson, 31 Oct. 1829.
[42] SBA/1303/5/462, Craig/Tod & Romanes, 20 Oct. 1829.
[43] NRS, Scott of Gala papers, GD477/105/21.
[44] SBA/1303/6/463, Craig/Sanderson, Bemersyde, 17 Mar. 1833.
[45] SBA/1303/5/29, Craig/Tod & Romanes, 1 Mar. 1827.
[46] Hall, *History of Galashiels*, 90–1.
[47] NRS, Scott of Gala papers, GD477/122/2 (caul and dam account); GD477/122/12 (draft lease, 11 Apr. 1826).
[48] SBA/1303/6/430, Craig/Gala, 7 Aug. 1829.

away, some 'putts' were lost, and some roads made hardly passable.[49] The situation would have been worse but for the exertions of the locals. They cut down and threw into the water sixteen large alder trees, tied with strong ropes, which caused an eddy and preserved the bank:

> There would not have been a stone of Miss Mercers house left but for the causewayed embankments of last Spring & Lees' caul giving way at a right part for her. Sanderson's machinery house & improven haugh was in the greatest jeopardy but the whole town having turned out & raised a strong stone & tree embankment saved it. In several places of the flood dyke on Netherbarnshaugh the water was within an inch of being over when most of his turnips & new limed land would have gone.[50]

Craig, reporting all this to Gala, added that the River Leader to the north was even worse, with 'two bridges at Carrolside & all the mill cauls carried away'. In Galashiels, the clothiers immediately began temporary repairs.

From August 1829 a furious correspondence was kept up with Gala who had to find a way forward with all interested parties: his neighbours; his feuars (particularly in Hemphaugh and Bemersyde which had the greatest flood risk); the Selkirkshire Road Trustees and the equivalent body in Roxburghshire. Craig immediately recommended a plan, 'so decidedly preferable to every other plan that now it is divulged there is but one voice on the subject', which apparently 'arose by accident' when a number of people gathered on Hemphaugh Bridge.[51] The local MP Alexander Pringle of Whytbank wrote to Torwoodlee, pointing out that the exact boundary between Roxburghshire and Selkirkshire was 'doubtful', despite what any maps might say, but he was happy for Torwoodlee to arrange matters with the county authorities together 'with Gala and Mr Craig'.[52] He did suggest, however, reserving the right to move the road away from the water 'at any time the water makes such encroachment as to render that more expedient than keeping up the embankments'.

Gala, to protect his tenant and feuars as well as the security of transport and the mail, adopted a generous approach. The road would be redirected where required to reduce the risk of flooding. Gala accepted £60 each from the Selkirkshire and Roxburghshire Road Trustees in return for work on embankments (particularly at Hemphaugh) and roads, which he had been paying for since August 1829. This was subject to future maintenance of the embankments being at the equal expense of all three parties, with Roxburghshire maintaining the road surface.[53]

[49] Putts were 'stones loosely piled in the interior, but finished on the surface after the manner of a pavement, and shaped like the fore half of a shoemaker's last, pointing up the stream, and forming with the bank an angle of 45°: NSA, 'Galashiels', 13.

[50] SBA/1303/6/430, Craig/Gala, 7 Aug. 1829. The Mercers were at Wilderhaugh, on the north of the Gala estate. According to Paterson, trees were again employed in this way to defend against flood: NSA, 'Galashiels', 13–14.

[51] SBA/1303/6/436-7, Craig/Gala, 21 Aug. 1829.

[52] SBA/1303/695, Copy of Pringle of Whytbank/James Pringle of Torwoodlee, 24 Aug. 1830.

[53] SBA/1303/6/189.

Craig hoped that such a job might be made of the Hemphaugh embankment 'as not to require any keeping up in future'.[54]

In January 1831 Craig duly reported to the Roxburghshire road surveyor in Jedburgh, Andrew Spiers, that Scott was proceeding with the Hemphaugh embankment with twenty men 'filling up & causewaying', at the county's expense.[55] He supervised the work closely, particularly in relation to Galashiels Bridge. Craig told Speirs where stone may best be had for repairing the bridge and road and sought authority from him, on behalf of the Roxburghshire Road Trustees, 'to engage carts & horses & a mason or two'. He added that 'I have no hesitation in saying that if this necessary repair is not immediately set about, a flood of half the size of the last would endanger the bridge'.[56] When the Hemphaugh work was completed in April, Craig invited the road surveyors for both counties to inspect it and report so that Scott could recover the promised funds.[57]

Following a 'remarkably floody' winter in 1833–4, Craig was concerned about threats to his 'embanking' work when, in June 1834, Spier's employees removed stones and dug a channel at part of the road adjoining Galashiels Bridge. This had been done without informing Craig, Torwoodlee or Gala, and Craig apprehended 'very great danger to the expensive embankments on the estates of both these Gentlemen from the very first heavy flood that occurs on the Gala', reserving their right to take action against the trustees for damages.[58] The road was being repaired but there were nearby quarries which offered better stone for the job and Craig, typically, demanded an explanation. He added the following:

> P.S. To prevent any mistakes of this kind occurring in future, I tell you plainly that I will turn off the first cart of yours that appears in the water & apply for an Interdict from the Court of Session. The quantity of stones carried off on the present occasion is I understand about 200 cart loads, which I shall recommend to the 2 proprietors & the manufacturers for protection of the Caul to replace from wherever they can find them, at the Trustees' expense, & which I have no doubt they will do.[59]

Here is Craig in the role of defender of his principals' properties and, he might argue, the wider interests of local people. When the fencing of the road proved inadequate, and cows were killed due to gaps, he again made his feelings known to Spiers, demanding 'for the sake of the public' that appropriate fencing be put up.[60]

Craig never let up his vigilance against potential floods, nor did landowners such as William Clark of Longhaugh who complained in 1835 that tenants were

---

[54] Ibid.

[55] SBA/1303/6/131, Craig/Andrew Spiers, road surveyor, Jedburgh, 22 Jan. 1831.

[56] SBA/1303/6/148, idem, 25 Feb. 1831.

[57] SBA/1303/6/170, idem, 13 Apr. 1831; ibid., Craig/T. Mitchell, surveyor, Selkirk.

[58] SBA/1303/6/453, Craig/Andrew Cranstoun WS, 30 Jan. 1834.; SBA/1303/6/487, Craig/Mr Speirs, road surveyor, Jedburgh, 7 Jun. 1834.

[59] SBA/1303/6/488.

[60] SBA/1303/7/208, C&R/Andrew Spiers, 3 Apr. 1836.

taking stones from his side of the river 'to the danger of my embankment'.[61] He eventually let the caul to Adam Brown in 1836 for eleven years, with the consent of Gala, Torwoodlee and 'manufacturers and millers on the dam'.[62] A stipulation of the lease, however, was that 'no stones for mettling the road, or for any other purpose, are to be taken from the bed of the river within 350 yards of the causeway'.

Further north, Fairholme's tenant in Stow, James Hogg, was reminded by Craig of the urgent necessity

> of employing all your men and horses to embank the water at the rear below your house, otherwise you will assuredly lose the road betwixt the rear and the dyke which now that you have so much arable land to the south would be a loss the farm would never recover.[63]

Praising the work of a nearby tenant of Innes of Stow in protecting his side of the Lugate Water, Craig reassured Hogg that if Miss Innes had contributed to that endeavour he was sure that Fairholme would bear the same proportion of Hogg's expenditure.

Craig's vigilance, unfortunately, had little permanent effect. Flooding in Galashiels continued, notably in 1839, 1846 and 1891.[64] Craig himself noted the 'great damages' done by the 'excessive' flooding in September 1839.[65] There was damage to 'the road below Wilderhaugh near the Wire Bridge' and the bridge itself, only the second suspension bridge to be completed in Britain, was destroyed.[66]

Water Rights

The flow of rivers, disturbed by new mills and other encroachments, affected the interests of opposite and downstream landowners. Thomas Bruce of Langlee complained to Tod & Romanes in 1829, having been informed by Craig about the development of two new factories which might affect the flow of the Gala Water near his property. The complaint was that Gala had acted unilaterally and Bruce wanted to know the legal basis for his doing so. After all, he noted,

> I was under the Impression that where a River is the mutual Boundary of two conterminous Heritors, such as Gala water is betwixt Mr Scott and me, that neither Heritor can appropriate to himself the use of that River or any part of it, without the consent of his opposite neighbour.[67]

---

[61] SBA/1303/7/68, Clark/George Blaikie, Muirhouse, 19 May 1835.

[62] SBA/1303/7/133, Craig/George Scott, road surveyor, Jedburgh, 31 Dec. 1835.

[63] SBA/1303/8/355, C&R/James Hogg, Nethershiels, Stow, 15 Oct. 1838.

[64] Hall, *History of Galashiels*, 93, 105, 153.

[65] SBA/1303/8/575, Craig/William Colvin, London, 23 Sep. 1839.

[66] SBA/1303/8/571, Craig/Andrew Spiers, Road surveyor, Jedburgh, 16 Sep. 1839; Hall, *History of Galashiels*, 93.

[67] NRS, Scott of Gala papers, GD477/138/4, Thomas Bruce, 2 Glenfinlas Street, Edinburgh/Tod & Romanes, Great Stuart Street, 16 May 1829.

Craig met Bruce and personally showed him where the factories were to be built. He also provided him with a sketch. The development, according to Craig, was 'further proof of the enterprise of the Galashiels clothiers': one factory was being built by Robert Gill & Son and the other by J. & H. Brown together with George Roberts junior.[68] A dam would be built within the flood dyke and the 'houses' (the factories) placed close by each other, with Gala keeping in view 'both that little of the valuable haugh might be encroached on & also that the Factories might be in the least conspicuous part of it'. Gala's nearby tenant, Anderson of Netherbarns, had agreed to the work with some allowance made to him for the use of ground which he had leased and, according to Craig, Gala 'with his usual liberality to the Clothiers, means to be moderate in his demands for the Falls & ground to be set apart on permanent leases'.

Craig was in the opposite camp when a similar concern was voiced about a mill built on the Eden Water near Gordon which was 'on too large a scale for the supply of water afforded by the Eden'.[69] Craig's client, George Fairholme, refused to accept the 'slightest encroachment or alteration' in the flow of the water. As soon as the mill began operation, Craig suggested, Fairholme and the owner of a mill downstream would have no difficulty obtaining interdict from the sheriff substitute in Greenlaw.[70] Six months later, he proposed that the parties, their agents and their witnesses, meet on the spot in the hope of agreeing the 'future regulation of the water, [and] if not then let us try the case'.[71]

RESOURCE MANAGEMENT

Agriculture

Through his regular visits to clients' properties across three counties, Craig knew the local geography and landscapes intimately. He displayed a level of farming knowledge which befitted him as a paid-up member of the Lauderdale Agricultural Society.[72] He believed fervently in the improving philosophies pioneered in the Borders by William Dawson in the second half of the eighteenth century: drainage, lime and the drill cultivation of turnips for cattle feed, had become orthodoxy.[73] So confident was Craig in his understanding of agricultural principles that he did not shirk from contradicting advice offered to Alexander Monro by David Lowe, professor of agriculture at the University of Edinburgh.[74]

Craig had become used to guiding Monro in farming matters. When he inspected his farm at Cockburn for the first time in 1825, he sent him a full report

---

[68] SBA/1303/5/394, 5 May 1829; the original letter is in NRS, GD477/138/14.
[69] SBA/1303/3/443-4, Craig/John Gibson of Gordonmill & Robert Swan, Kelso, 19 Dec. 1823.
[70] Ibid.
[71] SBA/1303/3/488, Craig/John Gibson, 9 Jun. 1824.
[72] SBA/1303/8/131, Craig/John Romanes, Lauder, 27 Feb. 1839.
[73] J. S. L. Waldie, 'William Dawson, 1734–1815' 26 (1951) *Agricultural Progress*, 94–98.
[74] SBA/1303/7/28, Craig/Dr Monro, 7 Nov. 1834.

largely praising his then tenant, George Logan. As a farmer, he thought Logan capable of making the most of the land, 'perhaps more than any farmer in Berwickshire, as far as his present system of management goes', although, needless to say, there were aspects which Craig felt needed improvement.[75] Craig had not drafted the lease (this was done by Monro's Edinburgh agent, William Patrick WS) and he considered the land 'too high rented', recommending a 15 to 20 per cent rent reduction.

In relation to Logan's method of crop rotation, Craig commented in detail:

> The best parts of the lands happen by rotation to be in white crop, in all about 300 acres, three fourths of which will be oats the rest barley & wheat, & still after going over the fields they will not average 4 bolls an acre. The arable lands are managed under the 5 shift rotation vizt. [videlicet] Oats – turnips & potatoes – oats or barley with grass seeds – Hay – & pasture which sometimes lies 2 years & even longer. Whether this is the rule laid down by the lease I do not know, but it is as good a one as I know, & which I prefer to summer fallow & wheat for any part of the farm, the whole being a light soil.[76]

On the farm were thirty-two score of Cheviot sheep. With the aid of turnips and early grass, Craig valued them at £8 per score. In his view, however, the number of cows was too few (Logan had six, with another four or five owned by the local hynds). This would not produce the required amount of dung and Craig suggested a remedy. As he noted,

> two well watered grass parks, the nearer the Onstead the better of about 20 acres each (to shift week about) which should always be in grass which would keep 18 or 20 cows, & these to be taken into the byres from 10 o'clock forenoon till 5 o'clock afternoon every day from the 1st of May till the 1st of September only, would produce more dung than is bred on the farm at present the whole year; in every instance I know of where this has been done its beneficial effects have been acknowledged . . .[77]

To compensate for the lack of fertiliser, Logan cut and burned heath to make ashes. Craig's suggestions for improving cattle husbandry were accompanied by his recommendation to build a flour mill; confident assertions about the quality of the dykes and advice to remove all the Scots fir from the plantation.

In 1829, Craig discussed with Monro his expectations of a new tenant. Referring to his favoured five crop rotation, he set out his requirements:

> The incoming tenants to leave a fifth in fallow & a 5th in new sown grass which is not to be parted after the cutting of his waygoing crop & the fallow to get one furrow before the Christmas preceding his removal. The whole years dung to be left at the Whitsunday & paid for to him at the same rate as he paid to the outgoing tenant & 16 bolls of lime per acre to be laid on the fallow break every year once over.[78]

[75]   SBA/1303/4/220, Craig/Dr Monro, 1 Aug. 1825.
[76]   SBA/1303/4/220-1; cf. NRS, Scott of Gala, GD477/463/18.
[77]   SBA/1303/4/221. The 'onstead' refers to farm outbuildings, as distinct from the farmhouse.
[78]   SBA/1303/5/344, Craig/Dr Monro, 10 Jan. 1829.

As the name suggests, a waygoing crop was grown by a tenant whose lease was coming to an end. He had the right to enter the land after the expiry of the lease (the 'ish' in Scots terminology) and take the crop, otherwise there would have been no incentive to grow anything in the last months of his tenancy. The new tenant would sow the next crop and in turn was entitled to a waygoing crop when his lease ended.

Despite admiring his farming skills, Craig encountered problems with George Logan whose debts to Monro kept growing. By the autumn of 1828, Craig told Monro outright that '[a]s a Banker I certainly would not take George's *ipse dixit* that his debt would be paid at the end of his lease, nor would any man of common sense'.[79] That was not an assessment of Logan's honesty, merely the capacity of the farm to produce enough to justify the high rent despite reductions that had already been made. Craig doubted that another tenant could do much better or, given the economic circumstances, whether one would be willing to expend more capital to achieve better results. As he candidly informed Monro, 'your writing me you must have money will not bring it a wit faster, all I have to do is to watch we get what we can'.[80]

Evidently, this did not satisfy Monro. Although his lease was intended to run until 1835, Logan was in arrears and replaced by John Wilson in 1829 after the property was advertised for let.[81] Wilson had plans for improvement and Craig assured Monro that if these were executed Cockburn 'will be a very different property at the end of the lease'.[82] Sure enough, Wilson soon extended the barn and erected cattle sheds.[83] Craig had identified the need for a flour mill and granary in 1825, noting that if it could not be arranged with the present tenant 'it should be kept in view for the next one'.[84] He got his way. Similarly, Wilson was a more effective stock breeder than Logan and his proclivities seem to have been more in step with Craig's own, a reflection of Craig's efforts to know the land and understand the views and abilities of prospective tenants before engaging them.

Craig knew, or thought he knew, what worked in agricultural lets and sought tenants with the right ideas. It was part of his job to ensure they could pay their rent. When a young man of his acquaintance missed out on a let 'for want of the needful' (i.e. an inability to pay the rent), Craig hoped to find him something smaller because he was convinced he would be a good tenant.[85] He also kept a sharp eye on land improvement and was unsparing when George Smibert fell behind in delivering cartloads of lime to Gibson of Ladhope's property: 'unless the whole is forward in ten days he [Gibson] will not begin to spread any of it but prosecute you for the value of the whole turnip crop'.[86]

---

[79] SBA/1303/5/312, idem, 25 Oct. 1828.
[80] SBA/1303/5/87, idem, 13 Jul. 1827.
[81] SBA/1303/5/337, idem, 22 Dec. 1828.
[82] SBA/1303/5/366, idem, 3 Mar. 1829.
[83] SBA/1303/5/151, idem, 7 Mar. 1831.
[84] Ibid.; SBA/1303/4/222, idem, 1 Aug. 1825.
[85] SBA/1303/4/152, Craig/Robert Bruce, bailie of Kelso, 7 Feb. 1825.
[86] SBA/1303/4/199, Craig/G. Smibert, Dryburgh, 6 Jun. 1825. Smibert regularly supplied Walker of Bowland: e.g. NLS, MS14079, fo. 52.

Lease Conditions

Craig sometimes discussed details of leases. A general condition in agricultural lets, due to its importance as fertiliser, was that the outgoing tenant had to leave accumulated cattle dung for the use of the next tenant. The lease of Plenploth, by Stow, which Craig had not himself drafted, provides an example. It set out that 'neither straw or hay or dung can be carried off the farm either during the Lease or at the ending of it, the whole belong to the Landlord who may treat with his incoming tenant for them'.[87] Reductions in rent might sometimes be made in respect of this, but not when the farm in question had not been properly farmed or fully stocked.[88]

Dung was required for turnips, a staple over the winter for sheep, but there was never a sufficient supply. As Craig informed Dr Monro, 'nine tenths of the farmers in Scotland' had the same problem.[89] William Colvin's former tenant at Mitchelston farmhouse, John Harper, had the value of dung left on the farm deducted from the rent. This was independently 'measured and valued' by a neighbouring tenant, with the measurement and value turning out to be twenty-four cubic yards at 4s 3d each.[90] That was the normal procedure and remedial steps were necessary if a tenant removed the dung, as George Haldane did when he left for his new tenancy at Whitebanklee. Before he was allowed to claim his waygoing crop, Haldane had to sign an obligation 'to bring back a sufficient quantity of dung from Whitebanklee every year in May for the turnip break' which Craig calculated to be thirty-four cart loads, the number to be checked by 'Mr Fair the printer as the carts pass'.[91]

Some conditions were less strictly enforced than others. John Scott of Galashiels, for instance, was permitted to sublet land to the baker Thomas Brown, even though his lease excluded assignation (transfer) and subletting. This was done, however, on the proviso that Scott 'continue to pay the rents & see the land properly farmed & perform all the other conditions of the Lease in the same manner as if you had not sublet'.[92] Leases often made allowance for repairs to farm buildings but, if this proved insufficient, there was always room for negotiation. James Jeffrey, tenant at William Colvin's farm at Mitchelston, was allowed a set sum 'to put my whole onstead & dwellinghouse in "complete & substantial repair"' and more to repair his fences, but he argued that 'it is out of the power of any man living to put the whole in the state required by Lease for the sum'.[93]

---

[87] SBA/1303/3/219, Craig/Alexander Wilson, 1 Aug. 1823.

[88] E.g. SBA/1303/6/48, Craig/James Primrose, Edinburgh, 27 Apr. 1830.

[89] SBA/1303/6/23, Craig/Dr Monro, 23 Feb. 1827.

[90] SBA/1303/8/181, Craig/D. Gardner, writer, Dalkeith, 10 Mar. 1838; SBA/1303/8/105, Craig/John Harper, tenant, near Penicuik, 11 Dec. 1837.

[91] Ibid., Craig/George Haldane, Whitebanklee, 6 Sep. 1827. A cart load was not the most precise measurement. See R. A. Dodgshon, 'Land improvement in Scottish farming: marl and lime in Roxburghshire and Berwickshire in the eighteenth century' 26 (1978) *British Agricultural History Society*, 4.

[92] SBA/1303/3/257, Craig/John Scott, Galashiels, 9 Oct. 1823.

[93] SBA/1303/5/262, Copy letter Mr Jeffrey/Mr Craig, 6 Jun. 1828; ibid., Craig/William Colvin, 10 Jun. 1828.

Craig sent Jeffrey's letter on to Colvin adding the comment 'you will know if Mr Jeffrey is right'.

In most respects strict adherence to leases was demanded, the reason being the landlord's right of hypothec which was a tacit right in security in crops and farm equipment. This gave the landlord an important preferential right if the tenant built up rent arrears and other debts. As Craig explained to Dr Monro, 'in estimating a *Farmers* credit, we must always take into account the Landlords *right of hypothec* to the exclusion of all other creditors'.[94]

In the case of Gala's tenant, John Dods, for example, Craig was able to order a petition for sequestration and to instruct the Melrose writer Robert Thomson to enter the property and

> inventory the growing wheat on the land, potatoes & turnips . . . horses, cows stocks & all principal implements of husbandry at the offices, & any articles within the Mills & bring the whole to sale as soon as possible.[95]

The question of whether to persevere with a struggling tenant, or remove him, depended on several factors, including the current value of the land and the likelihood of getting a higher rent or a better tenant. Craig was capable of delicacy in taking legal steps to recover rent arrears when necessary. He asked Grieve, the new tenant at Plenploth, to agree in a letter to pay to the landlord the value of the waygoing crop of the failed former tenant, David Bell. This avoided the use of the landlord's 'unquestionable' right of hypothec, and Craig asked Grieve not to mention the letter to Bell 'as I do not wish David's feelings to be hurt'.[96]

A different circumstance arose when Rev. Nathaniel Paterson received a letter from Charles Riddell, the duke of Buccleuch's chamberlain of Eskdale and Liddesdale, about his father-in-law, Mr Laidlaw, the duke's tenant. Paterson came to Craig 'as a friend & not as a man of business' to assist in the matter.[97] Laidlaw wanted to obtain security for his rent arrears, sell his sheep at Whitsunday (May), his corn at Lammas (August) and then sublet his farm without the duke resorting to his hypothec. This was declined. That left no option but for Laidlaw to sell off his stock and crop and quit the premises at Whitsunday.[98]

Farming could be brutal and when it came to removing tenants Craig was himself no shrinking violet. He scorned the complaint of James Wight's subtenants at Bankhouse about not being warned of their removal by the landlord, William Tait of Pirn. He told Wight that 'Mr Tait treats with you alone for the giving up of the lease & has nothing to do with any of your lodgers or cottars. They have to do with

---

[94] SBA/1303/5/315, Craig/Dr Monro, 25 Oct. 1828. The emphasis is Craig's.
[95] SBA/1303/5/34, Craig/R. G. Thomson, writer, 12 Mar. 1827. The creditor in the sequestration was John Scott of Galashiels, but Craig arranged to have the landlord's hypothec assigned to him via a deed prepared by Robert Haldane: SBA/1303/5/40, Craig/Robert Haldane, 22. Mar. 1827.
[96] SBA/1303/7/97, Craig/Mr Grieve, Plenploth, 4 Sep. 1835.
[97] SBA/1303/6/140, Craig/Charles Riddell, Branxholm, Hawick, 7 Feb. 1831.
[98] SBA/1303/6/145, idem, 19 Feb. 1821.

you.'[99] Wight himself was only permitted to take the current growing crop on conditions imposed by Tait. These included that he agreed to pay up the rent arrears 'out of the first & readiest of the sales of stock & crop from the farm'; that the houses and fences were in a 'proper tenantable condition of repair' at his expense and that he and his lodgers and dependents immediately removed without process of law.[100] The following year, Craig hired tradesmen to repair 31 broken panes of glass before the entry of a new tenant. The breakages were 'destroying the house' and Wight was warned that he would be 'found liable in damages'.[101]

Animal Husbandry

A copy of a sketch of Newhall farm, contained in Craig's letter book, relates to a letter to Robert Darling in Kelso in 1829. Discussing the farm, Craig took the view that unless the marshy parts of the fields could be drained it would be wiser to turn them permanently to grass.

> The present *dry* arable parts do not amount to more than 42 acres which is quite little for a pair of horses. The Hill in like manner only keeps 11 score of sheep which is not half employment for a Herd & by throwing the whole farm into *pasture* it would keep 24 or 25 acres which at 6/1 perhaps would be £144 of rent, which is more than I can make it by £2 valuing the 42 acres of arable at 20/ & the swampy parts & old pasture at 12/.[102]

Craig did not dismiss the possibility of drainage but favoured stock farming. He also preferred the sitting tenant, Mr Elder, who was 'employed as a wool buyer for an English house' and would produce as much rent as any other man Darling could 'find and shape'. Shaping tenants was clearly something Craig saw as part of his own role as a land agent.

Craig had a good knowledge of horses and farmed animals, but, as importantly, he could recommend experienced breeders to his clients. In 1821, for example, he advised George Fairholme that, when it came to cows, he could

> employ no such hand as little Watherstone at Earlston – he passed this way with a dozen of Ayrshires for Greenlaw fair the other day – I was not at home or I would have been apt for to buy two as I heard they were all young and handsome.[103]

Craig had approved of John Wilson's initial plans, when he took over Cockburn, to improve its capacity for livestock. Two years later, he reported that Wilson had been draining the land and using lime and bone dust for fertiliser to improve pasture. He was also allowing sheep to eat turnips on the ground and

> keeping fewer of the short-horn cattle than his predecessor, as being rather fine for the situation; he has been successful for the 2 seasons in a cross breed from the Angus Cow

---

[99] SBA/1303/3, Craig/James Wight, Bankhouse, 25 Jun. 1822.

[100] SBA/1303/3/3-4, W[illiam] T[ait]/James Wight, 25 Jun. 1822.

[101] SBA/1303/3/147, Craig/James Wight, 2 Mar. 1823.

[102] SBA/1303/6/247, Craig/Robert Darling, Kelso, 14 Jun. 1829.

[103] SBA/1303/2/46, Craig/George Fairholme, 23 May 1821.

& the Tees Water Bull of which he began with a score – the calves go with their mothers in the new sheds till Whitsunday at turnip of which he has already 11 calved; the mothers are annually fed off at 3½ years old & arrive at about fifty-five stones – they are a beautiful breed & I have no doubt in a few years will be generally reared in all the higher districts of the Country.[104]

Wilson was by no means the only stockbreeder in the area. When Charles Robson and his brothers were sequestrated in 1827, Craig lamented that he should be brought low by an excess of zeal 'in agricultural pursuits, particularly in stock'.[105] As he was 'confessedly the best breeder in the south of Scotland', Craig even suggested that the county, given 'his improvements in that line', should make good any deficiencies in the repayment of his debts.

Poor weather always caused concern for livestock. In 1838, after 'such a storm as few remember the like of' and unable to speak to farmers, Craig feared that even 'the most skilful managers' could not have saved all their sheep.[106] So harsh was the weather that Monro's tenant, Robert Purves, made the 'quite unusual' request to be permitted to fell trees from the Cockburn plantation to use their branches to feed his sheep. Craig refused, hoping that Purves had not been driven to it by having sold any of his hay.

> In this quarter I have had no such demand, but at once the farmers remove their stock to the Lothians where abundance of provender is to be had, and take it for better or worse, as a casualty[107] that will happen to them only once or twice in their lives, and that every year is not to be like the winter of 1837/8.[108]

Sheep, unsurprisingly, often appear in the correspondence, both as asset and nuisance. A tenant was warned that 'the number of sheep in Ladhope park without turnips is making it like redland' and Mr Gibson, the landlord, wanted them 'away immediately'.[109] Less common is discussion of rabbits, but Craig did lease out rabbit warrens at Monro's farm at Cockburn. He proved to be a shrewd negotiator. An offer from Peter Black in Dunbar for a seven-year lease 'of the rabbits of Cockburn', with the option of giving up after one year if the venture failed to pay, was rejected by Craig because the risk was all on Monro's side.[110] As he did not offer more if it did pay, Black would simply have to take his chance on the full lease like any other tenant.

Despite his connections to farming, there is apparently only one reference in the correspondence to the 'Union Agricultural Society', the forerunner of

---

[104] SBA/1303/6/151, Craig/Dr Monro, 119 George Street, Edinburgh, 7 Mar. 1831. Teeswater cattle were a short-horned variety.

[105] SBA/1303/6/62, Craig/LBC, 7 May 1827.

[106] SBA/1303/3/121, Craig/LBC, 8 Feb. 1822; SBA/1303/3/122, idem, 10 Feb. 1822.

[107] 'Casualty' in the sense of casual or chance occurrence.

[108] SBA/1303/8/165, Craig/Robert Purves, Oatliecleugh, Duns, 24 Feb. 1838.

[109] SBA/1303/6/266, Craig/Mr Roxburgh, Ladhope, 20 Feb. 1832. 'Redland' was land that had been ploughed or had its crop removed.

[110] SBA/1303/5/319, Craig/James Black, shoemaker, Dunbar, 8 Nov. 1828.

the Border Union Agricultural Society which still exists today.[111] This arose in a letter to the writer, John Smith, in Kelso who was asked to put William Walker of Bowland in touch with the secretary, Mr Currie, because he wished to subscribe to it.[112]

Dykes

Livestock had to be contained and this was partly done by the stone dyke walls which remain a feature of the Borders landscape. Their construction and maintenance was a regular discussion topic. Dykes and fences were of two kinds: those which an owner placed on his own property to subdivide it and those which were placed on the boundary between two properties (known as 'march dykes'). The latter were regulated by 1661 legislation which required heritors, at either side of the boundary, to share the expense of maintenance equally even if the dyke only benefited one of them.[113]

In a properly drafted lease, the obligation to renew march dykes lay with the tenant, not the landowner. Tenants normally entered agricultural property that was in 'tenantable repair': in other words, it was in such a state that it would, with ordinary care, last until the ish.[114] At that point, properties were often given a new roof (straw or even heather sometimes being used), and new 'cupples' (sloping rafters) or lintels might be provided.[115] In the case of fences and dykes, however, it was recognised that they may require to be renewed earlier and the tenant's obligation was to ensure that the property at the ish remained in the same tenantable state as it had been received. A landowner was not entitled, during the currency of a lease, to create any new subdividing fences. However, any owner could compel his neighbour to erect a march dyke at their mutual expense. Moreover, tenants in their leases could be made liable to maintain dykes of either kind, although in the case of a march dyke the expense was shared with the neighbour.

Craig recorded detailed arrangements in 1827 and 1837 relative to march dykes bordering land owned by Torwoodlee and Pringle of Whytbank. In the first case, Whytbank's tenant George Haldane called on him to repair the march dyke between Whitebanklee and Crosslee (possessed by James Brydon, Torwoodlee's tenant). Whytbank duly asked Torwoodlee to meet half the expense. Craig noted that the matter was a small one but 'still troublesome & quite necessary'.[116] He reminded Brydon that it was he, as Torwoodlee's tenant, who was liable for the

---

[111] The Border Union Agricultural Society's records date back to 1813: SBA, D/73.

[112] SBA/1303/8/87, Rutherford/John Smith, 21 Nov. 1837. William Stuart Walker was the son and heir of General Alexander Walker of Bowland (an estate purchased in 1809).

[113] RPS, 1661/3/148; ibid., 1669/10/54; G. C. H. Paton, ed., *Baron David Hume's Lectures, 1786–1822* (6 vols, Edinburgh, Stair Society, 1939–1958), III, 413.

[114] J. Rankine, *A Treatise on the Law of Leases* (Edinburgh, 1916), 222.

[115] E.g. SBA/1303/8/566, Craig/W. S. Walker of Bowland, 7 Sep. 1839.

[116] SBA/1303/5/161, Craig/James Brydon, 8 Dec. 1827.

cost and urged him to liaise with Haldane quickly in order to prevent any 'law expenses' that might be created in case of delay.

A decade later, another issue arose between the same parties, this time with the march dyke that ran along a turnpike road past Whytbank farm. Whytbank demanded that Torwoodlee renew the dyke wall. According to a report commissioned from James Bell, an experienced dyker, the whole wall, extending to 364 roods, required to be renewed and raised in height.[117] His cost estimate was just over £43. Again, it was the respective tenants on both sides who were liable. Craig, however, thinking it 'hard' that their tenant should be called on to meet this expense when he only had nineteenth months left on his lease, intended to propose to Torwoodlee that Brydon only pay a share of the expense.

Like any good factor, Craig did not rely on a single estimate and he also understood the rudiments of building practice. In advising tenants on the building of dykes, he insisted that they advertise for estimates in the press. In 1836, we find him advising James Hogg at Watherston, in Stow, on the construction of an appropriate march dyke as follows:

> See that the dyke is of sufficient breadth at the bottom, in such a high Country, tapering it to the top in a proper degree, and that a Bondstone is laid close along the centre the whole way.[118]

Under an Act of 1669, when two contiguous estates were to be separated by a dyke, and the marches were 'crooked or unequal' or unable to bear a dyke, then it was lawful for one of the proprietors to invite the sheriff to visit the marches and apportion the relevant areas of ground necessary to build the dyke with the least prejudice to either party.[119] When George Fairholme's tenant wanted to build a dyke between his farm and that of neighbouring Fawside, Craig, keen to avoid the expense of an application to the sheriff, suggested inviting a local farmer 'to point out the stance of the dyke'.[120] This offer was ignored. Indeed, so anxious was the tenant to have the dyke built that 'a summons of marching' was served on the neighbouring proprietors.[121] This process led to expenses for Craig, including the production of a plan and a report, which he was still trying to recover three years later.[122]

Landowners often quibbled over details. Craig records a debate between Torwoodlee and Gibson of Ladhope in which the former favoured 'a feal cape',

---

[117] SBA/1303/8/62, Craig/James Brydon, Woodlaw, 10 Oct. 1837. A rood was a Scots measurement of area. One Scots acre was four roods.

[118] SBA/1303/4/295, Craig/James Hogg, 18 Nov. 1836. A bondstone, also known as a perpend stone, extends through the width of the wall from outer to the inner wall. This 'bonds' the two layers of the wall together.

[119] RPS, 1669/10/54.

[120] SBA/1303/7/237, Craig/Robert Darling, writer, Kelso, 12 Jul. 1836.

[121] SBA/1303/7/278, idem, 25 Oct. 1836. Also SBA/1303/7/368, idem, 20 Feb. 1837; fo. 413, 7 Apr. 1837.

[122] SBA/1303/8/463, Craig/Robert Darling, 26 Mar. 1839.

in other words a stone dyke topped with turf, whereas the latter wanted the dyke capped with stone.[123] The dimensions, at least, were agreed: '18 inches thick at 4 feet, 15 inches thick at top or other 6 inches; 6 inches thick of feal or stone cope'. The cost, whether feal or stone, was apparently the same.

A more acquiescent attitude is found in correspondence between Gala and Torwoodle. This related to Torwoodlee's proposal to build a drainage ditch near a mutual boundary on land Gala and Craig had inspected the year before. Noting that a fence would be to the advantage of tenants on both sides, Gala was happy to take 'any line of fence or exchanging so that you may have full benefit of the Drain you propose', suggesting an excamb (exchange) of a few acres.[124] Craig, in sending on Gala's letter, added his agreement to the idea of a march dyke being built along a particular line (running 'along the upper or south side the whole way from Kilknowe park to Sanderson's Stockyard') and, to create the best line, suggested that Torwoodlee part with an equivalent amount of land from Caddonlee to compensate.[125]

There was usually scope for flexibility in making such arrangements. Another example of this occurred when Fairholme's tenant in Greenknowe, George Bruce, demanded that a march dyke be built between the land he farmed and that belonging to William Ford at Riccarton Gate. Ford was given a choice. He would either pay half the expense, or 'as the practice has all along been in Gordon if Mr Fairholme gives the stance of the dyke, the feuar is [at] the whole expence'.[126] In other words, if the necessary land upon which the dyke was to be built was transferred to the neighbour, the neighbour bore the cost of building the dyke.

Plantations

Tree husbandry was another important aspect of country life and Craig frequently refers to tree plantations and 'wood roups' (the sale of timber at auctions). He even wrote, with a hint of disapproval, to George Wood, a Lauder wright, remarking upon his absence from a wood roup at Torwoodlee which all the other neighbourhood wrights had attended.[127]

Many references to plantations relate either to their insurance or inspection. When visiting Gordon in 1826, he noted that at least half the muir had either not been planted or, if planting had taken place, that the trees were dead. The locals blamed late planting and lack of subsequent rain, with Craig remarking that this would be a difficult thing for the tenant to remedy '& worse for the proprietor as a year or two lost is so provoking & cannot be made up'.[128] In the same year,

[123] SBA/1303/5/329, Craig/Thomas Bruce, 28 Nov. 1828.
[124] SBA/1303/7/25, Copy letter, Scott of Gala/Pringle of Torwoodlee, 28 Oct. 1834. The letter was copied only because a meeting was impossible due to Gala's horse not being 'fit for his work'.
[125] Cf. SBA/1303/7/557, Craig/W. S. Walker of Bowland, 22 Aug. 1839.
[126] SBA/1303/4/509, Craig/William Ford, 16 Dec. 1826.
[127] SBA/1303/8/399, Craig/George Wood, Lauder, 31 Dec. 1838.
[128] SBA/1303/4/408, Craig/G. Shillinglaw & Son, Redpath, 23 Jun. 1826.

concerned about the Galahill plantation, he wrote to Donald McLaren, grieve (estate manager) at Argaty near Doune, about a man there he had heard of 'who roots out Rabbits effectually for nothing but the Rabbits he kills', asking him to be sent to deal with one or two hundred rabbits threatening the young trees.[129]

On a later visit to his own plantation at Gordon, Craig observed from a tower that the larch trees were too thick. To maximise his profit, he arranged orders for 310 sheep flakes (wooden racks for carrying fodder in winter) and wrote to the local forester, Thomas Robertson, instructing him to cut trees the following spring and to bargain locally to have such racks made.[130] The forester in Galashiels, he informed him, obtained 2s 3d per flake and, if there was any doubt 'as to the making of them' Craig offered to come down to assist personally. In return, he expected Robertson to send him sale proceeds. It is clear from the same correspondence that Craig himself also arranged for the sale of trees and bark.

Income from the sale of timber was important to some of Craig's clients. In August 1833 Alexander Monro's tenant at Cockburn, John Wilson jr, marked out 220 Scots fir and larch trees and he intended to return a month later to mark out 'as many more as form a sale to the amount of £50', an order already having been received.[131] He added that every year, at Martinmas, they estimated that they might be able to sell £20 worth of timber. The effort to develop the woodland, however, seems to have been overdone. In 1837 Craig referred to the young trees as being 'too thick'.[132]

Purchasers used wood for various purposes including leather-making. Paterson the tanner, for example, bought it by the ton and expressed interest in Walker of Bowland's trees. Craig presumed this was because the wood was young and Paterson was willing to pay the latest market price – 'oak perhaps 135/ per ton and larch 75/ or 80/', he estimated.[133] In 1835 he wrote to the Dalkeith wood merchants, Thomson & Philip, that as there was 'a good number of old Oak trees to mark this season both at Gala & Torwoodlee', rather than roup them, it made sense for the merchants to come and see them '& try to make a bargain for the whole, either you cutting & peeling or the proprietors'.[134] George Tillie would be on hand at Torwoodlee to show them the trees and, if Craig was absent, Robert Rankine would do it in Galashiels. In August 1833 he personally offered to conduct Mr Caldwell, a mill-owner from Tushie Bridge, to see the birch trees on Gala's estate and at Greenknowe and was prepared to conclude a bargain before the Martinmas public sales.[135]

Various species of tree are referred to in the correspondence. Craig complained when Walter Ormiston, who ran a nursery in Melrose, sent more shrubs and trees

[129] SBA/1303/4/494, Craig/Donald McLaren, grieve, Argaty, Doune, 21 Nov. 1826.
[130] SBA/1303/7/100, Craig/Thomas Robertson, forester, Gordon, 12 Sep. 1835.
[131] SBA/1303/6/409, Craig/Dr Monro, Edinburgh, 19 Aug. 1833.
[132] SBA/1303/8/60, Craig/John Wilson, Cockburn, by Duns, 10 Oct. 1837.
[133] SBA/1303/8/223, Craig/W. S. Walker of Bowland, 16 Apr. 1838.
[134] SBA/1303/7/51, Craig/Thomson & Philip, wood merchant, Dalkeith, 13 Mar. 1835.
[135] SBA/1303/6/407, Craig/Mr Caldwell, Holy Power Mills, Tushie Bridge, 8 Aug. 1833.

to Gala than he had ordered. Gala was happy to keep what he ordered and the remainder of the shrubs were 'sheughed in' (furrowed) until Ormiston could collect them. He kept 'all the American plants' and there is reference to 200 beech, 200 spruce, 60 silver firs and 3,000 thorns (500 of which were returned).[136] On behalf of Gibson of Ladhope, Craig ordered seventeen acres of larch to be planted above Ladhope House by another nurseryman, William Lamb of Selkirk.[137] More unusually, in 1838 Mr Scott of Mossilee bought fifty black Italian poplars.[138]

Mining

Evidence of mining activity in Craig's correspondence is limited, however there was some attempt to revive copper mining at Cockburn. Craig had visited the 'copper working a little up the Whittader [Whiteadder] from Edenford on the East side of the water' in 1826, but nobody was there.[139] Having been told that samples had been sent to England, he collected a piece of rock and sent it to Monro, describing the workings he had encountered.

Neighbouring owners, Molle and Turnbull, had been approached for the right to work their lands.[140] Monro was also approached, by Thomson & Company, but Craig rejected their proposed lease as being 'too general'.[141] He set out twelve conditions he thought should be added. This included an exclusion on subletting; no erection of a steam engine without Monro's approval of the site; indemnity against surface damage; any new roads to require written approval and be at the company's expense; at least six men to be employed in mining and the method of determining Monro's one-eighth share to be established and the money remitted bi-annually. Craig warned, in respect of those behind company, that Mr Gandy of Kendal, 'a most respectable man & acquainted with most of the characters of the North of England, & who is at my hand at this moment, never heard of one of them'.

The following year Craig was asked to review a lease that Monro's neighbour, Turnbull, had entered into. He was also sent a copy of a pro-forma lease drafted, for an English lead mining company, on which he commented 'whatever it might be in its own country, I think in ours the most absurd thing I ever read'.[142] Turnbull's lease (with the Newcastle Mining Company) was better but unsatisfactory. Craig thought it required to be more explicit:

> In pointing out the manner of ascertaining, & also of paying the 1/8th part. *Where* is it ascertained & how is it paid? Is it in kind or do they remit you by a Banker's Draft from

---

[136] SBA/1303/3/133, Craig/Walter Ormiston, Melrose, 7 Mar. 1823.
[137] SBA/1303/8/163, Craig/Lamb, 23 Feb. 1838.
[138] SBA/1303/8/224, Craig/Messrs Lamb, Selkirk, 18 Apr. 1838.
[139] SBA/1303/4/444, Craig/Dr Monro, 1 Sep. 1826.
[140] William Molle of Mains WS; Turnbull is possibly John Turnbull of Abbey St Bathans, or his son, George (d. 1855), who was also a WS.
[141] SBA/1303/4/456-7, Craig/Dr Monro, 15 Sep. 1826.
[142] SBA/1303/5/87, idem, 13 Jul. 1827; SBA/1303/5/102, idem, 6 Aug. 1827.

the nearest place of smelting – & who determines your just proportion? Is it themselves or a third party – In other respects the Lease appears feasible enough.

It is unclear if any contract was agreed. In any case, the revival of copper mining in the area was short lived.[143]

CONCLUSION

Change was a constant theme of life in the Borders of the period and the environment was anything but static. New development, new farming methods, new divisions and enclosures were appearing regularly. In 1826 Elliot Anderson even referred to a 'commission of survey' which sat to examine 'the practicability of bringing Tweed into Gala by the way of Clovenfords & down by Torwoodlee'.[144] The scheme reflects high ambitions, but turned out to be impossible.

Craig made great efforts to know the land and the people. A visit to Cockburn, for instance, was more than a chance to speak to one tenant: it involved an inspection of land, buildings and livestock and getting to know local people. He was also alive to new prospects for his clients and his acquaintances. He wrote the following to George Logan, suggesting an opportunity for a mutual acquaintance:

> Col. Thornhill of the 7th Huzars [Hussars], at present quarters in Jocks Lodge barracks, who was inspecting the Selkirkshire Yeomanry in this Parish lately, stated after the Mess that he had thoughts of retiring from the army, and commencing farmer but whether in England or Scotland he did not say, he appears a very gentlemanly person, and I have heard since of good fortune. It is known that he has advertised for an Overseer; and I think Mr Ord should lose no time in waiting upon him, & hearing the Colonels views, I understand it will be a good situation in point of emolument to a person thoroughly qualified.[145]

Ord was Logan's brother-in-law with whom, that autumn, Craig had inspected the cornfields at Cockburn.[146] Again, this points to Craig's usefulness to those who knew him.

A comparison of Wood's town plan of 1824 and the 1858 Ordnance Survey plan demonstrates how much the caul on the Gala Water at Buckholmside had been extended. Craig was assiduous and relentless in its development and protection. When it came to other infrastructure projects, such as plans for a new Edinburgh–Newcastle road in 1829, he similarly sought to protect local interests. On that occasion, since Edinburgh would benefit substantially, he told Robert Shortreed, sheriff substitute in Jedburgh, that the 'writers & merchants' there should take a lead and offer £10,000 for the project with Newcastle putting in

---

[143] See https://canmore.org.uk/site/71550/elba (accessed 3 Mar. 2022).
[144] SBA/1303/4/417, Anderson/George Mercer, Edinburgh, 14 Jul. 1826.
[145] SBA/1303/4/480-1, Craig/George Logan, Cockburn, 4 Nov. 1826.
[146] SBA/1303/4/444, Craig/Dr Monro, 1 Sep. 1826.

£5,000.[147] Relying on the local statute labour force – which was derived from the annual period of compulsory labour required of local tenants and cottars under an Act of 1669 – would 'never do & would be a very unpopular measure'.

Craig influenced those who worked the land through his legal knowledge of leases; his understanding of building methods and in other ways. His ideas on farming, dyking, drainage and pasture were formed over many years of interaction with farmers and shepherds across the Borders and reflect the wisdom of those he had known. This influence had practical consequences in shaping the local environment. While lawyers are recognised as having the potential to affect their community, Craig's correspondence show the less obvious ways in which their work can affect the landscape and our built heritage.

[147] SBA/1303/5/354, Craig/Robert Shortreed, 28 Jan. 1829.

Chapter 5

Scottish Provincial Bank Agent

I am grievously affronted at the fright and jealousy you have expressed to the only man I do business with, which must do me more harm in all my future transactions than I can name.[1]

James Hogg

Thus the poet James Hogg, the Ettrick Shepherd, complained to publisher William Blackwood about a dispute into which he had drawn Hogg's banker, George Craig. The affair, over what Craig referred to with exasperation as the 'mighty matter' of a £50 debt owed to Hogg, led to handwringing on all sides.[2] At this juncture Craig was highly experienced in banking after succeeding his father as agent for the Leith Bank. Hogg described him perceptively as 'a most honourable and disinterested man', although 'noted for a sort of stubborn perverseness when in the least crossed'.

The years after the Napoleonic Wars saw declining prices for agricultural produce and there was an economic depression from 1819–1822.[3] As a result, bank failures in the 1820s were common.[4] The Leith Banking Company was not one of Scotland's major banks and it faced growing competition, particularly as larger competitors, such as the Bank of Scotland and the British Linen Company Bank, developed their branch networks. The financial crash of 1825, which so badly affected Sir Walter Scott (whose main bankers were Sir William Forbes and Company and the Bank of Scotland), largely resulted from speculative investment but it also had implications for Craig and his clients.

Many of Craig's letters relate to banking: in fact, there are more letters to bankers than any other category of correspondent. For the first six months of 1827, for example, 21.7 per cent of all his correspondence was addressed to bankers. Nearly two-thirds of these letters went to the Leith Bank, but that should not disguise the variety of bankers across the country with whom he corresponded. Many of these letters are short, cast in the efficient, laconic language of banking professionals speaking of bills of exchange received, remittances sent, and protests for non-payment made. Craig's office spent much time chasing debtors, employing

---

[1] Hughes, ed., *Collected Letters of James Hogg*, II, 104, Hogg/William Blackwood, 19 Aug. 1821.
[2] Craig's letters shed some light, but the underlying story is here: P. Garside, 'James Hogg's Fifty Pounds' 1 (1990) *Studies in Hogg and his World*, 128–32; also ibid., 'Three Perils in Publishing' 2 (1991) *SHW*, 45–63.
[3] C. W. Munn, *The Scottish Provincial Banking Companies 1747–1864* (Edinburgh, 1981), 72.
[4] A. Cameron, *Bank of Scotland 1695–1995* (Edinburgh, 1995), 109.

diligence (legal procedures to elicit the payment of debts) and attempting to avoid the need for formal enforcement by cajoling payment through encouragement or threats.

Craig was a pragmatic creditor. If there was a prospect of payment, he normally forbore formalities. An example is a postscript in a letter to his Edinburgh agents in 1823:

> P.S. A letter from Hunter, Biggar promises to pay a part of bill of £16 due 21st & the rest if allowed a little time, which I think it will be better to grant as he seems inclined to pay – you will therefore please to delay using diligence till we see how he comes forward.[5]

This concerned a bill (discussed further below) and Craig asked the debtor in question, William Hunter from Biggar in Lanarkshire, for an immediate payment of £5 warning that if he failed to comply he would instruct his Edinburgh agents to allow legal measures to recover payment to take their course.[6] Later that same year, recognising that 'every kind of farm produce is still selling very ill', he showed equal understanding to James Brydon in Woodlaw, advising him to 'send what you can at present' in payment of an overdue bill.[7]

Ultimately, debts had to be enforced. While this might be finessed and delayed in individual cases, it had to be done dispassionately. As Craig wrote to William Turnbull in Peebles – unusually putting into writing the Borders dialect of Southern Scots which he used in everyday speech – banks had to deal 'alike wi' ane alike wi' a'' (the same with one as with all) in how they treated the recovery of debt.[8] As we shall see, he did not always live up to this sentiment.

BANKERS

Many local lawyers in Scotland diversified into bank agency in the nineteenth century.[9] Craig's profile was perfect for the role. Success depended on identifying opportunities for lending and understanding local people and their circumstances well enough to be a good judge of their potential as savers and borrowers. It needed someone with a good local reputation, entrepreneurial spirit and a willingness to take calculated risks.

Banks had local agents in different towns across the Borders, although only Craig was operating in Galashiels in the middle of the 1820s.[10] Indeed, this allowed him to serve areas, such as Selkirk, Earlston and Lauder, which had no banks. In Kelso, James Darling was agent for the Bank of Scotland (followed by his son, Peter) and John Waldie agent for the Commercial Banking Company

---

[5] SBA/1303/3/128, Craig/Tait & Bruce WS, 19 Feb. 1823.
[6] Ibid., Craig/Hunter, 19 Feb. 1823.
[7] SBA/1303/3/263, Craig/Brydon, 23 Oct. 1823.
[8] SBA/1303/5/91, Craig/William Turnbull, 19 Jul. 1827.
[9] Finlay, *ARNP 1800–1899*, I, pp. xii–xiii.
[10] *Pigot's Commercial Directory 1825–6*, 657.

of Scotland.[11] The firm of Dickson & Davidson acted in Hawick for the British Linen Company Bank and William Fair (later Fair & Shortreed) did so for the same bank in Jedburgh.

Craig also dealt with bankers more widely, from Newcastle, Carlisle and Berwick, to Paisley, Perth and beyond. He wrote to the British Linen Company's agent in Elgin, for example, to obtain payment of a bill that had been indorsed by two parties, one in Orkney and the other in Elgin (indorsement and delivery of the bill making them both liable for payment).[12] Craig was as censorious in his banking correspondence as he was in other aspects of business. He complained in one case to his fellow writer and banker, David Spence in Melrose, that by lending to allow a borrower to pay off existing debt Spence was engaging in 'a bad practice and one we never encourage'.[13] Craig's attitude to Spence was condescending, almost that of master to pupil, despite Spence having been successful as a bank agent from about 1810.[14] On another occasion, he mused that a draft on a cash account sent to him by Spence would not be accepted by the banker on whom it was drawn, because 'it is quite unusual for Bankers to do so'.[15] His conjecture proved correct.[16]

Craig kept apprised of developments in the banking world, particularly the entry of new banks and the demise of old ones. For example, in 1823 he wrote to the Commercial Bank of Scotland branch agent in Kilmarnock with a bill payable at the Kilmarnock Bank, adding that he 'did not know that there had been a Kilmarnock Bank for some years past' and asking him to mention this, presumably to the payee.[17] The Kilmarnock Bank, founded in 1802, had, indeed, been restructured in 1819 but had sold out in 1821 to Hunters & Company, an Ayr bank.[18] This kind of detail mattered to Craig, particularly when dealing, as here, with an agricultural bank which issued its own notes.

THE GALASHIELS SAVINGS BANK

'I approve of Savings Banks much' Craig told Dr Monro in 1838.[19] This is unsurprising given that he was the treasurer of the Galashiels Savings Bank which was established in 1815 at the height of the savings bank movement.[20] According to

---

[11] Darling (b. 1801) was the son of James Darling and Margaret Stormonth. Waldie (b. 1788), the son of Charles Waldie and Christian Dawson, was nephew of William Smith, writer in Kelso.

[12] SBA/1303/2/145, Craig/A. Brander, British Linen Co., Elgin, 22 Oct. 1821.

[13] SBA/1303/2/43, Craig/David Spence, Melrose, 18 May 1821. On Spence's background, see Catherine Magarey, *Unbridling the Tongues of Women: A Biography of Catherine Helen Spence* (Adelaide, 2010), x–xi.

[14] Spence was a freemason and sometime master of Melrose Ancient Lodge, but Craig's affiliation is unknown: *The Courier* (Hobart, Tas.), 3 Apr. 1845, p. 4. He was successful as agent for Borthwick, Gilchrist & Co.: Spence, *Tenacious of the Past*, ed. King & Tulloch, 37, 41.

[15] SBA/1303/2/162, idem, 24 Nov. 1821.

[16] SBA/1303/2/168, idem, 3 Dec. 1821.

[17] SBA/1303/3/127, Craig/J. Paterson, Commercial Bank of Scotland, Kilmarnock, 18 Feb. 1823.

[18] Munn, *Scottish Provincial Banking Companies*, 73.

[19] SBA/1303/8/259, Craig/Alexander Monro, 4 Jun. 1838.

[20] The first Savings Bank in Scotland was established at Ruthwell in Dumfriesshire in 1810: Munn, *Scottish Provincial Banking Companies*, 146.

a handbill Craig produced in 1839, the bank had been 'found to be of the greatest use to the Labouring Classes' (Figure 5.1). As the name suggests, a savings bank held savings accounts only and, unlike the Galashiels Friendly Society, it did not lend money. The deposits were modest, reflecting the intended market. The bank, situated at Craig & Rutherford's office, was open 10am until 4pm every lawful business day. Each depositor had a passbook and the firm's accounts record an entry in August 1839 for £18 paid to Thomas Brown 'for making pass books for lodging money'.[21] Forty copies of the 1839 handbill were printed and twenty-nine

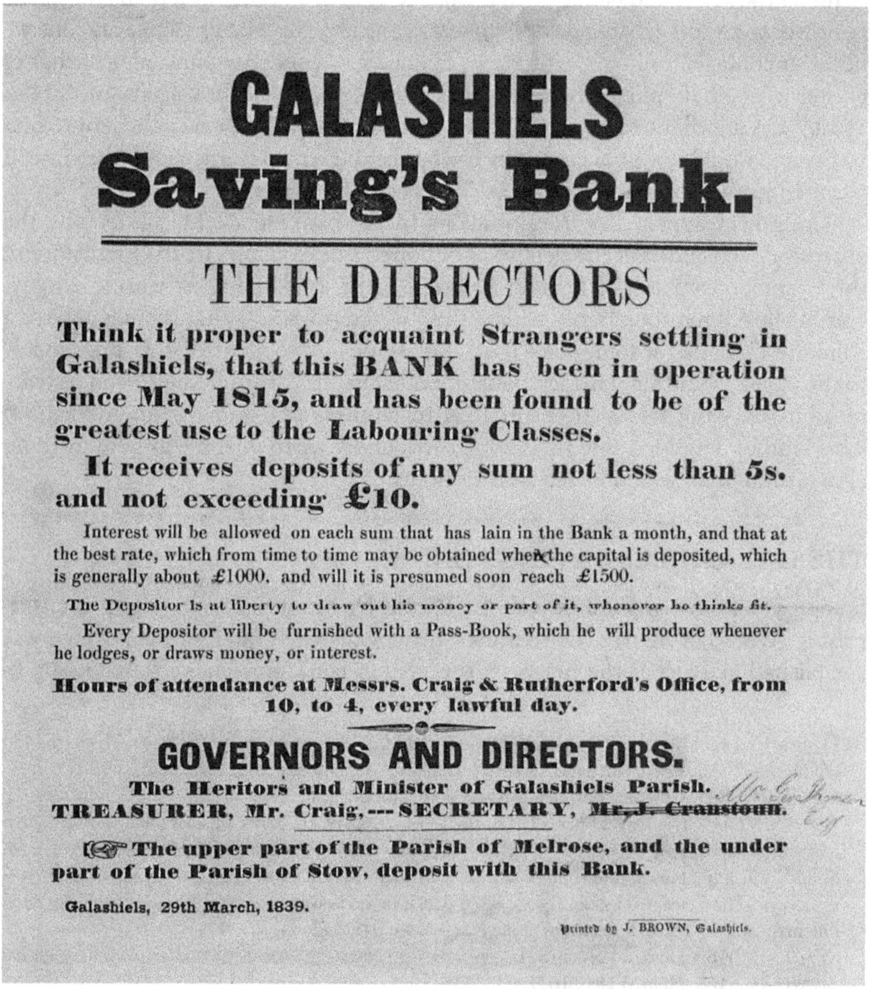

GALASHIELS
Saving's Bank.

THE DIRECTORS

Think it proper to acquaint Strangers settling in Galashiels, that this BANK has been in operation since May 1815, and has been found to be of the greatest use to the Labouring Classes.

It receives deposits of any sum not less than 5s. and not exceeding £10.

Interest will be allowed on each sum that has lain in the Bank a month, and that at the best rate, which from time to time may be obtained where`the capital is deposited, which is generally about £1000. and will it is presumed soon reach £1500.

The Depositor is at liberty to draw out his money or part of it, whenever he thinks fit.

Every Depositor will be furnished with a Pass-Book, which he will produce whenever he lodges, or draws money, or interest.

Hours of attendance at Messrs. Craig & Rutherford's Office, from 10, to 4, every lawful day.

GOVERNORS AND DIRECTORS.
**The Heritors and Minister of Galashiels Parish.
TREASURER, Mr. Craig, --- SECRETARY, Mr. J. Cranstoun.**

☞ **The upper part of the Parish of Melrose, and the under part of the Parish of Stow, deposit with this Bank.**

Galashiels, 29th March, 1839.

Printed by J. BROWN, Galashiels.

Figure 5.1 Galashiels Savings Bank advertisement. SBA © John Finlay

[21] SBA/1303/9/99, 14 Aug. 1839.

were sent to named individuals, with one put up publicly in Galashiels.[22] Those sent a copy included Nicol Milne in Faldonside and Richard Dennistoun WS, the tenant at Gala House. Beyond that, however, Craig's letter book is largely silent on the everyday business of the Savings Bank which was presumably recorded elsewhere.[23]

The Savings Bank accepted deposits of sums between 5s and £10, offering interest 'at the best rate'.[24] At the end of 1822 this was declared to be 5 per cent annually, but the Leith Bank apparently lowered it to 4 per cent in 1826 without informing Craig.[25] Once a customer's account reached the £10 limit, the money was supposed to be withdrawn and lodged in a Leith Bank deposit account at a preferential rate of interest.[26] In 1828, however, Craig complained that this was not being done properly. His branch was by then paying 4 per cent interest, but part of the account was being credited with only 3 per cent by the Leith Bank. He demanded corrective action, 'as this account by agreement 12 years ago was to have a preference – To encourage it I have taken £30 worth of trouble and expence every year for 12 years *for* nothing.'[27] From 1829 to 1832 Craig paid 3.5 per cent, only to find that the Leith Bank was again underpaying interest by giving only 3 per cent. This left £2 19s 3d to come out of Craig's 'private pocket' leading him again to complain:

> I cannot suppose it possible that you would alter this arrangement by withholding 2 or 3 pounds from so excellent an institution, particularly at present when every encouragement should be held out to them, as in England where 4 per cent is provided by Government authority.[28]

If the discrepancy was made up, Craig agreed to pay 3 per cent from 1 March.[29] There are scattered references to the rate of interest thereafter.[30]

The Galashiels Savings Bank was successful to judge by its longevity. Many customers of the Selkirk Savings Bank were women and the same is likely true of Galashiels given similar trends elsewhere.[31] Craig and Anderson also ran the Ettrick Forest Savings Bank on identical principles to that in Galashiels, with

---

[22] SBA/1303/8/468, 1 Apr. 1839.

[23] Other books are mentioned occasionally e.g. 'see ledger No. 2': SBA/1303/4/253, Elliot Anderson/J. Fairgrieve, Galashiels, 18 Oct. 1825.

[24] SBA/1303/8/467b. The advertisement, printed by J. Brown, Galashiels, is dated 20 Mar. 1839.

[25] SBA/1303/4/319, Craig/LBC, 6 Feb. 1826.

[26] SBA/1303/5/361, Craig/LBC, 16 Feb. 1829.

[27] SBA/1303/5/194, Craig/LBC, 21 Jan. 1828.

[28] SBA/1303/6/268, Craig/LBC, 5 Mar. 1832.

[29] SBA/1303/6/270, Craig/LBC, 12 Mar. 1832.

[30] E.g. SBA/1303/7/368, Craig/LBC, 20 Feb. 1837.

[31] SBA, SBA/8/1, Selkirk Savings Bank, Cash Day Book 1835–1839. More than half (seventeen out of thirty-three) of the transactions in Aug. 1836, for example, involved women. Women also feature heavily in Yarrow: SBA, SBA/200/20, Yarrow Parish Savings Bank, Cash Book 1815–1838. For further evidence, see L. Perriton and J. Maltby, 'Working-class households and savings in England, 1850–1880' (2015) *Enterprise & Society*, 413, esp. 413–21.

money deposited in the Leith Bank once the balance reached £10. This is apparent from a surviving passbook, belonging to Miss Isabel Harper in Bowshank, whose account was active between 1823 and 1837.[32] Until 1835, most of the entries bear Elliot Anderson's initials.

The Leith Bank itself certainly had its local women savers. Craig added this note in an 1832 letter to the bank's managers:

> You ask of whom I received so much Bank of England paper. It was from the fair hand of Miss Brodie for many years one of our greatest money lodgers: she paid in £170 of the same kind on Saturday.[33]

There was more than one Miss Brodie, probably sisters, one of whom transferred a £1,000 deposit receipt to the British Linen Company Bank in 1835.[34] These were not Savings Bank customers, but the evidence suggests that Craig took his obligations as a banker to 'the Labouring classes' seriously. There is nothing to indicate whether he received a salary for doing so although it is certainly possible. In Selkirk the treasurer of the Savings Bank, James Murray, received £20 per annum.[35]

THE LEITH BANKING COMPANY

The development of local bank networks in Scotland was precocious, thanks to the initiative of the Bank of Scotland after 1774.[36] The Leith Banking Company, a private bank, was established in 1792 and began trading on 1 January 1793.[37] Its head office was in Bernard Street, Leith and it developed a modest network of branches including one in Carlisle.[38] Bankers, like law agents, required a licence and an annual stamp duty of £30 was charged on licences under the Stamp Act 1815.[39] Banks which issued notes at branches had to take out a licence for each branch as well as for the mother bank.[40] Robert Henderson, the local surveyor of taxes at Selkirk, sent Craig a demand for duty of £1 in 1827 but this was remitted when Craig certified that he was included in the Leith Bank's licence and was not liable personally.[41]

Craig acted independently for the bank within a defined sphere. He was authorised to engage procurators, such as the Edinburgh solicitor-at-law, James Mack,

[32] NRS, Scott of Gala papers, GD477/463/5; see also SBA/200/20.
[33] SBA/1303/6/270, Craig/LBC, 12 Mar. 1832.
[34] SBA/1303/7/61, Anderson/LBC, 20 Apr. 1835; 67, idem, 13 May 1835.
[35] SBA, SBA/8/1, Selkirk Savings Bank, Cash Day Book, 25 Nov. 1839.
[36] S. G. Checkland, *Scottish Banking: A History, 1695–1973* (Glasgow, 1975), 196.
[37] W. J. Logan, *The Scottish Banker* (Edinburgh, 1839), 3.
[38] John Russell, *The Story of Leith* (Edinburgh, 1922), chapter 30; Munn, *Scottish Provincial Banking Companies*, 178.
[39] Stamp Act 1815, c. 184, Sched. 1. The charge for a law agent at that date was only £25.
[40] HC, *Report on Fictitious Votes*, 413 (per Henry Burgess, q. 5154).
[41] SBA/1303/5/169, Craig/LBC, 19 Dec. 1827; also SBA/1303/5/179, Anderson/Robert Henderson, Selkirk, 26 Dec. 1827.

to defend bank-related litigation.[42] He also employed writers and messengers to carry out specific tasks whenever necessary. While he was trusted with capital from the bank, he undertook transactions at his own risk. There is no indication in Craig's letters what his remuneration was or who his guarantors were. It is possible, as with Archibald Scott who worked as agent for the bank at Langholm and then at Carlisle, that he was paid a sum (in Scott's case, £1,250) annually from which he had to defray his own running costs.[43] Like Scott, Craig received regular parcels of notes from Leith, signed by the accountant and cashier of the bank.

Craig wrote to the bank typically more than once a week. As he informed William Fleming of the Clydesdale Bank his 'weekly states arrive at The Bank on the Tuesday about 2 o'clock'.[44] These weekly states (statements of transactions), for no apparent reason, ceased to be added to the letter book after July 1838 but must have been recorded elsewhere.[45] There is a reference in 1825 to 'private memorandum books kept of transactions connected with the Bank'.[46] Craig also occasionally visited the bank's head office in Leith. The main managers of the bank during the period of the letter books were Henry Johnston and James Ker and there is correspondence from Craig to both of them. He also corresponded with John Bisset SSC, a partner in the bank. At some point, Craig himself became a partner and, having begun with eighteen partners, it had only four (Johnston, Ker, Bisset and Craig) when it was sequestrated in 1842 with loss to its creditors.[47]

Craig expressed his views vigorously to the bank's managers. When they forbade him to provide letters of credit, he disputed their interpretation of the Stamp Act, noting that, 'so far as I can construe English', the relevant section, aimed at undated and unstamped drafts, had no application to such letters. He added, with a hint of sarcasm, that, if drafting them was wrong 'will you be pleased to say if we are to refuse all such sort of things that are drawn & issued by other Bankers; as I observe that if the one is wrong the other also subjects us to a penalty of £20 for being "knowingly received"'.[48]

Parcels of money came in and out of the branch constantly. Something of the working relationship between Craig and his clerk, Elliot Anderson, can be seen from an error that occurred in 1827. Anderson was at dinner when Craig, using

[42] SBA/1303/5/39. James Smith Mack was admitted to the Society of Solicitors at Law in Edinburgh on 1 Nov. 1816: Edinburgh Central Library, Accession 848697601, Register of the Society of Procurators of Edinburgh.

[43] *In Re Hobson*, *The Times*, no. 14291, 29 Jul. 1830, p. 3. The Lord Chancellor regarded the Carlisle office as the place of issue of the Leith Bank's notes, in contravention of the Bank of England's statutory monopoly on producing notes in England.

[44] SBA/1303/8/399, Craig/William Fleming, manager, Clydesdale Banking Company, Edinburgh, 31 Dec. 1838.

[45] SBA/1303/8/298, Craig/LBC, 23 Jul. 1838. This entry is incomplete in the letter book but was probably copied and completed in another volume.

[46] SBA/1303/4/191, Anderson/John Orr, writer, Edinburgh, 16 May 1825.

[47] *London Gazette*, no. 20099 (13 May 1842), 322; A. W. Kerr, *History of Banking in Scotland* (London, 1918), 202.

[48] SBA/1303/5/186, Craig/LBC, 5 Jan. 1828; Stamp Act, 1815, s. XIII.

Anderson's desk, paid an order on the Selkirkshire Yeomanry account of £200. Among the notes was a parcel of 100 guineas (amounting in value to £105) 'tied in the manner they always come from the Bank'.[49] Later that afternoon, Anderson balanced his money and found it correct. George Rodger, who was the yeomanry paymaster, wrote next morning that the parcel he had received contained twenty-shilling notes, rather than guinea notes. That would have left him £5 short in his payroll. In the previous ten days, Anderson had only had one parcel of twenty-shilling notes from Craig, and was still working through it, therefore he wrote to Rodger indicating he must have been mistaken. Rodger, however, had opened the parcel in front of his nieces and remarked on the error, and had paid out the notes as twenty-shilling notes. Anderson concluded that the bank may have sent the wrong parcel:

> The thing seems to me very extraordinary as it would imply both that Mr Craig had committed a mistake about the notes & that I had committed another error in paying away money without getting a receipt or overpaying some person to that extent none of which things so far as I am concerned ever has happened before – & what makes it more extraordinary still Mr Rodger's letter desired Guinea notes to be sent.[50]

Anderson wanted to know if the head office had noticed a surplus of £5 among any of the balances at the bank.

Rodger later informed Alexander Pringle, captain in the Selkirkshire yeomanry (and the future MP), who complained to the bank.[51] The bank denied liability, taking the view that Rodger should have credited the yeomanry account with the value of his order and adjusted the matter in Galashiels. Anderson, who customarily updated Pringle on the state of the yeomanry deposit account, informed him that Rodger should have 'restored the notes that we might have been satisfied how the mistake had arisen, & which of us should bear the loss'.[52] There the matter apparently rested.

When Anderson did make an error, in 1824, he appealed for help to the commissary clerk Andrew Lang. Anderson had paid Lang the proceeds of a deposit account of the late Walter Forsyth, but the Leith Bank refused to release the funds because the right to the money was in question. They had informed Lang's brother, William Lang WS, that they would only release the money in return for a formal discharge with security. Anderson had assumed that any doubt had been resolved when Forsyth's executor obtained a sheriff court decree of confirmation. His premature payment led him to ask Lang to provide a formal discharge 'as I observe the whole blame will attach to me personally, which places me in a very

[49] SBA/1303/5/101, Anderson/Mr Duncan, Leith Bank, 6 Aug. 1827.
[50] Ibid.
[51] SBA, Walter Mason archive, WM/10/1/3, Alexander Pringle/George Rodger, 4 Nov. 1826.
[52] SBA/1303/5/201, Anderson/Alexander Pringle, 28 Jan. 1828. On the deposit a/c, e.g. SBA/1303/5/302, Anderson/Captain Pringle, Yair, 1 Oct. 1828; also, SBA/1303/5/66, Anderson/Alexander Pringle, 31 Home St., Edinburgh, 21 May 1827.

awkward situation & which I have no doubt you will most readily do everything in your power to remove'.[53] The danger, however, soon passed when the confirmation was found to have been regular. This led to a letter from Anderson to the bank containing a measure of bravado: 'as to *me* being personally responsible for any trouble or loss the Bank might be put to fifty years hence, that is quite out of the question; not that I should apprehend it'.[54]

Security

With much cash on hand, Craig was naturally concerned about its security both within his premises and in transit to and from Leith. He was prompted to think about this in 1822 when he heard about the robbery of the Commercial Bank agent in Dunkeld. After enquiring in Edinburgh, he learned that the agent and his assistant were being blamed for negligence. They had kept £1,800 in their desks and £3,000 in the safe and, since they kept the key to the safe on a nail in the office in plain sight, the robbers would have escaped with everything but for 'a catch on the keyhole which they could not find a way of moving'.[55] In the event, they took the £1,800 plus bills and Craig, although not regarding himself as guilty of such 'supineness' as his Dunkeld colleagues, saw this as a warning to all country agents to take greater care. To minimise risk, he asked the bank for a better safe than the 'small useless thing' he currently had, referring to a 'Crieff safe' they had formerly promised him which he intended to place 'in a room off my bedroom'. When it arrived, six months later, he proclaimed it 'an excellent piece of workmanship'.[56]

Craig worked from home. This was not unusual for a banker or law agent, a similar example being John Romanes, writer and Bank of Scotland agent at Lauder.[57] Romanes moved to another building, soon after opening his branch office in 1833, but it is unclear whether Craig ever did so. According to the firm's cash book, after the partnership of Craig & Rutherford was formed they began paying £4 as a share of the annual rent to the bank for a bank office.[58] As these sums were repaid by the bank, this suggests that the payments were nominal and that the firm owned the branch premises.

Attending the fairs that were commercially so important in the Borders and the north of England required large amounts of cash on hand. The bank's directors were clearly nervous of the security of the large sums transported south. In May 1823, for example, Craig asked for £5,000 to be sent. This was an unusually large sum, but it was the 'term week' when leases were being negotiated and a

[53] SBA/1303/4/110, Anderson/Andrew Lang, 29 Oct. 1824.
[54] SBA/1303/4/112, Unsigned (Anderson)/LBC, 1 Nov. 1824.
[55] SBA/1303/3/64, Craig/LBC, 21 Oct. 1822.
[56] SBA/1303/3/139, Craig/LBC, 17 Mar. 1823.
[57] E. Brandeschi, *The Hidden History of the Royal Burgh of Lauder* (Selkirk, 2021), 57.
[58] SBA/1303/9, fo. 260 (14 Jan. 1839).

multitude of payments made for goods and services. He received, however, only
£2,500 via the carrier, John Young, who alternated with his son, William, in transporting cash from Leith.[59] Craig, left short of cash to pay the tenants and factors
of the duke of Buccleuch, was quick to complain:

> As the Dukes people will at least require £2500 there will be such a song tomorrow by
> people from Ettrick & Yarrow as we have not heard for 20 years. If your only excuse is
> the want of confidence in John Young with so large a sum as the £5000 required, you
> had better have said so in time that some other remedy might have been fallen upon.[60]

Craig's reputation depended on working effectively with the bank's managers and
shortcomings of this kind affected his goodwill. Yet the sum involved was a huge
one to be entrusted to one carrier. In purchasing power, £5,000 in 1823 was worth
just over £287,000 in 2017.[61]

Craig anticipated local demand, particularly on term days, and would ask the
bank's managers for extra supplies of cash when required. As he noted before the
principal fair of Selkirk, held on 5 April, it was 'a market at which a great many
payments are generally stipulated to be made'.[62] He was also quite specific about
the nature of what was needed. In May 1838 he asked for £2,500 'as the payments
will be large for the two ensuing weeks', plus he required some silver, and £60 in
Bank of England notes or sovereigns for a friend going to London and a further
£40 similarly for another travelling to Wales.[63]

Despite his precautions, Craig occasionally ran out of banknotes. A week
before Christmas in 1825 he was 'much disappointed' not to have received a
supply and had none left.[64] He looked to the bank's managers because it was
'absolutely necessary to keep us full handed at the [sic] season of the year'. Not
long after this, he added this postscript to another of his letters to the bank: 'Mr
Anderson very properly says that it is needless my mentioning what you are to
send since you pay so little attention to it'.[65]

When it came to smaller sums, Craig was happy to receive this by whatever
means the bank's managers had available. In one case, for example he asked them
to 'send £50 in silver by the Guard of the mail on Tuesday morning and either
E[lliot] A[nderson] or I will be at Fords waiting for it'.[66] While Craig mostly dealt
in letters of credit and bills, he was not averse himself to sending cash through
the post. One example is five-pound notes which he posted to George Fairholme
when the latter was at Castle Forbes. He took the precaution of recording the

[59] E.g. SBA/1303/3/10, Craig/LBC, 8 Jul. 1822.
[60] SBA/1303/3/176, Craig/LBC, 21 May 1823.
[61] According to TNA, currency convertor: www.nationalarchives.gov.uk/currency-converter/.
[62] SBA/1303/5/45, Anderson/LBC, 2 Apr. 1827.
[63] SBA/1303/8/247, Craig/LBC, 14 May 1838.
[64] SBA/1303/4/289, Craig/LBC, 19 Dec. 1825.
[65] SBA/1303/4/325, Craig/LBC, 13 Feb. 1826.
[66] SBA/1303/7/22, Craig/LBC, 18 Oct. 1834. This may be a reference to the Blucher which ran from
Jedburgh to Edinburgh: Hall, *History of Galashiels*, 118.

date and serial number of each note in an accompanying letter.[67] He did the same soon after when he sent Bank of England notes to Margaret Lindsay in London, having heard from her mother that she was unwell and probably requiring funds from her account until able to resume her employment.[68] On another occasion, having been asked for £50 by George Fairholme in Bemersyde, he sent Anderson to deliver it personally proclaiming that he 'will be the better of the ride'.[69]

Forgery

Forgery also affected security of commerce. In a letter to the bank in 1822 Craig mentioned a forged Aberdeen £1 note.[70] He had never heard of a forgery on that particular bank and asked the managers to let him know immediately whenever forgeries came to light because 'trusting to newspapers is useless unless it is in them all'.[71] He included an addendum reflecting his agency agreement with the bank: '[i]n cases like this you ought at all events to bear the half of the loss as they are by no means considered by our present agreement'.[72] The same year, the bank alerted Craig to a forged £1 note of Sir William Forbes & Company's bank.[73]

Craig's practice was to count parcels of notes and bills before his clerk sent them to the bank, but he did not always have time and, in one case, managed to miss a forged note of the Commercial Bank of Aberdeen which he was unaware of until the bank returned it.[74] He did allude to 'ill done' forgeries of 20 shilling Royal Bank notes in 1823, commenting that he did not remember the Royal Bank 'having advertised this forgery or having seen any notice of it otherways'.[75] Lack of notice was always concerning; Craig had no notice of forged Bank of Scotland £5 notes in 1831, although he was aware of stolen National Bank of Scotland notes being in circulation.[76]

So severe was the problem becoming that Elliot Anderson wrote to the bank in 1822 in the following terms:

> The forgeries are so numerous it would appear that we are obliged to lay down every note flat upon counting which is a great trouble ... I wish some of the fellows were caught & made an example of.[77]

[67] SBA/1303/3/45, Craig/G. Fairholme, Castle Forbes, Alford, Aberdeen, 10 Sep. 1822.
[68] SBA/1303/3/50, Craig/Margaret Lindsay 9 Arling St., Piccadily, London, 18 Sep. 1822.
[69] SBA/1303/2/107, Craig/George Fairholme, Bemersyde, 23 Aug. 1821.
[70] It is not made clear which Aberdeen bank was the issuer. One-pound notes were more susceptible to forgery because smaller notes attracted less scrutiny: Checkland, *Scottish Banking*, 187.
[71] SBA/1303/2/44, Craig/George Fairholme, 9 Sep. 1822.
[72] Banks were not legally obliged to give value for forged notes. Practice varied as to whether banks actually gave value for their own forged notes: Munn, *Provincial Banking Companies*, 145. Craig clearly expected to take a share (but no more) of the loss in such cases.
[73] SBA/1303/2/6, Craig/George Fairholme, 1 Jul. 1822.
[74] SBA/1303/3/166, Craig/LBC, 5 May 1823.
[75] SBA/1303/3/183, Craig/LBC, 31 May 1823.
[76] SBA/1303/6/202, Anderson/LBC, 18 Jul. 1831.
[77] SBA/1303/2/60, Anderson/LBC, 14 Oct. 1822.

Walter Scott's neighbour, Nicol Milne, clearly felt the same way. A letter from him to law agents in Hawick is preserved in Craig's letter book.[78] It relates to a forged £1 note of the Dundee Union Bank which Milne had received, in part payment for lambs, from a Hawick farmer named Andrew Wilson. It was in a parcel of £75, the only note not issued by the British Linen Bank. The forgery was detected on presentation to the Forbes & Company Bank but Wilson refused to take it back. Milne asked the agents to summon him to the next JP court to be held in Hawick and was prepared to swear an oath that he got the note from him.

In an age of regular bank failure, banknotes of defunct institutions were another problem. The East Lothian Banking Company, which was wound up under a trust deed after its cashier, William Borthwick, embezzled its funds in 1822 and escaped to America, is a case in point.[79] Craig, at the time, hoped 'the young vagabond' Borthwick would be delivered up 'suppose he does reach the continent both for the sake of the Bank proprietors & the public'.[80] The bank's debts, however, were paid in full by its trustee. In June 1824 an 'old woman', Nelly Clark of Midholm, left five guineas of the East Lothian Bank in Craig's office to see if anything might be done with them.[81] The Leith Bank arranged with the trustee for payment, placing the equivalent sum in a deposit receipt at their head office in favour of Margaret Clark (presumably Nelly's daughter).[82] The sudden failure of the Northumberland Bank in November 1821 also came out of the blue.[83] Craig, whose branch had 'always been in the way of receiving considerable sums' of their notes, was glad that at the time they had very few but expressed concern for 'Bank agents farther down' who were more exposed.[84]

Coinage caused fewer difficulties, although in 1818 the county fiscal, George Rodger, had people taken into custody at Selkirk for 'issuing base coin'.[85] The Leith Bank did refuse to take a sovereign that was 'deficient in weight'.[86] This had been supplied to Anderson by James Middlemas of Stow who had been fore-warned that this may be the case and was required to replace it with a £1 note.

Credit Referencing

An important branch function was assessing the creditworthiness of local individuals and businesses. In 1826 Craig sent to Leith a copy of a partnership contract between six clothiers who sought £2,000 of credit. One of the challenges in the

---

[78] SBA/1303/4/449, N. Milne/Messrs Oliver & Elliot, Hawick, 7 Sep. 1827.
[79] Munn, *Scottish Provincial Banking Companies*, 73–4; N. Munro, *The History of the Royal Bank of Scotland 1727–1927* (Edinburgh, 1928), 164–5.
[80] SBA/1303/3/237, Craig/LBC 20 Apr. 1822.
[81] SBA/1303/4/55, Craig/LBC, 30 Jun. 1824; fo. 57, idem, 5 Jul. 1824.
[82] SBA/1303/4/64, Craig/Nelly Clark, 16 Jul. 1824.
[83] M. Phillips, *A History of Banks, Bankers and Banking in Northumberland, Durham and North Yorkshire* (London, 1894), 163.
[84] SBA/1303/2/162, Craig/LBC, 24 Nov. 1821.
[85] RPLB fo. 85, Rodger/Hugh Warrender WS, 21 Jul. 1818.
[86] SBA/1303/4/34, Anderson/James Middlemas, 22 May 1824.

woollen industry was the cost of apparatus and machines were generally shared or owned in common.[87] Grouping together to form a 'cloth company', as these individuals intended, Craig thought sensible, particularly because it prevented competition between them. The group was 'well selected' from the general body of clothiers in Galashiels 'as embracing none of them who aspire at great things but are content to live by fair & honest industry alone'.[88] Most had been in business for many years and had brought themselves forward 'from small beginnings to very reputable credit & active employment'. To reassure the bank further, Craig mentioned that 'Mr Anderson & I will be welcome at all times to look at their Books & general management of the concern but which from their own careful habits I hope may be seldom necessary'.

Despite Craig's recommendation, the bank wanted more details of the borrowers who included William Thomson, John Lees, Thomas McGill and the Clapperton brothers. He described the latter as

the eldest sons of old Thomas Clapperton who is by degrees giving up his business to them – who draws £100 of rents with not much debt upon a machinery house of which he has the one half, the whole being at least worth & could be sold tomorrow for £3000.[89]

In short, these men were a good risk and Craig underlined this by pointing out that 'they are all Galashiels men, bred & born to the same business – never any of them failed or are likely to do'.

In that difficult year for textiles, 1829, however, Thomas Clapperton did fail, 'to the amount of £3000', along with two other clothiers. Craig held many of their bills but expected no loss to the bank. Even so, the circumstances meant delay in recovering their value and he found this vexatious 'the more so when I was flattering myself' that each bill 'was as good as the Bank of England'.[90] To make matters worse, some of Clapperton's transactions were suspected of being fraudulent.

Craig's recommendations were not made only for the Leith Bank but extended very broadly. An example is his assessment, requested by Alexander Macartney, general manager of the Commercial Bank of Scotland, of the local merchant William Laidlaw. Laidlaw was generally 'doing well, tho he might not always be punctual in his payments & this with some additional buildings lately put up may press upon his capital – he is sober & attentive to his country business'.[91] A typical recommendation was that given for William Haldane, Alexander Martin and William Ovens. They were all in a similar line of business: keeping shops and 'a sort of private public houses [sic]' with Haldane running the post office 'which

[87] C. Gulvin, *The Tweedmakers* (Newton Abbot, 1973), 61.
[88] SBA/1303/4/501, Craig/LBC, 27 Nov. 1826.
[89] SBA/1303/5/19, Craig/LBC, 12 Feb. 1827; also SBA/1303/5/521, idem, 8 Jan. 1827.
[90] SBA/1303/5/461 Craig/LBC, 19 Oct. 1829.
[91] SBA/1303/4/370, Craig/A. Macartney, Commercial Bank of Scotland, Edinburgh, 17 Apr. 1826. On Macartney, see Checkland, *Scottish Banking*, 291–3.

appears to be well managed'. Martin 'has a pension of £25 or so from Government as a disabled gunner' and Craig supposed that they could 'be safely trusted with £30 or £40 of goods'.[92]

If necessary for a reference of this kind, inquiries would be made. Elliot Anderson responded on Craig's behalf to a query about Messrs Blaikie & Clark, a firm of building contractors. Anderson had enquired with 'a respectable person of my acquaintance' and formed the conclusion that the firm 'cannot be trusted with any feasibility such a sum as £100 on their *own* credit'. He went on

> Indeed I never heard their names before altho' the most of people [sic] in that line are known to *us* in one way or other. Clark not long ago was a Journeyman Wright with Messrs J.& S. Smith. To be brief, *whatever sums* your friend trusts them he should require security.[93]

Of course, information flowed both ways and Craig took advantage of his contacts in Leith to find out more about Edinburgh traders. Thus he inquired whether John Kerr & Co and Alexander Shaw 'all clothiers or Haberdashers', were 'Respectable people'.[94]

In his regular updates to the bank, Craig also shared local intelligence. The emphasis was on trading conditions and business at the fairs. For example, in July 1822 he reported that

> [t]he wool market opens very slowly; at two or three neighbouring fairs little or nothing done, & what was [done was] at 3/. or 4/s less than last year per stone of Cheviot – St Boswell's will decide it which is on Thursday the 18th.[95]

In 1831 Elliot Anderson wrote that it was being conjectured that 'the advance on the price of wool today would be from 30 to 40 per cent on last years [sic] prices', a reflection of economic recovery from a very difficult trading period, many woollen goods producers having experienced insolvency in 1828–30.[96]

London Bankers

Craig drew upon the Leith Bank's London bankers, Barnetts, Hoare & Company.[97] His use of them was multifaceted and not always business-related. For instance, through Barnetts he paid his private subscription to the weekly newspaper, *The Examiner*, as well as to the *Literary Gazette*.[98] He also asked them to use their

---

[92] SBA/1303/3/183, Craig/LBC, 31 May 1823.
[93] SBA/1303/5/172, Elliot Anderson/Robert Johnston, Leith Bank, 20 Dec. 1827.
[94] SBA/1303/8/251, Anderson/Robert Johnston, 21 May 1838.
[95] SBA/1303/3/10, Craig/LBC, 8 Jul. 1822. The quality of Cheviot wool was in decline and becoming unsuitable for manufacturing fine cloth: Gulvin, *The Tweedmakers*, 64.
[96] SBA/1303/6/202, Anderson/LBC, 18 Jul. 1831; Gulvin, *The Tweedmakers*, 68.
[97] J. W. Gilbart, *A Practical Treatise on Banking* (London, 1927), 59.
[98] SBA/1303/4/163, Anderson/E. Ranoe, 2 Mar. 1825; SBA/1303/4/166, Craig/John Hunt, 5 Mar. 1825; SBA/1303/5/5, Anderson/W. A. Scripp, 16 Jan. 1827.

influence with Lord Reay to recommend a local, John Horsburgh, to the duke of Sutherland as his new factor in 1825 and, within a fortnight of Horsburgh's death in 1837, he wrote again suggesting a replacement.[99] This time he recommended 'much the same kind of man', William Laidlaw who had been Sir Walter Scott's 'land steward and amanuensis' until Scott's death in 1832. Laidlaw, Craig's 'intimate acquaintance', had settled near Beauly in Inverness-shire. Craig was in no doubt that if influence with the duke's London bankers or agents brought him the situation, he would welcome it.

As bills of exchange were often drawn on Edinburgh or London, Barnetts was a useful resource for credit referencing just as the Leith Bank was more locally. In one case Craig refused to give value to an indorser of a bill on a London bank until the Leith Bank had sent it to Barnetts to see if it was 'a bill likely to be paid', since the last indorser, though 'respectable', might be 'put about were it returned with protest'.[100] It was Barnetts who told Craig of the insolvency of Thomas Rutherford in 1827. Craig informed Charles Robson who was directly affected by Rutherford's failure, telling him he was 'very sorry for this catastrophe on you & your brothers'.[101] Robson had already set up a trust for his creditors and Craig, knowing him to be highly respected in Roxburghshire, regretted that his commitment to stockbreeding should have so damaged his business.[102]

An interesting example of Craig's use of Barnett's arose in 1836 when he sent them a note from the wife of Lieutenant William Clark, who was called suddenly to Plymouth by the unexpected arrival of her husband's ship for repairs. Craig arranged a letter of credit for Mrs Clark in case her husband required money and asked Barnetts to honour any draft Clark made upon him and send it through the Leith Bank. He also made an enquiry. Clark donated to the Royal Naval School (in the expectation of having his son educated there), but he did not know 'what similar young gentlemen like himself[,] Lieutenants in the R.N. in commission are in the habit of paying annually towards the School as he would like to be neighbour like and not more'.[103] Craig asked Barnetts to investigate as a preliminary to setting up an annual payment to be remitted through them. Clark later wanted this adjusted to one day's pay, in line with other officers, but Craig, ignorant of what that was, wrote to the receiver of subscriptions at the Naval School asking him to inform Barnetts of the sum so that they could make the arrangements.[104]

Craig's legal knowledge also proved useful to Barnetts. As he explained to them on one occasion, in Scotland, in order to preserve recourse (the right to

[99] SBA/1303/7/395, Craig/Barnetts, Hoare & Co., London, 22 Mar. 1837. The 1825 letter is not in the letter book and has not been traced. Jane, the daughter of Patrick Sellar, factor to the first duke of Sutherland, was Andrew Lang's daughter-in-law.

[100] SBA/1303/7/464, Craig/LBC, 3 Jun. 1837.

[101] SBA/1303/5/68, Craig/Charles Robson, 23 May 1827.

[102] SBA/1303/5/62, Craig/LBC, 7 May 1827.

[103] SBA/1303/5/251, Craig/Barnetts, Hoare & Co., London, 10 Aug. 1836; cf. SBA/1303/6/335, copy letter W. Clark/Lt. C. Brand, Royal Naval School, 29 Nov. 1832.

[104] SBA/1303/7/496, Craig/J. M. Hope, 7 Jermyn Street, St James, London, 10 Jun. 1837.

demand payment) against parties who had failed to pay a bill, it was necessary, within six months of the bill falling due, that it be registered in the Books of Council and Session.[105] In any such case, Craig had to have the original bill in his possession in time to register it.

The relationship with Barnetts, however, was not always smooth. To Craig's frustration, they more than once objected to Elliot Anderson signing drafts on his behalf.[106] He asked the Leith Bank in 1825 to investigate, having thought the matter previously resolved.[107] Anderson had signed fifty drafts 'without a word' prior to the most recent objection being raised. Craig's annoyance reflected his dependency on Anderson, who superintended some significant accounts, including that of the London drysalters R. & E. A. Whytt. In 1830 Craig complained to the partners in that firm when a number of their drafts to locals in Galashiels had to be referred to Barnetts to pursue payment, noting that such failure to pay timeously affected their goodwill locally. He also emphasised that 'such a steady person as Mr Anderson' was 'quite qualified' to look after their interests.[108]

BANKING SERVICES

Despite his regular need for cash, Craig's core banking activities involved negotiable instruments, particularly promissory notes and bills of exchange. An example will easily explain a typical transaction involving a negotiable instrument. While the language is that of the banker, it would have been well understood by their clientele. Here is a letter to James Robson, a stocking-maker in Peebles:

> Sir, B. Lawrie's P[romissory] Note to you, dated 12 Jan[uary] last at 4 m[onths] £39.10/ indorsed by you to the Bank fell due 15th cur[ren]t & is this night ret[ire]d prot[este]d for non pay[men]t cha[rge]s 11/10d for w[hic]h you will immediately provide.[109]

The meaning is straightforward. In January Lawrie, also a hosier by trade, had promised in writing to pay £39 10s to Robson four months from the date of his note. This promissory note became due on 15 May 1821. Robson had negotiated the right to receive the sum to the Leith Bank by indorsement (i.e. he had transferred the right to receive payment to the bank and signed the note to that effect). The bank then sought payment from Lawrie who failed to pay. Therefore, the bank had had drawn up a document, known as a protest, in the appropriate legal form authenticated by a notary public. There was a charge for this, specified as being 11s 10d, which was added to the debt. While Lawrie was the principal obligant (the main debtor), because this was a negotiable instrument everyone

---

[105] SBA/1303/5/60, Craig/Barnetts, Hoare & Co., Bankers, London, 4 May 1827.
[106] A 'draft' was a bill prior to its acceptance by the drawee.
[107] SBA/1303/4/175, Craig/LBC, 28 Mar. 1825.
[108] SBA/1303/6/35, Craig/Barnetts, Hoare & Co., 17 Mar. 1830; SBA/1303/6/14, Craig/E.A. Whytt, 27 Jan. 1830; SBA/1303/6/36, Craig/E.A. Whytt, 17 Mar. 1830.
[109] SBA/1303/2/44, Craig/James Robson, 19 May 1821. Contractions are obviously indicated here.

who had signed it was liable upon it on a joint and several basis. In other words, Robson, who had received value for the note from the bank, was liable to the bank for the debt expressed in the note plus the charges. If Robson made payment, he would be entitled to relief (i.e. to recover his outlay) from Lawrie. The Leith Bank need not waste time trying to recover from Lawrie, whose solvency they apparently thought questionable (he was, soon after, thought to be contemplating bankruptcy), when they could recover from Robson.[110]

A promissory note was a simple form of instrument involving an unconditional written promise to pay a defined sum to a certain party at a determined or determinable future date. Such notes, like all negotiable instruments, could be transferred to different payees without any requirement to inform the creditor. Thus Craig wrote to the poet James Hogg, in June 1827 about a promissory note to him for £30 by 'P. Phillips', presumably his father-in-law Peter Phillips, which Hogg had indorsed to Adam Laidlaw and Laidlaw had indorsed to the bank.[111] This was a typical example of the bank acting as collecting agent, having bought the note at a discount (see below). Craig drew up a formal notarial protest for non-payment when the note fell due and sought immediate payment from Hogg as indorser. He made no effort to allow Hogg additional time to pay, for this was a debtor of whom he had previous experience. Indeed, in his letter to Hogg he also demanded at least partial payment of a separate note that had fallen due the year before.[112]

Bills of exchange were slightly more complex instruments. They would, however, have been as familiar to the bank's customers as credit cards now are for modern consumers.

Inland Bills

The main business of the typical bank agent, as Checkland noted, lay 'in discounting bills drawn usually on Edinburgh or London, transferring money to and from other parts of the country, and in receiving deposits'.[113] Provincial banks dealt largely with inland bills, that is bills drawn in Scotland where payment was obtained by sending them to a bank agent in the town where the bill was drawn.[114] The creditor who drew the bill, known as the drawer, obliged a drawee (the debtor) to pay to him or a third-party payee a certain sum at a defined date (known as the bill's maturity). The drawee would 'accept' the bill (i.e. sign it to acknowledge the debt) and, until accepted, a bill was known as a draft. As 'acceptor', the drawee was then bound to pay when the bill matured. If the drawee was

[110] SBA/1303/2/50, Anderson/Tait & Bruce WS, 1 Jun. 1821; see also, SBA/1303/2/162, Craig/J. S. Mack, solicitor-at-law, 26 Nov. 1821.
[111] M. G. Garden, ed., *Memorials of James Hogg* (3rd edn, Paisley, 1903), 111–12, 153.
[112] SBA/1303/5/73, Craig/James Hogg, Mount Benger Knowe, 6 Jun. 1827.
[113] Checkland, *Scottish Banking*, 196–7; L. S. Pressnell, *Country Banking in the Industrial Revolution* (Oxford, 1956), 292–3.
[114] Munn, *Scottish Provincial Banking Companies*, 121. Any bill payable abroad, including in England, was a bill of exchange which may also be used as a generic term.

a bank then, under Scots law, if it possessed the funds to pay the draft, the draft operated as an assignation (transfer) of the sum for which it was drawn, in favour of the party holding it, from the date it was presented for payment.[115]

Before maturity, the drawer might negotiate (i.e. indorse and transfer) the bill to a third party. If he wanted cash earlier than maturity, he might sell the bill to a bank which would buy it at a discount (e.g. if the debt was £100 the bank might purchase it for £96 anticipating £4 profit). The bank would then present the bill to the drawee for payment when it matured and receive the full amount of the debt. If the bill was not paid by the drawee, the bank would have a right of relief against the drawer or any intermediate holder of the bill.

A bill presented but not paid was said to be 'dishonoured'. The party presenting it would have a notary draft an instrument of protest. An example from Craig's correspondence involved a guest of Sir Walter Scott, Villiers Surtees, visiting Abbotsford, who drew on the account which his uncle, Rev. Mathew Surtees, rector of North Cerney in Gloucestershire, held with the bankers Ladbroke & Company of London for £26 5s.[116] On the strength of this, Craig paid him cash at a discount. When Ladbroke refused to pay, the bill was returned dishonoured. Craig informed Scott that the dishonour 'will have arisen from want of advice from the Divine to the Bankers' (in other words, Ladbroke had not been notified of, or accepted, the draft from the nephew who was not the account holder). He asked Scott for the address of the young man and his uncle and wrote to Gloucestershire seeking a remittance for the amount owed plus charges of £1 11s 6d. Rev. Surtees, brother-in-law of the judge Lord Eldon and 'a man of a peculiarly odious disposition', sent a new draft.[117] However, he took so long that Craig had meanwhile heard from the drawer (presumably advised by his uncle) that the bill, on being presented again to the bank, would be paid including the charges. Since the bill was by then in the hands of the Leith Bank, Craig simply instructed them to obtain payment and debited the head office in his accounts for the amount.

In practice, bills sometimes went awry. For example, if the payee's name was incorrect, then a draft would not be honoured. A draft from the duke of Buccleuch in favour of Nicol Milne of Faldonside, was mistakenly drawn on the London bankers Coutts & Co. in favour of 'Mr Park' rather than Milne. Craig informed the duke that it would be necessary to alter 'the word Park into Milne before it will be paid in London' and asked him to return the amended draft.[118]

A fundamental principle in all negotiable instruments was that every signatory was jointly and severally liable for payment. Anyone who had indorsed or

[115] *Gavin v Kippen & Co. and others* (1768) Mor. 1495; G. J. Bell, *Principles of the Law of Scotland* (4th edn, 1839), 315, 1495. Assignation required intimation to the debtor, but in case law notarial protestation for non-payment of the draft was the equivalent of intimation.
[116] SBA/1303/3, Craig/Sir Walter Scott, 5 Sep. 1823.
[117] H. E. Litchfield, ed., *Emma Darwin, Wife of Charles Darwin. A Century of Family Letters* (2 vols, Cambridge, 1904), I, 7, 34; SBA/1303/3/248, Craig/LBC, 17 Sep. 1823; SBA/1303/3/249, Craig/LBC, 20 Sep. 1823.
[118] SBA/1303/5/296, Craig/the duke of Buccleuch, 3 Sep. 1828.

transferred a bill was liable upon it if it was dishonoured by the drawee. Sometimes latitude might be given to the drawee. An example arose in 1831 when Craig sent a routine bill to Mr Macfarlane at the Bank of Scotland in Falkirk. The bill, drawn by D. Hodge on J. Lyon, was one week from reaching maturity.[119] Lyon had accepted the bill and Craig required Macfarlane to receive payment from Lyon and remit the sum to the Leith Bank. Craig had obtained the bill from a Mr Paterson, who had indorsed it and so was liable upon it if Lyon failed to pay. The Bank of Scotland was merely collecting agent on Craig's behalf. Just after writing to Falkirk, however, Craig received a letter from Paterson intimating that Lyon was not in funds to meet the whole bill. He could however,

> . . . satisfy any person in Falkirk that there would be no loss in the transaction as he has monies due to him for part of the goods sold, & still has part of them on hand, & will pay if a little time is allowed.[120]

Craig authorised Macfarlane, if he thought payment likely, to allow Lyon 'any reasonable extra time to collect his debts & sell his goods'.

Enforcing Bills

Craig did not treat all debtors the same and, depending on the debtor, might even allow a bill to 'lie over' and be partly paid, with interest being charged on the sum outstanding. An instructive example is a bill owed by William John Napier, 9th Lord Napier (1786–1834), that fell due on 9 July 1824. Napier told Craig to obtain payment from his agents, Hunter, Campbell & Cathcart WS.[121] Craig's natural first resort was to protest the bill and threaten diligence.[122] The Edinburgh agents, in response, offered to pay a third of the bill and the remainder at a later date. This surprised Craig who regarded the proposition as 'quite a new one & one which as agent for the Bank I can by no means fall in with'.[123] The drawer of the bill, Samuel Oliver, and J. Little, Napier's grieve, who had indorsed it, were liable but if they could not pay then Craig was determined 'to make the payment effectual'. He was, however, willing to relent if the agents provided him with their own promissory note for the balance to be paid in five or six months.[124] When they demurred, he threatened to arrest Napier's rents.[125] This, however, was a bluff. Craig, instead, followed his usual rule of granting more time when a debtor was likely to pay.[126] Since Napier, who had been absent from home for months,

[119] SBA/1303/6/177, Craig/A. Macfarlane, Bank of Scotland, Falkirk, 10 May 1831.
[120] SBA/1303/6/179, Craig/A. Macfarlane, 11 May 1831.
[121] SBA/1303/4/67, Craig/LBC (with copy letter from Napier), 22 Jul. 1824; SBA/1303/4/74, Craig to Hunter, Campbell & Cathcart WS, 5 Aug. 1824.
[122] SBA/1303/4/79, Craig/Hunter, Campbell & Cathcart WS, 16 Aug. 1824.
[123] SBA/1303/4/82, idem, 23 Aug. 1824.
[124] SBA/1303/4/85, idem, 26 Aug. 1824.
[125] SBA/1303/4/111, idem, 1 Nov. 1824.
[126] SBA/1303/4/131, idem, 16 Dec. 1824.

was likely to return in a month or two, Craig accepted one-third plus interest and charges, asking the agents to pay it into his Leith Bank deposit account and to send him the receipt so that he could mark the payment on the back of the bill. This was done, but not instantly.[127] In August 1825, the balance had not been settled and Craig reminded the agents that the interest 'will now be considerable upon it'.[128] Five months later, the balance still unpaid, the Leith Bank insisted on diligence being carried out.[129] Yet this was also bluster. Even when Napier was known to have paid off all his local accounts around Selkirk, no formal action was taken.[130] Instead, Craig wrote to Napier 'earnestly' requesting payment.[131] Elliot Anderson even suggested to one of the bank's partners that it might be useful to present Napier's receipt '*again* if you or any of the other Gentlemen passing *that* way will take so much trouble'.[132]

Napier, naval officer turned diplomat, was well connected. His father Francis, lieutenant in the county of Selkirk, had commissioned Gala as his deputy lieutenant in 1813.[133] Napier himself was a representative peer in the House of Lords between 1824 and 1832, before being appointed Chief Superintendent of Trade at Canton in 1833 where he died the following year.[134] While both the Leith Bank and Craig occasionally pressed and insisted, there was reluctance to undertake legal steps to recover his debt, in marked contrast to the treatment of other debtors who owed much less. In 1834, whether in connection with this or another unpaid debt is unclear (the sum was £193), Craig had written to Napier and expressed to his agents that he 'would be the last man in the County to put him [i.e. Napier] to any inconveniency & therefore requested that he would send only £25 merely to show to the bank that I was not altogether neglecting it'.[135] He kept abreast of Napier's trade mission to China, wishing him well but commenting that 'the Chinese are a selfish stubborn people, & have not yet had Reform to fight with & break them down'.[136]

This is a far cry from a statement Craig made in 1822 to the writer John Paterson that he 'will never allow any Bill belonging to the bank to ly over, on any account' and a similar comment to indorsers of a bill payable at four months in Stow that 'the Bank never allow long bills to ly over'.[137] Napier's bill was payable

[127] SBA/1303/4/136, idem, 28 Dec. 1824.
[128] SBA/1303/4/233, idem, 23 Aug. 1825.
[129] SBA/1303/4/301, idem, 12 Jan. 1826.
[130] SBA/1303/5/9, idem, 25 Jan. 1827.
[131] SBA/1303/5/47, Craig/Napier, 9 Apr. 1827; SBA/1303/5/195, 21 Jan. 1828; SBA/1303/5/281, 22 Jul. 1828.
[132] SBA/1303/5/172, Elliot Anderson/Robert Johnston, Leith Bank, 20 Dec. 1827.
[133] NRs, Scott of Gala, GD477/463/9.
[134] J. Laughton & A. Lambert, 'William John, ninth Lord Napier of Merchistoun (1786–1834)', *Oxford Dictionary of National Biography* (accessed 4 May 2022).
[135] SBA/1303/6/448, Craig/Hunter, Campbell & Cathcart WS, 3 Jan. 1834.
[136] SBA/1303/7/46, Craig/William Scott, 4 Feb. 1835 (Napier was already dead by this date).
[137] SBA/1303/3/19, Craig/John Paterson, writer, 23 Jul. 1822; SBA/1303/3/112, Anderson/G. & J. Boyd, Stow, 22 Jan. 1823.

at two months yet remained unpaid for years. This was hardly 'alike wi' ane alike wi' a', but while it opens Craig up to the charge of hypocrisy, his approach often varied according to the financial status of the debtor.

Discounting

As Elliot Anderson reminded David Spence in Melrose, no draft could be discounted unless it had first been accepted.[138] The Leith Bank would not discount any bill payable more than five months from the date it was drawn.[139] It was also a rule, as Craig informed the clothier Robert Lees at Bemersyde, 'to which our Bank adheres strictly of giving no discounts whatever to parties who keep their accounts at other Banks'.[140]

Discounting depended on the likelihood of full payment being received. That was a question of commercial judgment made in reliance on the character of the parties involved and the nature of their business.[141] Local knowledge mattered. When the Kendal card manufacturer John Wade sought cash in return for Andrew Boyd's promissory note to him, Craig gave him short shrift:

> The bill is good enough – but the Banks [sic] Branches are not in the custom of discounting to English people, preferring to keep their funds in the district to which they belong, and you have omitted to Indorse it at any rate. I therefore inclose it and debit you 1/8d of postage.[142]

Craig reiterated this advice to a Newcastle correspondent the following year, noting that while the Leith Bank did not discount to English or Edinburgh houses at its local branches, it would do so at Leith 'when the parties are known & the reason is obvious'.[143] If an English house did obtain a discount in Edinburgh, the Edinburgh banker would send the bill to the country branch to collect the debt.

Craig's Langholm colleague, Archibald Scott, was 'exposed to English paper of all descriptions' and Craig expressed concern for him in 1825 during a disruptive period for London and Yorkshire banks.[144] Craig himself refused provincial English bank notes, although Elliot Anderson made an exception for some notes of the Tweed Bank supplied by the builders Sanderson & Paterson.[145] This, however, was conditional on Sanderson bearing the risk of the notes being rejected in Edinburgh.

[138] SBA/1303/2/114, Craig/David Spence, Melrose, 6 Sep. 1821; cf. SBA/1303/4/272, Craig/W.A.& G. Maxwell, Liverpool, 21 Nov. 1825, where a draft was 'indorsed in place of accepted' by the drawee and would have to be accepted by him before it could be discounted.

[139] SBA/1303/1/15, Craig/R. & E.A. Whyte, London, 5 Nov. 1819.

[140] SBA/1303/5/276, Craig/Mr Lees, Bemersyde, 12 Jul. 1828.

[141] Munn, *Scottish Provincial Banking Companies*, 123.

[142] SBA/1303/2/36, Craig/John Wade, 8 May 1821.

[143] SBA/1303/3/223, Craig/Robert Usher, Newcastle, 9 Apr. 1822.

[144] SBA/1303/4/289, Craig/LBC, 19 Dec. 1825.

[145] Ibid., Anderson/Sanderson & Paterson, 20 Dec. 1825. The Tweed Bank was the name adopted by the Berwick bankers Batson, Berry & Company with whom Craig had occasional correspondence: Munn, *Scottish Provincial Banking Companies*, 73.

Further information on discounting to Edinburgh houses can be gleaned from correspondence with the printer James Ballantyne in 1821.[146] Ballantyne had a bill, drawn by Sir Walter Scott, for £580 payable at three months and he sought a discount. Craig replied:

> It is quite irregular for Country Branches to discount to Edinburgh houses, & a thing never done. When Sir Walter draws on houses in town & applies the money in the Country, it is a different thing and we discount them.[147]

In this instance Craig was willing to make an exception but, having sent the bill to Leith for the managers to discount it, they sent it back making the same observation.

Craig and Anderson normally discounted bills only if they were likely to be paid without difficulty. As Anderson explained to James Burnett, 'we never discount bills that we know will not be paid regularly', in this case the drawer had only been in business a short time and Anderson expected 'a good deal of trouble' in retiring the bill.[148] Craig thought that banks had to show a mixture of flexibility and firmness. Noting in 1822 that other banks had moved to reduce the discount rate for bills of exchange to 4 per cent, he pointed out to the bank's managers how unwise it was 'to stand out', particularly as he anticipated that parliament would legislate to make 4 per cent the general rule. It was better to discount at that rate now 'with a good grace as then with a bad one' and, in fact, reducing it even further would help to generate 'more lively business' from the landed interest than 'has been derived from it for these last eight or ten years'.[149]

CONCLUSION

Craig's banking correspondence is not always dry and businesslike. For example, when Elliot Anderson responded to a complaint about the payment of orders by Rev. Cormack of Stow, he injected some fun. Anderson explained that the bank had nothing to do with the timing of orders for payment, all it had to do

> is to *pay them* when they are *presented* taking care only that their date is not *subsequent* to the day on which they are *paid*. If we had committed the 'sin' you mention & charged your account of the dates of the Orders it would have been a 'sin' of *Interest* & not of *Commission* (in the mercantile sense of the word) the being guilty of which would have cost you 8d.[150]

According to Clifford Gulvin, banks played 'only a small part in the Scottish woollen industry before the 1820s'.[151] Craig's correspondence provides evidence

---

[146] This was the elder brother of John Ballantyne, Scott's confidante, who died on 16 Jun. 1821.
[147] SBA/1303/2/101, Craig/James Ballantyne, 3 Heriot Row, Edinburgh, 10 Aug. 1821.
[148] SBA/1303/5/188, Anderson/James Burnett, Edinburgh, 15 Jan. 1828.
[149] SBA/1303/3/16, Craig/LBC, 13 Jul. 1822. The Bank of England decided in July to discount bills at 4 per cent and Craig became aware of this quickly: Munn, *Scottish Provincial Banking Companies*, 186.
[150] SBA/1303/6/457, Anderson/Cormack 20 Feb. 1833.
[151] Gulvin, *The Tweedmakers*, 62.

of bankers' burgeoning interest in that and other industries. His activities reinforced his position as a lynchpin between his clients, particularly in the local merchant community, and the Leith Bank. His commitment to banking required careful attention and long hours. When the carrier was to leave early next day, he was happy to stay up until midnight in order to ensure that he sent 'what may be worth while' to Leith.[152]

Craig's letters reflect serious engagement with banking matters and place him firmly within a banking fraternity that included new institutions such as the Clydesdale Bank and bank agents across the country.[153] He communicated regularly, for example, with Robert Paul, general manager of the Commercial Bank of Scotland in Edinburgh, a notable figure in contemporary banking.[154] Operating a bank agency was a very different experience from that of other practitioners who, like the Hamilton writer Thomas Dykes, engaged in sheriff court litigation on behalf of local bank branches. When Dykes described himself as 'Agent of the Paisley Union Bank' he did not mean branch agent.[155] He meant simply that he had a mandate to represent the bank in sheriff court litigation and, consequently, his letter books are much less bank orientated than those of Craig.

Banking, however, could be a hazardous business. There is no direct evidence as to when Craig took the fateful decision to become a partner in the Leith Bank. In 1833, in a letter to the bank's Henry Johnston, he expressed sorrow at hearing of a court decision Johnson had mentioned 'as to N.P.'s who are partners of Banks'.[156] He noted that James Erskine, of Curle & Erskine, who was visiting his office as he wrote, had heard of the case (his partner was a notary) but been told by the British Linen Company Bank that no final decision had been taken.[157] The decision referred to must have been the Outer House judgment in a case involving the Leith Bank which was later reported on appeal.[158] The judgment was to the effect that a notary public could not validly protest the non-payment of a bill which he had personally drawn and indorsed (the protest being a formal procedure involving a notarial instrument of protest). The decision, however, did not prevent notaries functioning as partners in banks (as evidenced by Craig's own promotion as partner in the Leith Bank). That Craig did personally protest bills as a notary is attested by a letter in 1827.[159]

At the head office, Craig found his business partners to be like-minded. He was not shy in expressing his political principles to them. In 1835, after the formation

---

[152] SBA/1303/2/151, Craig/LBC, 5 Nov. 1821.
[153] E.g. SBA/1303/8/399, Craig/James Fleming, manager, Clydesdale Banking Company, Edinburgh, 31 Dec. 1838.
[154] E.g. Checkland, *Scottish Banking*, 362–3, 441–2.
[155] Glasgow City Archives [GCA], T-DY/1/1/5, Dykes/Allan Fullarton, writer, Glasgow, 19 Nov. 1823.
[156] SBA/1303/6/385, Craig/Henry Johnston, 27 May 1833.
[157] Erskine's partner, James Curle, was admitted as a notary on 12 Feb. 1812: Finlay, ed., *ARNP 1800–1899*, I, no. 592. Sir Walter Scott, as clerk of session, subscribed the certificate of Curle's taking the oath of admission: NLS, Acc. 9430, fo. 92. On James Erskine, see above, p. 126.
[158] *Leith Bank v Walker's Trustees* (1836) 14 S. 332.
[159] SBA/1303/5/6, Anderson/Gibson & Hector WS, 19 Jan. 1827.

of Robert Peel's first (minority) government, he told the bank's managers that 'I could not figure a better Ministry than the one now formed & the Country is of the same opinion though too many of its inhabitants don't wish to acknowledge it'.[160] While he occasionally disagreed with the managers, he respected them and, as their agent, deferred to their opinion. When William Currie in Linthill, in the parish of Lilliesleaf, made a novel request in respect of his account, Craig indicated that he was willing to allow him to be overdrawn for small sums when they could soon be replaced. If the measure he had proposed were to apply generally, however, it would 'not only be departing from all established rules in a Bank but might in many instances prove hurtful' and it was a matter for head office whether to allow it.[161]

More commonly, however, Craig was assertive, if not imperious, in the banking side of his activities. Regular failures meant he well knew the risks of banking; indeed, as late as 1832, he himself still had a claim on the trustee for the Falkirk Union Bank which had failed as long ago as 1816.[162] Unfortunately for him, the creation of further joint-stock banks in the 1830s, and the expansion of branch networks by existing banks, brought too high a level of competition for the Leith Banking Company to survive.[163] The Bank of Scotland, for example, more than doubled its number of branches between 1807 and 1850.[164] In becoming a partner Craig was exposed to unlimited liability and, despite his confidence and wise words of advice to others, it was his involvement in banking that led to the disaster that engulfed the last year of his life.

---

[160] SBA/1303/7/42, Craig/LBC, 5 Jan. 1835.
[161] SBA/1303/3/67, Craig/William Currie, Linthill, 23 Oct. 1822.
[162] SBA/1303/6/336, Craig/A. Macfarlane, Falkirk, 29 Nov. 1832.
[163] Munn, *Scottish Provincial Banking Companies*, 86.
[164] H. M. Boot, 'Salaries and career earnings in the Bank of Scotland, 1730–1880' 44 (1991) *Economic History Review*, 629, 631.

Chapter 6

Borders Law Agent

Craig's letters illustrate the everyday concerns of a provincial law agent, demonstrating familiarity with all aspects of legal practice even if Craig himself did not carry them out personally. They show him undertaking tasks typical of writers, such as acting as a professional trustee, and operating as part of a professional network with other law agents. In 1837, however, Donald Horne made the erroneous claim that Craig did not 'practise as a writer generally'.[1] Prior to becoming a political agent in January 1833, Horne does not seem to have known Craig.[2] It may be that Craig, in his fifties when his partnership with William Rutherford began in 1836, focused on banking and the affairs of his major clients while Rutherford took on the bulk of the more general work and this may have influenced Horne's perception. Even if true, in earlier years, Craig certainly undertook general practice. He described himself as a writer in newspaper advertisements and contributed to the local writers' widows' fund.[3] In 1815 he was designed 'writer' in a civil action and John Paterson referred to him variously as 'writer' and 'banker' in his firm's letter book.[4] Craig, as usual, obtained an attorney certificate in 1835 which was sent to Andrew Lang to be recorded.[5] The following year, now working in partnership, he neglected a certificate but he took one again in November 1838.[6]

Setting aside his banking correspondence, Craig's letter books show similarities to those of contemporary local law agents, like Thomas Dykes (1792–1876) in Hamilton and James Russel (c.1788–1858) in Falkirk, although as procurators their focus was not identical to his.[7] His grasp of agricultural leases was discussed in an earlier chapter, but the range of his work reflects an understanding of the disparate areas of law relevant to his clients' needs.

---

[1] House of Commons, *First Report from Select Committee on Fictitious Votes (Scotland)* (1837), Minutes of Evidence, 259.

[2] Craig's earliest letter to Horne is in 1834: SBA/1303/7/14, Craig/D. Horne, 23 Sep. 1834. On Horne, see Hutchison, 'Party Principles in Scottish Political Culture', 396.

[3] E.g. *Caledonian Mercury*, 12 Feb. 1818, p. 5; SBA/1303/3/194, Craig/William Reid, writer, Jedburgh, 19 Jun. 1823. On the Borders society of lawyers, see Chapter 1.

[4] NRS, Scott of Gala papers, GD477/122/18; SBA, D/45/35/2, RPLB 1818–1820, fos. 20, 113, 278, 286, 292, 315, 316, 337.

[5] SBA/1303/7/116, Anderson/Andrew Lang, 14 Nov. 1835. George Rodger paid 8s for his procurator's certificate in Nov. 1818: RPCB, fo. 7.

[6] SBA/1303/7/299, C&R/William Turnbull, 24 Nov. 1836; SBA/1303/8/393, idem, 21 Dec. 1838.

[7] GCA, T-DY/1/1-4; Falkirk Archives, Callendar House, Falkirk, A1887.002, A1887.003.

LEGAL EDUCATION

Nothing specific is known about Craig's legal education but the experience of his early acquaintance, William Jerdan (1782–1869), son of a baron bailie of Kelso, was perhaps not dissimilar to his own. Jerdan trained in law before moving to London where he became famous as editor of the *Literary Gazette*.[8] According to his autobiography, he spent part of his youth 'scribbling in the office of Mr James Hume a writer (as attorneys or solicitors in Scotland were called) and distributor of stamps for Berwickshire'.[9] Hume entertained clients at home and Jerdan benefited from exposure to 'a good deal of good company', perhaps including Craig and his father. It is possible that, like David Spence in Melrose and the Jedburgh sheriff clerk William Rutherford, he passed some time working in an Edinburgh law office.[10]

Craig's apprentice master (most likely his father) would have tutored him in the creation and transmission of heritable and personal rights. He would have been taught about the regulation of feudal rights; the different forms of landholding (such as ward-holding, blench-holding and burgage tenure in burghs), and about charters, sasines and warrandice. Instruction in the various types of legal obligation, and the deeds by which they might be constituted, would have been given, as well as the technical training necessary to understand and draft the various essential clauses required in common types of bonds, contracts and securities. He would have been shown how to draft the substantive and formal parts of instruments, such as instruments of sasine in which it was necessary to understand the respective roles of feudal superior (or his bailie), the vassal (or his attorney) and the notary.[11] He would also have learned the essentials of book-keeping and banking practice.

Professional competence is obvious from Craig's correspondence, but was formally attested by his completion of an apprenticeship (at an unknown date) and, at the age of twenty-two, his admission as a notary public.[12] While the latter did not involve a particularly rigorous examination, it provided the status to authenticate certain types of deed and to participate fully in conveyancing and commercial matters. His cautioner (guarantor) upon admission was Archibald Gibson of Ladhope WS who, unusually, was also one of his examiners and later became his client.

Key to training and future practice would have been access to books, but little is known of Craig's library. He probably owned much of it before the surviving correspondence begins. There are letters to the Edinburgh bookseller Alexander Peat but these relate to sealing wax and the return of unwanted books, such as

---

[8] SBA/1303/3/106, Craig/W. A. Schipp, London, 11 Jan. 1823. Craig was happy to hear that Jerdan was 'making such a respectable figure in the world'.

[9] W. Jerdan, *Autobiography of William Jerdan* (London: Hall, Vertue & Co., 1852), 23.

[10] Spence, *Tenacious of the Past*, ed. King & Tulloch, 36.

[11] Cf. Glasgow University Library, Special Collections, MS Murray 330, fo. 83.

[12] Finlay, ed., *ARNP 1800–1899*, I, no. 199.

'Glen on Bills' and 'Connell on the Law of Parishes', rather than books purchased, although he had ample opportunities to supplement his book collection.[13] Craig would have held manuscript volumes containing pro-forma styles of document in common legal use, such as leases, bonds and documents required in conveyancing. Some bonds in local use reflected 'what the practitioners hereabouts have always adopted from the Juridical Styles', suggesting variance in detail from equivalent bonds elsewhere.[14]

Craig kept up with case law, sometimes referring to recent Court of Session decisions, and had access to law reports and statutes as well as detailed case reports in the local press. Occasionally he was confident of the law but struggled to find relevant authority. In one case, involving ownership of a crop in circumstances where a tenant was being removed, he told Thomas Scott that their client should be able to prevail 'as I have read of similar decisions I think altho' I cannot just now turn them up'.[15] Research materials were certainly available and amongst his professional brethren Craig both borrowed and lent books and other resources.

Resort was occasionally made to Counsel's opinion. In one case William Rutherford, convinced the sheriff depute was wrongly applying new rules introduced under the Bankruptcy (Scotland) Act 1839, obtained both counsel's opinion and that of William Alexander WS who had published a book on the legislation.[16] The sheriff's error, he complained, 'is likely to lead us all into a great deal of ill-paid trouble if nothing worse'. Such criticism is characteristic of contemporary litigators' correspondence. Sheriffs substitute, particularly, were sometimes accused of adopting 'very absurd' and 'quite wrong' positions.[17]

CRAIG'S NETWORK

Craig's correspondence places him within a network of lawyers whose services he required. He needed others (particularly writers to the signet) to draft documents which he could not lawfully draft; to speak for clients in courts where he had no right of audience (procurators); to execute legal instruments in places he lacked time to visit (messengers-at-arms); to supply him with materials, such as stamped paper, essential to his business (distributors of stamps); and to carry out specific tasks, such as the registration of documents (keepers of local registers). In some contexts, he had a choice about whom to employ, and indeed he employed a variety of procurators, writers to the signet and messengers on an ad hoc basis, but

---

[13] SBA/1303/3/250, Craig/A. Peat, bookseller, Edinburgh, 22 Sep. 1823; SBA/1303/4/26, idem, 9 Aug. 1824.

[14] SBA/1303/6/279, Anderson/Adam Paterson WS, 19 Apr. 1832.

[15] SBA/1303/6/214, 17 Aug. 1831, Craig/Thomas Scott, writer, Melrose.

[16] SBA/1303/8/605, Rutherford/William Rutherford, sheriff clerk, Jedburgh, 18 Oct. 1839; William Alexander, *Digest of the Bankrupt Act for Scotland, 2d and 3d Victoria, cap. XLI* (Edinburgh, 1839).

[17] E.g. GCA, T-DY/1/1/5, Dykes/Allan Fullerton, 11 Jul. 1823; ibid., Dykes/Captain Cross, Woodhead, 17 Nov. 1823.

it was sensible to use trusted individuals or firms repeatedly to deal with routine business and that is generally what he did.

Lawyers were therefore regular correspondents, including his own Edinburgh agents, Tait & Bruce WS and Gala's agents, Tod & Romanes WS. Writers to the signet were generally based in Edinburgh where, as members of the College of Justice, they enjoyed a number of privileges, not least the right to draft certain documents for use in conveyancing, debt recovery and Court of Session litigation.[18] Members of the WS Society, and other Court of Session agents, facilitated and advised across Scotland upon a wide range of legal business.[19] Locally, Craig especially relied on the firms of Rodger & Paterson in Selkirk and Erskine & Curle in Melrose (Tory political agents like himself), as well as George Reid in Jedburgh, Thomas Scott in Lauder and John Spence in Earlston.[20] Politics were no obstacle, however, since he also employed Whigs, such as the Melrose firm Spence & Thomson and the Galashiels writer and banker Robert Haldane.

Town clerks and sheriff clerks feature prominently, chief among them the Selkirkshire sheriff clerk, Andrew Lang.[21] Lang, whose father, John, had also been sheriff clerk and whose brother, William (1791–1837), was a WS, corresponded regularly. He kept the commissary court book in which inventories of estates were recorded.[22] Also in Selkirk was George Rodger of Bridgelands, law agent and town clerk, and his son, Peter, who was for some time, as his father had been, procurator fiscal. In Jedburgh, there was the sheriff clerk William Rutherford who administered the affairs of the local society of writers.[23] There were also lawyers whose function made them essential. John and William Smith, writers in Kelso, kept the particular register of sasines for Roxburgh, Selkirk and Peebles. William Turnbull, in Peebles, supplied the stamped paper upon which such sasines and other transactions were recorded. As well as these, Craig dealt with clerks to road trustees and clerks of supply. Sometimes he sent circulars to several parties, as he did when trying to discover who had subscribed, in Melrose, Peebles, Kelso, Jedburgh and Lanark, to a survey promoting a Newcastle to Glasgow railway line in 1837.[24]

---

[18] See J. Finlay, *The Community of the College of Justice* (Edinburgh, 2015), chapter 6.

[19] On the SSC Society, see Barclay, *The S.S.C. Story*.

[20] Erskine & Curle became the firm of Curle & Erskine after the death of Charles Erskine in 1825: SBA/1303/4/154, Craig/LBC, 14 Feb. 1825. Curle, admitted as a procurator in the sheriff court of Roxburgh on 16 Jul. 1811, took over the firm: NRS, Roxburgh sheriff court, roll of procurators, SC62/27/2. Charles's son James Erskine (1810–1875), later Curle's partner, was admitted to the same court on 14 Mar. 1835 and became a notary in 1836: Finlay, ed., *ARNP 1800–1899*, I, no. 1873. John Spence (1787–1852), writer in Earlston, was elder brother of David Spence: Spence, *Tenacious of the Past*, ed. King & Tulloch, 30, 62.

[21] Lang was sheriff clerk, commissary clerk, sub-distributor of stamps and clerk to the Selkirkshire Road Trustees.

[22] E.g. SBA/1303/8/180, Craig/Andrew Lang, 9 Mar. 1838.

[23] This William Rutherford, a friend of James Curle, was apparently related to Craig's partner but the family background is obscure. Craig's partner was son of the Jedburgh writer, Alexander Rutherford (c.1760–1845).

[24] SBA/1303/8/14, 14 Aug. 1837.

Craig's legal work often involved debt recovery. This might arise from straightforward loans that had not been repaid; accumulated arrears of rent, or non-payment for goods or services. He was also involved in buying, selling and leasing land and buildings. Sometimes he did this with a political end in view, since voting was based on a property qualification and he helped clients qualify to vote if they were the 'right sort of' people.[25] He also dealt with property law problems, such as encroachment on land and succession to property. Whenever he sent deeds to be signed and witnesses, he gave clear instructions to ensure proper attestation.[26]

Craig's correspondence tells us about clients and their affairs but also reveals the wider community of Borders lawyers. Some, like him, were also bank agents. Robert Darling, agent for the Bank of Scotland in Kelso, is an example, as are John Welsh of the British Linen Bank in Peebles; David Spence agent in Melrose for the private Edinburgh bank of Ramsay, Bonar & Company, and Thomas Bowhill of the Commercial Bank of Scotland in Eyemouth.[27] Some practised primarily as messengers-at-arms, such as Gilbert Amos in Hawick (messengers were essentially debt collectors, but Amos, as we shall see, apparently forgot that the payments he collected belonged to others and not himself). Some were procurators, active before the local courts, and Craig employed them to plead in cases on behalf of his clients.

Craig and his colleagues also worked with writers in distant counties, employing them and being employed by them in turn. This included places such as Glasgow, Musselburgh, Perth and Aberdeen.[28] Elliot Anderson asked a correspondent in Biggar in Lanarkshire to put a bill

> into the hands of a respectable Writer to recover payment as I have long since lost track of the professional Gentlemen in your 'gude toun' – I should suppose Mr Lamb to be a good hand if he does business of that kind.[29]

This referred to John Lamb, a writer in Lanark, of whom Anderson clearly had prior experience.[30]

In such cases normally what was required was enforcement action, but Craig did not always know the correct jurisdiction in which a debtor resided. An interesting example involved his own future client, Dr William Colvin, who was living in Brierybank in Berwickshire in 1823. Craig wanted to serve an arrestment on

[25] SBA/1303/7/322, Craig/William Kerr-Loraine, Manse, Musselburgh, 2 Jan. 1837.
[26] E.g. SBA/1303/6/227, Craig/John Thorburn, Merchant 75 Hanover St [Edinburgh], 3 Oct. 1831; SBA/1303/6/351, Craig/Rev. William Harper, Leven, 26 Jan. 1833.
[27] Craig mentions Spence's appointment in 1823: SBA/1303/3/206, Craig/LBC, 7 Jul. 1823; for Bowhill, SBA/1303/7/525, 685. Spence had earlier been agent for Borthwick, Gilchrist & Co., see, above, p. 101.
[28] E.g. SBA/1303/5/96, Craig/Munn & Smith, writers, Glasgow, 23 Jul. 1827; SBA/1303/3/200, Craig/Thomas Wright, solicitor, Musselburgh, 2 Aug. 1823; SBA/1303/3/271, Robert Peddie, writer, Perth, 11 Nov. 1823; SBA/1303/2/35, Anderson/John Ewing, advocate in Aberdeen, 7 May 1821.
[29] SBA/1303/4/421, Anderson/Mr Thomson, Castle Yett, 19 Jul. 1826.
[30] Finlay, ed., *ARNP 1700–1799*, II, no. 2769.

him and, thinking Brierybank might be in East Lothian, asked Tait & Bruce to employ the Haddington writer Archibald Todrick to deal with it.[31] Todrick, agent for the Bank of Scotland, was already familiar to him.

The Buckholmside Brewery

Networking can also be seen early in Craig's career when, in 1809, he wound up the unsuccessful Buckholmside Brewery.[32] He employed the Selkirk firm Rodger & Paterson to undertake diligence to recover sums owing to the brewery's partners (himself included).[33] There were some 224 debtors to be written to and, in some cases, taken before Selkirk commissary court to recover sums outstanding.[34] For cases before the commissaries of Lauder, Thomas Scott, procurator in that burgh, was instructed to summon debtors resident there and in Earlston, Gordon, and neighbouring areas. Likewise, procurators were paid to bring actions in the sheriff courts at Peebles and Edinburgh.[35] Also involved in these processes was the firm of Gibson, Oliphant & Cleghorn WS.[36] Here we find the link to Edinburgh lawyers that was essential in debt recovery procedures. What is worth noting, however, is continuity: over a decade later, Craig still worked with almost all these lawyers.

LAWYERS AND LITIGATION

Edinburgh Agents

Why were so many Edinburgh lawyers correspondents? There are several reasons for this. Many were Court of Session practitioners with a monopoly on the provision of documents required in conveyancing and debt recovery procedure. Secondly, as we have seen, these practitioners were a good source of funds to be lent locally to clients. Thirdly, they could provide or obtain authoritative opinions on difficult points of law. Finally, they could also undertake a range of services in Edinburgh, including debt collection and the recording of deeds in central registers.

Craig worked most closely with his own agents, Tait & Bruce WS, until that firm was dissolved at the end of 1827.[37] He then worked with Gibson & Hector WS which, in the course of 1826, succeeded in business the long-standing firm of

---

[31] SBA/1303/3/135, Craig/Tait & Bruce WS, 12 Mar. 1823. Similarly, in 1834 Elliot Anderson assumed Mayshiel was in the commissariat of Haddingtonshire: SBA/1303/6/456, Anderson/Todrick, 18 Feb. 1834.

[32] See Chapter 1.

[33] SBA, Copy state of accounts between Craig and Rodger & Paterson, D/45/13/13.

[34] SBA, Business account, Craig to Rodger & Paterson, D/45/13/7.

[35] James Cairns in Peebles and the Edinburgh solicitor at law John Gray were the writers employed.

[36] SBA, Account of business Mr George Craig to Rodger & Paterson, 13 Apr. 1810, D/45/13/8.

[37] The winding-up of Tait & Bruce is mentioned in passing: SBA/1303/5/177, Craig/Thomas Gibson, Windydoors, 27 Dec. 1827. Partnerships at this period tended to last five to ten years.

Gibson & Oliphant WS (the two partners in which had been in business together since 1797, albeit for some of that time with a third partner, David Cleghorn).[38] He later recommended Gibson & Hector to a Glasgow correspondent who was one of several executors involved in administering an estate:

> I could recommend none more respectable than these Gentlemen who succeeded in business to one of the oldest & most respectable Firms of WSs about 15 years ago.[39] I would far recommend the propriety of this in order that the whole management might be under *one House*, both as being less expensive than employing different agents, & also as avoiding the risk of these agents differing in opinion among themselves upon the different points that may arise.[40]

Key players in these firms were Archibald Gibson of Ladhope (1760–1845) and his son John (1789–1879). The latter was Torwoodlee's Edinburgh agent with whom Craig exchanged accounts annually and to whom he sent extracts from the Torwoodlee cash book.[41] In the later 1830s, Craig also worked closely with Donald Horne WS in a range of business, not simply related to politics, and also his brother-in-law Robert Laidlaw SSC. Many others, however, feature whenever business brought them within Craig's orbit.

What is notable, but not surprising, is the extent to which his closest contacts were, like the Gibsons, local men. Tait & Bruce, for example, comprised Craig's second cousin, John Tait of Pirn (1783–1838) and Thomas Bruce of Langlee (1785–1850) who, in 1824, became a depute clerk of session as his father had been before him. Tait became a WS in 1808, having apprenticed under Archibald Gibson, while Bruce entered the WS Society in 1810 following apprenticeship with Archibald Tod of Drygrange. Gibson had, of course, been Craig's cautioner when he became a notary public in 1805. So closely connected were Tait & Bruce to the region (Bruce lived at Langlee when not in Edinburgh) that they had their own direct business arrangements with local practitioners. For example, the Selkirk messenger John Paterson had an 'understanding' with them in relation to fees.[42] Gala's Edinburgh agents, John Tod WS & John Romanes, similarly had many local connections and counted Hawick burgh council among their clients.[43]

---

[38] The firm originated in 1797 with Archibald Gibson and Charles Oliphant (1771–1852): NRS, GD443/11. David Cleghorn (1775–1840), who later became crown agent, was briefly a partner (c.1809–1812).

[39] This places the dissolution of Gibson & Oliphant around 1820, which is too early.

[40] SBA/1303/7/49, Craig/William Piccary, stationer, Dumbarton, 24 Feb. 1835. The sense here is that each executor should not employ their own Edinburgh agent; it was best to act as a body with one firm providing advice.

[41] E.g. SBA/1303/5/204, Craig/John Gibson WS 31 Jan. 1828; SBA/1303/5/103, Craig/Gibson & Hector WS, 9 Aug. 1827. The partners in Gibson & Hector were John Gibson and David Hector (1802–1874).

[42] SBA/1303/3/180, Craig/Tait & Bruce WS, 27 May 1823.

[43] HC Report, *Municipal Corporations*, 84.

In his trips to Edinburgh, Craig often stopped at the offices of Tait & Bruce and other lawyers as well as at the Leith Bank head office. His relationship with his Edinburgh agents, however, was not always smooth. On one occasion he was upset at having been inveigled into a collusive arrangement to bring an action. Having 'lent' Tait & Bruce his name, he was found liable for expenses despite having had nothing to gain from the outcome ('for the loan of my name to serve my friends, I am now asked to pay down £70 not a penny of which will ever be recovered').[44] However, mutual interest, and a shared understanding of local people, geography and Borders affairs, ensured the longevity of his most important relationships with Edinburgh agents.

Local Writers

Craig maintained contact with many local and provincial writers. In the first six months of 1827, for example, he wrote to eleven legal practitioners in Edinburgh and thirteen who practised variously in Melrose, Kelso, Galashiels, Duns, Lauder, Hawick and Glasgow. Of particular importance were James Curle of Curle & Erskine in Melrose; John Welsh in Peebles and John Romanes in Lauder.

Craig and the local writers he employed periodically rendered accounts to each other for monies collected and disbursed. Thomas Scott in Lauder, for instance, having been asked to collect money from a roup, was expected to send a statement of account and to credit himself with the amount collected.[45] Scott had been a procurator in Lauder burgh court and Greenlaw sheriff court before moving to Melrose (and seems to have been very prominent locally); afterwards, Craig employed another writer, Alexander Crawford, to bring cases in Lauder and Greenlaw.[46]

Deeds and other papers were borrowed from other local offices when required and lawyers generally had good systems for record retrieval. Craig instantly knew that Gala's ancestors had the exclusive right of salmon fishing at a particular spot between the mouth of the Ettrick and Rinkhaugh, where Torwoodlee's servant was caught fishing in 1839, because that right 'was clearly described in the Gala Title deeds'.[47] These papers, held between Craig's office and that of Tod & Romanes, were very familiar to him.[48] Instant retrieval, however, was not always possible. Craig elsewhere mentions 'the great labour' of collecting scattered deeds relating to Longhaugh 'from different offices in Edinburgh'.[49] In 1837, he tried to recover the papers in a process between George Fairholme and the Gordon

---

[44]   SBA/1303/4/132, Craig/Tait & Bruce, 17 Dec. 1824.
[45]   SBA/1303/3/51, Craig/Thomas Scott, writer, Lauder, 21 Sep. 1822.
[46]   SBA/1303/7/410, Craig/Alexander Crawford, 6 Apr. 1837. See also the report of a 'long historical sketch' given by Scott at a dinner in honours of Sir Thomas Makdougall Brisbane in Kelso: *Kelso Mail*, no. 1836, 3 Mar. 1836. Scott was a procurator successively in Berwickshire and Roxburghshire.
[47]   SBA/1303/7/549, Craig/Gala, 7 Aug. 1839.
[48]   SBA/1303/8/491, Craig/Curle & Erskine, 11 May 1839.
[49]   SBA/1303/3/185, Craig/Tait & Bruce WS, 3 Jun. 1823.

feuars undertaken in the period 1824–1826 in Lauder burgh court and asked Alexander Crawford to find them. They were not with Thomas Scott, Fairholme's then procurator, but Craig thought they were probably in the burgh clerk's office.[50] There was always a risk of documents going missing, perhaps by being used in court and then mislaid. While looking out a process requested by a client, Elliot Anderson informed Robert Haldane that he had noticed 'that some of the papers appear to be your property' and he sent them on.[51] He also noted that Haldane had made copies of certain papers for which the client had not paid him, offering him payment if he sent in his account.

Writers did not necessarily make a living from the law, however flexible they might be in the services they provided. In 1826 Anderson described the writer Walter Hogg, son of a Selkirk manufacturer, as having 'almost no business & no funds, I should suppose, of any kind'.[52] When the Galashiels writer John Paterson died in December 1823, he left a widow and six young children living in a house only half of which he had owned (Craig, on Gala's behalf, had negotiated the lease of his garden in 1819).[53] As Craig told a correspondent, 'I have not heard how his affairs are likely to turn out but I should suppose not well'.[54] Law agents were occasionally sequestrated and this occurred to David Spence whose personal bankruptcy, following poor investments, dissolved the Melrose firm of Spence & Thomson in 1839.[55]

Procurators

Procurators were writers who had been formally admitted to plead in the local courts, a task which required knowledge of court procedure. Some procurators known to Craig had long experience. Charles Erskine in Melrose, for example, was practising in Jedburgh sheriff court as early as 1800 (this was the year Sir Walter Scott, describing him as 'an excellent young man', commissioned him as his sheriff substitute).[56] Other familiar names in Craig's correspondence were the Kelso writers William Smith, Robert Bruce and James Darling; the Hawick writer, John Oliver, and the Jedburgh writer, Francis Harkness. With insufficient business for court practitioners to confine themselves to litigation, they often described themselves in admission books as 'procurator, notary public and conveyancer' reflecting the broader scope of their activity.

[50] SBA/1303/8/17, Craig/Alexander Crawford, writer, Lauder, 18 Aug. 1837.
[51] SBA/1303/6/311, Anderson/Robert Haldane, Galashiels, 4 Apr. 1833.
[52] SBA/1303/4/371, Anderson/Sir William Forbes & Co., Edinburgh, 18 Apr. 1826. The first reference to Hogg jr is on 22 Jan. 1825, SBA/1303/4/146.
[53] NRS, Scott of Gala papers, GD477/455/43 (17 Apr. 1819).
[54] SBA/1303/3/292, Craig/Robert Roy WS, 20 Dec. 1823. This John Paterson is not to be confused with the Selkirk writer and messenger John Paterson.
[55] NRS, CS230/SEQNS/S/3/16. Spence's partner was Robert Gillon Thomson (b. 1795).
[56] NRS, Jedburgh sheriff court, Register of Law agents, SC62/27/1, fo. 7 (14 Jan. 1800); Chisholm, *Sir Walter Scott as a Judge*, 8; NRS, Buccleuch papers, GD224/663/6/29. Erskine was slightly older than Scott.

As court practitioners, procurators borrowed up processes, drafted petitions and defences, and brought and defended legal actions competent to the court in which they worked. The Edinburgh law agent William Duguid mistook Craig for such a procurator in 1833, apparently asking him to get hold of a process depending in Peebles. He was soon corrected:

> I never resided in Selkirk, nor do I act as a procurator before the sheriff court of Peebles, & I am sorry at having as little connection with that County that I cannot name any writer there to borrow up the process . . .[57]

If a summons were to be raised for court action, Craig would directly instruct a procurator to raise it or advise his client to do so. An example is his advice to James Brydon in Woodlaw when Brydon's fellow joint tenant, Goodfellow, sold their crop by auction solely in his own name. Craig suggested raising an action immediately to recover Brydon's share and making an arrestment in the purchaser's hands, adding 'Mr Paterson writer here will do this for you on sending him a state of it, or any other procurator before the Sheriff Court at Selkirk'.[58] In an action involving George Fairholme in 1825, when Craig was dissatisfied with the sheriff substitute's interlocutor, he sent a representation to the writer George Reid in Jedburgh asking him to present it in court.[59] All things being equal, Craig might leave the choice of court to the procurator's discretion, as he did in 1831 when he sent the correspondence in the case to Spence & Thomson in Melrose and thought them the better judge of whether the summons should be 'before the sheriff or the Justices'.[60] In his typical style, however, he gave them a hint favouring the latter.

The roll of procurators in the sheriff court of Selkirkshire, presided over by Sir Walter Scott at the time, does not survive before 1825.[61] When John Paterson, whom Craig had employed for Selkirk sheriff court business, died in early December 1823 there was 'some talk of another procurator or even two' settling locally.[62] The only three admissions recorded in the period 1825–1843 were Peter Rodger (1825), Robert Paton WS (undated) and Craig's partner, William Rutherford (1836). Paton was procurator fiscal of Selkirk in the 1840s and secretary of the Selkirk Savings Bank. The later letter books contain considerable correspondence with him as a private practitioner both from Craig and, to a greater extent, his partner Rutherford. Rutherford was an active litigator but he also dealt with other

---

[57] SBA/1303/6/366, Craig/William Duguid, solicitor, Edinburgh, 18 Mar. 1833.
[58] SBA/1303/2/88, Craig/James Brydon, 11 Dec. 1822. An arrestment was taken in the hands of a debtor's debtor, meaning simply that the purchaser, in this case Mr Hall, would be prevented from handing over funds to Goodfellow pending court action which might result in part of the arrested fund being paid to Brydon.
[59] SBA/1303/4/165, Craig/George Reid, 5 Mar. 1825.
[60] SBA/1303/6/242, Craig/Spence & Thomson, Melrose, 11 Nov. 1831.
[61] NRS, Roll of Law agents practising before the Sheriff Court of Selkirkshire, SC63/17/1/1.
[62] SBA/1303/3/289, Anderson/William Turnbull, Peebles, 17 Dec. 1823. Walter Hogg (mentioned *infra*) may have been the procurator mentioned.

matters, including aspects of land management and notarial work.[63] He employed Paton to cover for him, when he had to attend 'the appeal court' in 1839, asking him to 'get out a small debt summons' against a party and have it executed.[64] Such co-operation between procurators was characteristic of the profession.

An interesting matter thrust into Craig's hands by the innkeeper William Dickson prompted a letter to Paton in 1837 and gives a flavour of some of the issues before the sheriff court. It was one of many cases involving horses.[65] Dickson had been informed by Paton of alleged damage to the tail of a horse, belonging to a man named Tenant, when it was kept in Dickson's stable a month before. Dickson strongly denied any damage, claiming that the horse's tail was 'as long when it went out as when it came in'.[66] He instructed Craig 'to say he will not pay one penny of damages and Mr Tenant will at once raise this threatened action without troubling him with any more letters'. If no action was raised within ten days, Craig was instructed to recover his expenses.

As befits a member of the Abbotsford Hunt, Craig demonstrated good equine knowledge. An instance occurred when one of a pair of carriage horses purchased by Thomas Tod of Drygrange turned out to be a 'riggling' unfit for purpose. With Tod about to leave for London, it was left to Craig to write to his brother, John Tod WS, to resolve the matter. Craig noted that the seller had warranted that both horses were 'sound & free of blemish, but everyone knows that a Riggling is what is termed in horse flesh *an unclean horse* so quite within his warrandice'.[67] Later the same year, Craig found himself looking for a stout pair of cart horses for the same client, one of the many ancillary tasks a law agent might find himself performing from time to time.[68]

Litigation

Thanks to Rutherford's recruitment in 1836, Craig & Rutherford undertook sheriff court litigation for which Craig, in the past, would have employed other procurators. That does not mean that Craig himself was uninformed about litigation or court strategy. He usually had firm views about whether to litigate and the appropriate legal points to emphasise when doing so; he certainly 'perused' procurators' replies and answers before they went to the sheriff court.[69] Some clients proved anxious litigants, including Robert Fyshe who, when 'short of funds' in 1823, engaged in an action in Edinburgh to recover fees from the parent of one of his pupils. Elliot Anderson corresponded at length with the Edinburgh

[63] E.g. SBA/1303/8/663, C&R/John Henderson, Innkeeper, Gordon, 19 Dec. 1839.
[64] SBA/1303/8/437, Rutherford/Paton, 26 Feb. 1839. It is not clear which 'appeal court' was meant.
[65] Cf. sale of a partially blind horse: SBA/1303/4/276, Craig/James Curle, Melrose, 25 Nov. 1825.
[66] SBA/1303/8/77, Craig/Robert Paton, 6 Nov. 1837.
[67] SBA/1303/5/72, Craig/John Tod WS, 1 Jun. 1827. A warrandice is a guarantee.
[68] SBA/1303/5/141-3, Craig/Thomas Tod, Edinburgh, 17 Nov. 1827.
[69] E.g. SBA/1303/6/330, Craig/William Aitchison, Cockburnspath, 8 Nov. 1832.

practitioner J. S. Mack about it, noting that Fyshe had become 'impatient' and his enquiries 'from their frequency of late have become rather troublesome'.[70]

The language of court procedure peppers the correspondence more regularly after Rutherford became a partner and there is more discussion of litigation strategy. In one case the sheriff had given an interlocutor (i.e. made an order) which Rutherford thought was wrong, although the expense could not justify further procedure to try to have it altered. Instead, he urged his client, the Hawick skinner George Watson, to put the defender to his oath of verity and sought a mandate from him 'to authorise a reference to be put into the process to that effect'.[71] It is due to Rutherford that we find the military metaphors so beloved of contemporary litigators. In one case, for instance, he noted that the defender 'on seeing the Proof in the case has struck his flag and offered terms of capitulation'.[72]

Law could be a harsh business. Warm words sometimes disguised brutal truths. This was particularly true when it came to the removal of tenants. On the same day in 1839, for example, Rutherford wrote two letters about it. The first, to Mrs Murray at Millbank, informed her that unless she immediately paid a considerable sum towards unpaid rent the firm would be under the 'disagreeable necessity of sequestrating your effects and warning you away from the ground'.[73] The second, to Donald Horne WS, related to farms at Redfordgreen in the parish of Kirkhope west of Hawick. The outgoing tenants were being replaced by liferenters to create votes, a practice recognised as lawful in the courts.[74] Rutherford required the tacks (leases) of the former and title deeds of the latter to bring actions of removing. He added, perhaps in case another might be employed, 'I am the only procurator connected with these matters practising before the Sheriff Court of the County where the farms are situated'.[75] To add to his admission in Selkirk, he was admitted before the sheriff of Roxburghshire in 1836.[76] Admission to multiple courts, however, was not uncommon.

Fees

Craig's income from his work as a law agent is unknown but it was probably substantial. David Spence in Melrose, when he married aged twenty-six, was reputedly 'making £600 a year and had £1600 on his books'.[77] Fees for specific items of business are mentioned in Craig's correspondence, sometimes quite casually (e.g. 'fees as usual 7/6 at your debit').[78] His charge for writing a letter was typically

---

[70] SBA/1303/3/150, Anderson/J. S. Mack, Edinburgh, 11 Apr. 1823.
[71] SBA/1303/8/276, Rutherford/George Watson, 25 Jun. 1838.
[72] SBA/1303/8/225, C&R/John Rutherford, Jedburgh, 19 Apr. 1838.
[73] SBA/1303/8/429, C&R/Mrs Murray, 12 Feb. 1839.
[74] NRS, Buccleuch papers, GD224/581/15, Horne/Buccleuch, 19 Dec. 1840.
[75] Ibid., C&R/Donald Horne W, 12 Feb. 1839.
[76] NRS, Roxburgh sheriff court, roll of procurators, SC62/27/2 (28 Jan. 1836).
[77] Spence, *Tenacious of the Past*, ed., King & Tulloch, 48.
[78] SBA/1303/6/371, Anderson/James Curle, Melrose, 4 Apr. 1833.

2s 6d.[79] The fee for 'drawing' (drafting) a precept of *clare constat* was a guinea and for extending it (i.e. writing it out formally) was 7s 6d.[80] Fees for notarial activities may be estimated from the records of other writers, such as William Smith in Kelso.[81] A proper record of fees would have been kept in Craig's 'Business Day Book' but it does not survive.[82] Accounts were regularly reconciled, as when Anderson asked Tait & Bruce to send a state of their accounts up to 31 December so that they might be compared and checked 'with my book'.[83]

Craig had a financial relationship with the writers and messengers he employed or who employed him. Any sum recovered for a client they were to remit to him and, in return, he paid their fee once they presented an account of their charges. He then charged this outlay to the client. Some of his costs involved fees for obtaining or lodging documents in court. The Court of Session regulated the fees of sheriff clerks and sheriff officers by means of acts of sederunt and by the same method in 1833 a new table of fees was authorised for procurators in sheriff courts.[84]

When William Colvin objected to James Robertson, an Edinburgh agent, twice charging him a shilling for making up his account, Craig replied that he was entitled to do so under the rules. Prior to 1833, he said, these procurators were

> entitled to what was called 'a procurator fee' but this fee was found to be so oppressive that it was abolished and the table referred to put in its place, and which is upon the principle that for every piece of business done, however small, a sum is allowed for it, and the shilling charge is warranted by the Table. As to the other items of the account we consider them moderately charged.[85]

The accounts from the Buckholmside Brewery cases clearly show the various fees Rodger & Paterson charged on this head and such fees could mount up.[86] The Kelso writer William Smith, complained that, as bailie of Kelso, he 'never realized more than about eight pence farthing a day, while the procurators who attended the Court, had never less than ten times, and frequently more than twenty times the amount' on a typical court day.[87]

---

[79] E.g. SBA/1303/5/283, Anderson/Thomas Scott, Abbotsmeadow, 26 Jul. 1828.

[80] SBA/1303/2/11, Anderson/John Spence, writer, Earlston, 9 Apr. 1821.

[81] E.g. SBA, D/3, William & John Smith client papers, suggests 5/1 was the fee for a notarial protest (17 Oct. 1829).

[82] SBA/1303/3/166. One of Rodger & Paterson's Day Books does survive: SBA, D45/35/1.

[83] SBA/1303/4/150, Anderson/Tait & Bruce, 2 Jan. 1825.

[84] NRS, Court of Session, Books of Sederunt, CS1/24, fo. 159 (sheriff clerks); CS1/25, fo. 60 (procurators) fo. 98 (sheriff officers). The procurators' fee table, taking up fifty folios, came into force for one year from 12 May 1833 but was renewed thereafter.

[85] SBA/1303/7/335, Craig/William Colvin, Wood Street, Woolwich, 12 Jan. 1837.

[86] SBA, Walter Mason Collection, D/45/13/8, Business account, George Craig/Rodger & Paterson, 13 Apr. 1810.

[87] SBA, Papers of William Smith, SBA/183/10, Smith/Roxburgh, 29 Nov. 1814.

Craig had already explained to Robertson the local custom, in dividing the account between drafting the summons and presenting the arguments in court, whenever an agent such as himself employed a local court practitioner:

> In the counties around us when one agent employs another the agent employing his friend is allowed the Drawing and the agent who is the Procurator in the county gets the presenting and agency and we trust you will do the same with us.[88]

Fees could be slow in coming. An extreme case saw Craig pay a fee of £2 10s to John Spence in Earlston in 1837 for obtaining a decreet on behalf of Glasgow merchants in March 1821. Spence had unsuccessfully sought payment from the client at the time; Craig, having paid, requested reimbursement.[89]

If disputed, fees and charges relating to litigation were taxed by the sheriff clerk and, in Selkirk sheriff court, Andrew Lang audited these expenses. In 1834, for instance, objection was taken to John Paterson's charges because he had allegedly executed a horning in Selkirk while claiming the expense of executing it elsewhere.[90] When William Colvin objected in 1831 to the fee of an agent who had defended sequestration proceedings against his tenant at Mitchelston, Elliot Anderson sent him all the accounts and explained that he had examined them carefully before paying them and 'did not observe anything in the least exceeding the printed regulations that govern all writers charges'.[91] He clarified that 'the charges in sequestration cases are regulated by the amount of the rent'.[92]

Sheriff clerks had a number of administrative duties which included copying documents into their court books so that their contents were preserved. It was perhaps for a similar purpose that the papers of the Galashiels writer John Paterson, including material held on behalf of clients, were taken to Lang's office in Selkirk after Paterson's death.[93] Craig's letter books, on the other hand, were not surrendered to the sheriff clerk but retained by his partner, William Rutherford.

Arbitration

Many disputes were decided amicably by arbiters without resorting to courts. Those selected as arbiters were sometimes lawyers but often not, with a tenant farmer or a tradesman chosen by the parties to make a binding settlement. If the arbiters disagreed, a third party or 'oversman', mutually chosen by the parties or the arbiters, would decide. Submissions to arbitration are regularly mentioned in

[88] SBA/1303/7/192, C&R/James Robertson, solicitor, Edinburgh, 31 Mar. 1836.
[89] SBA/1303/8/38, Craig/Roll & Kidstone, merchants, Glasgow, 7 Sep. 1837. Why Craig took on this liability is not made clear.
[90] SBA/1303/7/114 Elliot Anderson/P. Rodger, Selkirk, 4 Nov. 1835.
[91] SBA/1303/6/134, Anderson/William Colvin, Forquhan, 22 Jan. 1831.
[92] SBA/1303/6/135.
[93] SBA/1303/3/310, Craig/McMillan & Grant WS, Edinburgh, 17 Feb. 1824.

Craig's correspondence and both Elliot Anderson and Craig acted as arbiters.[94] In a dispute between George Blaikie and his mother in 1822, in which Craig and John Paterson were the arbiters, unusually they passed one of the issues (concerning property tax) directly to Archibald Gibson WS 'from a wish to give the parties the benefit of the opinion of their learned oversman'.[95]

Craig encouraged arbitration and sometimes advised clients on appropriate arbiters. He advised Adam Fairholme, for example, not to nominate Robson at Blainslie but to go for 'John Smith or William Paterson (Sanderson & Paterson) as persons of more weight than Robson'.[96] Either choice, he thought, would do a better job than Robson of nominating an oversman.

Offering arbitration was a useful counter to threats of legal action. Anderson wrote to the writer Robert Haldane with such an offer regarding a dispute over house repairs, noting that his client was willing to 'submit the matter to respectable tradesmen'.[97] In another case, Craig's client was happy to refer the value of a threshing machine 'to tradesmen such as people constantly employed in that line like John Aimers and William Bathgate millwrights Galashiels or any other of equal respectability'.[98] Other issues commonly left to amicable settlement included the respective rights of outgoing and incoming tenants, as with the exit of George Logan from Cockburn farm. Part of the dispute was about the fallow break and whether Logan was entitled to leave the field 'in lea in place of stubble'; the former being more common in East Lothian and Berwickshire.[99] Arbitration, however, was no panacea and Craig was sometimes critical of how specific articles in submissions to arbitration were treated. In another case related to Cockburn, dealing with a subtenant, the oversman made no proper allowance for the dung that the tenant ought to have left behind 'but on the contrary mentions it to the account of *general loss*'. This appeared to Craig 'to be the most extraordinary doctrine I ever heard of & what I will not agree to'.[100]

Much reliance was placed upon the integrity of an arbiter. In a dispute over damaged corn mills, Gala and the Road Trustees referred their dispute to Thomas Bruce of Langlee despite him being Gala's neighbour. As a lawyer, Bruce was experienced in arbitration and, as a gentleman, was unquestioningly relied upon for an impartial opinion.[101]

[94] SBA/1303/2/200, Note of Messrs F. Oliver, E. Anderson, J. Murray & Thomas Frier, arbiters met at Keadslie, 28 Feb. 1822.
[95] SBA/1303/3/71, Craig/Archibald Gibson, Ladhopeburn, 6 Nov. 1822. Other elements of the case were decided by them, e.g. SBA/1303/3/41, Craig and Paterson/G. Blaikie, Kilknowe. A matter was remitted to Oliver & Anderson for a report: fo. 64, Craig and Paterson/Oliver & Anderson, Langlee & Netherbarns, 18 Oct. 1822.
[96] Ibid. fo. 46, Craig/Adam Fairholme, Chapel, 11 Sep. 1822.
[97] SBA/1303/4/298-9, Anderson/Robert Haldane, 10 Jan. 1826.
[98] SBA/1303/3/185, Craig/Mrs Tod, Drygrange, 2 Jun. 1823.
[99] SBA/1303/6/57, Craig/J. McGregor, Pit Street, 19 May 1830. 'Lea' meant land left for pasture; 'in stubble' meant that cornstalks were left in the ground after harvest.
[100] SBA/1303/6/170, Craig/John Wilson jr, Preston, 12 Apr. 1831.
[101] SBA/1303/8/37, Craig/Andrew Lang, 7 Sep. 1837.

DEBT RECOVERY

In the important sphere of debt recovery, Craig was often the middleman. The authority to proceed to diligence (the legal procedures used to recover unpaid debts) relied upon documents provided by Edinburgh lawyers, while the process itself required someone local to the debtor to carry out the necessary procedure.

When recovering debts owed to the Leith Bank, Craig normally employed his own Edinburgh agents. Sometimes he used James Smith Mack, solicitor-at-law in Edinburgh, for legal work on the bank's behalf.[102] Mack died in 1828 and, in later years, Craig relied upon his brother-in-law Robert Laidlaw SSC in such business. The procedure required letters of horning under the royal signet, signed by a Court of Session practitioner. If the client was already such a practitioner, or employed one, then so much the better. For instance, Adam Paterson WS was sent a protested bill payable to his own father, a Galashiels merchant, so that he may obtain the horning and send it to the messenger, John Paterson, in Selkirk who could enforce it against the debtor.[103] Likewise, having obtained a sheriff court decree in a case for Gala, Craig sent it directly to Gala's Edinburgh agents, Tod & Romanes WS, with a request for a horning.[104]

Letters of horning were addressed to local messengers-at-arms ordering them to require the person named in the letters to make payment under pain of rebellion and being 'put to the horn' (i.e. declared a rebel). They authorised the arrestment of funds in the hands of anyone who owed money to the debtor and also the poinding (seizure) of the debtor's goods and ultimately their sale to satisfy the debt. Thus Craig & Rutherford employed the Hawick sheriff officer, John Wilson, against Gala's former tenant, John Hobkirk, who owed rent. They instructed him 'to bring back his furniture here which you will do immediately if he does not arrange the payment', though if Hobkirk offered security for the payment Wilson was to take it.[105]

If payment failed to materialise, then a caption, another type of writ under the signet, could be obtained. Captions proceeded on the basis that the debtor had become a rebel and was subject to imprisonment. They authorised the debtor's apprehension for failure to obey a horning and imprisonment until they did so. In 1823, for example, the Galashiels Burgher minister Rev. James Henderson was apprehended under a caption at the instance of the Kelso writer John Smith and carried off to Jedburgh jail.[106]

---

[102] SBA/1303/6/39. Solicitors-at-law practised before the inferior courts in Edinburgh. See J. Finlay, 'The lower branch of the legal profession in Early Modern Scotland' 11 (2007) *Edinburgh Law Review*, 31, 60–61.

[103] SBA/1303/6/137, Anderson/Adam Paterson, 31 Jan. 1831. Paterson senior lent to Scott of Gala as well as others: NRS, Scott of Gala papers, GD477/105/19, Tod and Romanes/Craig, 16 Jun. 1829.

[104] SBA/1303/7/313, Craig/Tod & Romanes, 15 Dec. 1836.

[105] SBA/1303/8/177, C&R/John Wilson, 5 Mar. 1838.

[106] SBA, Receipts relating to William and John Smith, SBA/183/10, Expense of incarcerating Revd. J. O. Henderson at Mr Smith's instance, 28 Oct. 1823; on Henderson, see Hall, *History of Galashiels*, 253–4.

Craig used hornings flexibly. He sent one to John Paterson in Selkirk in 1824 instructing him not to serve it but '*to intimate only* in some menacing way' that upon failure to pay the balance by the following Monday 'the Horning will be executed to be ready for caption'.[107] He could obtain them quickly. In one case Robert Laidlaw in Edinburgh was asked to 'forward us a Horning, first coach' which Craig, two days later, duly sent on to Paterson in Selkirk.[108] By this point Craig had been sending hornings to Paterson for nearly thirty years. He had asked him as early as 1809, whenever he charged one of his hornings, to mark '*at the foot*' of the document the expenses of charging.[109]

Caption was always a last resort. It followed a build-up of pressure, as in the case of the clothier John Gledhill.[110] Instructed to poind his goods, and knowing Gledhill was out of Galashiels, Elliot Anderson told the messenger to do it 'as privately as you can, as I hope he may be able to settle the matter when he returns & would not therefore wish to injure his credit'.[111] This initial 'delicate' approach to poinding was common.[112] In this case, Anderson justified the 'quiet' execution to the Glasgow instructing agent on the basis that

> there does not seem to be many Goods in his immediate possession he having been lately travelling the East Country with all those finished, & had neither as I am respectably informed brought back much money nor the Goods themselves, so that we could not find out in all probability where they were deposited.[113]

A further consideration was that, while Gledhill had property (including 'a fourth share in one of the best machinery houses'), the Bank of Scotland was known to have old claims against him which might swallow up his assets. Since that bank had 'a professional man here who formerly attended to their claims' his Glasgow creditors would derive no benefit from publicity. Eighteen months later, however, another creditor was pressing and a more aggressive approach was necessary. Having had a horning executed, Craig took the view that 'Gledhill would not be the worse of a fright with a caption'.[114] When this was arranged, and the instructing agent (this time in Edinburgh) insisted on full payment, Craig informed the messenger that without immediate payment 'the caption must just take its course'.[115] It did not, however, because Gledhill successfully questioned the amount of the debt and thus avoided incarceration.[116] Another debtor, this

---

[107] SBA/1303/4/52, Anderson/John Paterson writer Selkirk, 25 Jun. 1824.

[108] SBA/1303/8/117, C&R/Robert Laidlaw, 28 Dec. 1837; SBA/1303/8/117, C&R/John Paterson, messenger, Selkirk, 30 Dec. 1837.

[109] SBA, D/48/56/10, Craig/Paterson, writer, Selkirk, 21 Mar. 1809.

[110] Another example, Thomas Clapperton, is discussed in Chapter 7.

[111] SBA/1303/3/53, Anderson/Mr Paterson, writer [John Paterson, writer, Galashiels], 25 Sep. 1822.

[112] E.g., SBA/1303/4/101, Anderson/Haldane, 2 Oct. 1824.

[113] SBA/1303/3/54, Anderson/D. Hood, writer, Glasgow, 25 Sep. 1822.

[114] SBA/1303/4/302, Anderson/Andrew Paterson SSC, Edinburgh, 31 Jun. 1824.

[115] SBA/1303/3/311, idem, 17 Feb. 1824.

[116] SBA/1303/3/317, Anderson/John Lauder, Silvermills, Edinburgh, 24 Feb. 1824.

time for a much larger sum, soon emerged, prompting Craig to take peremptory action against Gledhill's property.[117]

Elliot Anderson was very much alive to the challenges of dealing with local debtors. Andrew Clarkson, pursued for debt by a Lanarkshire writer, denied having signed the bill constituting the obligation. Anderson, however, considered this 'a singular piece of hardihood'. While he was prepared to poind his goods, he warned:

> Although he drives a horse & cart, which I suppose to be his own, yet I am not sure that it would be worth while to risk the expenses of a prosecution, as he seems to be in debt to a number of people in this neighbourhood & is I should think otherways very poor . . .[118]

This was one of those cases where the legal costs might outweigh any return.

Space precludes discussion of heritable debt. However, Craig naturally recognised the vital importance of obtaining heritable security. When there was a sequestration, he noted, 'in 90 cases out of a 100 the personal creditors get little or nothing at all while the heritable creditors run off with everything'.[119] Sometimes even putting in a claim in order to rank with other personal creditors was risky because, by doing so, the creditor became liable for a share of the expenses of the sequestration yet might recover none of their debt.

Lawyers and Messengers

Missives to messengers-at-arms were often brief. Typically, they would inclose letters of horning, ask the messenger to charge the relevant party or parties and return the letters with a note of their fee. Numerous writers and messengers feature in the correspondence, including James Stalker in Earlston; John Paterson in Selkirk and, later, Haldane & Lees in Galashiels. Sheriff officers are also mentioned, such as John Wilson in Hawick and John Taket in Melrose. Sometimes the same creditor might act against multiple debtors at once meaning that the same instructions would be sent simultaneously to messengers in different districts. Thus, in June 1837 hornings at the instance of Ker & Johnston (of the Leith Bank) caused letters to go out to three messengers: William Allan in Kelso; John Paterson in Selkirk and Thomas Oliver in Jedburgh.[120]

Messengers worked within particular jurisdictions and there was an etiquette to employing them. When Peebles writer Alexander Bartram, acting together with Craig, employed his own messenger to come to Galashiels to serve a process, Craig thought this 'extremely improper in every point of view'.[121] The cost of

---

[117] SBA/1303/4/59, Craig/Gledhill, 7 Jul. 1824.
[118] SBA/1303/3/227, Anderson/William Walkinshaw, writer, Lanark, 15 Aug. 1823.
[119] SBA/1303/6/262, Craig/Adam Paterson WS, 31 Jan. 1832.
[120] SBA/1303/7/466, C&R/various messengers, 5 Jun. 1837.
[121] SBA/1303/3/192, Craig/A. M. Bartram, writer, Peebles, 16 Jun. 1823. On Bartram, see Finlay, *ARNP 1700–1799*, II, no. 2907.

importing a messenger would be disallowed on expenses because 'we have a respectable messenger here whom I always employ for this neighbourhood' (meaning John Paterson) and only the charge of employing the nearest messenger was permitted. That was not true in cases heard in the sheriff court in Edinburgh, however, since sheriff officers were sometimes sent out from there to undertake diligence and Craig even met them from the coach to facilitate their business.

The physical recovery of money, from registered protest against non-payment to court action, was a lengthy business and could go awry. Craig's relationship with those he employed depended on mutual trust. In 1821 he complained about the Hawick writer Gilbert Amos whom he had instructed to recover a debt.[122] Rather than transmit any sums obtained, Amos retained the partial payment he had collected, claiming that he had placed it to Craig's account.[123] Craig instructed another Hawick writer, Andrew Oliver, to execute a caption against the debtor and threaten Amos that if he did not transmit the money thus far received then an action would be raised against him before the Lord Lyon (messengers and their cautioners were subject to the Lyon Court for malversation of office).[124] Craig had already threatened to make Amos' cautioners liable.[125] Considering Amos 'awkward and unbusinesslike', Craig told Oliver to bring proceedings and regarded himself as free to come upon the debtor 'a second time'.[126] Six months later, not having received payment either from Amos or Oliver but being informed that they had recovered the debt in full, Craig instructed the separate Hawick firm of Oliver & Elliot to pursue a claim on his behalf against both writers.[127] They recommended an action before the Court of Session, something Craig was happy for them to pursue with their Edinburgh agent as a means of 'bringing these two pettyfoggers forward'.[128] Trouble of this kind, particularly with local messengers, was not unusual. The Hamilton agent, Thomas Dykes, for example, even threatened to advise his client to pursue the Lanark messenger James Young for the debt when the latter failed to execute diligence.[129]

When a query arose over an unpaid account following the death of Alexander Bartram in 1830, Craig's attitude was more relaxed. He examined their correspondence going back to 1813 and discovered three instances where Bartram held dividends or other sums for him apparently without remitting them. He acknowledged that 'I have always considered that Mr Bartram would rather be in

[122] Amos was admitted as a procurator and conveyancer in Roxburghshire sheriff court in 1811: NRS, SC62/27/2, 30 Jul. 1830.

[123] SBA/1303/2/103, Craig/Andrew Oliver, writer, Hawick, 15 Aug. 1821. See also SBA/1303/2/59, 69.

[124] SBA/1303/2/106, idem, 22 Aug. 1821; *The Records of the Parliaments of Scotland to 1707*, ed. K. M. Brown et al. (St Andrews, 2007–2019), 1672/6/57. See also, ALSP, Arniston collection vol 80, no. 38, *Information for John Campbell-Hooke of Bangeston Esq; Lord Lyon, etc.*, 23 Jun. 1765.

[125] SBA/1303/2/105, Craig/Amos, 18 Aug. 1821.

[126] SBA/1303/2/109, Craig/Andrew Oliver, writer, Hawick, 28 Aug. 1821.

[127] SBA/1303/2/210, Craig/Oliver & Elliot, writers, Hawick, 12 Mar. 1822. The firm of Oliver & Elliot was entirely separate from Andrew Oliver who was a sole practitioner.

[128] SBA/1303/3/20, idem, 24 Jul. 1822. See also SBA/1303/2/90, 93.

[129] GCA, T-DY/1/1/5, Dykes/Young, 24 Jul. 1823 (no pagination).

my debt than me in his, but if a balance can be satisfactorily ascertained between us it would be desirable to have it settled'.[130] In 1836 he was still trying to recover sums paid out in respect of litigation in which Bartram had acted.[131] Similarly, he instructed the Lauder writer John Elliot to obtain payment of an account from his fellow practitioner, William White, that had lain so long it had accrued seven years' worth of interest.[132]

As the Amos incident demonstrates, Craig abhorred dishonesty or unprofessionalism in other practitioners. This came to the fore in complaints he made against the Leith Bank's agent, John Patison WS (1784–1832). Craig had instructed Patison to obtain the proceeds of a bill, retired to him by the Leith Bank, on which Andrew Gardner was liable as acceptor. Patison, however, was owed money by the Leith Bank and therefore kept for himself what he recovered from Gardner. Craig was unimpressed, telling Gardner that the bank's debt to him was 'quite foreign to my business' and repeatedly calling on him to pay the amount recovered into his account.[133] Craig was infuriated when Patison cut off communication with him. He required his Edinburgh agents 'to get up the Bill & Diligence, & cash received & if refused to raise an action against Mr Patison immediately', informing the Bank that he hoped 'not a day will be lost in prosecuting him to the utmost before the Court'.[134] As he later explained, Craig knew from Gardner that full payment was unlikely but he wanted to ensure that all partial payments Patison had obtained were put in his account. Having clarified that, he reiterated his position: 'unless the whole sum is paid in there by Wednesday first, I positively order you to give him a summons for recovery – Gardner will furnish you with a Note of the several payments'.[135] A Court of Session action was raised but Craig was keen to transfer it to the sheriff court to have it heard more quickly.[136] His aggression bore fruit, with Patison proposing a settlement which was eventually agreed, although Craig had initially refused it 'without ample security'.[137] Craig, 'ill pleased about this business', was indefatigable in asserting his rights; intolerant of what he considered improper behaviour, and showed, in Hogg's phrase, his 'stubborn perverseness'.[138]

CONVEYANCING

When land was bought and sold an instrument of sasine was prepared and normally sent to William and John Smith, in Kelso, who kept the register of sasines.

[130] SBA/1303/6/86, Craig/D. Cormack, accountant, Edinburgh, 31 Jul. 1830.
[131] SBA/1303/7/201, Craig/T. & H. Snoddy, leather merchants, Carlisle, 15 pr. 1836.
[132] SBA/1303/5/68, Craig/John Elliot, 23 May 1827.
[133] SBA/1303/3/182, Craig/John Patison, 31 May 1823.
[134] SBA/1303/3/189, Craig/Tait & Bruce, 9 Jun. 1823; Craig/LBC, 9 Jun. 1823.
[135] SBA/1303/3/192, Craig/Tait & Bruce, 16 Jun. 1823.
[136] SBA/1303/3/222, idem, 5 Aug. 1823.
[137] SBA/1303/3/226, idem, 13 Aug. 1823.
[138] SBA/1303/3/200, Craig/LBC, 30 Jun. 1823; Hughes, ed., *Collected Letters of James Hogg*, II, 104.

Craig was occasionally involved in conveyances beyond the local area. In 1837, for instance, he had sent a disposition of an Edinburgh property, drawn by Tod & Romanes in favour of Thomas Darling of Longhaugh, to Robert Laidlaw so that he could take sasine on it locally. Laidlaw had then to return it with a memorandum narrating that the ceremony of sasine (involving symbolical delivery of earth and stone) had taken place, so that Craig could prepare an instrument of sasine.[139] The instrument was quickly returned to Laidlaw 'for the notary's docquet & signature of the witnesses'.[140] It is interesting that a process carried out entirely in Edinburgh should have involved Craig at all, although Darling was his client and Craig could claim a fee for extending the instrument of sasine even if another notary authenticated it.

Craig advised, and implemented the directions of, feudal superiors. If a new vassal required a charter of confirmation, the superior might set conditions before granting it. In Gordon, the villagers traditionally had the servitude right of casting peats at the local peat moss (i.e. they exerted the right, as feuars, to take peat from any part of the moss). The superior, George Fairholme, however, had persuaded most of them to discharge their right in return for gaining the feu (effectively ownership) of one half of the moss.[141] Some, however, held out, including a youth named John Darling who continued to cast peats wherever he pleased. Darling, however, had asked for a precept of *clare constat* as heir to his late father. This was a deed by which a superior recognised the right of his vassal's heir to enter land held of him. As this was in Fairholme's gift, Craig regarded Darling as being 'under our thumb' – unless he discharged his right to cast peats generally, no precept would be granted.[142] Once this was done, Craig thought they could buy off the other objectors. This is a significant indicator of social change because local reliance on the moss was traditional; historians have noted the impact which the division of commonties and mosses, and the removal of common land, had on the decline of cottar life.[143]

Drafting a precept of *clare constat* was no small task and Craig charged a guinea for doing so.[144] To make the draft, unless he already possessed it, he had to borrow the instrument of sasine relating to the property when it was last conveyed. For the same purpose, Craig himself lent out deeds to his fellow practitioners when needed.[145] Co-operation of this kind was always forthcoming, as it was if a deed, for example, required authentication by two notaries. An instance is found in a note to the Melrose writer James Curle, never actually sent, congenially asking

[139] SBA/1303/8/65, Craig/Robert Laidlaw SSC, Edinburgh, 12 Oct. 1837.
[140] SBA/1303/8/70, Craig/Laidlaw, 24 Oct. 1837.
[141] SBA/1303/7/276, Craig/John Romanes, writer, Lauder, 21 Oct. 1836.
[142] SBA/1303/7/286, Craig/George Bruce, Greenknowe, by Earlston, 5 Nov. 1836; also, SBA/1303/7/371, Craig/John Romanes, 21 Feb. 1837; SBA/1303/8/86, Rutherford/John Smith, 21 Nov. 1837.
[143] E.g. T. M. Devine, *The Scottish Nation* (London: Penguin, 2012), 148.
[144] SBA/1303/2/11, Craig/John Spence, writer, Earlston, 9 Apr. 1821.
[145] E.g. SBA/1303/8/168, C&R/Spence & Thomson, Melrose, 19 Feb. 1837.

him to come up 'to sign Notary with me to a woman's Settlement who cannot write – if you come to dinner so much the better'.[146]

Interesting conveyancing issues arose periodically, sometimes affecting a property's selling price. James Stirling's house, built in 1823 and only a few years old when he attempted to sell it, was subject to a ninety-nine-year lease which, unusually, was not automatically renewable. The lease was granted at a time when 'noise was made about the legality of building leases extending beyond a certain number of years', although normal practice (involving automatic renewal clauses) had quickly resumed.[147] To compensate, the rent per acre was reduced across the ninety-nine-year term but potential buyers regarded that as insufficient compensation. Craig asked Gala to assist Stirling by agreeing to automatic renewal to bring his property into line with the rest of Galashiels and to grant 'a letter or an obligation on the back of the lease that it will be done in 1923'. In return, any purchaser was to pay the usual rent rather than the discounted rate. When particularly difficult issues of interpretation arose, specialist opinions were sought, generally from writers to the signet. In 1838, for instance, Craig twice sought the opinion of Alexander Douglas WS (1780–1851), the son of a Kelso physician, telling him that he had 'great confidence in you as a conveyancer'.[148]

THE STAMP OFFICE

Craig was sub-distributor of stamps for Galashiels (in Selkirk, Andrew Lang was sub-distributor).[149] He had the privilege of distributing stamped paper in respect of transactions in Selkirkshire and Peeblesshire.[150] This extended to the sale of the Ladhope estate in 1838 which was actually in Roxburghshire but, as Craig told John Lindsay WS, it was 'in our neighbourhood'.[151] Under the Stamp Acts, certain types of legal document, commercial paper, insurance documents and a range of other deeds, even including 'hawkers licences', required for validity to be written on stamped paper.[152] The Leith Bank, for instance, refused payment because of an instrument 'not being drawn on a stamp'.[153]

Craig was supplied by the distributor William Turnbull in Peebles to whom he regularly remitted funds. The correspondence with Turnbull, engaged in by both Craig and Elliot Anderson, is rivalled in regularity only with that of the Leith

[146] SBA/1303/2/45, Craig/Curle, Melrose, 22 May 1821.

[147] SBA/1303/6/470, 5 Nov. 1829.

[148] SBA/1303/8/212, Craig/A. Douglas WS, 17 Drummond Place, Edinburgh, 4 Apr. 1838.

[149] *Fifteenth Report of the Commissioners of Inquiry into the Collection and Management of the Revenue of Ireland, Scotland etc*, 262 H.C. (1828) (13), XIII.1 [Henceforth, HC, *Report on Collection of Revenue*].

[150] SBA/1303/8/431, C&R/Donald Horne WS, 1 May 1837.

[151] SBA/1303/8/163, Craig/John M. Lindsay WS, 23 Feb. 1838; SBA/1303/8/160, Craig/Turnbull, 20 Feb. 1838. Interestingly, Craig acted for the buyer, not for the seller Archibald Gibson.

[152] SBA/1303/8/365, C&R/Turnbull, 1 Nov. 1838.

[153] SBA/1303/3/32, Anderson/William Bathgate, Buckholmside, 22 Aug. 1822.

Bank. It is a strange mixture of frustration (on the numerous occasions when no or insufficient stamped paper was sent) and humour. There is also correspondence with the stamp offices in London and Edinburgh.

The local demand for stamped paper was high.[154] When Turnbull refused to supply due to an unremitted balance that was owed, Anderson thought this a 'paltry pretence' and told him he would apply to Edinburgh instead, adding that he would complain 'how ridiculous it is to keep a manufacturing town such as this, with a Bank Office, for three weeks upon such a supply' unless Turnbull immediately sent his order.[155] On another occasion, Anderson chided Turnbull:

> It is I have often thought a great pity that the pericraniums of many people are so constituted as to be sensible of no fault but those of their neighbours: this is a moral axiom that I shall feel particularly obliged by your considering on those manifold occasions when you do not send thence half of the stamps I order.[156]

In 1833, Anderson wanted Turnbull to give Mr Fair, a local stationer, the right to sell stamps, describing him as 'a most respectable person & quite incapable of conniving at any fraud'. Illustrating the local commercial upturn, he noted:

> Indeed it is our mutual Interest that he should be licensed, as I observe that the sale of Bill Stamps has increased very much from accommodation a shop like his affords to mercantile Travellers by being accessible at *all hours*, which Mr Craig's house you are aware cannot be; & this being now the great thoroughfare of the Carlisle road, makes it the more necessary that some place should be provided where strangers & passers by could get stamps at all times . . .[157]

Queries on points of law concerning stamp duty could be sent directly to the Edinburgh Stamp Office.[158] Inventories of estates were lodged with Andrew Lang as Selkirk commissary clerk, a process which sometimes involved interaction with the Stamp Office or the solicitor of stamps.[159] Craig also had to account to the Inspector of Stamps, providing an 'inventory of stamps & cash on hand', as he did in 1822.[160] In an emergency in 1821 he wrote to the inspector, James Waddell, requesting a £50 sheet of stamped paper for an inventory to be signed at Selkirk by people who all resided 'at great distance from one another'.[161] Rather than rely on Turnbull at short notice, he asked Waddell to send out a sheet the next day.

Accounts were carefully kept to ensure that the appropriate duty was paid. Executry matters could be particularly complex. In one such case Craig stressed

---

[154] E.g. SBA/1303/5/183, Craig/Andrew Lang, 3 Jan. 1828.
[155] SBA/1303/4/54, Anderson/Turnbull, 29 Jun. 1824.
[156] SBA/1303/5/53, Anderson/Turnbull, 2 May 1827.
[157] SBA/1303/6/431-2, Anderson/Turnbull, 13 Nov. 1833.
[158] E.g. Craig/William Kenny, Stamp Office, Edinburgh, 4 Jan. 1826.
[159] E.g. SBA/1303/2/52, Craig/James Bremner, solicitor of stamps, Edinburgh, 4 Jun. 1821.
[160] SBA/1303/3/41, Craig/James Waddell, Inspector of Stamps, Edinburgh, 3 Sep. 1822.
[161] SBA/1303/2/8, idem, 2 Apr. 1821.

that a delay in paying legacy duty arose because the executors 'refuse to sign –
through ignorance'.[162] In an 1826 case he stuck to his guns in a dispute with James
Bremner, solicitor of stamps, and William Renny WS, solicitor for the Inland Revenue. The late William Young had made a transfer to his wife before he died and
Craig, on the executor's behalf, demanded the solicitors identify 'the section of
the Act of Parliament which obliges a husband or wife possessing under a *mutual
settlement* to render an account at the death of either'.[163] He was prepared to insist
on counsel's opinion being taken unless the relevant authority was provided to
justify the Stamp Office's approach.

An insight into Craig's relationship with Turnbull occurred when the farm at
Mossilee fell vacant in 1836 following the death of the tenant, George Ballantyne.
Ballantyne was a nephew of George Ballantyne of Walthamstow, an elder brother
of Trinity House (a master mariner), who had died in 1822.[164] Ballantyne received
a substantial legacy from his uncle and Craig did some drafting work in regard to
another of the legatees.[165]

Of interest is a request Craig made to James Ballantyne, the residuary legatee,
on behalf of Turnbull and also for himself. Turnbull, he wrote:

> hopes that the Return that you have to make yourself as Residuary Legatee to the
> Stamp Office for the duty of 3 per cent & also the Sheet of Stamp paper which cost
> several hundred pounds might be ordered through him, so that we might not lose the
> small commission due to him, & myself as his sub distributor . . . it is only by such occa-
> sional circumstances coming our way, that we are in any way compensated as Servants
> of the Revenue for our great trouble daily in the Stamp department, the Commission
> on them alone being so small in ordinary sales.[166]

He pointed out that whether the duty was paid in Peebles, Galashiels or London
made no difference to Ballantyne and, since he came from Craig's district, strictly
speaking the return should have been made through him.[167]

CONCLUSION

In general, country lawyers and Edinburgh correspondents worked together
smoothly. Exceptions, of course, occurred such as a dispute between Dr Murray of
Philiphaugh's Edinburgh and country agents in relation to which of them had to

---

[162] SBA/1303/4/493, Craig/William Turnbull, 20 Nov. 1826.
[163] SBA/1303/4/394, idem, 26 May 1826.
[164] TNA, Will and Testament of George Ballantyne of Walthamstow, Prob/11/1663/1.
[165] SBA/1303/6/389, Craig/Sir Robert Wigram & Ors, trustees under the will & testament of the
       late George Ballantyne, 12 Jun. 1833. This may have been Dorothea Laidlaw's younger brother,
       William (b. 1795).
[166] SBA/1303/6/390, Craig/James Ballantyne, Osborne's Adelphi Hotel, London, 13 Jun. 1833.
[167] Craig later refers to charging a 7.5 per cent commission on receipts for stamped paper sold:
       SBA/1303/8/578, Craig/Turnbull, 24 Sep. 1839.

pay his feu duties – 'the former alleging the latter should pay them & *vice versa*'.[168] Craig cut this particular Gordian knot simply by ignoring the lawyers altogether and laying an arrestment on Murray's principal tenant.

Craig's relationships with local lawyers were normally positive. Personal comments occasionally appear, as when he congratulated Robert Bruce in Kelso for entering 'the happy state of matrimony', regretting only that he had 'been so long about it'.[169] Craig was alive to variations in local practice and knew that practitioners might take different approaches to aspects of business. When a landlord refused house rent, when it was proffered at Earlston Fair, on the basis that he would only accept it if paid in Lilliesleaf (thirteen miles distant), Craig was incredulous. He thought the refusal of payment 'absurd' and unprecedented when the landlord had no additional claims against the tenant. Even so, he did not reject the possibility that the demand might be pursued, although he wanted the landlord's agent to set out the grounds for doing so – whether 'it be specified in the Tack or if it be the practice of your place – as it is not the custom here'.[170]

When it came to sharing information, for example about the public burdens affecting an area of land, then he relied on fellow practitioners and they could rely on him.[171] In many aspects of business, there was a co-operative spirit between lawyers built on mutual trust and a shared professional identity. Formal links, such as joint membership of a professional body, are not a particularly strong feature of Craig's correspondence. There was no shared library at the heart of legal practice, as there might have been in Edinburgh, although there is evidence of the sharing of books and legal sources when needed. What is evident, however, is working engagement with fellow lawyers, an understanding of professional standards and a collegiate approach to matters of business.

Living up to his notarial motto, *veritas* (truth), Craig was often candid with clients, particularly about the fact that legal action was sometimes 'tardy & expensive'.[172] He also, as both lawyer and banker, exhibited a strong sense of propriety. Suspecting that 'certain underhand securities' were being granted by several property owners in the town, he instructed Gibson & Hector WS to investigate. While he had little involvement directly with the parties, he expressed himself 'unwilling to be taken advantage of by my neighbours either in my own account or that of others for whom I act'.[173]

A sheriff court process against Gala and Craig, as his factor, survives from 1815.[174] A number of residents attempted to interdict them from closing a road and hampering access to a well after building works had already allegedly inconvenienced the petitioners' access to water in the upper part of Galashiels.

---

[168] SBA/1303/6/334, Craig/R. Cunningham, Coldstream, 24 Nov. 1832.

[169] SBA/1303/4/219, Craig/Bruce, 19 Dec. 1825.

[170] SBA/1303/4/208, Craig/John Paterson, Selkirk, 1 Jul. 1825.

[171] E.g. SBA/1303/8/268, Craig/Spence & Thomson, 14 Jun. 1838.

[172] SBA/1303/3/232, Craig/Shakespeare G. Sikes, Huddersfield, 29 Nov. 1823.

[173] SBA/1303/5/471, Craig/Gibson & Hector WS, 10 Nov. 1829.

[174] NRS, Scott of Gala papers, GD477/122/18.

Quite naturally, John Paterson, the Galashiels writer and procurator, drafted and subscribed the petition on their behalf. Adverse actions of this kind, brought on behalf of clients, had no effect on working or personal relationships within the profession.

In sum, Craig's correspondence identifies an interesting group of lawyers, some of whom had discrete functions and all of whom operated under a common understanding of legal practice and the business needs of their clients. Craig's expectations of his professional colleagues were high, his criticisms withering and, despite occasional errors which he acknowledged, his own competence as a law agent beyond question. That does not mean to say that his clients never complained. For example, one was 'grumbling sadly' at the delay of a summons being executed; Elliot Anderson responded robustly to another, blaming a delay on his correspondent's own 'constant interference' rather than 'any inattention on my part'.[175] Such complaints, however, were part and parcel of the business of the law.

[175] SBA/1303/7/316, Craig to George Main, writer, Kelso, 21 Dec. 1836; SBA/1303/4/257, Anderson to Richard Richardson, Selkirk, 20 Oct. 1825.

Chapter 7

Manufacturing and Commerce

This chapter considers Craig's attempts to promote commercial activity. The Galashiels population, which was 1,545 in 1821, rose quickly in the following decade and it was said in 1825 that few towns in Scotland were 'advancing more rapidly', although this was before a financial crash the following year.[1] Later came the very difficult year of 1829 which saw 'numerous failures' in Galashiels.[2] There was then a boom thanks to the success of tweed products from 1830 onwards. During Craig's time as bailie, therefore, trade fluctuations created challenges, particularly in textiles where a transition to lighter products, made of finer wool not typical to the region, brought in its wake several local bankruptcies at the end of the 1820s.[3]

Craig had his own youthful experience of commercial failure with the ill-fated Buckholmside Brewery.[4] He had a banker's understanding of the strengths and weaknesses of local businesses. In a credit reference for a local building contractor in 1827, Elliot Anderson casually mentioned that most people 'in that line are known to us in one way or other'.[5] So were many weavers, artisans, millworkers and overseers all of whom might benefit from Craig's network of contacts.

Craig's correspondence tells us much about how local commerce operated and shows how useful his contacts might be. In October 1819, for instance, he wrote to the law agents Taylor & Gardner in Glasgow, mentioning that he had heard of the failure of the Glasgow merchant John Stewart. Stewart had recently visited the area and bought goods in Galashiels and Hawick, particularly from the Hawick yarn manufacturers. One such firm, Waldie, Pringle & Co., sold him £500 worth of goods on credit. Hearing of Stewart's failure, they sent people to Glasgow who, as Craig put it, 'were so rash as carry off goods to a great extent from Stewart's premises on the ground that he was only their agent'.[6] Craig asked his Glasgow colleagues to investigate, rightly noting that, unless there was a contract of agency, the Hawick firm had prejudiced Stewart's other creditors and rendered themselves vulnerable to a legal action.

---

[1] *The Scotsman*, 16 Nov. 1825, p. 735; Hall, *History of Galashiels*, chapter X.
[2] SBA/1303/6/279, Craig/Adam Paterson WS, 19 Apr. 1832.
[3] Hall, *History of Galashiels*, 344; B. Lenman, *An Economic History of Modern Scotland 1660–1976* (London, 1977), 12; see also Chapter 5.
[4] See above, pp. 7, 128.
[5] SBA/1303/5/172, Anderson/Robert Johnston, Leith Bank, 20 Dec. 1827. See also Chapter 5.
[6] SBA/1303/1/10, Craig/Tayler & Gardner, writers, Glasgow, 29 Oct. 1819. Also SBA/1303/1/18.

THE TEXTILE INDUSTRY

From insuring weavers' houses to the development of mills and factories, Craig was involved at all levels of cloth-making. This is not surprising as Torwoodlee, one of his closest connections, had strongly supported the building of the Cloth Hall in 1791 as had a number of individuals from families with which Craig himself later had much involvement.[7] Hall lists twenty-eight firms engaged in the Galashiels woollen trade in 1825 and many of them appear in Craig's correspondence, such as James & Henry Brown, Thomas Clapperton, William Brown, Robert Gill & Son and John Gledhill.[8] An undated document, in which Elliot Anderson demonstrated a firm understanding of the manufacturing process, makes it clear that visiting manufacturers were impressed by the high quality of product, particularly flannel, which Galashiels weavers were able to produce.[9]

Craig's ambitions and entrepreneurial spirit are demonstrated by his engagement with drysalters, dealers in the dyes that were widely used locally. In April 1823 he was contacted by the London firm, R. & E. A. Whytt, and he encouraged them to send any travelling salesman they might have in the north of England to Galashiels because business there was 'better than for some years' due to cheap labour which allowed manufacturers to make savings even if 'demand was less'.[10] A salesman, he advised, would benefit them much more than simply sending samples of indigo, particularly as 'numerous' representative of other firms already visited local cloth manufacturers and dyers.

Having received samples of indigo and puce, Craig distributed them to local clothiers 'none of whom appear to be in immediate want' but, in July, he anticipated orders for a chest or two in due course.[11] Craig had also spoken to 'one or two likely hands to further your views in the quarter' but had learned that the present lack of orders could be attributed to 'the approaching monthly sale at the India House . . . as they [the local clothiers] expect Indigo to be down [in price]'.[12] Craig took the matter up further with the clothier William Brown who discussed with him the indigo samples and found them to be 'of a coarser copper than that generally used here, as our manufacturers prefer the violet copper & of a finer quality than those forwarded by you'. The business terms offered by Whytt were also unhelpful, since Glasgow and Leith firms took bills payable at six and eight months from the date of invoice, whereas Whytt was offering only three

[7] Hall, *History of Galashiels*, 303–4.
[8] Ibid., 338.
[9] NRS, Scott of Gala papers, GD477/201/8.
[10] SBA/1303/3/154, Craig/R. & E.A. Whytt, London, 17 Apr. 1823.
[11] SBA/1303/3/214, idem, 26 Jul. 1823. Craig evidently also received samples of tea from another supplier: SBA/1303/3/251, Craig/Adam Scott, Mr Fiddes', 3 Great St. Helens, Bishopsgate, London, 23 Sep. 1823.
[12] SBA/1303/3/214, Craig/Whytt, 26 Jul. 1823. The sale was on 1 Aug., *The Scotsman*, 30 Jul. 1823, p. 488. The price of indigo, in the period 1823–1828, showed considerable variation and importers warehoused it waiting for a favourable market. 'Blue claith', considered old-fashioned, proved hard to sell around this time: Hall, *History of Galashiels*, 339.

or four months, while other London suppliers gave six months' credit and then took a bill for three months.[13] Nonetheless, if Whytt were willing to amend their terms, and send on a few chests 'of the violet copper kind', Brown was willing to help procure them a share of the local trade. This was quickly done and Craig had several follow-up meetings with Brown, but it emerged that 'the number of riders lately here in the same line has been more than in any former year', with some of them selling cheaper and on easier terms.[14] According to Brown rival suppliers from Liverpool had appeared for the first time. It was a Glasgow seller, however, offering deals on Guatemalan indigo, who had done best, supplying enough to satisfy the short-term needs of clients who reckoned the price of indigo was declining. The local area consumed between 150 and 200 chests of indigo annually and Craig suggested that a permanent agent, able to supply a variety of types of indigo at quantities less than a full chest, might be worth appointing since this would provide a better regular service than the occasional bulk supply by 'contending houses'.[15]

In 1828, Craig told Robert Whytt that the local clothiers, who had been 'going on wonderfully considering the times' (perhaps an optimistic view), were much involved with foreign wool.[16] He confessed that he was not the man to obtain orders, refusing to meddle since he knew 'nothing about the qualities of indigo' and also because visiting salesmen did deals on the spot. He ascertained from James & Henry Brown that Galashiels clothiers did not have a positive record with English mercantile houses, although Elliot Anderson was well connected with the clothiers and they were willing to make a trial if Whytt was prepared to send further samples. This seems to have been a success. Craig later suggested a further improvement if local manufacturers 'had a more ready method of purchasing the finest kinds of *foreign wool*'.[17] If Whytt could select 'the best London house in the line' to send samples of different kinds of wool, it 'would confer a great obligation on the place' which was currently relying on samples from Leeds and Liverpool.

Due to a decline in profitability of agricultural lending, some of Craig's clients attempted to commercialise their estates and develop alternative sources of income.[18] Improving the trade in textile manufacture became a priority. Gala, for example, tried to exploit the industrial opportunities afforded by the Gala Water. In addition to leasing out Buckholm Mill, Craig was heavily involved in

[13] SBA/1303/3/216, Craig/R. & E.A. Whytt, London, 29 Jul. 1823.

[14] SBA/1303/3/229, idem, 21 Aug. 1823.

[15] SBA/1303/3/236-7, idem, 4 Sep. 1823.

[16] SBA/1303/5/275, Craig/Robert Whytt, London, 10 Jul. 1828. They had petitioned the House of Commons against duty on foreign wool the month before: *The Scotsman*, 18 Jun. 1828, p. 388. In fact, only about 5 per cent of consumption in Galashiels in the 1820s was of imported wool: Lenman, *Economic History of Modern Scotland*, 124.

[17] SBA/1303/5/322, idem, 11 Nov. 1828.

[18] On estate improvement, see R. H. Campbell, 'The landed classes', in T. M. Devine and R. Mitchison, ed., *People and Society in Scotland*, vol. 1 (Edinburgh, 1988), 91–108.

his attempts in 1829 to dam the river and build two new factories or mill houses at Netherbarns (see Chapter 5).[19] The promoters, local textile manufacturers (including J. & H. Brown) bore the cost of construction in return for permanent leases from Scott on reasonable terms.[20]

When the water wheel at Buckholm Mill needed repair, Craig naturally pointed out that it was the tenant's responsibility 'to keep up the wheel, & everything else connected with the mills during his Lease'.[21] The Mill itself, a corn and flour mill, was destroyed by fire in October 1839 causing loss to the Caledonian Insurance Company with whom Torwoodlee had insured it. The claim, Craig reckoned, would amount to about £700 plus £300 for the ground and unground victual inside. As well as noting that the miller, Mr Hume, habitually inspected the mill every evening at 9pm and had found nothing amiss, he described him as 'a most respectable and correct man'. The effects, as Craig informed the insurer, were much wider:

> a number of people who are accustomed to buy victual at Roups and get it ground at the mill unfortunately had it there while this calamity occurred, these of course the office have nothing to do with but we are also to get a list of them and should some of them turn out to be poor people, the directors might perhaps consider their case.[22]

Innovation itself often raised legal issues. On hearing that John Hislop in Galashiels was 'about to erect a Steam Engine of considerable power on our property', Craig asked him, on Gala's behalf, to send him a sketch of it. He needed to know where it was planned to be positioned and wanted to know the probable effect 'on horses passing along the turnpike road or any injurious effects by smoke or noise' that may be caused to his neighbours or to the town in general.[23]

In 1826 there is reference to the creation of six additional fulling mills which were all to be under one roof. Captain Pringle, then residing in Bath, had objected but Craig explained the project in more detail and told him that his father, Torwoodlee, was in favour:

> fulling mills are merely waulk mills and Galashiels could employ a great deal more than even these six additional, But at present the clothiers are going to continue their fulling mills where they are, and all we want is your concurrence to a Manufactory house like R. Lees down at the cauld pool, and the corn mill to be converted into one also.[24]

In waulk mills wool was cleaned and made thicker as part of the process of cloth manufacturing. Their expansion indicates that the textile industry was prospering relative to the period immediately following the end of the Napoleonic Wars.

[19] SBA/1303/5/136, Craig/Alexander Scott, Newtoun Mill, 8 Nov. 1827.
[20] NRS, Scott of Gala papers, GD477/138/16, Scott/Craig, 8 Apr. 1829.
[21] SBA/1303/6/196, Craig/G. Richardson, Buckholm Mill, 27 Jun. 1831.
[22] SBA/1303/8/609, Craig/John Moinet, 23 Oct. 1839.
[23] SBA/1303/4/452, Craig/John Hislop, Galashiels, 11 Sep. 1826.
[24] SBA/1303/4/302, Craig/Capt. Pringle R.N., Norfolk Buildings, Bath, 13 Jan. 1826.

Converting the corn mill into a manufacturing house was evidently a change to which Torwoodlee had been 'pressed by our manufacturers' to consent.[25]

The clothiers had an obvious interest in maintaining their riverside mills against flooding and to this end they formed a 'Committee for managing Galashiels caul and dam'. Gala's view was that he had granted the land for the use of the caul 'principally with a view to serve the Clothiers & eventually relieve his tenants from a heavy annual assessment in supporting a Cauld from which they derived no benefit'.[26] Maintaining the dam was up to the clothiers; but in 1831 Gala proposed an annual assessment of £25 'on the tenants & Mills until the whole debt of the Cauld is extinguished'.[27] This is another example of co-operation between the laird and cloth manufacturers.

William Blair of Sanquhar

Brief but interesting correspondence relates to William Blair who was a cloth manufacturer at Yochan Mill in Sanquhar in Dumfriesshire. Blair had been financially assisted by Craig's client, William Colvin of Torquhan, whom Craig described as 'a Gentleman of considerable estate in this neighbourhood'.[28] Blair, in the 1820s, established a spinning mill on a farm run by one of the duke of Buccleuch's tenants without ever obtaining a lease from the duke. In 1835 Colvin, regarding Blair as 'a very deserving man', wished to give him further financial assistance but wanted heritable security in the mill. Craig therefore wrote on Colvin's behalf to Thomas Crichton, the duke's chamberlain at Drumlanrig (and also Blair's factor), seeking a lease in Blair's name. He also asked Crichton, should he live near Blair, to 'be so good as read this letter to him with Mr Colvins compliments & my own'. The duke was happy to grant this, but under his entail it could not be done earlier than Whitsunday 1838.[29]

Blair had a cash account with the Leith Bank which Colvin apparently guaranteed. The bank certainly pressed Colvin for payment of Blair's debts in May 1836 when Craig wrote to Blair asking to meet him at the Crook Inn, near the head of the River Tweed, so that they could make a plan to relieve Colvin of liability. Craig identified two options on the basis that Blair could not proceed without further assistance and that:

> unless you can get as much spinning from Glasgow or other Houses as would keep the Factory going under your management that the next best thing would be to advertise it to let immediately for two years; by spinning wool alone for others you will

---

[25] SBA/1303/4/294, Craig/J. Murray, Kittlebrig, Ancrum, 3 Jan. 1826.

[26] SBA/1303/6/229, Craig/The Committee for Managing Galashiels Caul & Dam, 4 Oct. 1831.

[27] SBA/1303/6/245, Gala[?]/idem, 17 Nov. 1831. The author is not stated, but the wording suggests it was a copy letter from Gala.

[28] SBA/1303/7/113, Craig/T. Crichton, Esq., Dalton, Sanquhar, 2 Nov. 1835.

[29] SBA/1303/7/212, Craig/William Blair, 7 May 1836. On the strict Buccleuch entails, see B. Bonnyman, *The Third Duke of Buccleuch and Adam Smith: Estate Management and Improvement in Enlightenment Scotland* (Edinburgh, 2014), 60–3.

perceive that you require no money and this method is not unfrequently resorted to in this manufacturing town when individuals like yourself have run short of capital.

Colvin was keen to assist, but not at a loss to himself. Craig favoured the Glasgow connection, recommending that Blair devote himself 'entirely to the spinning of Black faced sheep wool for carpet manufacturing' which would allow him to avoid any further advance of money for a while.[30] In this episode Craig, once again, is cast in the role of adviser and would-be problem solver. It would be interesting to know the link between Colvin and Blair but, alas, the correspondence does not reveal it. What it does reveal is that Colvin did indeed obtain security and to protect that interest had Blair's mill and dwellinghouse insured through Craig.[31]

Solvency and Debt

Craig's letters demonstrate the ups and downs of commercial life. The Galashiels weaver Thomas Clapperton exemplified the latter. Clapperton had gone into business with others, including the clothiers Hugh Sanderson and James Sime, in the erection of a mill in 1797 which became known as the Botany Mill.[32] According to Hall, when this development was extended, in 1829, Clapperton 'was under the necessity of assigning his share of the buildings to George Craig, the Baron bailie, for behoof of his creditors'.[33] From March 1827 until November 1829, bills drawn by Clapperton were protested for non-payment on twelve separate occasions. Craig investigated two bills signed by James Sime & Co. which lay in his office unpaid and he informed Clapperton that 'it appears on enquiry at some of the parties interested that you are the sole cause of their not being paid'.[34]

While some of these bills would have been paid, this was an indication of a trader in trouble and Craig had particular reason to be alert as a result of one bill which Clapperton had drawn on his son, Andrew. This, he wrote to Clapperton, had been

indorsed by you to me & for which you obtained money from Mr Anderson my Clerk on a most false & clandestine statement to him . . . Of course not an hour will be lost in raising Diligence against you & your son if the money is not paid by Saturday at 12 o'clock & followed to the utmost height by imprisoning you both & detaining you there at my own instance untill [sic] that sum with interest and expenses are all paid.[35]

[30] SBA/1303/7/126, Craig/William Colvin, Torquhan, 16 Dec. 1835.
[31] SBA/1303/8/560, Craig/William Blair, 30 Aug. 1839; SBA/1303/8/564, idem, 5 Sep. 1839; SBA/1303/7/332, Craig/John Moinet, 11 Jan. 1837.
[32] Hall, *History of Galashiels*, 397–8.
[33] Ibid., 398.
[34] SBA/1303/5/90, Craig/Thomas Clapperton, 17 Jul. 1827.
[35] SBA/1303/5/459, idem, 16 Oct. 1829.

He also investigated whether other protested bills by Clapperton that had fallen due with the Leith Bank had been paid.[36]

As Craig commented to William Brown in Stow, when trying to recover sums owed to Brown's creditor, '[i]n cases of Bankruptcy like the present too much punctuality cannot be observed after the debt is once put in a way of being settled'.[37] As was discussed in Chapter 6, in taking steps to obtain the payment of debts time was often of the essence; when a business was in trouble, creditors usually arrived in a group and raced to obtain payment before formal steps were taken.[38]

An example of an enterprise which ran out of road, particularly because it reveals an aspect of the relationship between Craig and Gala, is revealed by an exchange of correspondence in 1829 concerning John Dods, the Galashiels miller. On Friday 27 February Craig intimated that unless Dods paid his rent arrears, he would sequestrate him the following Tuesday.[39] Before proceedings followed on the sequestration, Dods went to the laird to plead his case as his tenant, asking him to write to Craig to review the state of his affairs. Gala was not enthusiastic. Dods had four years of his lease of the mill to run and his 'former friends seem not disposed to come forward in future' to act as his guarantors. Gala cited rent arrears as being significant in the decision as to whether to re-let the property, noting that he would certainly not proceed without security for payment and lamenting that Dods himself 'never was active'.[40] Craig, in reply, was clear and determined, noting that doing anything for Dods 'is of no use' and that he would 'do wisely to go away at this time'.[41] He had been sequestrated every year for rent, and relieved each time by a different person, and 'now when they are all tired of him he goes to try what you will do as Landlord'. As he was more than £80 in debt Craig regarded Dods' circumstances as hopeless and ended his letter by reminding Gala that 'they are bad cases indeed when I order sequestration'.

Burnhouse Mill

Each thread of correspondence, when teased out, reveals something of contemporary commercial reality. Craig knew his way around mills in terms of building them, leasing them and running them. For example, he recommended the millwright, John Aimers, to Duns as having long been in 'the practice of making machines for the manufacturers' in Galashiels.[42] Just as with the farm leases, he inserted conditions into leases for mill tenancies.[43]

[36] SBA/1303/5/458, Anderson/LBC, 14 Oct. 1829.
[37] SBA/1303/3/156, Craig/William Brown, 18 Apr. 1823.
[38] See Chapter 6, pp. 138–142.
[39] SBA/1303/5/364, Craig/James Dods, Galashiels Mills, 27 Feb. 1829.
[40] NRS, Scott of Gala papers, GD477/138/18, Scott of Gala/Craig, 18 Mar. 1829.
[41] SBA/1303/5/376, Craig/Gala, 21 Mar. 1829.
[42] SBA/1303/6/75, Craig/Robert Laidlaw, depute sheriff clerk of Duns, 29 Jun. 1830.
[43] E.g. SBA/1303/4/260, Craig/J. Scott of Yetholm Mills, 26 Oct. 1825.

As for running mills properly, Craig's ideas on the type of person to fit that role were made clear in relation to Burnhouse Mill in Stow parish. Craig acted as local factor for the owner, John Thomson. Thomson was from Oxton, near Lauder, but had moved to Edinburgh and Craig worked with his Edinburgh agents, Cranstoun & Anderson WS. On their behalf he regularly inspected the mill and its offices. In 1831, having noticed a threat from recent flooding, he ordered that 'a very severe encroachment . . . which threatened nothing less than a total change of the water course' be prevented with stones.[44] Two years later, he was back organising work to prevent 'the Gala from making an encroachment on the Millhaugh'.[45]

The mill itself, run by Walter Niel, was not successful and Craig described Niel, in November 1829, as 'getting worse and worse'.[46] By then Craig had taken an offer for the mill from John Mitchell (also from Oxton) who was previously unknown to him. Of Mitchell, he wrote:

> He appears to be a plain steady looking man – has been in a mill under Mr Usher at Quarryford in East Lothian who I know well & who writes me a good character of him. Mitchell also brought one from Mr Mason of Justice Hall near Lauder.[47]

Niel was sequestrated for unpaid rent. Unusually, a sheriff officer was sent out from Edinburgh and Craig personally went to meet him as he alighted from the Blucher coach. According to Craig, Walter could 'only have himself to blame as I have done every thing for him to prevent so unpleasant a step'.[48] Niel thought some financial allowance should be made for his having put up 'an excellent new big outer wheel' and making repairs to machinery at the beginning of his lease, but that was for his landlord to determine.[49]

Mitchell, however, proved to be a disappointing tenant and fell into arrears. In the summer of 1832, Craig inspected the mill and offices and found the latter to be 'in a miserable condition'.[50] The offices comprised 'a stable, a barn & a byre' but Mitchell had failed to maintain the roofs even when Craig personally offered to provide the wood; marked out the trees and pointed out a quarry where stone could be obtained.[51] He also came up with the idea of building a new suite of offices in nearby Plenploth Park but this would require investment. Mitchell lacked both 'capital and enterprise' and Craig advocated removing him at Martinmas.[52] Craig's comments on him reveal what he thought requisite in a miller:

> Mitchell has not been lucky in a Miller, who requires to be a steady honest man, & good at his work: I impressed upon him yesterday the necessity of his finding such a person

[44] SBA/1303/6/235, Craig/Cranstoun & Anderson WS, 27 Oct. 1831.
[45] SBA/1303/6/395, idem, 1 Jul. 1833.
[46] SBA/1303/5/475, idem, 13 Nov. 1829.
[47] SBA/1303/5/475, Craig/Cranstoun & Anderson WS 14 Nov. 1829.
[48] SBA/1303/5/478, idem, 18 Nov. 1829.
[49] SBA/1303/5/479, idem, 23 Nov. 1829.
[50] SBA/1303/5/311, idem, 11 Jul. 1832.
[51] SBA/1303/7/84, Craig/Anderson, Cranstoun & Trotter WS, 11 Jul. 1835.
[52] SBA/1303/6/312, Craig/Cranstoun & Anderson WS, 11 Jul. 1832.

immediately when four times more business might be done: At present it will not do more than pay the Millers wage, whereas 1000 bolls of meal ought to be made yielding between £55 & £60.[53]

Craig was as clear in his ideas about the yield of a corn mill as he was about agricultural yields and the value of other rights attached to land. As for Mitchell, egged on by his agent (as Craig thought), he proved troublesome to remove and made counterclaims against his landlord as a pretext to avoid arrears of rent; Craig nonetheless thought he should be sequestrated.[54]

BORDERS FAIRS

Craig's mobility was not restricted to visiting local farms and estates or his bank's head office in Leith; he assiduously attended the many local fairs across the Borders.[55] His need for cash on such occasions has already been noted (see Chapter 5); the link was usually explicitly made, as when he warned in July 1834 that there would be heavy demand 'for a few weeks till the wool markets are over', the summer being 'the season of the wool markets'.[56] The fairs were where shepherds, labourers and servants, in a highly mobile labour population, looked for employment; animals and crops were sold; lawyers met clients and land agents and bankers undertook financial transactions.[57] Melrose Fair, for instance, held in the middle of August, was, according to Elliot Anderson, a 'sort of "settling day" in this quarter'.[58]

An anonymous memorialist of the middle of the nineteenth century evoked the hiring fairs he attended in 1827 at Duns, Dunbar and Haddington:

> I went to the hiring market at Dunse, with a piece of whip cord in the ribbon of my hat, and a piece of straw in my mouth, as signal that I wanted to be hired. But with the exception of one person, nobody even asked how much wages I expected. Men were more plentiful than masters. Men of full years, and experience as carters and ploughmen, were only offered from three pounds to four pounds ten shillings, with their victuals, for the half-year.[59]

The 'Great Hiring Days' were timed to coincide roughly with the Whitsunday and Martinmas term dates.[60] The 'term time generally produces extra demands',

---

[53]   SBA/1303/6/314, idem, 25 Jul. 1829.

[54]   E.g. SBA/1303/7/61-62, Craig/Cranstoun, Anderson & Trotter 22 Apr. 1835; SBA/1303/7/85-85, idem, 10 Jul. 1835; SBA/1303/7/121, idem, 10 Dec. 1835.

[55]   Douglas, *General View . . . Roxburgh*, 206–9.

[56]   SBA/1303/6/1, Craig/LBC, 28 Jul. 1834; SBA/1303/3/207, Elliot Anderson/William Turnbull, Peebles, 14 Jul. 1823.

[57]   On Lowland labour mobility, see Devine, *The Scottish Nation*, 464–5.

[58]   SBA/1303/7/88, Anderson/LBC, 5 Aug. 1835.

[59]   Anon., *Autobiography of a Working Man*, 103.

[60]   M. Robson, 'The Border farm worker' in T. M. Devine, ed., *Farm Servants and Labour in Lowland Scotland 1770–1914* (Edinburgh, 1984), 79. The Whitsunday term date was 15 May; Martinmas was 11 November.

as Craig informed the Leith Bank.[61] A gap of a day in the letter book, such as 12 August 1823, the day of 'the principal fair of the year at Melrose', suggests that Craig and his colleagues all attended.[62]

Craig comments often about being present at fairs, particularly on bank business. He would note in passing how successful a fair had been. As an illustration, when writing to James Laidlaw in Inverness, he ended curtly by informing him 'there has been a bad Yetholm hog fair'.[63] Two years later, he noted the success of the 'great lamb fair in Eildon Hills'.[64] In 1834 he reported to his bank that

> St Boswells fair was a good one for the farmers wool sheep & lambs & cattle all high priced & much business done. The Galashiels clothiers have bought wool largely in Northfield Liddesdale & Selkirkshire keeping the Englishmen in cheque [sic].[65]

Different fairs, depending on their timing, provided a market for specific goods. In 1827, for example, Craig told Alexander Monro that his tenant, George Logan, was setting off for Whistonbank Fair at Jedburgh to sell 200 'Ewe & Wedder hogs' (female and male year-old sheep) and would send the price to Galashiels when he returned.[66]

In 1823 Craig reported to the Leith Bank on the wool market held at Rink, lying in the Tweed valley between Galashiels and Selkirk, one of a series of such markets:

> The wool market at Rink on the Border on Saturday was rather brisker though prices for inferior sorts were much the same or perhaps 1/ or 18d lower than last year. One of our Clothiers bought a parcel of Cheviot of 70 pack @ £750 so high as 18/ but it was the best in the market; 11/.12.13.14. & 15/ will be the prices. St Boswells is on Friday. The wool staplers are going about you may make the remittance large . . .[67]

Craig was at the St Boswells fair in 1827 when, at 7pm, Elliot Anderson wrote to the bank what he had heard during the day about the state of the market.[68] Lambs were selling slightly above the previous year's prices, but there was no indication of 'any wool being bought', though Craig, according to Anderson, would probably report further to the bank on his return.

Transactions undertaken at fairs regularly generated correspondence and sometimes legal actions. In 1831, for example, Craig wrote to Thomas Scott,

61 SBA/1303/5/396, Craig/LBC, 11 May 1829.
62 SBA/1303/3/221, Craig/LBC, 4 Aug. 1823.
63 SBA/1303/5/417, Craig/James Laidlaw, 3 Jul. 1829.
64 SBA/1303/6/212, Craig/LBC, 15 Aug. 1831.
65 SBA/1303/6/499, Craig/LBC, 21 Jul. 1834.
66 SBA/1303/5/69, Craig/Alexander Monro, 28 May 1827.
67 SBA/1303/3/208, Craig/LBC, 14 Jul. 1823. Wool staplers purchased wool from tenants, graded its quality and then sold it on. The meaning suggested by the text is that the clothier purchased a lot comprising a large number of bags, each of which contained seventy fleeces of Cheviot wool, which at eighteen shillings per stone were together heavy enough to be valued in total at £750.
68 SBA/1303/4/90, Anderson/LBC, 18 Jul. 1827.

writer in Gattonside, about 'an unsound broken winded horse' which Torwoodlee's overseer, John Tillie, had purchased at the Earlston Fair.[69] He wanted him to raise an action at Greenlaw before the sheriff of Berwickshire against the seller Robert Aitchison, described as 'tenant and horsedealer' at Mellowlees. Aitchison, according to a note written in pencil which Tillie had asked him to write, had warranted the horse 'to be sound except a grass cough' but had refused to take it back. Inevitably, horse-related transactions are not uncommon in Craig's correspondence. He wrote to George Eckford at Birkhill Mill in Earlston telling him that the farmer, Rob Paterson, had given him an 'account against you concerning exchanging a horse at Melrose Fair'. Paterson sought a prosecution, though Craig wanted Eckford's side of the story.[70]

Fairs were occasions to gather information and passing conversations there often also had consequences. In 1837, for instance, William Rutherford attended the Stow Fair on 14 March where he learned that William Colvin's shepherd, not having heard from him, had 'hired himself elsewhere'.[71] He found a replacement, subject to Colvin's approval, in the form of John Thomson from near Pathhead who appeared 'a very likely hand'. Rutherford was also told by Blackie of Muirhouse that he had had the Braeside grass park in Torquhan measured and it was much less than the thirty-five acres it was thought to be, leading to the firm writing to the Stow schoolmaster, James Jackson, asking him to confirm the measurement.[72]

TRANSPORT INFRASTRUCTURE

Roads

Sir Walter Scott complained about 'the common plague of country gentlemen' in the Borders which he termed 'roadmania', although he succumbed to it himself, hosting at least one meeting on the subject of roads at Abbotsford to which Craig was invited.[73] The development of new roads was something in which Craig was heavily involved, alongside Gala and Torwoodlee. His correspondence includes a copy letter from Gala, at the request of his 'Selkirkshire friends' to the duke of Buccleuch in 1830 seeking support for an alteration of the Edinburgh to Carlisle road.[74] The plan involved building two bridges, one over the Tweed and another over the Ettrick, and completing a road from them to Galashiels. The estimated cost was £2,500.

Building bridges was controversial. According to Craig, Torwoodlee had mentioned to him at church one Sunday that 'A. Pringle' (probably Alexander Pringle of Yair) and Andrew Lang as agent for Robert Pringle of Fairnilee 'had been laying

[69]   SBA/1303/3/204, Craig/T. Scott, writer, Gattonside, 6 Jul. 1831.
[70]   SBA/1303/8/326, Craig/Eckford, 6 Sep. 1838.
[71]   SBA/1303/7/388, C&R/William Colvin, 15 Mar. 1837.
[72]   SBA/1303/7/389, C&R/Jackson, 15 Mar. 1837.
[73]   SBA/1303/6/118, Craig/Gala, 20 Nov. 1830; Anderson, ed., *Journal of Sir Walter Scott*, 688, Grierson, ed., *Letters of Sir Walter Scott*, XI, 416.
[74]   SBA/1303/6/58-9, Gala/duke of Buccleuch, 24 May 1830.

their heads together to start objections to our new road bill'.[75] They were particularly 'hostile' to the positioning of any bridge over the Ettrick.

Roads needed legislation and this was where Craig's links to London lawyers were useful in theory, although in fact Charles Scott WS, of the family of Scott of Woll, was particularly engaged as a focal point on this subject. As Sir Walter recognised, the road projects in 1830 were 'a kind of Scott question' involving Scott of Gala, Scott of Woll and others – none more so, however, than Craig whose letters provide great detail on the whole question of road development. In a letter to Charles Scott, Craig pointed out the practical challenges in this particular project, listing those likely to subscribe, including Sir Walter Scott and his own clients Walker of Bowland and Torwoodlee. He also suggested getting John Piper of the coach company on board since any road improvements had implications for mail and passenger transport.[76]

In 1833, in his *Statistical Account of Scotland* entry for Galashiels, Rev. Nathaniel Paterson regarded the 'greatest improvement in buildings' since the last volume of that publication to have been these two new bridges over the Tweed and the Ettrick respectively.[77] Craig's local co-ordinating role, too detailed to be recounted here, seems to have been pivotal. As early as 1827, at the request of Torwoodlee, he offered to point out to the road surveyor 'the lines of road in this neighbourhood' which Gala wanted included in the next roads bill, although he had already anticipated the expiry of existing road bills and the presentation of a new one.[78] His correspondence with road trustees, in relation to this and other projects, was extensive. Craig paid for repairs to roads and bridges on behalf of the Roxburghshire trustees, since time was often of the essence, recovering his outlay in due course.[79] He was also involved in collecting subscriptions for works such as the new bridges.[80]

Roads, of course, affected the economy of all the local burghs but not to the same extent. Trying to apportion the expense of them was a difficult task. Craig also had to deal with 'noise' about roads, such as when it was complained that a road had become 'so deep that unless something is done to it, it will not be passable during winter'.[81] He lobbied for minor road alterations. In petitioning to alter a road at Old Longhaugh, he asked James Curle to support, on Melrose's behalf, one third of the expense.[82] When, in 1835, Craig was asked to grant a letter about a road alteration, he told the Edinburgh lawyer John Cant that 'the Road clause' should be kept out of any contract relative to the work.[83] It is not clear what the

---

[75]   SBA/1303/5/245, Craig/Gala, 4 May 1828.
[76]   SBA/1303/5/63, Craig/C. B. Scott WS, 26 May 1830.
[77]   Paterson, 'Galashiels', NSA, III, 17.
[78]   SBA/1303/5/36, Craig/Andrew Speirs, 13 Mar. 1827; cf. SBA/1303/4/481-3, Craig/Tod & Romanes, 4 Nov. 1826.
[79]   E.g. SBA/1303/8/50, C&R/Geo. Scott, 6 Oct. 1837.
[80]   SBA/1303/6/318, Elliot Anderson/Nicol Milne, 4 Aug. 1832.
[81]   SBA/1303/3/82, Craig/Torwoodlee, 27 Nov. 1822.
[82]   SBA/1303/5/185, Craig/Curle, Melrose, 4 Jan. 1828.
[83]   SBA/1303/7/50, Craig/John Cant SSC, Edinburgh, 2 Mar. 1835.

clause required, but he noted that in 'this quarter over the last 3 years we have been full of similar work & no such clause or letter were ever mentioned'.

New roads being 'metalled' or surfaced is referred to from time to time.[84] This sometimes involved work to make room for the road. The new road from the south being 'metalled' in 1832, for example, required demolition of 'the old kiln, storehouse, part of the byre & the stackyard of the Galashiels Corn Mills'. The tenant, Mrs Dods, was entitled to damages to be assessed by two neighbours acting as referees. The offices to be replaced were to be exactly the same size as those removed to avoid undue expense to the Road Trustees. However, this was complicated by the fact that the new ones had to be built upon 'the run of the dam from the Corn Mill bridge up to the Mill door, which will consequently have to be arched over for the new Offices to stand upon'.[85] If a superior roof was to be constructed, with 'slate in place of thatch & tile', that was, so far as Craig was concerned, purely a matter for Gala and the Road Trustees to negotiate.

While roads feature heavily, footpaths and pavements do not. There is at least one reference, however, which perhaps is indicative of Craig's duties as bailie. In 1825 he wrote to the Kelso paver, William Brough, asking him to 'causeway the sewer in Bridge Street' in Galashiels the following week because 'the edge stones of the foot path' were being put up the next day.[86] Bridge Street, in Darlingshaugh, was, according to Hall, 'said to have been planned by Mr Craig'.[87]

Coach Transport

In 1821 Craig wrote to John Piper, an Edinburgh mail coach contractor. He informed him that the locals had expressed a desire that the new coach which was intended to pass through Galashiels on the road to Carlisle should be called the *Sir Walter Scott*, it being 'needless to say that a more popular name than Sir Walter's is not to be found in the Kingdom'.[88] He urged Piper to advertise the coach's schedule in the papers of Edinburgh, London, York, Carlisle and Dumfries to encourage more traffic north to south and ended by saying that if there was a bridge over the Tweed at Boldside then the new coach would 'supersede both the Mail & Blucher'. By advertising improved accessibility, he sought to enhance local trading circumstances.

Craig refers often to the mail coach or the passenger coach and made use of them himself. When he had to be in Edinburgh on business, he mentioned to the bank that he planned to 'take a seat in this days coach if I can get one' to transport money which he would send to the bank on arrival.[89] More prosaically, the remarkable propensity for nineteenth-century people to be killed in transport

[84] E.g. SBA/1303/6/319, Craig/Archibald Lang, 7 Sep. 1832.
[85] SBA/1303/6/319, Craig/Andrew Lang, Selkirk, 7 Sep. 1832.
[86] SBA/1303/4/193, Craig/Brough, 20 May 1825.
[87] Hall, *History of Galashiels*, 99.
[88] SBA/1303/2/138-9, Craig/J. Piper, Mail coach contractor, Edinburgh, 19 Oct. 1821.
[89] SBA/1303/3/129, Craig/LBC, 22 Feb. 1823.

accidents is not missing from the correspondence. This was the fate of Martha Hill's husband, John, an innkeeper, which led to a dispute about his estate.[90]

Stevenson's Railway Project

The major economic barrier to development in Galashiels was recognised as 'its great distance from coal and lime, and the principal market; all of which would be brought nearer by a rail-road'.[91] Coal, virtually the only source of fuel that was used, was transported over twenty miles to Gala from Middleton by cart. It was therefore expensive. The desire to bring lime and coal into the Borders more cheaply was the chief motivation behind a railroad linking Dalkeith to Galashiels and Selkirk, however none was created in Craig's lifetime.[92] Enthusiasm was such, however, that the possibility was investigated by forward-thinking speculators who commissioned the civil engineer Robert Stevenson (1772–1850) to undertake a survey and prepare a report on a section of what was known as the Roxburgh and Selkirk Railway.[93] At this juncture, Stevenson generally planned waggonways (rails for waggon traffic pulled by horses), rather than the heavier track required for locomotives, but the descent into the Gala valley was too great a challenge for horse-led traffic which required lesser gradients.[94]

The route of Stevenson's plan was from St Boswells to Dalkeith. An 'Acting Committee' was established which included Lord Napier, Sir Walter Scott, and Gala, and the survey which they directed was undertaken between 1818 and 1822. Craig was the agent for the enterprise, and it was through Craig that Stevenson sought payment of his account from the project's subscribers. His report appeared in 1822 but, while the line remained in contemplation, Stevenson delayed pressing for his account, partly it seems because of a supposition that the duke of Buccleuch would contribute to his costs (Sir Walter Scott was not keen on pressing the duke and said he would rather pay out of his own pocket).[95] In 1827, however, Stevenson, armed with recent English authority and the opinion in a similar Scottish case given by the dean of the Faculty of Advocates, took a firmer line. The law, as he took it to be, was that 'when once men got into these companies, there they must remain, with all their liabilities, till they were fairly got out' even when they had no contract and the company had not been regularly founded.[96]

Craig's view was that Stevenson had to be paid and he thought that the latter's suggestion, of raising the money 'by assessing the subscribers according to a fair & equitable rate of the annual value of their properties', was preferable to discussing

---

[90]   SBA/1303/7/1, Craig/Robert Laidlaw, Edinburgh, 28 Jul. 1834.
[91]   Paterson, 'Parish of Galashiels', NSA, III, 28.
[92]   C. J. A. Robertson, *The Origins of the Scottish Railway System 1722–1844* (Edinburgh, 1983), 37.
[93]   See Hall, *History of Galashiels*, 100. Robert Stevenson, grandfather of Robert Louis Stevenson, was best known for the Bell Rock Lighthouse.
[94]   Robertson, *Origins of Scottish Railway*, 35–6.
[95]   SBA/1303/5/75, Craig/Robert Stevenson, civil engineer, 9 Jun. 1827.
[96]   *Sir J. Perring v Hone*, 4 Nov. 1826, 4 *Bing*. 28.

their liability in a court.[97] In this way, the liability was modest, the lowest sum being £1 and the highest, that of Scott of Harden, £28. Moreover, attempting to make the committee personally liable, given that they had acted for the public good, would have been a hardship. As Craig explained to John Tod WS (whose own liability was assessed at £2), Lord Napier had the idea for the project and 'the moment it took wing every one ran to put down his name'.[98] While they imagined the survey would cost no more than £100, in the end it cost £366 and, in the absence of any formal meeting or agreement, they were all jointly and severally liable as Stevenson's employers.

A circular, dated 20 June 1827, was sent around the subscribers setting out their assessed contributions. Craig attempted to engage in correspondence with them but this had mixed results, as he advised Stevenson in October, confessing himself 'at a loss to advise'.[99] Nonetheless, he suggested that Stevenson write to the non-payers once again, setting a deadline for payment to be made to Craig's deposit account in the Leith Bank of 19 November, under the threat of court summonses subsequently being sent. He also identified some Edinburgh agents Stevenson should visit who might encourage their clients to pay. This was unsuccessful, with seven subscribers agreeing to pay and thirty-three not, leaving Craig confessing to Napier that he was 'more at a loss how to settle with Mr Stevenson than ever'.[100] While Craig did not think the survey wasted, it was in fact for another generation, and a different plan adopted by the North British Railway Company, to develop the first line linking St Boswells to Dalkeith via Galashiels which opened in 1849.

EXPLOITING THE LAND

Peat

Peat was an important fuel, particularly given the cost of transporting coal to the Borders. Notable trade in peat had once been carried on from Gordon, from where it was sent to Kelso market by horseback. In 1824 Craig referred to this practice as having long been carried on but 'given up about thirty or thirty five years ago'.[101] He was writing to Robert Bruce, the bailie of Kelso, inquiring, on George Fairholme's behalf, how many horse loads of peat equated to a cart load. He asked Bruce to search the stent-masters' books (stent-masters were the burgh tax collectors). He thought it likely that

> the collectors of the Town Revenue would have the charge of it in the same way that they have now of coal, by seeing them weighed or measured, or at least a rule for it at their Public Weighhouse.

[97] SBA/1303/5/83, Craig/Tods & Romanes, WS, 4 Jul. 1827. A copy of the 1827 circular, setting out this authority, can be found in NRS, GD477/138/5.
[98] SBA/1303/5/92, Craig/John Tod WS, 20 Jul. 1827.
[99] SBA/1303/6/124, Craig/Robert Stevenson, Edinburgh, 12 Oct. 1827.
[100] SBA/1303/6/187, Craig/Lord Napier, 11 Jan. 1828.
[101] SBA/1303/3/315, Craig/Robert Bruce, 21 Feb. 1824.

This suggests an attempt to resurrect the trade. Craig had clearly been consulting the records, referring Fairholme to a book indicating the 'number of horse loads' belonging to each of his feus at Gordon moss and suggesting that if he decided to sell the feus 'I suppose you would keep the purchasers out of the moss altogether'.[102]

Within the year a legal dispute had arisen between Fairholme and the Gordon moss feuars over the question of access to the moss and Fairholme brought a sheriff court action with Craig employing the Melrose writer Thomas Scott to present Fairholme's case. He offered to meet Scott in Gordon in November 1824 to discuss the question on the spot.[103] Fairholme produced a printed address, to which the feuars responded by forming a committee and presenting demands.[104] Craig was anxious to have the question of the feuars' right to work the moss, and the quantity of moss to which they were entitled, referred to arbitration but evidently it was, according to Fairholme's address, for the feuars to seek arbitration and not Fairholme's representatives.[105] The action rumbled on and Craig's employer, anxious to keep on top of the costs, had him complain to Thomas Scott for failing to render his account.[106]

The peat moss at Gordon was an important resource but it was not isolated; most of the proprietors for whom Craig acted had peat mosses on their lands and they fell within Craig's purview. In 1825, for instance, he asked the Selkirkshire road surveyor, Thomas Mitchell, to attend to the drain at Parkhouse moss to ensure it was strong enough to bear the weight that was placed on it. If the drain gave way, he warned, this would 'fill the moss again & cost ten times more after, than now, in preventing it'.[107]

The importance of peat was why Craig & Rutherford took an immediate interest when Rob Gill, a local clothier, gave them a letter, drawings and specimens from James Buchanan of Glasgow who had invented 'machinery employed in the process of making peat into fuel'.[108] The estates of Gala, Torwoodlee, Bowland, Chapel and Greenknowe had considerable amounts of peat moss, and they asked Buchanan for more details of the cost of a licence under his patent, the cost of the machinery and its potential output. They also wanted more samples and listed more proprietors to whom Buchanan might send the information, including Baillie of Mellerstain and the duke of Buccleuch. J. Buchanan & Company of Union Street were coachbuilders, founded in 1834, but no details of their patent are known.[109] Experiments with peat as a fuel were ongoing and still being carried

[102] SBA/1303/3/292, Craig/George Fairholme, Bemersyde, 19 Dec. 1823.
[103] SBA/1303/4/123, Craig/Thomas Scott, 24 Nov. 1824.
[104] SBA/1303/4/136, idem, 28 Dec. 1824.
[105] SBA/1303/4/137, idem, 31 Dec. 1824.
[106] SBA/1303/4/300, idem, 11 Jan. 1826.
[107] SBA/1303/4/170, Craig/Thomas Mitchell, 17 Mar. 1825.
[108] SBA/1303/8/171, C&R/James Buchanan, 52 Union St., Glasgow, 2 Mar. 1838.
[109] *Post Office Annual Glasgow Directory*, 1838–9, p. 255; *Glasgow and its Environs* (London, 1891), 170.

out a decade later by James Young, the founder of Scottish shale-oil.[110] Galashiels interest, however, soon cooled when Buchanan sent circulars but asked for £50 for each licence under his patent. None of Craig's clients would attempt a trial 'on such heavy terms'.[111] Gill was to take up the matter on his next trip to Glasgow but nothing more seems to be heard of it.

Innovation might also be near at hand. William Kemp, manager of the local gasworks, devised 'an apparatus for supplying the furnaces with coal tar and thereby, in a great measure, doing away with common coal'.[112] This 'valuable discovery', Craig thought, would 'soon become known and generally acted upon in similar works, and eventually in steam navigation'. He invited the scientist Sir David Brewster to examine it with a view to giving Kemp some 'public mark of approbation'. The device, however, was a failure.[113]

Shooting Rights

The sport of shooting game was much practised locally and shooting rights were lucrative. To remain within the law, it was necessary to obtain a game certificate and this was something which Craig dealt with for his leading clients. Each year he normally purchased all their certificates together in one go. In 1823, for example, he wrote to Andrew Lang, sheriff clerk at Selkirk, acknowledging receipt of game certificates for Torwoodlee, Gala, Adam Fairholme of Chapel, George Fairholme of Greenknowe, Archibald Gibson of Ladhope and William Clark of Longhaugh.[114] Most were in Melrose parish but he specified that Chapel was in the parish of Lauder and Greenknowe in the parish of Gordon. Since Torwoodlee was not shooting that season, his certificate was to be given to another. Craig also requested a further certificate for George Pringle at Torwoodlee. He paid for these seven certificates, each costing £3 14s 6d, by banker's draft.

Administrative tasks such as these were Craig's forte and attention to detail was vital. For instance, the gamekeeper at Torwoodlee was Robert Anderson, in respect of whom Sir James Pringle purchased a game licence. John Swanston also killed game for Pringle but, as he was gamekeeper for Sir Walter Scott, Pringle had no liability to pay for his licence.[115] It was also necessary to pay tax for any hunting dogs. Craig's regular returns to the surveyor of taxes in Peebles reflect the changing dog-owning habits of his clients.

Shooting rights, an incident of the ownership of estates, were a valuable commodity in the area given the extent of game locally. It was Craig's business to exploit them to his clients' best advantage and he advertised leases of the right

[110] J. Butt, 'James Young, Scottish Industrialist and Philanthropist' (University of Glasgow PhD thesis, 1963), 72.
[111] SBA/1303/8/216, C&R/James Buchanan, 6 Apr. 1838.
[112] SBA/1303/7/378, Craig/Sir David Brewster, 1 Mar. 1837.
[113] Hall, *History of Galashiels*, 352.
[114] This was Mr William Clark of Langhaugh.
[115] SBA/1303/8/311, Craig/John McGowan, surveyor of taxes, Peebles, 7 Nov. 1838.

to shoot in the press. For this, Craig in the 1830s normally used a national publication, *The North British Advertiser*, as well as the *Kelso Mail*.[116] His advice to
Alexander Monro, in relation to advertising the game at Cockburn, was to do
so once or twice in each of those publications.[117] Earlier, he had used the *Caledonian Mercury* for this purpose, an example being an advertisement in 1825 for a
five-year let of the game at Caddonhead, described as being 3,000 acres in Stow
parish, with the optional addition of the game at the nearby farm of Trinlyknowe
(900 acres) near Ettrick Forest.[118]

As Craig told a potential tenant, Torwoodlee wanted £60 annually for the
five-year lease of Caddonhead. The area had 'always been considered the best in
the country' and Torwoodlee and his friends habitually lived there for three weeks
or so every season.[119] According to Craig, the laird was unwilling to sign a shorter
lease 'because a party might destroy the Game very much having it only one season'. There was a house, split with that of a shepherd and his family whose quarters
were unconnected to the accommodation for the shooting party. This included
two beds, a peat fire, a kitchen and stables. A five-year deal was not struck,
however, and the commercial value of the shooting rights may have been over-
estimated. Torwoodlee was willing in 1831 to accept £30 per annum for a proposed two-year lease.[120]

It was typical for individuals taking the lease of a house in the neighbourhood
for a year or two to seek shooting rights. William Colvin's 1,000 acre estate at
Torquhan, on the Gala Water north west of Stow, was available to let for a year
in 1838 and there was interest from a friend of John Fraser who had leased Gala
House. The game on the estate was described by Craig succinctly as 'hares and
partridges, Black game plenty, Grouse not'.[121]

The decision to let out shooting was not simply a financial one. When Tod of
Drygrange was interested in gaining the right to shoot at Caddonhead in 1834,
the rights were then held by Robert Thorburn, a farmer at Juniper Bank and one
of Craig's clients whom he described as 'an expert sportsman'.[122] Thorburn apparently had the right to sub-let. According to Craig, some of Thorburn's friends were
of opinion that 'more damage would be done to the sheep by inattentive takers
of the Game than all the Rent you would receive', and that it ought not to be
let.[123] He described Tod, however, as a 'quiet gentle "shot"' for whom an exception
might be made for perhaps a day or two per week if Thorburn was happy to charge
a moderate rent. Craig also understood that Tod might be spending more time in

[116] E.g. Greenknowe game, SBA/1303/8/338.
[117] SBA/1303/8/445, Craig/Alexander Monro jr, 5 Mar. 1839.
[118] *Caledonian Mercury*, 6 Jun. 1825, no. 16,192, p. 1. There is no reference to this in Craig's letter
books. On Trinlyknowe, see Pringle, *The Records of the Pringles*, 245–8.
[119] SBA/1303/4/199, Craig/D. Lees, Council Chamber, Edinburgh, 4 Jun. 1825.
[120] SBA/1303/6/166-7, Craig/John Gibson WS, 30 Mar. 1831.
[121] SBA/1303/8/220, Craig/Fraser, Leamington, 10 Apr. 1838.
[122] SBA/1303/8/303, Craig/John Colquhoun, Langlee, 31 Jul. 1838.
[123] SBA/1303/6/482, Craig/Mr Thorburn, Juniper Bank, 26 May 1834.

the country in future, and therefore the rent to be expected from him might rise over time.[124]

Concern for local tenants was also evident when a request was made by William Walker at Bowland to hunt with harriers on the Gala estate. The then tenant, John Fraser, who had the right to game as well as occupancy of Gala House, was happy to give permission. However, he required Walker to consult with Gala's estate tenants, James Sanderson in Meigle, William Paterson at Kilnknowe, William Scott in Mossilee, Adam Arras of Rink and George Anderson at Netherbarns.[125] Fraser and his servants had had previous run-ins with the tenants for disturbing their sheep when greyhound coursing. Given that the proposed use of harriers was during lambing season, he suspected the tenants would baulk 'at the very Idea of Harriers' and that none would give Walker leave to execute his plan.

Fishing Rights

Fishing and shooting generally went hand in hand, particularly on estates such as Trinlyknowe where the 'fishings & shootings' were much in demand.[126] The right to fish was an important asset and the law on fishing was an area where Craig needed to be up to date. When he heard from the MP, Pringle of Whytbank, that changes in the fishery laws had been proposed he wrote to the Tory agent in Melrose, James Curle. Pringle had not specified the changes and, as Scott of Gala's interest in fishing was 'worth looking after' he asked Curle to write back immediately with a summary the proposals.[127]

It was with a view to protect this interest that Craig wrote to James Sanderson in Meigle in 1836. The fishing on the Tweed had been included under a lease of Meigle from 1806 which had expired in 1825 but Sanderson, the current tenant, did not fish. Craig told Sanderson that Scott claimed the fishing on both sides of the river at that point, and had not objected to the opposite proprietor occasionally fishing,

> but to establish our right, and as you do not fish yourself, we should be at pains to *let* it to a respectable tenant during your lease which I beg you will pay attention to which I will also do – you to draw the rent and protect the water along with the tenant.[128]

This was a wise precaution. What is surprising is that Craig seems to have overlooked it for a decade.

The value of the 'Tweed fisheries', at least so far as Craig was willing to admit, was low. Having been charged £2 by the clerk to the Commissioners of the Tweed

---

[124] Henry Scott and Mr Berwick of the Canongate were tenants in Caddonhead in 1832–3: SBA/1303/6/347, Craig/Henry Scott, Grieve & Scott, Edinburgh, 8 Jan. 1833.

[125] SBA/1303/8/179, Craig/William Walker WS, Bowland.

[126] SBA/1303/8/478, Craig/George Fairholme, Ramsgate, 18 Apr. 1839.

[127] SBA/1303/5/123, Craig/James Curle, Melrose, 11 Oct. 1827.

[128] SBA/1303/7/227, Craig/James Sanderson, Meigle, 11 Jun. 1836; for Curle as clerk, see NRS, Kelso procurator fiscal's papers, AD30/48.

Fisheries, James Curle, for protecting them, Craig asserted that Scott's fisheries were let to Anderson at Netherbarns farm and valued 'at *nothing at all*, as they had yielded nothing for several years'.[129] Torwoodlee's fisheries at Caddonlee and Laidlawsteel were valued at just over one pound annual rental, whereas Curle had valued Gala's at £20. Craig demanded it be reduced.

CONCLUSION

Craig was always on the lookout for enterprising individuals and he himself had an entrepreneurial spirit. Enterprise demanded that the potential of rail travel be explored and this was done, albeit with disappointing results. As Craig noted in 1824, his was 'the age of adventure', and he foresaw that if, via rail, 'all the East Country trade with Edinburgh & Dalkeith can be brought this way it will make a wonderful difference to Galashiels'.[130] In 1836 Craig 'had much pleasure' in chairing a meeting in the Assembly Room at Galashiels to garner support for a proposed line between Newcastle and Edinburgh.[131] This was aided by a speech in favour by another law agent, Thomas Scott of Abbotsmeadow, but, despite working out possible routes, he saw no result in his lifetime.[132] His dealings with drysalters also reflect a desire to promote commercial advantage.

Wherever he went, Craig was concerned to make the most of every opportunity. On a visit to Gordon to collect the rents, for example, he thought of building a sawmill and interested the locals in the idea despite the challenge of finding a suitable location near a quarry and water. This challenge was removed when Bruce of Greenknowe offered an old barn as a site. This had potential, as Craig informed George Fairholme, since

> we have only to put up a mill & by a very little conducting bring forward his thrashing [sic] mill water . . . I am sure that you will order it immediately when we shall have Gates, Flakes, paling, Stobs & all sorts of Country work for wood purposes constantly on hand for the market.[133]

Much of his work when it came to larger infrastructure projects revolved around administrative tasks in the co-ordination of meetings and explaining and gaining consent from the significant landowners whose interests would be affected by whatever the project happened to be. This was true of road, rail and bridge-building as well as in the development of mills and other enterprises.

---

[129] SBA/1303/7/4, Craig/Curle, 25 Aug. 1834.
[130] SBA/1303/4/134, Craig/LBC, 20 Dec. 1824.
[131] SBA, John Smith Scrapbooks, D6/2/441; *Kelso Mail*, no. 4105, 15 Aug. 1836.
[132] SBA/1303/7/532-4, Craig/Gala, 12 Jul. 1839.
[133] SBA/1303/6/461, Craig/George Fairholme, Ramsgate, 6 Mar. 1834. A flake was a wicker cage used for winter fodder; stobs were pegs for the support of paling.

Chapter 8

Insurance

Every description of Fire Business is transacted on the most moderate terms; losses are settled with promptitude; and Tables of Premiums, and every information given gratis, on application at the Office, and at the Agencies.[1]

The fit between law and insurance was a natural one. In 1836, of the fifteen directors of the Standard Life Assurance Company in Edinburgh, six were writers to the signet and one, George Patton, was an advocate.[2] The manager, James Cheyne WS, was also a lawyer. Albeit at a less exalted level, our knowledge of Craig's work as an insurance agent comes mainly from the correspondence which he and Elliot Anderson had with the Edinburgh accountant Henry David Dickie (1792–1863), secretary of the Caledonian Insurance Company. Despite becoming manager of the company in 1828, Dickie remained the main correspondent for Craig until the appointment of John Moinet in 1835 as company secretary.[3]

Insurance, like banking, required local knowledge, if risks were to be properly assessed, and Craig was much in demand for his services. In 1806, he had been one of the first agents appointed by what was then the Caledonian Fire Office (established in Edinburgh in 1805 and later describing itself as 'the oldest Scottish establishment but one').[4] That, together with his later employment by the London Union Assurance Company, obliged him to turn down an approach to act as agent for the Scottish Union Insurance Company.[5] He also refused an offer from Sir John Hope to become local agent for both the fire and life departments of the Guardian Assurance Company in Edinburgh.[6]

Craig was more at home in banking than insurance. Neither he nor Anderson can be described as insurance experts, although they expanded their knowledge and made efforts to understand the practice of head office, sending queries whenever clarification was required. Insurance was still a developing industry and the terms of policies were being adjusted as understanding grew about the quantum of

---

[1] Advert for the Caledonian Insurance Company, *Kelso Mail*, no. 4060, 7 Mar. 1836.
[2] SBA/183/27, bundle 1831–1839.
[3] T. A. Lee., *Seekers of Truth: The Scottish Founders of Modern Public Accountancy* (Amsterdam, 2006), 118; for Moinet's appointment as company secretary, see ibid., 261.
[4] SBA/1303/4/248, Craig/George Dunlop WS, Edinburgh, 3 Oct. 1825; *Kelso Mail*, no. 4060, 7 Mar. 1836. By 1836, Caledonian had nine agents in the Borders, including two other writers, John Romanes (Lauder) and William Archibald (Kelso).
[5] SBA/1303/4/153, Craig/A. Henderson, Edinburgh, 11 Feb. 1825.
[6] Cf. SBA/1303/3/285, Craig/G. Dunlop, Edinburgh 4 Dec. 1823; SBA/1303/4/94, idem, 16 Sep. 1824.

risk. Craig's practice was to write out the details of each policy in a memorandum book which apparently no longer survives. Occasionally a policy schedule drafted by head office, and sent to Galashiels, did not conform to Craig's memo and he had to request an amendment. In one case, for example, a policy was drafted covering 'household furniture' which, according to the memorandum book, was supposed to cover 'a dwellinghouse in Galashiels stone & sl[ate-roofed] tenanted'.[7] In the correspondence, clients were referred to by name and policy number and where the client held more than one policy all the numbers were included.

Craig and Anderson's efforts to familiarise themselves with the detail of insurance practice is evident. They were unclear, for instance, about the point at which Caledonian became liable on a policy. Having seen cases quoted in the newspapers of policyholders trying to recover sums insured in the event of accidents, Craig wrote asking whether, following an accident, the company was liable

> from the date of the agent taking the note of Insurance, or till he writes the office for the policy or till the policy is actually sent off, suppose no money in either of the three cases be paid?[8]

Whatever answer was made is not referred to, but in 1835 Craig counselled a client that 'the present practice' of the Caledonian Insurance Company was that no-one was insured until the head office issued the policy.[9]

While Craig and Anderson depended on Dickie or Moinet to draft and supply insurance policies for their clients, and to advise them on points of detail, as agents they were capable of forming their own view of the company's practice and written circulars. In 1827, when the company introduced a 'new plan for discontiguous premises', Anderson addressed Dickie candidly:

> I cannot of course pretend to understand the rules by which you are guided in your charges; but if I understand the printed circulars about your new plan . . . it seems to be plain enough that the premium remains the same as under the old mode, & that the duty only is different & the terms of the policy in point of expression.[10]

The context of that comment was Anderson's attempt to understand a policy in favour of Sanderson & Paterson, the builders, who had insured two separate drying houses. If fire took hold in one of them, both would likely be destroyed, and it was unclear to Anderson from the wording – and, he ventured, would be unclear to others ('however distinct your meaning may be to yourselves') – whether the £400 cover applied to each property or was the ceiling of liability in respect of both. In plain terms, he asked Dickie whether the policy meant that the company would pay £400 or £800 in the event that both buildings were destroyed by fire.

---

[7] SBA/1303/6/139, Anderson/Dickie, 2 Feb. 1831.
[8] SBA/1303/4/462, Craig/Dickie, 25 Sep. 1826.
[9] SBA/1303/7/108, Anderson/D. Thomson, Acklington, 14 Oct. 1835.
[10] SBA/1303/5/13, Anderson/Dickie, 3 Feb. 1827.

Anderson confessed that he knew Dickie disapproved when he took it upon himself to make alterations to polices, but he never corrected a policy without first consulting Craig and gaining his 'direct concurrence'. The 'new plan' was also mentioned in relation to a policy being prepared for the Gala manufacturer, William Thomson, the following year. Notably, Thomson's existing policy with Scottish Union had been forwarded to Dickie for him to use as the basis of the new policy with Caledonian.[11]

In another query, Craig wanted a better understanding of policies covering materials that were partly hazardous and partly a common risk. He cited as an example the merchant William Laidlaw (policy no. 18070). When Laidlaw specified that he had hazardous goods of one description in his stock, such as spirits, Craig wanted to know whether the failure to specify hazardous stock of a different description would raise any question. He assumed it would not, telling Dickie that, being 'quite aware of the miscellaneous stock of a country merchant you will generally regulate your charges accordingly and that their policies will be all quite correct and safe for both parties'.[12]

A further area of doubt surrounded the question of what was insurable. In 1827, Craig enquired whether gentlemen's 'plantations' might be insured, since he had it in mind to insure Gala's plantation for £1,000 and had discussed the matter with the neighbouring landowner, Bruce of Langlee.[13] He returned to the same question in 1832 in respect of his own plantation, of about twenty-six English acres, at Gordon in Berwickshire. Craig noted that it 'was planted in the droughty year of 1826, & as few of the plants came away I had it almost all to do over again'.[14] Having been successfully planted, the value of the land had increased but Craig did not know how to estimate its value for insurance purposes; evidently Dickie informed him, since a policy was arranged.[15]

While they closely followed advice from Edinburgh, that did not stop Craig and Anderson from offering their own opinions occasionally as part of a joint effort. This was all the more necessary because of the intense competition between insurers. In 1826, for example, a number of cloth manufacturers insured with Caledonian threatened to move to the Scottish Union Insurance Company, claiming that their agent could sell them similar policies at 7s for which the Caledonian was charging them 10s 6d.[16] One reason for this was a differing approach to risk: the agent for the Scottish Union treated manufacturing furnaces as common fireplaces whereas the Caledonian placed them in a higher risk category.[17] Anderson returned to this the following year. If Caledonian insisted on charging

[11] SBA/1303/5/191, Anderson/Dickie, 15 Jan. 1828.
[12] SBA/1303/5/54, Craig/H. D. Dickie, Edinburgh, 21 Apr. 1827.
[13] SBA/1303/5/6, Craig/Dickie, 19 Jan. 1827.
[14] SBA/1303/6/290, Craig/Dickie, 17 May 1832.
[15] SBA/1303/6/295, Craig/Dickie, 30 May 1832.
[16] SBA/1303/4/470, Anderson/Dickie, 18 Oct. 1826.
[17] SBA/1303/4/500, Anderson/Dickie, 25 Nov. 1826.

higher premiums for what other offices regarded as common risks, he noted, their premium had 'but little chance of being paid'.[18]

In the face of competition, Craig was not above poaching customers from other insurers. He persuaded George Fairholme to leave the Sun Fire Office, which had an agent in Kelso, and insure his estate at Greenknowe with Caledonian.[19] Commenting to Dickie in July 1821, Craig noted that Caledonian's dividend and bonus 'continued to be very respectable' but, as further competition was in prospect, the partners and those interested in the company 'must use their exertions so as we continue to thrive'.[20] It is no coincidence that other clients of Craig became insured with the Caledonian Insurance Office. Gala and Torwoodlee, for example, had their insurance managed through Craig.[21] His local contacts, after all, were one of the reasons he had been so sought after as an agent.

COMMERCIAL FIRE INSURANCE

Insuring mills against fire damage had initially been a challenge for insurance companies because the methods of building and heating factories, as well as the method of cloth production, affected the level of risk but not in ways they always clearly understood.[22] Better information, especially about the use of fires and stoves within industrial premises, made it easier to classify the level of risk and adjust premiums. Even so, there is evidence that underinsurance was common in some industries. This might be a deliberate method of allowing reduced premiums in a competitive market, particularly in circumstances, such as farm stock, where the risk of a claim was regarded as low.[23]

Through Craig's letters to Dickie considerable information about conditions in local mills and workshops can be gleaned due to a bias in the correspondence towards the discussion of policies of insurance on commercial property. For example, 'workhouses' in Galashiels were not to be thought of in the same way as factories, according to Elliot Anderson, and they did not represent more than an ordinary risk of fire. In the context of a policy for the clothiers Robert Gill & Sons, a major firm in Galashiels, he described such buildings as being merely

> places where they finish & dress the cloth or spin yarn on hand jennies, & [they] have nothing of particular risk – their press ovens are heated by furnaces built in to the

---

[18] SBA/1303/5/14, Anderson/Dickie, 3 Feb. 1827.
[19] SBA/1303/2, fo, 54, Craig/Mr Ballantyne, Sun Fire Office, Kelso, 8 Jun. 1821; Craig/G. Fairholme, 8 Jun. 1821; ibid./64, Craig/Dickie, 23 Jun. 1821.
[20] SBA/1303/2/87, Craig/Dickie, 23 Jul. 1821.
[21] SBA/1303/5/158 (cont. from 154), Anderson/Dickie, 5 Dec. 1827.
[22] P. G. M. Dickson, *The Sun Insurance Office 1710–1960: The History of Two and a Half Centuries of British Insurance* (London, 1960), 91.
[23] R. Ryan. 'The Norwich Union and the British fire insurance market in the early nineteenth century' in O. M. Westall, ed., *The Historian and the Business of Insurance* (Manchester, 1984), 45. See J. P. P. Higgins and S. Pollard, *Aspects of Capital Investment in Great Britain, 1750–1850* (London, 1971), 115.

walls of the house, & are not more dangerous than common chimneys, perhaps not so much so.[24]

As a result, Anderson thought them no more than a common risk. Dickie may have been unconvinced, since Gill & Sons returned a policy, charged at a higher rate 'of doubly hazardous', and took a new one at the common rate supplied by a rival company, the Norwich Union, whose Galashiels agent was the writer Robert Haldane.[25] This caused Craig to invite Dickie or one of his colleagues to come to Galashiels to carry out their own inspection of cloth manufacturers' premises, since he was convinced that they would better understand the level of risk involved.[26]

Another cloth manufacturing firm, John & Walter Cochrane, also questioned the level of risk, suggesting they had been overcharged.[27] Anderson regarded this as a matter for his employers to judge after careful inspection. However, he did note that the workshops and dye houses which Caledonian had previously reckoned to be hazardous seemed an unlikely source of fire, since they contained only woollen goods mostly in a wet state. On the other hand, the

> furnaces are all or nearly so on the outside & in stone gables with good vents, & sunk below the surface of the ground, & their furnaces in their press shops that are inside are all sunk below the level of earthen or stone floors & to all appearance much safer than any common fire place.[28]

Much trouble, he observed, would be saved in returning and altering policies if head office would send out an inspector to look at premises.

Craig, for his part, was sometimes prepared to overrule head office and make his own risk assessment. In discussing the consolidation of existing polices held by a client, Craig noted that Dickie had made an additional charge because the insured premises were near the corn mills. He regarded this as no reason to elevate the risk; in fact, Craig himself owned property much nearer the mills and did not think it ran any risk on account of it.[29]

When Torwoodlee's kiln at Buckholmside mill burnt down in February 1833, causing about £30 worth of damage, it was found that there had been wool drying on it, belonging to a tenant, which should not have been placed there.[30] Had it not been for the actions of about 100 young men, Craig related, the whole building, plus the wheat and flour within it belonging to a local baker, would have been lost. In appreciation, Craig ordered the firefighters a hogshead of ale, at the

[24] SBA/1303/4/293, Anderson/Dickie, 2 Jan. 1826.
[25] *Pigot's Commercial Directory*, 1825–6, 657.
[26] SBA/1303/4/336, Craig/Dickie, 27 Feb. 1826.
[27] On the Cochranes, see SBA, SBA/83/9, Sanderson, 'Old Galashiels;', 23–4.
[28] SBA/1303/4/500, Anderson/Dickie, 25 Nov. 1826.
[29] SBA/1303/3/117, Craig/Dickie, 1 Feb. 1823.
[30] SBA/1303/6/358, Craig/Dickie, 20 Feb. 1833. Wool is much less likely to ignite than grain, therefore was unlikely to have contributed as a cause of the fire.

insurance company's expense.[31] The building had cost Torwoodlee over £1,500 and he had insured it for £1,100. Craig feared that the policy might be rendered useless 'by a foolish act of his tenant' who was already in financial difficulties and had no means of repairing the damage. He had never heard of wool being dried on a kiln in the winter but had since learned that it was done in Galashiels as well as Buckholmside and immediately vowed to have it stopped.

Craig inherently had a conflict of interest, being agent of both Torwoodlee and the insurance company. He resolved this squarely in favour of Torwoodlee, raising as 'a question of doubt' whether wool or corn was more likely to ignite. Whatever the fact was, he informed Dickie that the popular view locally was that wool was much less flammable than grain, warning that it would be highly 'impolitic', in a relatively small claim, to encourage further discussion about the respective levels of risk 'in a place where the public have made up their minds that the difference was in your favour'.[32] Refusing the claim because of the wool, in other words, made no commercial sense because it would be seen as a pretext for avoiding the claim and damage the company's reputation locally.

Measures to improve conditions for workers, such as the introduction of a stove to provide heat, had to be carefully assessed in terms of additional risk. Complaints about the unfairness of high charges for stoves in machinery houses were of long-standing, but the head office seems to have taken little notice and queries concerning them arose frequently.[33] Stoves were sought in working premises (including between water wheels to be used in severe frost) but also, for example, in Stow church where some of the heritors thought one desirable.[34] Others, however, considered the church so damp that a stove would be of no comfort to the congregation. Craig instructed a firm of builders in Darnick to visit the church and report on the matter.[35]

Craig himself occasionally made site visits, sometimes accompanied by an experienced surveyor or tradesman, to make an assessment and recommendation to head office. As well as providing detailed descriptions, Craig and Anderson would also send plans and sketches of property as an aid to assessing risk.[36] It is worth quoting at some length a description which was sent to Dickie in 1825:

> In the 4th flat of the woollen machinery or factory house occupied by J. Sime & Son they propose to run a stove pipe along the Roof of the apartment from east to West the long length for the purpose of heating it only during the Winter Months for the comfort of the workers, and for no other purpose. This stove pipe is made of what is

---

[31] In another case, Elliot Anderson recommended a reward for those helping to fight a fire: SBA/1303/5/109, Anderson/Dickie, 3 Aug. 1827.

[32] SBA/1303/6/362, Craig/Dickie, 27 Feb. 1833.

[33] E.g. SBA/1303/3/118, Craig/Dickie, 1 Feb. 1823, re R. Lees' machinery house. Charges for 'small stoves in common vents', however, were not made until 1835: SBA/1303/7/77, Anderson/Dickie, 9 Jun. 1835.

[34] SBA/1303/4/274, Anderson/Dickie, 23 Nov. 1825.

[35] SBA/1303/8/88, C&R/Messrs Smith, 21 Nov. 1837.

[36] E.g. SBA/1303/5/22, Anderson/Dickie, 20 Feb. 1827.

called double rolled black iron of the 12th of an inch in thickness and is supported by iron hold-fasts from the joists all the way along 44 feet & terminates in the vent of the West Gable. Hislop the smith who I took to look at it does not think there is more risk from it than from a common fire place in a room.[37]

In the same letter, he noted that William Laidlaw required a small portable stove to be placed in his cellar when bottling his wine in the winter. This would be positioned on the earthen floor of the cellar, connected to a pipe that went through a stove vent in the back wall, a situation Craig thought should be safe, particularly as the stove only required to be heated for about ten days each year. The Simes were later were permitted a stove in another apartment of their factory for drying their dyed wool.[38]

A similar request was made by the manufacturing firm J. & H. Brown who wanted a small stove in their dye house which would 'dry their undyed webs' when required. They also asked for another stove to heat their wareroom 'for 2 or 3 hours in the forenoon only when they are beside it'. Anderson thought that both stoves were so small they posed no risk and that Dickie might indorse their policy accordingly.[39] Over time, James and Henry Brown extended their business. In June 1837, they obtained from the Selkirk magistrates a feu disposition of land which, by December, contained a woollen factory (the Dunsdale Woollen Factory) which was in full production, having been built at a cost of £12,000. The premises were insured with the Caledonian for £5,000 and the North British Insurance Company for £500. Craig's firm were happy to recommend them as 'respectable business people' to whom others could confidently lend money on security of these premises.[40] The arrangement of the insurance provides a reminder that Craig was very much an agent for Caledonian and in a subordinate position. When the Browns complained to him about a 'night work' clause that had been sent to them from Edinburgh but which had not been embodied in their policy when it was issued, Craig could do nothing but pass on their complaint to Moinet at the head office and transmit the reply to Selkirk.[41] The firm had no intention of engaging in night working but resented the fact that they were being prevented from doing so without consultation.[42]

In terms of fire insurance policies in relation to mills and houses, most transactions were routine, involving a mixture of new business and the amendment of existing policies as building development took place.[43] Naked flames in woollen mills made them particularly vulnerable to fire. Policy amendments to reflect

[37] SBA/1303/4/263, Craig/Dickie, 3 Nov. 1825.
[38] SBA/1303/5/154, Anderson/Dickie, 3 Dec. 1827.
[39] SBA/1303/4/277.
[40] SBA/1303/8/117, C&R/G. Hector WS, 28 Dec. 1837. This appears to have been the original building of Ettrick Mill.
[41] SBA/1303/8/85, Craig/Moinet, 18 Nov. 1837; SBA/1303/8/88, Craig/J. & H. Brown, 21 Nov. 1837.
[42] According to CRCB, Hugh Brown was still paying his premium (£11 14s 2d) in 1844: SBA/1303/9/684.
[43] E.g. the corn and flour mills of James Pringle of Torwoodlee in Melrose: SBA/1303/9/139, 15 Nov. 1827.

changed circumstances, such as requests for permission to use small stoves during the day in winter for drying dyed wool, were regularly sought.[44] Sometimes the business form changed, as when Marion Whale had the name on her policy altered to 'Miss M. Whale & Co. Thread Manufacturers'.[45] The letters reflect work being done to develop Galashiels; in one case Craig wanted to know whether the builders, Sanderson & Paterson, could insure a quantity of tar in a shed for a period of less than six months.[46] On behalf of the same firm, he later expressed discontent with the wording of a policy protecting their workshop and the stock within from fire. He noted that a stove, although situated very inconveniently for the workmen, had been placed 'with a view to safety alone', and that having a common fireplace in the building would be 'a hundred times more hazardous'.[47] Including a plan of the premises in his letter, he set out his client's instruction concerning an increase in the level of cover.

There are other examples of stock being insured. One is the Galashiels millwright William Bathgate who insured the working utensils, timber and other stock in trade in his shop, as well as spinning jennies, books, patterns, casting and woollen goods, which he also housed under the same roof.[48] Care was taken in another policy, in respect of a two-storey house which had been entirely turned into a wright's shop, to ensure that his tools were specifically covered.[49] Where a premium for insuring the property of one client was disproportionate to that charged for another, Craig or Anderson did not hold back from pointing this out to Dickie.[50] Similarly, where stock was underinsured, Craig was happy to indicate to a client if undue risk was involved, as in the case of John Henderson, a baker in Gordon. Henderson's premises, grain and liquors were, Craig informed him, insured for only £100, 'whereas I should suppose £500 would be little enough'.[51]

The dangers of kilns did not only affect mills, but also had an impact on the brewing industry. In 1823, when William Brown established a new brewhouse in Galashiels, Elliot Anderson sent a description of it to Dickie, so that he might be in a position to assess the level of risk involved in the operation. Each item insured was valued separately. According to Anderson,

> The kiln is formed by a large grate in the centre of a stone building about 16 feet square which contains nothing else, & the malt is dried on cast metal plates raised about 12 feet above that grate. Mr Brown therefore thinks no danger can arise from the Kiln & that consequently the insurance should be at a less hazardous rate.[52]

[44] SBA/1303/5/153-4, Craig/Dickie, 3 Dec. 1827; SBA/1303/5/163, 10 Dec. 1827. Thomas Mercer's mill burned down twice within six years: *The Scotsman*, 20 Mar. 1819, p. 92.
[45] SBA/1303/5/54, Anderson/Dickie, 21 Apr. 1827.
[46] SBA/1303/2/101, Craig/Dickie, 10 Aug. 1821.
[47] SBA/1303/5/8-9, Craig/Dickie, 24 Jan. 1827.
[48] SBA/1303/4/490 (cont. from 488), Craig/Dickie, 13 Nov. 1826.
[49] SBA/1303/8/271, C&R/Moinet, 18 Jun. 1837.
[50] E.g. SBA/1303/5/15, Anderson/Dickie, 5 Feb. 1827.
[51] SBA/1303/8/41, C&R/John Henderson, 16 Sep. 1837.
[52] SBA/1303/3/123, Anderson/Dickie, 10 Feb. 1823.

Again, the focus was very much on categorising the risk and attempting to achieve the best outcome for the client.

In practical terms, most clients seem to have insured personally with Craig, although others chose to do so directly at the head office in Edinburgh. The manufacturers G. & J. Boyd, in Stow, fell into the latter category, paying six guineas for £1,200 worth of cover for a number of years.[53] This was less than the going rate for factories in Galashiels and, when they applied through him for a policy, Craig imagined that Dickie would find an explanation for this in the company's books.

Craig's adventures in fire insurance prompted him to try to raise funds to acquire a fire engine for the town. Having investigated the cost in 1823, he was told it would be £150. A town meeting took place to discuss it.[54] Craig corresponded on the matter with William Braidwood in Edinburgh, the then manager of the Caledonian Fire Insurance Company, but nothing further is noted until 1836.[55] The immediate concern, as usual, was the jeopardy posed by kilns in the corn mills in Galashiels and nearby Buckholm which posed a significant risk of causing major damage. Craig wrote to Dickie to persuade Caledonian that a fire engine was in their interests.[56] He had thought through what was required, stating that an engine would have to be housed in a small building with slated roof and plastered walls in order to keep the pipes 'in a wholesome state'. Additionally, a small salary for a man to exercise the pipes once a month would be necessary.[57] Given a recent incident, which but for swift action would have involved a loss of £4,000, Craig hoped that support would be forthcoming. He was, of course, not disinterested, since he himself owned nine properties in the upper part of Galashiels. These were insured for £1,520 and, being relatively distant from a water source, they were highly vulnerable to fire damage.[58] For that reason, in 1831, he had tried a different tack by attempting to persuade Dickie's company to make a financial contribution to the effort to bring water to that part of the town.[59]

In relation to the fire engine, Craig's efforts were in vain. It was not until 1863 that Galashiels obtained its first fire engine and, until then, efforts to combat fire continued to rely on the alertness of locals able to ferry water from the nearest water supply.[60] This contrasts with nearby Kelso which had fire engines at a much earlier date. It was also made clear in the Kelso fire regulations that the bailie, who was then the writer John Smith, was responsible for directing operations in the event of fire and, in particular, for placement of the two fire-engines.[61]

---

[53] SBA/1303/4/463, Anderson/Dickie, 27 Sep. 1826.
[54] SBA/1303/3/108, Craig/Dickie, 15 Jan. 1823. Town meetings, sometimes chaired by Craig, were not unusual. See, e.g., See Hall, *History of Galashiels*, 113. It was said in 1826 that, typically, 'harmony prevailed' in the town's meetings: NRS, Scott of Gala papers, GD477/463/7, fo. 12.
[55] SBA/1303/4/194, Craig/Braidwood, 17 Jun. 1823.
[56] SBA/1303/7/167, Craig/Dickie, 18 Feb. 1836.
[57] SBA/1303/7/159-60, Craig/Dickie, 11 Feb. 1836.
[58] SBA/1303/6/163, Craig/Dickie, 25 Mar. 1831.
[59] Ibid. Craig sought a 450-gallon cistern for the upper district that would cost £50.
[60] Hall, *History of Galashiels*, 362.
[61] SBA, SBA/183/5, *Regulations for the Prevention of Fire in Kelso* (Kelso, 1814), 5.

NON-COMMERCIAL INSURANCE

In regard to non-commercial insurance, there was also much that was routine. Craig arranged policies for his clients which, once made, were later endorsed or cancelled as the occasion arose. An interesting example is a request Craig sent to Dickie to endorse a policy in favour of George Fairholme for a pianoforte which was then standing in the 'furniture wareroom' of the builders Sanderson & Paterson in Galashiels. The wareroom, he noted, was under the same roof as the firm's wrights' workshop in a two-story stone building, placing it at unusual risk.[62]

One of Craig's clients, Adam Arras of Rink, 'from considerate feelings towards their general welfare', made his servants insure 'their little all' with Caledonian. In this case, Anderson sought to have the premium reduced to its minimum and the policy charged strictly according to the sum insured to minimise stamp duty.[63] Arras, according to Craig, took 'a particular interest in keeping his servants right'.[64]

Through Craig's office, clients might arrange insurance of property locally and also elsewhere. The minister at Stow, for example, Rev. John Cormack, insured his furniture and books in the local manse for £300 and also at his house, 7 St Vincent Street in Edinburgh, for £200, and had this consolidated within a single policy.[65] The manse itself was insured by the heritors of Stow, although a misunderstanding over arrangements led to a curious incident in 1827 when a policy arranged by Craig had to be returned. It transpired that the manse and some other property held by the heritors had already been insured with the Edinburgh Friendly Insurance Company since 1814. The heritors had been unaware of this because Gilbert Innes of Stow, one of their number, had paid the premiums for thirteen years but made no demand upon the others to contribute.[66] As one of the wealthiest men in the country, and deputy governor to the Royal Bank of Scotland, the cost would have been inconsequential to him. Noting that the other heritors had taken out a second policy unnecessarily, Innes wrote directly to Henry Dickie at Caledonian noting that 'a double insurance without intimation to the Insurers would be fatal to one of the policies & might endanger both'. As a director of Friendly Insurance, Innes intended to continue doing business with them. Craig, on the other hand, was sympathetic to the other heritors due to Innes's lack of candour, thinking it 'no wonder' they had thought the property was uninsured.

Fires in domestic properties, if not insured by Caledonian, could be good for business, as could near misses. Anderson informed Dickie that he expected to have 'the pleasure of sending you a few more orders by & by' because the previous Sunday

> there was a thatched house burnt down in the centre of this town which created a considerable bustle among us all; as it was adjoining & to windward of a row of other

---

[62] SBA/1303/4/269, Anderson/Dickie, 17 Nov. 1825.
[63] SBA/1303/7/100, Anderson/Dickie, 26 Oct. 1835.
[64] SBA/1303/6/295, Craig/Dickie, 30 May 1832.
[65] SBA/1303/3/239, Anderson/Dickie, 5 Sep. 1823
[66] SBA/1303/5/93, Craig/Gilbert Innes of Stow, 21 Jul. 1827.

thatched ones, however the townspeople by their intrepidity & good arrangement saved the others & us of a probable loss likewise as we were interested in almost all the surrounding houses.[67]

Two other fires occurred the same afternoon destroying two shepherds' houses in different parts of the town.

TYPES OF PROPERTY INSURED

The correspondence provides details of the types of properties insured which tell us something of the living conditions and businesses of those who inhabited them. A note of a policy for Robert Paterson, a skinner in Bemersyde, mentioned that he held wool in two adjoining lofts containing a stove while the ground floor was 'tenanted by several families'.[68] The Galashiels baker, J. Brown, had a newly built house in 1821 of one and a half storeys which he insured for £100; the victual inside, however, was insured for £50 suggesting that the value of houses was not particularly high.[69] George Sommers, a Galashiels grocer, similarly insured a single-storey stone and slated house he owned in Darlingshaugh for £50 but groceries within it for £20, and 'wool woollen yarn & cloth' for £30.[70] Again, William Roberts' three-storey machinery house in Galashiels was insured for £200 but the machinery inside it was insured for £300, indicating buildings of comparatively modest value.[71] In contrast, the schoolmaster, D. Walker, had a two-storey stone and slated house which, with his household furniture, was insured for £150.[72] Thomas Bruce of Langlee insured the three-storey house, which he and his brother owned near Selkirk, for £350 and the neighbouring coach house and stable for £400.[73] The fact that some property may have been under-insured, however, makes meaningful comparison difficult.

LIFE ASSURANCE

In June 1823, on receipt of a circular from the accountant Archibald Gibson, the Edinburgh agent for the London Life Assurance Company, Craig replied expressing his enthusiasm for life assurance. Gibson was the son of Archibald Gibson of Ladhope WS and Craig wished him success. While observing that life assurance was 'a thing hardly known in the country', he offered his services and pointed out that he had many clients taking out fire insurance which, not many years before, had been 'as little attended to' as life assurance.[74] Norwich Union, which allowed

---

[67] SBA/1303/4/63, Anderson/Dickie, 13 Jul. 1824.
[68] SBA/1303/3/125, Anderson/Dickie, 14 Feb. 1823.
[69] SBA/1303/2/41, Craig/Dickie, 17 May 1821.
[70] SBA/1303/3/293, Craig/Dickie, 29 Dec, 1823.
[71] SBA/1303/7/123, Craig/Moinet, 14 Dec. 1835.
[72] SBA/1303/3/294, Craig/Dickie, 5 Jan. 1824.
[73] SBA/1303/7/133, Anderson/Moinet, 1 Jan. 1836.
[74] SBA/1303/3/191, Craig/Gibson, 14 Jun. 1823.

a division of profits amongst its insurers every seventh or tenth year, was at that time the local rival and, Craig noted, they offered life assurance. Craig's offer was taken up: he was, by December, an agent for London Union.[75]

When Dickie at the Caledonian Fire Insurance Company informed Craig in 1829 that he was thinking of extending his business to include life assurance, Craig, reflecting on his experience, stressed the limited local demand. Country gentlemen who could afford it, generally arranged such insurance in London or, more particularly, Edinburgh, where they took advice from their law agent as part of making a family settlement. Craig advised Dickie that if he was thinking of joining life assurance to fire insurance, the success of such a venture 'will depend much on your connection with WSs & advocates'.[76] Nonetheless, despite confessing that he had only managed to achieve the sale of two policies for London Union, he supported the attempt:

> I approve very much of Life Insurance in principle as there are few people whose situation in life is of any respectability at all who could not afford 20 or £30 per annum to secure a certain sum for one branch of their family or another; but in the Country among the more ordinary classes at least, it is surprising how little is done in that way even when the propriety of it is explained & enforced upon them.[77]

The Caledonian expanded into life assurance in 1833, but Craig for the time being continued as its agent for fire insurance only.

Craig worked for London Union through its Edinburgh agents. These were Gibson – latterly via his firm Burnet & Gibson in St Andrew's Square – and, from 1829, James Miller in Nelson Street. Business was limited and the attitude of the London head office does not seem to have chimed with what Craig considered reasonable.

A policy of assurance taken out on the life of Charles Rutherford provides an example of how these relationships worked. James Wilson of Otterburn, near Jedburgh, sought the policy in 1827, when Rutherford, the eldest son of Major Rutherford of Mossburnford, was aged thirty-two and described as 'in perfect health & of sound constitution'.[78] The policy, which was worth £330, was intended to secure a debt of the same amount.[79] Wilson, who later lived at Lindean, near Galashiels, wanted it for his sister, Miss Jean Wilson, who was presumably the creditor.[80] Rutherford was expected to succeed to some property but if he died without doing so then the amount would be covered by the policy. Craig

---

[75] SBA/1303/3/285, Craig/G. Dunlop, Edinburgh 4 Dec. 1823. It is possible that some letters to Gibson are unrecorded. There is, for example, reference on 28 June 1825 to a letter sent on 19 June which had gone unanswered but that earlier letter is not in the letter book and its content is unknown.

[76] SBA/1303/5/395, Craig/H. D. Dickie, 9 May 1829.

[77] Ibid.

[78] SBA/1303/5/66, Craig/Burnet & Gibson, 10 May 1827.

[79] SBA/1303/6/165, Craig/Dickie, 28 Mar. 1831.

[80] SBA/1303/6/144, Craig/James Miller, 18 Feb. 1831.

forwarded the request and asked, on Wilson's behalf, what the terms would be and whether they might be easier if paid annually or by means of a single payment for four or five years' of cover. Ten months later, the next mention is a letter stating that Craig's enquiry to Jedburgh to ascertain Rutherford's date of birth had elicited only the fact that he was born on 29 September and that he was unable to confirm whether it was 1779, 1780 or 1781.[81] Craig must have been uncharacteristically unclear in his letter to Jedburgh. The matter was not material, however, since the policy soon arrived at Craig's office and he sent an order for the premium which was £11 15s 7d.[82] The policy was taken out for three years on the basis of a premium paid annually, although when Craig sent the payment in 1829 he was unaware that James Miller had taken over as agent for the London Union and had to send a second bank order in his name.[83]

In March 1831 a request for a two-year extension to Rutherford's policy was declined. Craig and Wilson had gone down to have the necessary certificates completed for the renewal but been told by the local surgeon, Dr Hilson, that Rutherford had become asthmatic, although Rutherford was not present and none of his friends Craig spoke to was aware of the diagnosis.[84] Wilson still required the policy, therefore Craig wrote to Henry Dickie to see whether Caledonian would accept the risk, promising to send any required certificate to two respectable surgeons and adding his own view that 'there can be no objection to the policy'.[85] Caledonian did accept the risk, as Craig later informed Miller, 'on the same certificates', a clear criticism of the London office, although Dickie seems to have had the policy underwritten by the North British Insurance Company.[86] A second policy on Rutherford, with the North British, was instituted in 1835 when Craig himself, having just seen Rutherford in Jedburgh, commented that he was 'in perfect health, altho' one of his arms was tied up in a sling'.[87]

In 1829 Craig sent Miller the documents necessary to effect a policy on the life of the local minister in Galashiels, Nathaniel Paterson.[88] The policy was for £500 and the premiums were regularly paid.[89] Paterson hesitated on being charged extra 'on account of his bilious complaint' and Craig wondered whether, if he were free of the complaint, head office might permit a deduction.[90] He added that '[I]t is observed of bilious people that they are long lived though never enjoying

[81] SBA/1303/5/223, Craig/Robert Burnet, London Union Life Assurance Office, 11 Mar. 1828.

[82] SBA/1303/5/229, Craig/Burnet & Gibson, 22 Mar. 1828. The policy expired on 18 Feb. 1831, so must have been dated 19 Feb. 1831 and the timing suggests that it was sent directly to Craig from London.

[83] SBA/1303/5/358, Craig/Burnet & Gibson, 7 Feb. 1829; SBA/1303/5/360, Craig/James Miller, 13 Feb. 1829.

[84] SBA/1303/6/144-5, Craig/James Miller, 18 Feb. 1831; SBA/1303/3/165, Craig/Dickie, 28 Mar. 1831.

[85] SBA/1303/6/166, Craig/Dickie, 28 Mar. 1831.

[86] SBA/1303/6/177, Craig/Miller, 10 May 1831.

[87] SBA/1303/7/104, Craig/John Brashe, [North British Life Office, 1 Hanover St.], Edinburgh, 30 Sep. 1835.

[88] SBA/1303/5/386, Craig/Miller, 22 Apr. 1829.

[89] SBA/1303/6/379, Craig/Miller, 27 Apr. 1833; SBA/1303/6/472, idem, 18 Apr. 1834.

[90] SBA/1303/5/399, Craig/James Miller 16 May 1829.

perfect health, probably owing to the caution they observe more than others as to regimen & exercise'. Paterson's vote for the Tory candidate in the general election led to unrest locally that persuaded him, in 1833, to accept a translation to St Andrew's Church in Glasgow for which he left in December of that year.[91] In May 1834, he wrote to Anderson requesting a reduced premium. Anderson sent an excerpt of the letter to Miller, expressing his hope that the request would be granted given the perfect state of Paterson's health.[92] However, the London office refused a reduction and the policy was discontinued, leaving Paterson to make fresh arrangements in Glasgow.[93]

Craig, however, had already ended his relationship with London Union. It had never been as close as his relationship with the Caledonian and it is unsurprising that he abandoned it to take on Caledonian's life assurance business. In July 1833, he authorised Henry Dickie to subscribe on his behalf the necessary articles of agreement.[94] Caledonian's life assurance was promoted the following year by means of a circular which Elliot Anderson, on Craig's behalf, sent 'to all likely individuals' known to the firm. Like Craig, Anderson regretted that in their community 'this very obvious & simple method of leaving a family in comparatively comfortable circumstances seems to be either not understood or not duly appreciated'.[95]

Life policies seem, increasingly, to have been taken up. A note mentioning the situation of the respective firms' accounts as at Whitsunday 1838, with the balance in favour of the Caledonian Insurance Company of £166, bears reference to a life policy.[96] Such a policy, to the value of £200, was confirmed by the Caledonian directors for the Jedburgh grocer, Robert Lauder with another, in the same month in 1839, for Adam Arras in Rink.[97] Around the same time, efforts were made to canvass the Edinburgh agents for major insurance houses on behalf of William Stuart Walker of Bowland who, at the age of twenty-seven, sought life cover worth £5,000. Robert Laidlaw SSC was given a list of five offices to attend to find the best deal and was invited to mention any other 'respectable house holding out greater advantage' which he may have encountered.[98]

OFFICE PRACTICE

Insurance was, of course, a precise business and Craig's office made efforts to ensure accuracy and candour. Elliot Anderson, having added a memorandum to a

---

[91] Hall, *History of Galashiels*, 213–4.
[92] SBA/1303/6/485, Craig/Miller, 2 Jun. 1834.
[93] SBA/1303/7/59, Craig/Miller, 14 Apr. 1835.
[94] SBA/1303/6/401, Craig/Dickie, 13 Jul. 1833.
[95] SBA/1303/6/465, Anderson/Dickie, 23 Mar. 1834.
[96] SBA/1303/8/238, C&R/Moinet, 4 May 1838. The accounts were adjusted due to errors: SBA/1303/8/245-6, 249.
[97] SBA/1303/8/559, C&R/Robert Lauder, 29 Aug. 1839; SBA/1303/8/550, C&R/Mr Arras, Rink, 9 Aug. 1839; see also SBA/1303/8/547 for another example.
[98] SBA/1303/8/fo. 619, Craig/Robert Laidlaw, 4 Nov. 1839.

policy for a weaver's property indicating that there was 'no fire used in the premises', was therefore quick to correct any wrong impression he may have given.[99] He pointed out that a detached property with a slate roof which never used a fire would require no fire insurance. What he had meant to say was that the premises had no particular fire, other than a common fire for occasional use, and he had never meant to imply that 'weavers should be debarred the use of a common fire place or prevented from working by candle light', both of which the memorandum would have excluded.[100]

Precision ran both ways. When John Moinet was asked to recalculate a premium on a policy for a client who claimed it was 'about 1/4 too much for the year', he was told that 'our Galashiels people are very particular'.[101] This applied above all to price. After a fire at James Bathgate's premises was extinguished with minor damage, he noticed that he might be being over-charged on one of his policies because he paid a premium of £1 4s in respect of £200 cover for his dwelling-house while his neighbour paid only 19s for £350 cover.[102] Craig took this up with Dickie. For another client, Anderson asked Dickie if he could arrange the items in a policy in such a way that less duty was charged on it.[103]

As well as questions of price, Craig had to answer for head office errors, such as misaddressing policies. When Caledonian insured Charles Rutherford, for instance, it obtained a policy issued by the North British Life Assurance Office which it reissued; however the policy mistook Otterburn in Northumberland for Otterburn in Roxburghshire.[104] In another instance, a policy holder was designed 'innkeeper band' rather than tenant in 'Juniperbank' in Peeblesshire; and another was located in Galashiels instead of Housebyres.[105] Another type of error was misattributing cover. Thus £30 cover for Mr Elliot's workshop was intended as £15 cover for the shop and £15 cover for the tools and other furnishings within it.[106] Such mistakes often resulted from poor handwriting which could be exacerbated by the fact that handwritten comments were sometimes added directly to policies. Elliot Anderson, for instance, confessed to Dickie on one occasion that he was unable to follow 'the indorsations lately made' on a policy.[107]

Income

Craig appears to have made up his annual accounts with Caledonian's head office in May.[108] These were dealt with by the manager, Dickie, directly, rather than

[99] SBA/1303/4/470, Anderson/Dickie, 18 Oct. 1826.
[100] Ibid.
[101] SBA/1303/8/76, C&R/Moinet, 2 Nov. 1837.
[102] SBA/1303/3/108, Craig/Dickie, 15 Jan. 1823.
[103] SBA/1303/5/22, Anderson/Dickie, 20 Feb. 1827.
[104] SBA/1303/6/192, Anderson/Dickie, 16 Jun. 1831.
[105] SBA/1303/6/419, Anderson/Dickie, 23 Sep. 1833; SBA/1303/3/264, Craig/Dickie, 20 Oct. 1823.
[106] SBA/1303/6/128, Anderson/Dickie, 29 Dec. 1830.
[107] SBA/1303/6/51, Anderson/Dickie, 3 May 1830.
[108] SBA/1303/4/26, Craig/Mr Blaikie, Kilnknowe, 7 May 1824.

Moinet as company secretary. Craig received a commission as agent, rather than a fee and, according to their cash book, Craig & Rutherford's commission on the premiums paid by their clients in the late 1830s was 5 per cent.[109] In 1839 this amounted to a mere £3 2s 5d, with only four premiums regularly being paid. This suggests a substantial decline in business compared to the evidence of the 1820s. For the year ending 1837, Craig & Rutherford paid Caledonian a balance of over £150 which they owed following their transactions for the year.[110] This may have represented a settling of accounts as Craig transitioned from sole practitioner to partnership with Rutherford.

In 1824, Craig explained the rate of duty to George Fairholme: 'insurance is 2/ per £100 to the Office & 3/ per £100 to the Government in all 5/ per annum on £1200'.[111] In other words, Caledonian paid stamp duty at the rate of 3 per cent on premiums to the Deputy Collector of Stamp Revenue (John Gray) on behalf of Robert Hepburne who was appointed Head Distributor of Stamps in Scotland in 1805.[112] They retained 2 per cent of the premium, while Craig & Rutherford took 5 per cent on their own account as their commission.

This rate of 3s per £100 in stamp duty was regarded as high and the reason why poor people, particularly in rural Scotland, could often not afford insurance. The increase in the rate to 3 per cent had been widely criticised by insurance companies when it was imposed in 1815.[113] Thomas Pender, Comptroller of Stamps in Scotland, in evidence to a parliamentary commission, lamented the effect the 'very heavy duty' on insurance premiums had on the poor, noting that hardly any insurance for less than £100 was taken out. The cost of the duty was a deterrent since it outweighed the premium, to the extent that if no duty were charged at all in such cases the Revenue would be no worse off.[114]

It is impossible to say what contribution to Craig's income his insurance agency work made but success required agents with drive and in this he was not lacking.[115] The regularity of his correspondence with Dickie, however, suggests that the income must have been significant given the time devoted to it, even if it later declined. There is also the fact that Craig was providing a local service to his clients, one which he could not afford to neglect as a man of business. This extended to arranging insurance as factor on tenanted property which proved to be an efficient arrangement. An example is the insurance arranged for George Fairholme's tenants which was charged to them when their rents were settled, Craig thus simultaneously protecting his client's property and making money from his commission.[116]

[109] SBA/1303/9/353, 684.
[110] SBA/1303/7/447, Craig/Moinet, 17 May 1837.
[111] SBA/1303/4/138, Craig/Fairholme, 31 Dec. 1824.
[112] HC, *Report on Collection of Revenue*, 413.
[113] Dickson, *Sun Insurance Office*, 99.
[114] HC, *Report on Collection of Revenue*, 33.
[115] Higgins & Pollard, *Aspects of Capital Investment*, 195.
[116] SBA/1303/8/270, Craig/George Shiells, Kirkhill, Earlston, 18 Jun. 1838.

ANNUITIES AND OTHER TRANSACTIONS

Craig's firm was occasionally concerned in the management of annuities. In 1823 he wrote to Archibald Gibson, following an enquiry from a local man, James Stirling.[117] Stirling, described as 'a stout healthy man, aged 36', enquired what annual sum he would need to pay to secure an annuity of £30 for his seventeen-year-old son when he reached the age of thirty. Elliot Anderson had no experience of such transactions but assumed that Gibson, as agent for London Union, did. He asked to be informed, if such an arrangement could not be made, whether the same outcome could be achieved another way. The youth concerned was unable to walk in consequence of a severe fever which had, according to Dr Monro of Edinburgh, 'injured the spinal marrow'. His father was anxious to make provision in case of his own death or his son surviving beyond thirty, although Anderson added the comment that 'as an ordinary observer' he did not think that the latter was 'very possible'. A letter from John Moinet in 1838 reveals a similar attempt by another client to set up an endowment with Caledonian. This responded to a query concerning the annual premium required for a new-born child to receive £100 on attaining the age of sixteen, eighteen or twenty-one. If the age of sixteen was selected, the amount payable would, according to Moinet, be four guineas per year.[118]

Some of Craig's clients depended on financial arrangements made through family settlements or wills. These often feature intergenerational transfers of property subject to the payment of an annuity to a widow. Late payment, or non-payment, in such cases could cause significant distress. Craig was at his most imperious when chastising George Blaikie for his irregularity in paying such an annuity to his mother. According to Craig,

> she looks to me for its being regularly paid & if she grants you indulgence she does wrong as marring the understanding between her & me regarding it. I must say of all the piece [sic] of business I have ado with, this has been & appears to continue one of the most unpleasant & to me inexplicable on your part.[119]

In this case, £50 was payable yearly based on a settlement made by Mrs Blaikie's late husband.[120] The matter, however, was disputed and the accounts had been submitted to arbiters.[121] In a similar case, involving the payment of an annuity by George Lindsay in Earlston to his mother, who was 'much in want of it', the sum involved was a modest £2 10s.[122]

[117] SBA/1303/3/286, Anderson/Archibald Gibson junior, 6 Dec, 1823.
[118] SBA/1303/8/232, Moinet/C&R, 26 Apr. 1838.
[119] SBA/1303/3/208, Craig/G. Blaikie, Kilnknowe, 15 Jul. 1823.
[120] SBA/1303/2/19, Craig/Erskine & Curle, Melrose, 14 Apr. 1821.
[121] SBA/1303/3/14, Craig/George Scott, Tax Office, Jedburgh, 12 Jul. 1822.
[122] SBA/1303/7122, Craig/Lindsay, 10 Dec. 1835.

STORM DAMAGE

Craig's correspondence includes periodic mention of bad weather and severe storms. One such storm, which commenced on 1 February 1823, apparently did not cause the number of anticipated claims, despite Anderson fearing that it '*must certainly*' have occasioned losses.[123] Claims might have bypassed Craig's office and gone directly to Henry Dickie in Edinburgh, or perhaps the damage was largely to property, such as sheep, that was not insured. There was little correspondence with Dickie following the storm, although on 3 April a request was sent to see the policy for corn and hay which was kept in the stock yard at Torwoodlee.[124] The yard, insured for £100, comprised a constant stock of hay that was maintained for the benefit of tenants in case of bad weather. Craig, as he often did, enquired whether a policy for seven years might achieve better value in terms of premium than a series of annual policies.[125]

A similar stock was maintained by Arras of Rink who grew concerned that in the event of damage the corn in his granaries would not be included under the item listed as 'crop in stockyard'. As he had no wish to change the level of cover (£250), the matter was dealt with via a memorandum to head office detailing an adjustment. Arras wanted to transfer the risk from his stockyard to his granaries by rebalancing the cover 'to wit on corn in the granaries from 1 Feb. to 1 May £200 & in like manner for the remaining part of the year in the granaries £50'.[126] This was routine but demonstrates the importance of being able to tailor policies to meet the demands of the client.

CONCLUSION

Craig's involvement in insurance demonstrates the growth of industry in Galashiels and provides intimate detail of the living and working conditions of some policy holders. The phrase 'stone and slated' to describe property, such as a backhouse owned by James Stirling referred to in 1823, occurs with regularity.[127] According to Hall, when Craig took over as bailie in 1813, there were only 'eight or nine slated houses' in Galashiels and the letters thus show an improving and changing environment reflecting growing prosperity.[128] Insurance was an important indicator of wealth and Craig's correspondence would reward future research into the relative value of property owned by different classes in Galashiels across the period of two decades.[129]

---

[123] SBA/1303/3/124, Anderson/LBC, 12 Feb. 1823.

[124] Dickie was written to on 10 and 14 Feb., but this was routine business unrelated to the storm. The next letter was not until 3 Apr. (cited below).

[125] SBA/1303/3/148, Craig/Dickie, 3 April 1823.

[126] SBA/1303/5/22, Anderson/Dickie, 20 Feb. 1827.

[127] SBA/1303/3/240, Anderson/Dickie, 6 Sep. 1823.

[128] Hall, *History of Galashiels*, 98.

[129] See the discussion in B. Harris & C. McKean, *The Scottish Town in the Age of the Enlightenment 1740–1820* (Edinburgh, 2014), 296–300.

Making proper insurance arrangements was something every factor had to take into account and, provided they had property to insure to the value of £100 or more, Craig could do this directly for his clients.[130] He did so, however, in the face of strong competition from other agents locally, in Melrose, Selkirk and Kelso, including those of the Norwich Union, Edinburgh Friendly Insurance, Sun Fire Office, the Scottish Union Insurance Company, Hercules, the Norfolk Fire Office, Edinburgh Life Assurance and Guardian Exchange. The sheer number of local agents indicates the burgeoning market for insurance and some of Craig's regular correspondents, such as Andrew Lang in Selkirk and James Curle in Melrose, were insurance agents.

Craig himself was consistent in his allegiance to Caledonian, a company in which he owned four shares.[131] The regular contact between his office and Dickie, and then Moinet, reflect Craig's steadiness as an agent and is reminiscent of his involvement in banking. Craig proved keen to make enquiries on the ground and that fit neatly into his everyday commitments as factor, visiting estates owned by his various clients across the Borders counties. His more limited endeavours in life assurance for London Union demonstrated, as he was quick to acknowledge, local social and business realities.

As well as providing information about property, insurance arrangements incidentally tell us something of local community spirit. When fire caught hold, the local response was immediate. Elliot Anderson, who was heavily involved in the insurance side of the business, described to Dickie actions which saved a whole range of houses at Netherbarns in 1835. These would have burned down 'had Mr Anderson the tenant not been promptly on the spot & ordered the roofs to be separated, the repairing of which forms the main part of the damage'.[132] Elliot Anderson himself, when sitting up late reading, lent a hand, alongside 'three active young lads and a neighbouring servant girl', to restrict the damage to the local doctor's furniture when a couple of houses caught fire in the early hours of the morning.[133] In championing the purchase of a fire engine, Craig himself was also motivated by a sense of service to his community, not merely self-interest in reducing insurance claims.

Craig's engagement with the competitive world of insurance is no surprise. The evidence suggests that he was not as successful as some other local agents, due largely to the perceived inflexibility of the Caledonian Insurance Company, at least in the 1820s. It did, however, become more successful, eventually acquiring several domestic competitors and entering foreign markets. In the next chapter, we will investigate Craig's own engagement with the world outside Scotland.

---

[130] SBA/1303/4/470, Anderson/Dickie, 18 Oct. 1826.
[131] SBA/1303/5/381.
[132] SBA/1303/7/66, Anderson/Dickie, 6 May 1835.
[133] SBA/1303/5/97, Anderson/Dickie, 27 Jul. 1827.

Chapter 9

Furth of Scotland

Craig's concerns were usually local but that is not true of all of his correspondence. Analysis of a six-month sample of his letters suggests that as many as 5 per cent were addressed outside of Scotland.[1] There were also matters dealt with in Scotland which had a foreign element, such as bills drawn abroad or foreign probate. Early nineteenth-century emigration, often associated with the Highlands and Islands, was also a factor in depopulation in the Borders.[2] In his 1834 entry for Melrose in the *New Statistical Account of Scotland*, George Thomson noted not only the rise of the burgh's population, which he ascribed partly to agricultural improvements and the growth in manufacturing in nearby Galashiels, but also that this had been achieved despite emigration which 'has of late years been uncommonly great'.[3] As we shall see, Craig both facilitated emigration and had to manage the effects of it.

PROBATE

When Scots died in another jurisdiction, leaving behind property or legatees in their native country, this generated work for Scottish law agents. This type of work could be prolonged and complicated, made challenging by distance and unfamiliar procedures as well as the need to deal with foreign legal representatives. An example is the death of John Lindsay's stepbrother, Robert Haig, in Charleston, South Carolina, in December 1819.[4] Lindsay only had news of this belatedly, in April 1821, and indirectly via family members (merchants named Leckie) in Dunbar. It transpired that the High Court of Appeals in Charleston had been required to determine which of two surviving wills left by Haig was valid. Lindsay was found to be the beneficiary of a share in the residue of the

---

[1] Based on a sample (13 Jan.–30 Jun. 1827) in which 5.2 per cent of 299 letters were addressed to correspondents outside Scotland.

[2] See, for example, M. Harper, *Adventurers and Exiles: The Great Scottish Exodus* (London, 2003), 62, 122; E. J. Cowan, 'From the Southern Uplands from Southern Ontario', in T. M. Devine, ed., *Scottish Emigration and Scottish Society* (Edinburgh, 1992), 61–83; Devine, *The Scottish Nation*, 468–79; M. Prentis, *The Scots in Australia* (Sydney, 2008), esp. chapter 5; B. Wilkie, *The Scots in Australia, 1788–1838* (Suffolk, 2017), 31–50.

[3] *The New Statistical Account of Scotland* (William Blackwood and Sons: Edinburgh, 1845), III, p. 63.

[4] SBA/1303/2/32, John Lindsay/Whiteford Smith, William Watson & Robert Shand, Charlestown, America, 1 May 1821; also SBA/1303/3/51 (19 Sep. 1822), 138 (15 Mar. 1823), 148 (3 Apr. 1823).

estate and a power of attorney had to be transmitted to Haig's executors in Carolina in order for this to be paid. While payment was eventually obtained, Craig threatened the Leckies with legal action for not communicating information about the case.[5]

More straightforward was the case of Captain Ballantyne of Walthamstow who died in November 1822 leaving a widow in Scotland. Craig wrote to his then London agents, Robertson & Bullock, asking them to procure probate of the will from the appropriate court.[6] On discovering that the cost would be £4 or £5, Craig thought this high and asked if a simple copy of the will could be provided more cheaply since it would 'serve the same purpose to those wishing to have it'.[7] A copy was quickly provided.[8]

When a death occurred in Scotland, but a legatee lived elsewhere, the matter could also be straightforward. In 1837 Craig acted for Christian Laidlaw, the executrix for Helen Laidlaw (d. 1836) whose legatees included two nephews, Adam and Robert, who lived in Niagara, Upper Canada.[9] It was a simple matter for Craig to send the legatees a discharge along with instructions for signing and witnessing the document. Yet complications could also arise in such cases. The administration of the estate of William Anderson, who died at Netherbarns in 1820, was particularly difficult (it is discussed further below). One aspect of it was a £500 legacy to a natural child in Liverpool, also named William. In terms of the Stamp Act, according to Craig's clerk, a natural child must be 'looked on in law as an alien in blood', resulting in stamp duty at the high rate of 10 per cent., an interpretation he then confirmed with the Stamp Office in Edinburgh.[10] When the surviving executors were ready to make payment, they required a proper discharge in their name, drafted by a local Liverpool attorney. Noting the rate of government duty, Craig's clerk added:

> If it is necessary that the attorney should engross this in the Discharge by the English form it may be done, but the duty will be paid at the Stamp Office in Edinburgh along with the other duties according to their [sic] several degrees of consanguinity of the Legatees.[11]

On receipt of the discharge, a draft drawn on London for £450 was to be sent to the child's guardian in Liverpool.

---

[5] SBA/1303/3/51 (19 Sep. 1822); also SBA/1303/3/138 (15 Mar. 1823) and SBA/1303/3/148 (3 Apr. 1823). It is unclear why Craig had to operate through the Leckies.

[6] SBA/1303/3/107, Craig/Robertson & Bullock, London, 14 Jan. 1823. On Ballantyne, see above, p. 146.

[7] SBA/1303/3/115, Craig/Edward Bullock, London, 27 Jan. 1823.

[8] SBA/1303/3/128, idem, 19 Feb. 1823.

[9] SBA/1303/8/10, Craig/Robert and Adam Laidlaw, Niagara, 9 Aug. 1837. This branch of the Laidlaws, originally from Yarrow, might have a link to Craig's in-laws the Laidlaws of Drumelzier but this is not obvious. Robert (b. 1807) and Adam (b. 1817) were the sons of Alexander Laidlaw (b. 1775) and Janet Laidlaw who were married in 1800 at Yarrow.

[10] SBA/1303/3/153, Anderson/Mr Anderson, Netherbarns, 16 Apr. 1823.

[11] SBA/1303/3/169, Anderson/John Askew, Liverpool, 10 (dated 9) May 1823.

EMIGRATION

Poverty and unemployment often compelled Scots to emigrate. Robert Douglas pointed to depopulation caused 'by the union of farms, by the demolition of villages, and by emigrations to avoid oppressive laws'.[12] Agrarian changes put pressure on rural employment across Scotland and brought about a phenomenon so widespread it has been described as the 'Lowland Clearances'.[13]

This is reflected in the casual way emigration was sometimes mentioned in Craig's correspondence. When writing to Charles Orr WS in 1825 about a debt owed by Walter Frier and John Dobson, builders in Selkirk, for which an arrestment was executed in 1819, Craig thought the matter not worth pursuing. One of the partners, Frier, had gone to America and the other, Dobson, was in 'very indifferent' circumstances.[14] Another case involved a debt owed by Robert Henry, his son, Robert junior, and Archibald Elliot. Henry senior having been sequestrated, the creditors had to act against Elliot who had guaranteed payment of the debt in a bond of relief. According to Craig's clerk, Elliot was perfectly solvent and he advised their Edinburgh agent to inhibit his property. He described him as having 'a fidgety sort of temper', but suggested action was needed quickly because 'he is making preparations to follow the Henrys to America'.[15] In another case, legacies were paid out to individuals who 'were on the eve of emigrating to America', so that it was impossible to get from them any further documentation.[16] In another, Craig threatened to write to his 'agents in America' to recover a wood roup account owed by James Cessford's brother who had emigrated there, unless Cessford could be persuaded to pay it.[17]

In 1833 there is a less casual reference. Craig recommended two 'young agriculturists', keen to go to America, to James Gibson in London who was presumably an emigration agent. One was the son of a tenant of Tait of Pirn, 'as straightforward an enterprizing young man as I have seen', who had just embarked from Leith and planned

> to land at New York & remain there with a Mr William Somerville a Builder, & then proceed to Lake Erie to a Mr Thomas Taylor of Middlesex & after that either buy land to the extent of 3 or £400 or engage himself otherways.[18]

The other young man was the only son and namesake of John Fairburn, a former tenant of Baillie of Mellerstain and currently working as overseer with George

---

12 Douglas, *General View . . . Roxburghshire*, 219; Cowan, 'From the Southern Uplands from Southern Ontario', 66.
13 Devine, *The Scottish Nation*, 147–51, 459–61; ibid., *The Scottish Clearances* (Milton Keynes, 2018) esp. 83–101.
14 SBA/1303/4/173, Craig/Orr, 24 Mar. 1825.
15 SBA/1303/6/279-80, Anderson/Adam Paterson WS, 19 Apr. 1832. Inhibition was an order preventing the person subject to it from selling heritable property.
16 SBA/1303/7/56, Craig/Adam Paterson WS, 7 Apr. 1835. Note also the delayed emigration to America of the family of the late James Paris, mentioned in Chapter 2.
17 SBA/1303/7/112, Craig/J. Romanes, Lauder, 29 Oct. 1835.
18 SBA/1303/6/377, Craig/James Gibson, John's Coffee house, Cornhill, London, 24 Apr. 1833.

Bruce, the principal tenant of George Fairholme. Fairburn junior preferred 'trying his Fortune in America' and Craig had often had 'an opportunity of witnessing his skill & activity at Greenknowe', with Bruce speaking highly of him. Fairburn's father could only spare him £150 or £200 but Craig thought it might be to the mutual benefit of both young men, and Gibson, that he send him details. Both were aged about twenty-five and unmarried.

Of particular interest is a letter from 1823 to Torwoodlee from John Horsburgh, a tenant farmer at Caddonhead. Horsburgh thanked the laird for sending him a letter from Sir Henry Hay Makdougall of Makerstoun, in Roxburghshire, replying to one Torwoodlee had sent outlining Horsburgh's plan to go to New South Wales. Those going there without capital were at a great disadvantage, and Horsburgh had no capital. This was not, he said, from 'any want of industry or attention but solely from the peculiarly hard times the farmer has experienced for years past'.[19] As a result, Horsburgh could not go as a settler, intending to buy stock and farmland, but wanted a position as a government overseer, managing some of the land owned locally by the government for agricultural purposes. For that, he had to meet the expense of passage to New South Wales. Before attempting to raise the funds, however, he needed more certain information.

Makdougall maintained correspondence with his brother-in-law, Sir Thomas Makdougall-Brisbane, who had been, from 1821, the colony's governor.[20] Horsburgh sought to use this relationship by asking Magdougall, through Torwoodlee, to procure information from Brisbane as to his prospects of employment. Horsburgh described himself as a young man

> who has no capital, but has received a good education – has been regularly bred to farming – & could procure most ample testimonials of character, & of knowledge & experience of farming in all its branches, particularly the management of sheep stock as most approved in this country.[21]

Craig clearly thought well of him, since he also made another enquiry on his behalf and recommended him.[22] There is no trace of a response from Makdougall in Craig's letters, but Horsburgh was by no means in a unique situation. There was a line of patronage direct from Borders sheep farms to New South Wales during Brisbane's governorship which can only have expanded thereafter.

In 1834 Craig sent a note to Alexander Monro confessing that, through lack of notice, he had failed to find a young man willing to go to New South Wales with Monro's son Henry on a ship bound to sail from London on 30 May.[23] He did so with an air of surprise and despite having 'seen many shepherds at Nethertown roup on the 23rd & at Caddonhead delivery of stock on the 24th inst.' Shepherds

[19] SBA/1303/3/238, Horsburgh/Torwoodlee, 6 Sep. 1823.
[20] NRS, Scott of Gala papers, GD477/460.
[21] SBA/1303/3/239 Horsburgh/Torwoodlee, 6 Sep. 1823 [marked as 'dated 1 Sep.'].
[22] Ibid., Craig/A. Kinghorn, St Boswells, 6 Sep. 1823.
[23] SBA/1303/6/491, Craig/Monro, 26 May 1834. Netherton is in Northumberland.

and sheep farmers were clearly his target. Four years later, Amy Paterson, daughter of the late Bailie Paterson, called at Craig's office on behalf of George Lawson who was the son of her husband, the Burgher minister of Selkirk, by his first marriage.[24] She sought a letter of introduction from Dr Monro to his son Henry in Australia. Like Horsburgh, George planned to go to Australia without capital. He hoped to become apprentice or servant 'to some sheep farmer for the usual period of indentureship'.[25] In his note to Monro, Craig added as his own testimonial that the twenty-year-old was 'a very active and intelligent young man and well educated' with the enthusiasm in his chosen line of work to make a very good servant. Once his period of service was over, £300 or £400 would be sent him so that he could set himself up in farming.

This was the system that was generally employed. Craig's involvement lay in organising finance, although the amount of funding varied depending on the position of the would-be farmer. Craig explained this in some detail to George Fairholme in 1839 in relation to sending his third son, George Knight Erskine Fairholme (1822–1889) to Australia:

> The plan usually adopted with young men going to Australia as farmers (and many have been the instances in this quarter), is that they are placed under a respectable settler there for a year or two, in order that they may learn the rearing of stock and other matters and have their eyes about them for a suitable farm after which from £600 to £1000 is generally sent out for them to commence with and we would recommend that plan in Mr George's case rather than giving the £600 you mention out with him about this time twelvemonth. We should have thought that either Mr George Pringle or your brother would have advised you.[26]

Fairholme jr, who became famous as a watercolourist, left London for New South Wales in 1840 on the barque *St George*.[27]

While sheep farming in Australia held obvious potential for Borders farmers, the attraction of India was as strong in the Borders as it was anywhere else in Britain and occasional references reflect this. When Craig went to Jedburgh on an insurance matter, for example, he casually noted that a former local doctor, Dr Grant, 'had left and gone to India'.[28]

Not far from Galashiels lived Alexander Pringle of Whytbank (1747–1827), who had entered the East India Company and become a writer in the Madras civil service, and then a merchant, before returning to Scotland in 1790. Of his five sons, all but the eldest (Alexander, the MP for Selkirkshire, known as 'little Pringle' due to his diminutive height) also became writers in the Company.[29] Like

[24] On Lawson, see Hall, *History of Galashiels*, 250–1.
[25] SBA/1303/8/314-5, Craig/Monro, 18 Aug. 1838.
[26] SBA/1303/8/422, Craig/Fairholme, 1 Feb. 1839.
[27] W. R. F. Love, 'G.K.E. Fairholme, Gentleman, Scholar and Squatter' 12 (1984) *Journal of the Royal Historical Society of Queensland*, 55.
[28] SBA/1303/6/144, Craig/James Miller, Edinburgh, 18 Feb. 1831.
[29] Fisher, ed., *The House of Commons 1820–1832*, VI, 894–6.

William Chisholme in Jamaica, Pringle used his foreign-made wealth to repurchase his family estate at Yair, 'one of the loveliest little spots in Scotland' according to Robert Chambers.[30] He built Yair House in 1788, and his family resumed its long association with that of Sir Walter Scott.[31] When the Leith Bank made enquiries about the family, Craig informed them of what he knew. While he had had no opportunity to become familiar with their financial circumstances, he noted that Pringle was said 'to have considerable East India Stock not brought home with him' and that, besides his eldest son being a member of the Faculty of Advocates and commander of the Selkirkshire yeomanry, three sons were writers in India.[32] In short, from the bank's perspective, it was impossible to 'have a more respectable man' as a debtor.

Money was not the only thing locals brought back from India. In 1838, when Monro's tenant Wilson left Cockburn House, his brother-in-law, Major Smith, late of India, moved in.[33] Craig regarded Smith's family as sufficiently respectable that no notice need be taken of the change of resident, particularly as Wilson was an active tenant who would continue to work the land. According to Craig, Smith had furnished the house excellently, 'the furniture of most of the rooms being of teake [sic] and other beautiful woods brought by himself from India and manufactured by an Ingenious Upholsterer of Berwick of the name of Purves'.[34]

JAMAICA

Scottish involvement in the slave trade and colonial estate management have been the focus of much recent historiography, although it has long been recognised that the profits of estates built on slave labour in the West Indies and elsewhere flowed into the hands of Scottish merchants and entrepreneurs.[35] In the landmark decision in *Knight v Wedderburn* in 1778, the Court of Session adhered to a ruling that slave laws which applied abroad were not applicable in Scotland. As the Berwickshire judge Lord Kames put it, the Court of Session judges 'sit *here* to enforce right, not to enforce wrong'.[36] Even so, despite that declaration of Scots law, and even after the legislation which prohibited the importation of slaves in

---

[30] R. Chambers, *Picture of Scotland*, 144.

[31] Anderson, ed., *Journal of Sir Walter Scott*, 329.

[32] SBA/1303/4/160, Craig/LBC, 25 Feb. 1825.

[33] SBA/1303/8/236, Craig/Monro, 4 Jun. 1838.

[34] SBA/1303/8/368, idem, 5 Nov. 1838. This is a reference to the cabinet maker James Purves in Berwick-upon-Tweed: G. Beard et al., ed., *Dictionary of English Furniture Makers 1660–1840* (Leeds, 1986), 724.

[35] See, e.g., T. M. Devine, 'Did slavery make Scotia great?' 4 (2001) *Britain and the World*, 40–64.

[36] Sir David Dalrymple of Hailes, *Decisions of the Lords of Council and Session, from 1766–1791* (2 vols, Edinburgh: W. Tait, 1826), II, 777–80; J. W. Cairns, 'The definition of slavery in eighteenth-century thinking' in J. Allain, *The Legal Understanding of Slavery* (Oxford, 2012), 61 at 79; see also generally, ibid., 'After *Somerset*: the Scottish experience' 33 (2012) *Journal of Legal History*, 291–312.

1807, individuals occasionally brought their slaves to Scotland.[37] The slave trade itself continued until outlawed within the British Empire in 1834.[38]

Scots were heavily involved in the development, management and ownership of slave estates in Jamaica and elsewhere in the Caribbean. Many prominent eighteenth-century Scots lawyers had family and professional links to slave estates and some themselves owned slaves.[39] In Craig's day, some lawyers and law agents supported the slave trade, including the Tory sheriff Archibald Alison and, another Tory, the writer Colin Dunlop Donald who was secretary of the Glasgow West Indian Association.[40] Less is yet known of the lawyers who were involved in the closer management of overseas estates, although it is clear that Scots feature prominently as overseers and attorneys in Jamaica.[41] Given the prevalence of Scotland's connections with slave plantations, it is no surprise that Craig, at some point, should have come into contact with one. His brother lawyer in Melrose, David Spence, had himself journeyed to Jamaica in his youth where his uncle, who had lived there some time, kept slaves.[42]

Craig's involvement came via the affairs of the late William Anderson, formerly an overseer in Jamaica, whose death at Netherbarns, near Galashiels, on 12 October 1820 has already been mentioned.[43] Netherbarns was part of the Gala estate and Anderson would have been one of the laird's tenants.[44] Anderson, acting under a power of attorney (it is unclear whether he was properly an attorney in the common law sense), had managed the Jamaican estates owned by William (d. 1802) and then James Chisholme (d. 1812), who were originally from Selkirk.[45]

---

[37] 47 Geo. III, c. 36, *An Act for the Abolition of the Slave Trade*. An example of the importation of a slave occurs in Advocates Library Session Papers, Moncreiff Collection, vol. 32, no. 22, *The Petition of Robert Paul*, 3 Jul. 1815.

[38] 3 & 4 Will. 4, c. 73, *An Act for the Abolition of Slavery throughout the British Colonies*.

[39] J. W. Cairns, 'Slavery without a *Code Noir*: Scotland 1700–1778' in F. M. Larkin & N. N. Dawson, ed., *Lawyers, the Law and History* (Dublin, 2013), 148, 157–161.

[40] On Alison, see C. Hall, '"The Most Unbending Conservative in Britain": Archibald Alison and Pro-Slavery Discourse' in T. M. Devine, ed., *Recovering Scotland's Slavery Past: The Caribbean Connection*, (Edinburgh, 2015), 206–24; M. Michie, *An Enlightenment Tory in Victorian Scotland: The Career of Sir Archibald Alison* (East Lothian: Tuckwell, 1997); on Donald, see S. Mullen, *The Glasgow Sugar Aristocracy* (London, 2022), 37, 49–50.

[41] Devine, 'Did slavery make Scotia great?' 40, 53. On Scots involvement in the eighteenth-century trade, see J. W. Cairns, 'Importing enslaved Africans into Eighteenth-Century Scotland', in *Deutsches, Europäisches und Vergleichendes Wirtschaftsrecht: Festschrift für Werner Ebke zum 70*, ed, B. Paal *et al.* (Munich, 2021), 155, 157–59.

[42] Spence, *Tenacious of the Past*, ed. King & Tulloch, 30.

[43] See note 10; *The Scots Magazine* 88 (1821), p. 240. Bailie Thomas Paterson had a clerk called William Anderson in 1805: NRS, Scott of Gala papers, GD477/143/13. Was this the same man?

[44] George Anderson was the tenant there in 1838: SBA/1303/8/179, Craig/William Walker WS, Bowland, 7 Mar. 1838.

[45] William repurchased the family estate, including Chisholme House, near Hawick when he returned to Scotland: UCL, *Legacies of British Slavery* database, www.ucl.ac.uk/lbs/person/view/2146635823 (accessed 20 Mar. 2022).

Their property included the Trout Hall estate in Clarendon and an interest in the Green River estate.[46] Anderson himself was of a Borders family (a daughter of his drowned in the Ettrick Water in 1800), and, after retirement, settled at Netherbarns to be with his nephews and nieces.[47] Craig drafted Anderson's will and acted on behalf of his executors: his brother, James Anderson, and George and Thomas, his nephews, who were both farmers.[48]

Anderson left over £2,200 in moveable property in Scotland, in respect of some of which Craig provided a bond of caution to guarantee that it would be made available to those with an interest.[49] There was, however, a complication because Anderson had drawn a bill for £1,000 upon James Robert Scott of Cheltenham which Scott refused to pay when it matured. This led to protracted correspondence in which Craig had to send to Jamaica for the vouchers (receipts) proving the debt.[50] In April 1821 Craig transmitted to Donald McLean a power of attorney on behalf of Anderson's executors in Scotland, authorising James Miller, an attorney in Jamaica, and also McLean, who was himself an attorney there, to follow up the matter.[51] He also sent extracts of Anderson's will and the act of confirmation of his executors in Selkirk commissary court. He omitted, however, to have the extracts sealed, an oversight which the London agents noticed when the correspondence passed through their hands. This was a surprising failure on Craig's part, given his experience of English lawyers. He had to obtain a letter from the commissary clerk, Andrew Lang, explaining that the seal of the commissary 'is not known or used, being merely words of style'. Given the importance, however, of seals 'in English forms', Lang offered to put his personal seal to the extract of the will if required.[52]

Despite the fact that Scots overseers on colonial plantations had a reputation for cruelty, Craig clearly formed a positive impression of Anderson – at least as a businessman.[53] The accounts sent from Jamaica showed 'most satisfactorily' how the debt had arisen, and the accuracy of Anderson's books, and 'his general character as a man of business', left Craig in no doubt that he would have sent a copy

---

[46] James inherited a liferent in estates in Jamaica from his older brother William, who also left a legacy to the poor of Selkirk. The residue of William's estate was shared, inter alia, by his sister Margaret, mother of James Robert Scott (b. 1790): The National Archives, Kew [TNA], Prob 11/1382/360.

[47] *Edinburgh Magazine: Or Literary Miscellany*, vol. 17 (Edinburgh, 1801), 146.

[48] NRS, Wills and testaments, CC18/4/8, fos 229–32; SBA/1303/2/15, Craig/Robertson and Bullock, London, 12 Apr. 1821. George farmed at Netherbarns, Thomas at Sundhope in Yarrowdale.

[49] NRS, Wills and testaments, CC18/4/8, fos 236–41. There is later mention also of consolidated annuities (presumably part of his estate in England) which Craig wished to convert to stock in the Bank of Scotland or Royal Bank: SBA/1303/5/392, Craig/R. B. Andrews, 8 May 1829. According to www.officialdata.org, in 2020, £2,200 in 1820 had the purchasing power of about £214,000.

[50] SBA/1303/2/238-9, Craig/Robertson and Bullock, London, 18 May 1822.

[51] SBA/1303/2/18, Craig/Donald McLean, Jamaica, 14 Apr. 1821. This was sent via Robertson & Bullock in London. For Scots as attorneys in Jamaica, see I. D. Whyte, *Scotland and the Abolition of Black Slavery* (Edinburgh, 2007), 49.

[52] SBA/1303/2/28, Craig/Robertson and Bullock, London, 26 Apr. 1821.

[53] Whyte, *Scotland and the Abolition of Black Slavery*, 61.

of the account to Scott when he drew the bill.[54] Nonetheless, the original bill was retired in Jamaica when its holder, Mr Adams of the firm Adams, Robertson & Company in Kingston, transferred it to his company and Miller then paid it (presumably at a discount).[55] Adams had since returned to England. Miller obtained authority from the company to take up the bill from Adams and transmit it to Craig. To that end, Craig instructed Robertson & Bullock, of Lincoln's Inn Fields, to obtain the original bill from Adams, who then resided in Bath, so that it might be pursued for payment against Scott who, as the drawee, was ultimately liable for payment.

Scott had inherited land in Clarendon from his uncle, William Chisholm. His scruple in refusing to pay appears to have related to the underlying transactions by Anderson which the bill was intended to clear. In Craig's view, however, Anderson's accounts with Chisholm were perfectly transparent: Anderson had drawn on Scott to pay debts which Scott owed. Craig sought a personal interview with Scott, enquiring with his Edinburgh agent, William Gardner WS, as to his whereabouts.[56] In July 1822, hearing that McLean had set sail for London, Craig attempted to engineer a meeting between McLean and Scott so that the former could fully explain the debts underlying the bill and bring 'this unpleasant matter to an end'.[57] It was not until February 1823, however, that Craig received the relevant vouchers evidencing the debts. Writing to Scott's agent, William Gardner WS, Craig's tone was pleading: 'These accounts & vouchers appear to be so distinct that I am convinced Mr Scott or you only require to see them to be satisfied of their accuracy & justness.'[58] He offered to send them to London or to meet Gardner at Torsonce, near Stow.[59] Evidently this was not enough for Gardner. A letter of October 1823 indicates that Scott was then willing to pay but this was subject to his agent being satisfied with the vouchers received from Jamaica.[60] Gardner was not satisfied and prolonged legal action in London against Scott followed. It was pursued by the attorney Richard Andrews of Furnival's Inn, with the advice of English counsel.[61]

[54] SBA/1303/2/236, Craig/William Gardner WS, 35 York Place, Edinburgh, 13 May 1822.
[55] SBA/1303/2/231, Craig/Robertson & Bullock, London, 3 May 1822. J. A. Delle, *The Colonial Caribbean: Landscapes of Power in Jamaica's Plantation System* (Cambridge, 2014), 155. To retire a bill means to pay it before it falls due. The payee, in return for receiving the money early, may allow the party making payment a discount on the sum paid.
[56] SBA/1303/2/243, Craig/William Gardner WS, 29 May 1822.
[57] SBA/1303/3/13, Craig/Milligan, Robertson & Co, 11 Jul. 1822.
[58] SBA/1303/3/122, Craig/William Gardner WS, 6 Feb. 1823.
[59] This suggests that Gardner (d. 1836) lived in the Borders. His father, an Edinburgh writer, has been deputy Treasurer's Remembrancer in the Exchequer: Finlay, ed., ARNP 1800–1899, I, no. 434.
[60] SBA/1303/3/259, Craig/William Gardner WS, 15 Oct. 1823; see also SBA/1303/3/150, SBA/1303/3/195.
[61] SBA/1303/5/377-8, Craig/R. B. Andrews, London, 26 Mar. 1829. For conference with counsel, see SBA/1303/5/274 (8 Jul. 1828). Counsel is not stated. Counsel for the Andersons in 1825 was Clement Tudway Swanston, who was himself linked to the slave trade: TNA, Court of Chancery: Six Clerks Office: Pleadings 1801–1842, C13/2608/4, *Anderson v Scott*.

It had been Craig's idea to have the matter brought before an English court rather than a Scottish one, because this would allow Anderson's executors 'the advantage of getting their claim attended to by Gentlemen versed in West India matters'.[62] The case first appeared in the Court of Chancery in 1825.[63] Craig was informed in 1829 that the opportunity of a further hearing might not come for another twelve months, and asked Andrews for copies of the depositions to be sent to him, although the matter rumbled on, as was usual with Chancery cases.[64]

There is an interesting postscript illustrating the trouble this case caused. Following the death of one of Anderson's executors, Craig had to obtain an affidavit from the minister of Peebles in order to explain to an English audience why the deceased, James Anderson, who had been ordinarily resident in the county of Peebles, was buried at St Mary's burial ground in the county of Selkirk. The Peebles minister, Alexander Affleck, had to certify that his parish kept no burial register and Craig had to explain that 'it is the general practice in Scotland for families to have their burial places in the parish where their ancestors lived however distant that may happen to be from their present residence'.[65] St Mary's was, he continued, 'sacred to recollections which belong to the period of the Reformation of the Scottish Church'.

This correspondence is related in detail because it demonstrates how pervasive the Scottish diaspora was. Its reach extended well beyond the ports and major trading centres. In this case, a provincial Galashiels agent had to engage directly, during a period of more than two years, with leading attorneys in Jamaica (including Donald Mclean, originally from North Uist, who himself was a slave owner), a firm of solicitors in London, a company of West Indies merchants also in London, and a writer to the signet in Edinburgh, all in respect of a domestic executory case involving a single bill of exchange and all because of the repatriation of the drawer of the bill and the reluctance of the drawee to honour it.[66] While Craig admired Anderson, his own views on slavery are not mentioned. Nor do his letters demonstrate involvement in an 1830 petition, from the inhabitants of Galashiels, supporting the abolition of the slave trade.[67]

MILITARY SERVICE

For an inland lawyer in peacetime, extensive correspondence with the military authorities might seem unexpected but other law agents, such as Thomas Dykes in Hamilton, are known to have written to the Admiralty, the secretary of state for

[62] SBA/1303/4/188, Craig/Messrs Bullock, Andrews and Brooke, London, 9 May 1825.
[63] TNA, Court of Chancery, C/13/2608/4, *Anderson v Scott*, 1827. The complaint was brought in 1825 and the matter was revived in 1833.
[64] SBA/1303/5/393, Craig/R. B. Andrews, 8 May 1829.
[65] SBA/1303/5/433, Craig/R. B. Andrews, 13 Aug. 1829.
[66] Mclean is recorded in the UCL *Legacies of British Slavery* database, www.ucl.ac.uk/lbs/person/view/2146632971 (accessed 20 March 2022).
[67] *House of Commons Journal*, p. 122, 22 Nov. 1830; *House of Lord Journal*, p. 140, 30 Nov. 1822.

war, the paymaster general and even the commander in chief, the Duke of York, in relation to widows' pensions and other matters.[68] Unlike Galashiels, nearby Kelso had been a parole town during the Napoleonic War.[69] Craig's correspondent in Kelso, John Smith, was agent for French prisoners of war in the area.[70] This has left considerable material in the archives, but no issues affecting these prisoners are referred to in Craig's letters.

The Borders was traditionally a strong army recruiting ground and it is possible, had earlier letter books survived, that they might contain regular letters to the Admiralty, the War Office and military agents. Craig however, was no military agent and such correspondence would have been incidental to his regular work. This is reflected in such examples of his interactions with the military authorities as do survive. In terms of the army, there is correspondence with the military agents Cox and Co. in London connected with the sons of the labourer James Ainslie who both served in the 92nd regiment.[71] One, John, was a corporal and the other, Robert, a private, and both were stationed at Fort Manoel in Malta. Robert sought to be discharged. He calculated the cost of his discharge and return home to be £25. Craig sent Cox a bill for this sum drawn on his London banker, asking the agents to inform the regimental paymaster that they had obtained the price of Ainslie's discharge. There are occasionally other references to individuals on military service abroad, such as George Fairholme's eldest son, William, who served in the 71st Regiment. He was normally based in Dublin but in 1838 he was posted to Canada.[72] It was possibly the same son who drew on a London bank (probably his father's account) from Jamaica during the same year.[73]

In some cases, Craig had to make enquires concerning the effects of dead servicemen. Thus he wrote to the War Office in London in 1827, in relation to the settlement of William White, of the Bengal Artillery, who had died at Nagpur in 1823.[74] In his letter book is preserved correspondence relating to the effects of the late Adam Thomson who had served on HMS Dolphin and HMS Melville. Thomson's father, William, wrote to the inspector of seamen's wills at the Admiralty in London.[75] Prompted by a circular from the Navy's accountant general, the letter was sent along with a claim form in respect of wages and prize money which had been due to his son. As Thomson's agent, Craig wrote to the secretary of

[68] E.g., GCA, T-DY/1/1/3, Dykes/Frederick, duke of York, 8 May 1820; T-DY/1/1/4, Dykes/Admiralty, 27 Dec. 1821; T-DY/1/1/5, Dykes/Viscount Palmerston, 29 Nov. 1823; Dykes/Paymaster General, 20 Dec. 1823.

[69] I.e., a town where prisoners were quartered on their word of honour that they would not attempt escape. On this, see generally I. Macdougall, *All Men are Brethren: Prisoners of War in Scotland, 1803–1814* (Edinburgh, 2008).

[70] SBA, SBA/183/27, Robert Walker of Wooden/William Smith, Kelso, 30 Oct. 1810.

[71] SBA/1303/8/27, Craig/Cox and Co., 28 Aug. 1837.

[72] SBA/1303/8/248, Craig/LBC, 14 May 1838. G. Fairholme, 'Notes on the Family of Greenknow'.

[73] Ibid./134, Craig/LBC, 27 Jan. 1838. Dr Monro's son, Alexander jr, served with the Rifle Brigade: SBA/1303/8/358, Craig/Alex. Monro jr, Tower of London, London, 22 Oct. 1838.

[74] SBA/1303/5/30, Craig/Secretary at War, London, 3 May 1827.

[75] SBA/1303/8/582, William Thomson/Inspector of Seamens' Wills, Admiralty, 27 Sep. 1839.

the Admiralty in response to a reply to the original letter, seeking a remittance.[76] Admiralty bills for lost wages were duly received, but Thomson wrote again in respect of prize money 'from the capture of one or more slave ships by the Dolphin'. He also wanted his son's personal effects, which he listed with his letter.[77] For the purpose of this correspondence, and to satisfy the Admiralty's forms, Craig signed himself 'Chief Magistrate'.[78]

THE NORTH OF ENGLAND

Craig naturally had correspondents in the north of England as part of his daily business. Cross-border traffic was regular, some of it connected to business trips to the county fairs. Craig refers to having visitors, such as Mr Gandy of Kendal, in Cumbria, of Gandy and Sons, woollen merchants and drysalters; or to cattle dealers heading south, some of whom were regular bank customers.[79] As a banker, however, he did not keep large amounts of Bank of England notes on hand and ordered them only when required.[80]

The most obvious reason for Craig to correspond with English attorneys was debt enforcement. In 1827, for example, he wrote to the Alnwick attorney, John Lambert, on behalf of the Leith Bank regarding the sequestration of Henry Martin, giving him full power to prosecute the bank's claims.[81] Another Alnwick attorney, William Pringle, was engaged by Craig when acting for the executors of the late Thomas Fairholme of Bolton in Northumberland (Adam and George Fairholme) whose property had been sold in May 1816.[82] Pringle had evidently been recommended to him by a Mr Milne, an Alnwick baker, whose brother James may have been a Galashiels resident.[83] Large sums owed by two purchasers of goods from the estate, businessmen William Cook of Alnwick and Thomas Cook of Bainsforth, were still unpaid in 1824. The matter had been in the hands of the bank agent, George Bolton of Wooler, but he had died in January 1823.[84] Payment had been delayed by the Cooks' bankruptcy and Craig engaged Pringle in February 1824, after hearing from a local source about a creditors' meeting that had occurred the previous December. Pringle quickly ascertained that Thomas Cook's funds would yield nothing, while William's estate produced only a small dividend (1s 1d per pound). This had been paid into the Alnwick branch of the Newcastle Bank but a question had arisen over whether the executors, to receive this money, had

---

[76] SBA/1303/8/651, Craig & Rutherford/Secretary of the Admiralty, 10 Nov. 1839.
[77] SBA/1303/8/687, Thomson/Secretary of the Admiralty, 17 Jan. 1840.
[78] SBA/1303/8/572, Craig/Accountant General of the Navy, London, 19 Sep. 1839.
[79] SBA/1303/4/157, Craig/Dr Monro, 15 Sep. 1826.
[80] SBA/1303/3/66, Craig/LBC, 23 Oct. 1822.
[81] SBA/1303/5/105, Craig/Lambert, 15 Aug. 1827.
[82] SBA/1303/3/311, Craig/William Pringle, attorney, Alnwick, 18 Feb. 1824; SBA/1303/2/157, Craig/
     George Bolton, 17 Nov. 1821.
[83] SBA/1303/3/290, Craig/Mr Milne, baker, Alnwick, 18 Dec. 1823.
[84] *The London Gazette*, issue 61992, 470.

to provide formal letters of administration to the bishop of Durham's court or whether it would suffice to provide a warranty to the bank agent who made payment. Craig had 'never heard of letters of administration to a bankrupt's effects before' and needed local advice.[85]

The administration of Fairholme's estate required Craig, who had entrusted to George Bolton the task of chasing up payment following the sale of Fairholme's effects, to write to Clement Pattison, a solicitor at Berwick, in 1826.[86] He had been informed that Pattison now held Bolton's papers, and, with the executors anxious to bring matters to a close, he asked Pattison for a statement of Bolton's intromissions with Fairholme's estate plus any balance that he had held in favour of the executors.[87] Matters of this kind could drag on for years. In 1836, Craig enquired as to a dividend in the sequestration of the Berwick corn merchants, Clunie & Son, in which Adam and George Fairholme had ranked as early as 1821.[88]

There were inevitably cross-border family relationships, beyond probate, that could generate legal work. In 1829, the schoolmaster Robert Fyshe, a near relative of eighty-four-year-old weaver James Tait, a copyhold tenant of Lord Tankerville in Berwick, was asked by Tait to manage his property. Due to his age, Tait wanted Fyshe to take possession of his houses and land in return for an annual annuity. This required Tankerville's consent, therefore Craig wrote to his agent, Willoughby, in Berwick, to gain the appropriate sanction and also for advice 'regarding the preliminary steps to be taken'.[89]

What emerged from this was a relationship with the firm of Willoughby & Hume (latterly Willoughby & Son), attorneys in Berwick. It was through these lawyers that Craig arranged a conclusion to Dr Monro's relationship with his erstwhile tenant, George Logan, who had moved from Cockburn to New Haggerston. Logan owed £279 in rent arrears plus interest, and Craig wanted proceedings raised, although he instructed the attorneys to accept £100 if offered in settlement.[90] Monro had reduced Logan's rent but continued to charge interest on the arrears, an arrangement Craig had to explain carefully to his agents. 'It is quite common in Scotland', he noted, 'to charge interest on arrears of Rent, which is only in terms of the Lease besides a heavy penalty for not punctual payment. In short, interest is no compensation for the want of regular payment'.[91] When Monro settled for £100, Craig wrote to Berwick that 'Logan may congratulate himself on having got off on such easy terms'.[92] It had been stipulated that Logan should pay Willoughby & Hume's expenses and, as

[85] SBA/1303/3/319, Craig/William Pringle, attorney, Alnwick, 27 Feb. 1824.
[86] SBA/1303/4/353, Craig/Clement Pattison, solicitor, 20 Mar. 1826.
[87] He evidently received the papers: SBA/1303/4/371, Craig/Adam Fairholme of Chapel, 19 Apr. 1826.
[88] SBA/1303/7/198, Craig/Willoughby & Son, Berwick, 13 Apr. 1836.
[89] SBA/1303/5/460, Craig/J, Willoughby Esq., Berwick, 17 Oct. 1829.
[90] SBA/1303/6/239, Craig/Willoby [sic] & Home, 5 Nov. 1831.
[91] SBA/1303/6/289, idem, 12 May 1832.
[92] SBA/1303/6/319, idem, 7 Sep. 1832.

part of that, Craig asked them to apply for £10 for his own 'considerable' trouble and expenses in the matter.

While Craig used attorneys to prosecute debts across the border, he was also employed by English creditors to the same purpose. An example is a letter to the banker Shakespear Garrick Sikes in Huddersfield. Sikes sought payment of a debt from John Gledstanes, but the latter proved rather wily. Gledstanes promised to pay up soon, but Craig noted that 'He seems quite aware of the advantage he has of making the debt altogether desperate should legal measures be adopted against him which I am afraid would be too much the case'.[93]

Sometimes Craig's cross-border correspondence was with individuals in similar straits to George Logan, having moved south pursued by creditors. An example is a letter to Robert and John Patterson, skinners who had moved to Liverpool in the challenging economic time of 1824. They left their business, and their creditors, behind, along with their sister, Anne, who was unaware of whether they intended to return. Given that their creditors intended to apply for sequestration to the Court of Session, Craig wrote to them noting the 'very great' expense this would involve and asking them to confirm their intention quickly.[94] His advice, if they did not intend to return, was to empower two or three of their friends locally 'to dispose of your property & effects for the benefit of your creditors . . . at a comparatively small expense'. Sending such an authority, Craig asserted, would be the 'much more honourable' course of action.

A number of letters, generally involving financial matters such as the payment of bills of exchange, related to merchants in Liverpool, Carlisle and elsewhere in the north of England.[95] One of the firms Craig had the most correspondence with was Harrison & Latham, one of the main Liverpool cotton importers from Portugal and Brazil.[96] This included an exchange of commercial intelligence. In 1826, Craig sought information from them when he disliked the appearance of a transaction entered into by a local farmer at Yetholm Fair.[97] He wanted to know if there was a firm in Liverpool called H. Levin & Co. and what it did; a man purporting to be from the firm had drawn a bill on a London firm and indorsed it to the farmer. On another occasion, he asked them to trace a journeyman millwright who had entered into a lease with Gala but had not signed it.[98] Craig noted 'you may have difficulty in finding him out in a place like Liverpool – but I hope you will cause enquiry to be made' since the matter was to the lessee's advantage.

[93] SBA/1303/3/231, Craig/Sikes, Huddersfield, 26 Aug. 1823.
[94] SBA/1303/3/40, Craig/Robert and John Paterson, 75 High Field St., Liverpool, 3 Jun. 1824.
[95] E.g., SBA/1303/4/272, Craig/W.A. & G. Maxwell, Liverpool, 21 Nov. 1825; SBA/1303/6/431, Craig/Mr Samuel, 75 Paradise St., Liverpool, 9 Nov. 1833; SBA/1303/6/131, Craig/R. Ferguson, Sons & Co., Carlisle, 10 Jan. 1831.
[96] A. Krichtal, 'Liverpool and the Raw Cotton Trade: A study of the port and its merchant community 1790–1815' (MA Thesis, University of Wellington, 2013), 62.
[97] SBA/1303/2/71, Craig/Harrison & Latham, Liverpool, 3 Jul. 1821.
[98] SBA/1303/4/366, Craig/Harrison & Latham, Liverpool, 11 Apr. 1826.

LONDON AGENTS

A significant feature of Craig's business lay in his correspondence with London law agents. The fact that the two firms with which Craig was most heavily involved had a strong connection to the Borders was coincidental. The firms, Spottiswoode & Robertson and Richardson & Connell, had links across Scotland and between them enjoyed the lion's share of the appellate and agency business that was referred to London by Scots law agents.

Spottiswoode & Robertson operated from at least 1803 until 1853 but the business originated with John Spottiswoode (1741–1805), who owned the Berwickshire estate of Spottiswoode, entered the Inner Temple in 1765, and established a successful practice in London.[99] His younger brother, Robert, entered Inner Temple in 1773. The firm Craig knew comprised John Spottiswoode jr (1780–1866) and David Robertson whose origins are obscure although he may have been a clerk of the elder John Spottiswoode.

The firm of Richardson & Connell also had a strong local link through John Richardson (1780–1864). Originally from Gilmerton in Midlothian, Richardson was a friend of Sir Walter Scott, who described him as having 'the highest character in his profession as an honest & able solicitor'.[100] In 1829 he purchased the estate of Kirklands, near Ancrum, which Scott regarded as 'beautifully compact' and an 'excellent' property.[101] An earlier attempt to buy property in the Borders had miscarried. This was around the time Richardson gained entry to the WS Society in 1827.[102]

These firms had developed partly in response to the extraordinarily high number of appeals from the Court of Session to the House of Lords.[103] An important aspect of their work, however, was their status as parliamentary agents facilitating the passage of bills through parliament. Alongside individual Scots London agents, such as Alexander Mundell (1769–1837) and Thomas Longlands (1743?–1820), these were the people with whom Scottish town councils and landowners usually dealt if they wanted information about prospective legislation or had draft bills to be enacted.

Craig is likely to have known Richardson personally. While their dealings largely centred on clients' properties in London, or the payment of bills, in 1832 Craig had a less usual request. He asked Richardson to trace a 'Dr Mudie' (described as 'a tall thin man aged 70') and his wife who, having left Edinburgh in 1830, were thought

[99] On his estate, see D. Hall and T. Barry, *Spottiswoode: Life and Labour on a Berwickshire Estate (1753–1793)* (East Linton: Tuckwell, 1997).

[100] Grierson, ed., *Letters of Sir Walter Scott*, VII, 73.

[101] Ibid., XI, 237, 248.

[102] Ibid., X, 264, 485; xi, 58. Scott's comment at the time was that 'any one who goes plainly and frankly to work in this country to bargain for land is generally flung'. Signet Library, WS Society, Sederunt book 1819–1829, fo. 490; Minute Book of the Commissioners for the Clerks to the Signet, fo. 261 (13 Nov. 1827).

[103] See J. Finlay, 'Scots lawyers and House of Lords appeals in Eighteenth-century Britain' 32 (2011) *Journal of Legal History*, 249, 253.

to be in Paris or London.[104] Mudie had departed to avoid getting caught up in his son-in-law's affairs, that son-in-law being Robert Dunlop WS.[105] Dunlop had run into financial difficulties and apparently had a bond of relief against Mudie and also against Robert Laidlaw, Craig's brother-in-law, with whom he had entered into a partnership in 1827.[106] These gentlemen, Craig suggested in 1829, 'shall certainly both go to Jail & be detained there all winter at least'.[107]

When Craig wanted to know the status of the firm Bullock, Andrews & Brooke of Furnival's Inn, to whom he had sent vouchers in the Anderson case but from whom he had received no reply, he wrote to Spottiswoode & Robertson. Given the importance of the claim against a West Indies estate, which the late Edward Bullock had managed and had now been succeeded by the firm, he wanted his correspondents 'confidential opinion of those Gentlemen as the matter under their charge should be immediately pursued to a close & it would appear not improbable that the case may be ultimately put into your hands'.[108] Evidently having received a satisfactory response, a few months later Craig wanted the business moved on and urged Bullock to serve a subpoena if counsel agreed. He asked them to employ Spottiswoode & Robertson 'if you do not yourselves practice before the Court', although it appears that they did and the latter firm was not employed.[109]

An aspect of business in which Spottiswoode & Robertson were certainly engaged was legislation concerning roads and it was no doubt through them that Craig gained his knowledge of the Standing Orders of the House of Commons. In November 1826, having received a letter from them, he wrote to Tod & Romanes in Edinburgh informing them that copies of notices had to be sent to London immediately because any petition 'must be presented within the first fortnight in the insuing session after the house shall proceed to business'.[110] Craig was alarmed because the Roxburghshire roads trustees had applied for a new bill without giving notice.[111]

In 1827 Craig wrote to John Richardson in Fludyer Street concerning a bill of exchange drawn by Charles Robson upon the London merchant Thomas Rutherford of Mossburnford which Rutherford had accepted. The bill had been indorsed by John Robson, a tenant in Belford. All three were bankrupt, with Rutherford imprisoned by his creditors, and Craig, anxious to find out what he

---

[104] SBA/1303/6/274, Craig/Richardson & Connell, Westminster, 31 Mar. 1832.
[105] Robert Dunlop married Helen Straton Mudie in Duddingston in Mar. 1822. 'Dr Mudie' was James Dunbar Mudie, a physician normally resident in Alford, Lincolnshire.
[106] Advocates Library, General Collection of Session Papers, 2 Feb. 1831, no. 308, Reclaiming Note of Robert Dunlop, *Laidlaw v Dunlop*. My thanks to Ms Angela Schofield for providing me with a copy of this document. See also *Laidlaw v Dunlop* (1830) 8 S. 307; (1831) 9 S. 579.
[107] SBA/1303/5/476, Craig/Gilbert & Hector WS, 14 Nov. 1829.
[108] SBA/1303/4/153, Craig/Spottiswoode & Robertson, 14 Feb. 1825.
[109] SBA/1303/4/188, Craig/Messrs Bullock, Andrews and Brooke, London, 9 May 1825.
[110] SBA/1303/4/485, Craig/Tod & Romanes, 5 Nov. 1826.
[111] SBA/1303/4/486, idem, 9 Nov. 1826.

could pay, asked Richardson to investigate.[112] The bill was payable at the office of J. J. Burns at Gray's Inn Square.[113] This case was no different from any other debt Craig pursued across the border; in fact, the same day he wrote to Ker & Leithead, attorneys in Alnwick, regarding another bill, this time drawn by John Robson on Charles Robson.[114] The following year, in another routine matter, he wrote to Richardson & Connell in connection with Harriot Randall's annuity from her late brother who had owned property in Strand. The property was to be demolished due to neighbourhood improvements, and Richardson was to liaise with the solicitor managing the estate to ensure that her life annuity continued to be paid by the residuary legatee (another brother) from any money awarded in compensation (Craig later noted that Government indemnities were being granted).[115] Craig again showed some knowledge of English form, seeking to avoid further probate by offering to accept an office copy of the part of her late brother's will which concerned his client.

Less routine was Richardson & Connell's involvement in the Brydon case (see Chapter 5), seeking reimbursement for funds disbursed to soldiers' wives from the War Office in London, and also in tracing the runaway father, George Brown in 1833.[116] It is fair to say, however, that Craig's London correspondence, despite its points of interest, was not particularly extensive. This reflects the nature of his business; he was not a court practitioner and had no involvement in appellate cases. While he was engaged in the development of roads which required legislation, and despite his political involvement, he was not brought into much direct contact with members of parliament in the ordinary course of his profession. Forwarding legislation was something more typically dealt with through Edinburgh agents. William Elliot Lockhart, MP for Selkirkshire, and his successor Alexander Pringle of Whytbank who was elected in 1830, were both correspondents, but his contact with them largely centred on more domestic concerns.

CONCLUSION

Craig's network beyond Scotland primarily involved lawyers and bankers in England, although he did claim to the Lauder writer, John Romanes, that he had 'agents in America' whom he might use to recover a debt.[117] His correspondence reflects a country where emigration was prevalent. The legal complexities arising from that situation would not typically have been the bread and butter of provincial law agents, but they did have implications for Craig, particularly in relation to New South Wales which was a destination attractive not only to Borders sheep

---

[112] SBA/1303/5/93, Craig/Richardson, 21 Jul. 1827.
[113] SBA/1303/5/97, Anderson/Richardson & Connell, 5 Fludyer Street, Westminster, 27 Jul. 1827.
[114] SBA/1303/5/93, Craig/Ker & Leithead, 21 Jul. 1827.
[115] SBA/1303/5/214-5, Craig/Richardson & Connell, 14 Feb. 1828; SBA/1303/5/280, idem, 21 Jul. 1828; SBA/1303/5/291, idem, 16 Aug. 1828.
[116] SBA/1303/6/110, Craig/Richardson & Connell, 29 Oct. 1830; on Brown, see Chapter 2.
[117] SBA/1303/7/112, Craig/John Romanes, Lauder, 2 Nov. 1835.

farmers. For example, William Walker of Bowland's brother, James, a lieutenant in the 88th regiment of foot, contemplated going there at a time when 'those wonderful cleaver [sic] people Messrs Craig & Rutherford' were transferring a bond in security to him in 1839.[118]

The international dimension is also revealed in other aspects of Craig's correspondence with clients who were absentee landlords living in England. These included Gala who spent some time in the south; George Fairholme who settled in Ramsgate, and also William Colvin of Torquhan who, from 1831, resided in Woolwich and for some time in Deal when, as Craig put it, he 'had the charge of' the Royal Naval Hospital.[119] Colvin was a ship's surgeon in Royal Naval service since 1804.[120] Colvin was given an additional appointment by the Admiralty in 1833 which required 'constant residence in London' at which point he told Craig simply that he had let Mitchelston House near Stow and that 'you will have to take charge of all'.[121] Finance was a factor in these relationships as much as law, since Craig often arranged with his London bankers to facilitate transactions with clients and others outside Scotland. Sometimes, as with a bill to be sent to Montreal, it was thought better to send a draft from the Leith head office rather than 'an agency' if it was 'to be negotiated abroad'.[122] Nonetheless, these arrangements are a reminder of the considerable advantage Craig enjoyed in the dual role of law agent and bank agent.

[118] NLS, Walker of Bowland papers, MS13961, fo. 87, James Scott Walker to W. S. Walker, 26 Jul. 1839. The phrase quoted may have been used sarcastically.
[119] SBA/1303/6/231, Craig/LBC, 17 Oct. 1831; SBA/1303/7/7, Craig/LBC, 25 Aug. 1834.
[120] TNA, ADM 196/68/434.
[121] SBA/1303/6/311, Craig/J McGowan, Peebles, 3 Apr. 1833.
[122] SBA/1303/4/515, Anderson/George Craig, Edinburgh, 26 Dec. 1826. This is the only letter *to* Craig in the letter books. He was on a visit to the Leith Bank.

Chapter 10

Conclusion

Craig's correspondence reveals many personal stories: a debt incurred or enforced; a property bought; a vote acquired; a dispute brought closer to resolution. It shows lawyers at the centre of their community and highlights their connection to municipal development, such as improvements to the water supply, gas lighting or the collection of subscriptions for building a new church.[1] Together, the letters build into a mosaic which brings into focus features of everyday life and gives us a portrait of a community.

Each letter written by Craig, Anderson or Rutherford reflects a moment in time but letters can also reveal continuity in relationships going back years. A reference in 1821 to the winding up of the innkeeper Thomas Sanderson's affairs '16 or 18 years ago', for instance, saw Craig cast his mind back to the relevant papers he had supplied long before 'to the late Mr Lang at Selkirk who carried on the adjudication of the property'.[2] This was John Lang, formerly sheriff clerk, whose son Andrew had become one of Craig's most regular correspondents.

Craig's lengthy working life, from his apprentice days at the turn of the century, meant that he often had a long association with a correspondent. Archival records testify to his enduring association with individuals such as George Rodger and John Paterson in Selkirk, while his letter books uncover his relationships with family members of some of his correspondents. For instance, he visited Pirn in 1822 and told John Tait WS (of Tait & Bruce) that he had left 'your father mother & Betty all in fine health & spirits'.[3] He mentioned in passing to John Gibson, when sending him an affidavit from his father Archibald Gibson regarding Sir Walter Scott's affairs, that he had found Archibald in bed following 'a violent attack of lumbago'.[4]

Tracing the correspondence of anyone of long acquaintance, such as Andrew Lang or Peter Rodger, provides a wealth of detail about their relationship. The almost casual way Craig or his associates might ask Rodger to look into the sheriff clerk's office at Selkirk to find a document required as the basis for a summons in the sheriff court, reflects long acquaintance.[5] A figure such as the sheriff-clerk

---

[1] The church (in Darlingshaugh) is mentioned several times e.g. SBA/1303/7/270; SBA/1303/8/52, 54. William Rutherford was secretary to the committee for erecting the new church: SBA/1303/8/58, Rutherford/Rev. James Cochrane, 6 Oct. 1837.

[2] SBA/1303/2/72, Craig/G. Dalziel, J. B. [at] Brodie's Esq. WS, 3 Jul. 1821.

[3] SBA/1303/2/237, Craig/John Tait WS, 14 May 1822.

[4] SBA/1303/5/174, Craig/Gibson & Hector WS, 24 Dec. 1827.

[5] E.g. SBA/1303/6/365, Anderson/Peter Rodger, 11 Mar. 1833.

Lang had great local standing (Henry Cockburn, for one, regarded sheriff-clerks as being 'respectable' and quite superior to town clerks who were 'wretched' and 'unworthy of trust').[6] Walter Scott praised Lang's speech and his 'decent & quiet good breeding' on the visit of Prince Leopold to Selkirk in 1819 to receive the freedom of the burgh, contrasting the impression he gave with the 'rabble' of the populace.[7] Craig, having been 'rummaging the store room for flower roots', wrote to Lang in 1825 that he had discovered eight volumes of the *Encyclopaedia Britannica* in a way that suggested this had recently been a topic of conversation between them.[8]

The letters also indicate familiarity with local family affairs. When Elizabeth Plummer of Sunderland Hall, the daughter of the erstwhile sheriff depute Andrew Plummer (Scott's 'excellent antiquarian'), died in 1839, for example, Craig knew all about the family's property arrangements which were subject to an entail.[9] This is perhaps unsurprising given that Andrew Plummer, who had died in 1799 and was replaced by Walter Scott, had married into the family of Pringle of Torwood-lee.[10] Craig noted that the estate went to Charles Scott-Plummer, son of the late C. B. Scott WS, who was then 'about 15 years of age', with his own family estate of Woll going to Colonel Scott.[11]

Some letters known to have been written by Craig are absent, suggesting that they were either not copied or copied elsewhere.[12] Of the thousands of copied letters in the letter books, very few originals survive.[13] The letter books alone demonstrate the sheer range of Craig's activities in banking, insurance and law. They show him to have been, to use the old Scots word, a 'doer', a law agent but with the wider connotation of 'man of business', a person who would manage things that needed to be managed.[14] As agent and baron bailie, for private clients or the wider community, this is essentially what he did.

Many things naturally fell within his purview and he took care of the details whether they involved tax matters; journal or newspaper subscriptions; changes to insurance documents, or alterations to roads regardless of whether he acted for individuals or as chair of town meetings. When William Clark of Longhaugh returned to the neighbourhood, after an absence of four years, he wanted to take a house near Peebles on an annual basis 'to be near the Schools for the education of

---

[6] Cockburn, *Letters Chiefly Connected with the Affairs of Scotland*, 335, 400.
[7] Grierson, ed., *Letters of Scott*, V, 505–6.
[8] SBA/1303/4/161, Craig/Lang, 28 Feb. 1825.
[9] W. Scott, *Minstrelsy of the Scottish Border* (3rd edn, 1806), 81.
[10] Sir Francis Grant, *The Faculty of Advocates 1532–1943* (Edinburgh, 1944), 173; NRS, Buccleuch papers, GD224/663/6/2.
[11] SBA/1303/8/434, Craig/William Colvin, 21 Feb. 1839.
[12] E.g. SBA, Walter Mason papers, WM/17/59, Craig/Peter Rodger, 12 Feb. 1835.
[13] E.g. NLS, Walker of Bowland papers, MS13961, fo. 9, recorded at SBA/1303/6/339, Craig/William Walker, 8 Dec. 1832.
[14] Cf. SBA, D/47/90/2, W. G. Innes to Peter Rodger, writer, Selkirk, 23 Aug. 1834, using the term 'man of business' in its narrow traditional sense of law agent.

his two boys'.[15] Craig sent a Peebles correspondent a description of Clark's requirements, seeking to know what such a house might cost if furnished or unfurnished.
This inquiry put Craig into land agent mode, but he gave the same careful attention to a diverse range of tasks.

What the letters do not reveal is what passed in face-to-face conversations,
held with locals in their familiar Borders dialect of the Scots language, although
the gist of some of that is sometimes recounted. The fact that someone was, or
had just been, in the office is often mentioned in a letter as having prompted the
writing of it. Likewise, 'Mr Pringle has handed me your letter to him' or some such
phrase might form the starting point.[16] Visitors to the office included clients like
Alexander Monro and lawyers such as John Tait and Archibald Gibson.

Craig's letters do not reflect his private views of laws or practices which some
of his contemporaries might justifiably have regarded as unfair or oppressive.
Business correspondence is not generally the place for philosophical discourse or
weighing up the quality, fairness or morality of the law. The reality of what had
to be done when rents were unpaid, or land poorly tended, was sometimes harsh.
Craig was not insensitive but he was, if anything, a realist. He was also the landowners' man, a later example of the class of 'superintendents of improvements',
keen to encourage agricultural improvement and local industry; prepared to
exploit sporting rights on behalf of absentee landlords, and facilitate emigration.[17]
To balance that, he did fulfil a responsibility towards the poor: the qualities of
forbearance, sympathy and understanding do show through. He cannot have been
unaware, however, that the consolidation of landholding and the improvement of
farming was detrimental to the labouring poor and a driver of depopulation.

CRAIG'S PERSONALITY

From any letter book, regardless how formal the writing or quotidian the subject
matter, must seep an element of the writer's personality and Craig's correspondence reveals a number of character traits. He was a forward thinker and a strong
believer in agricultural improvement. He understood the potential of rail for the
local economy and was open to the challenges of the insurance market and willing
to learn and experiment as he went along. In his clients and colleagues, Craig had
many strong and durable connections; he also had an eye for detail and a willingness to meet and get to know people from all walks of life.

He was very precise in his words and deeds and, while he freely acknowledged
his own mistakes, he could be scolding of those who failed to meet his expectations. If a charge or arrangement was 'quite ridiculous' or 'absurd' Craig would
say so plainly and not hide his displeasure.[18] Not being given to extravagance,

[15] SBA/1303/8/452, Craig/Walter Thorburn, Peebles, 14 Mar. 1839.
[16] SBA/1303/5/31, Craig/John Tait WS, 6 Mar. 1827.
[17] Devine, *The Scottish Clearances*, 145.
[18] E.g. SBA/1303/4/383, Craig/John Haig, Charlotte Sq., Edinburgh, 6 May 1826, where the extended
employment of a gardener unnecessarily would be 'quite ridiculous'.

he would not, for example, take counsel's opinion if it was unnecessary to do so. In one case, he told Adam Paterson WS that he chose not to take the opinion of counsel since 'yours is just as good' and there is no sense either of flattery or economy in that statement.[19] In another, he noted that his partner Rutherford was 'very much astonished' that a promise to pay two guineas for revising a deed, which a writer to the signet had made to him in no less a place than 'the writers to the Signets library', had not been kept.[20] Craig was willing to refer the truth of Rutherford's claim to the writer's 'word of honor as a professional gentleman'.

James Hogg regarded Craig as stubborn when crossed and his letters bear this out. In 1838 he had a disagreement with the local postmaster. Rutherford wanted his letters delivered when they arrived but Craig did not, preferring to collect them or to send a boy to do so. William Haldane, the postmaster, wanted to deliver all the letters together rather than be 'plagued' by having to deliver to one partner and not the other. Craig however, for once signing himself 'Baron Bailie of Galashiels', wrote to Sir Edward Lees, secretary of the Post Office, insisting that his preference be respected.[21]

Craig's own evaluation of others was often frank. The clothier John Gledhill, for example, he considered 'a shifty creature, perhaps too much so to support a high character as a trader'.[22] John Hislop was 'a slovenly sort of a man of business'.[23] He was quite often 'astonished' at the behaviour of some individuals. When Monro's tenant, Robert Purves, failed to pay a third party, Liddle, a sum for which allowance had been made to him in his rent, Craig was unhappy. He told John Stobie, Liddle's agent, that 'it is most indecent of him to allow such a demand to appear before me after the liberality that has been shown him'.[24] Again, this echoes Hogg's description of Craig.

An interesting vignette is a claim by one of Torwoodlee's tenants that he was entitled under his feudal disposition to wood for an axletree (a beam of wood, connecting the opposite wheels of a carriage). Even if he was, Craig was unimpressed by his conduct, as he told Torwoodlee:

> for it can never imply that he is to go to [a] Millwright and order one at your expense and as he has been so forward as to do so without consulting me he shall not only pay it but get a lecture for his impudence and if we are bound to give him one he will get notice at the proper season where it is lying cut.[25]

As this implies, Craig lived in a culture of hierarchy. He was baron bailie at the laird's gift. The authority he seemed to exercise so naturally was borrowed,

[19] SBA/1303/8/193, Craig/Adam Paterson WS, 17 Mar. 1838.
[20] SBA/1303/8/453, Craig/Robert Laidlaw SSC, 18 Mar. 1839. The WS was 'Mr Greig', possibly James Greig jr WS (1798–1850).
[21] SBA/1303/8/207, Craig/Lees, 2 Sep. 1838.
[22] SBA/1303/3/88, Craig/Shakespeare G. Sikes, Huddersfield, 12 Dec. 1822.
[23] SBA/1303/8/588, Craig/William Baillie, Edinburgh, 1 Oct. 1839.
[24] SBA/1303/6/451, Craig/John Stobie, writer, Haddington, 24 Jan. 1834.
[25] SBA/1303/5/153, Craig/James Pringle, Torwoodlee, 1 Dec. 1827.

devolved from Gala or another estate owner, the local heritors more generally, or his employers at the bank and the insurance company. He never lacked confidence in his status, however, and he trusted his instincts when it came to the community's well-being. A nuisance complaint in 1834 shows something of his spirit as well as the vivacity of his writing style. The issue was the danger posed by a watchhouse chimney which Craig wanted removed at the expense of those who had put it there. The watchhouse, presumably, was for the use of the constable who kept watch overnight.[26] Craig's stance upset the watchhouse committee but he was alert to a 'nuisance of a very dangerous description' which had already nearly set fire to the house of a widow, Mrs Paterson. As he wrote to the clerk to the committee:

> With regard to any *right* you or the Committee may think that they have in the matter, I only beg to repeat what I stated to you verbally, that no man can acquire a right to set fire to his neighbours house at midnight; & as it can be proved that Mrs Paterson's house has recently been twice in that danger, I therefore see no other mode of your avoiding the very serious damages that you may be found liable in than by your either immediately removing the house altogether, or building the chimney to such a height (at the sight of tradesmen) as would protect Mrs Paterson's property from risk.[27]

Craig was keenly interested in horses both as a huntsman and a lawyer. In trying to sell one of his own, he named a price and was determined to have it, telling the buyer that if he tried the pony for a few days he would soon agree because 'it has been so well broke it is more like a trained person than a horse'.[28] He regularly attended church and his role as treasurer of the Galashiels Bible Society has already been mentioned.[29] The president was Archibald Gibson of Ladhope and the vice-presidents were the ministers, Nathaniel Paterson and James Henderson. The Society supported the Scottish Missionary Society, the Gaelic School in Edinburgh and other activities. This may have been the object of a subscription to the 'religious society' in his accounts.[30]

We know little of Craig's literary tastes, although he may have been a member of a local literary society formed by the manufacturer James Sanderson.[31] He borrowed only one publication, the fourth volume of *The World*, from the Selkirk Subscription Library.[32] He was fond of art and conformed to the well-known pattern of the professional man who was also a cultural innovator.[33] He corresponded with the architect David Rhind who, in 1838, was responsible for the fluted

[26] Hall, *History of Galashiels*, 121.
[27] SBA/1303/6/486-7, Craig/Robert Brodie, clerk to Watching Committee, Galashiels, 7 Jun. 1834.
[28] SBA/1303/4/406, Craig/Mr Dickson, Pavilion, 19 Jun. 1826.
[29] See above, p. 31.
[30] SBA/1303/9/381 (6 May 1839).
[31] SBA, SBA/83/9, Sanderson, 'Old Galashiels', 16–17.
[32] SBA, S/PL/7/2, I owe this reference to Amy Thomson of Scottish Borders Archive. This is probably Adam Fitzadam, *The World* (4 vols, London, 1774).
[33] B. Harris, 'Cultural change in Scottish towns' 54 (2011) *The Historical Journal*, 105, 114–15.

Doric column upon which Sir Walter Scott's statue dominates Glasgow's George Square. This related to the Association for the Promotion of the Fine Arts in Scotland of which Craig was a member, as were a number of locals, including the builders Robert Hall and William Sanderson, the merchant George Clapperton and the writer Hugh Lees.[34] The Association involved an annual subscription of one guinea in return for which the member received a print and was entered into a lottery to win a painting. One print, *The Examination of Shakespeare*, made by Robert Graves in 1833 of a painting by George Harvey, is specifically mentioned in the correspondence. Another, sent in 1838, was *The Strayed Children* which Craig thought 'very beautiful', offering to distribute future copies to subscribers if they were sent to him.[35] He operated in the capacity of 'honorary secretary' of a local branch of the association.[36]

While Craig had no children, it is worth noting that the progeny of some of his closest associates made a significant mark. The Melrose writer James Curle married, in 1816, Isabella Romanes (probably linking him to the Romanes family in Lauder which contained a number of lawyers). Their grandson, also James (1862–1944), was a WS and noted amateur archaeologist who discovered the Roman site at Trimontium. His brother, Alexander (1866–1955), another WS with similar interests, became director of the National Museum of Antiquities in 1913. David Spence's daughter, Catherine (1825–1910), became a writer and journalist in Australia after the family emigrated in 1839 due to his sequestration after failed investments.[37] Spence himself became the first town clerk of Adelaide and his son chair of the state bank.[38] Of great renown also was Andrew Lang's grandson, also called Andrew (1844–1912), the folklorist, historian and classicist.[39] Craig's own partner, William Rutherford, as well as becoming senior magistrate, founded another partnership which continued in business until the middle of the following century without whose survival this book might not have been written.[40]

WIDER SIGNIFICANCE

What do Craig's life and letters reveal about wider aspects of Scottish society in the 1820s and 1830s? They show the nature of life for ordinary people and the domesticity of rural life. Craig's insurance activities illustrate the typical living accommodation for weavers and their families. Small details, such as the desire of the shepherd John Thomson, one of William Colvin's tenants, to have his

---

[34] SBA/1303/8/161, Craig/David Rhind, 11 Abercrombie [sic] Place, Edinburgh, 20 Feb. 1838.

[35] SBA/1303/8/180, idem, 8 Mar. 1838.

[36] SBA/1303/7/359, Craig/Rhind, 4 Feb. 1837.

[37] NRS, Court of Session, unextracted processes, CS236/S/34/8; *Western Mail* (Perth, WA), 9 Apr. 1910, p. 34; Magarey, *Unbridling the Tongues of Women*, 27.

[38] *Barrier Miner* (Broken Hill, NSW), 8 Dec. 1902, p. 2.

[39] Like his father, John (1744–1805), Andrew Lang's son, John (1812–1869), and grandson, Patrick Sellar Lang (1845–1900), served as sheriff clerk of Selkirk as did Lang himself: P. S. Lang, *The Langs of Selkirk* (Melbourne, 1910).

[40] See above, Note on Sources.

cow moved 'in order to be near his wife in milking it', demonstrate some of the domestic details which landowners were obliged to negotiate with their tenants.[41] Another letter, to the carrier John Young's servant, Catharine Scott, demanding that she return to his service or face being 'apprehended and incarcerated' until she found caution for doing so, shows the particularly vulnerable position of servants, especially women.[42]

On the other hand, we see women as agitators and saboteurs, egging on their husbands to acts of violence in the difficult economic circumstances of the early 1820s the hardship of which for many is evident in Craig's correspondence. Beside the radicalism, we also see women as keen supporters of savings banks which Craig facilitated. Through his banking correspondence and his letters to tenant farmers, the economic challenges that confronted many of Craig's clients are clear. As he sympathised in 1830 with the plight of farmers 'in these dull times' to Mr Clapperton in Caddonlee, he offered words of comfort, noting that apprehended difficulties 'are often greater than in reality they turn out to be' and that the circumstances which combine to produce worry might give place 'to more cheering ideas & prospects'.[43] There is also real and grinding poverty. Craig's activities as a debt enforcer show a combination of sympathy and ruthlessness, often depending on the prospects of payment.

The forces of history are far too nuanced and complex to posit Craig as a sole defining figure in the transformation of Galashiels, any more than such a claim might be made about Dr Douglas; the more prominent manufacturers, the Sandersons, Gills, Cochranes or Lees, or even Scott of Gala. What he has left behind, however, is an important source of information that helps to explain that transformation and which certainly demonstrates his own place in the history not only of the town but of the eastern Borders more generally. As with any lawyer, Craig's life experience carries to some degree the reflection of the experiences of his clients. He was one of what came to be many law and bank agents in nineteenth-century Scotland and, over time, he was surrounded by other professionals of the same type as bank branches expanded. Yet Craig, as a land agent and factor, was particularly attached to his local community in ways many others could scarcely have claimed. His influence, as an adviser, manager and lawyer, was unusually extensive. It gave him the ability to influence his environment in lasting ways and to bring about change, for good or ill, in people's lives.

Epilogue

> The estates of the Leith Banking Company, and of James Ker, Banker, in Leith; Henry Johnston, Banker there, George Craig, Banker in Galashiels, and John Bisset Solicitor in the Supreme Courts of Scotland, the surviving Individual Partners of that Company, and as Individuals, were sequestrated on the 7th day of May 1842.[44]

---

[41] SBA/1303/8/434, Craig/William Colvin, Woolwich, 21 Feb. 1839.
[42] SBA/1303/7/339, Craig/Catharine Scott, Kedzlie, 17 Jan. 1837.
[43] SBA/1303/6/98, Craig/Mr Clapperton, Caddonlee, 28 Aug. 1830.
[44] *The London Gazette*, no. 20099, 13 May 1842, p. 1322.

So runs the beginning of the legal notice signalling what may have been the last significant legal act in Craig's life. Sadly, his correspondence does not exist from this period but it would likely make sad reading. Craig & Rutherford's cash book reveals payments to 'Mr Craig's creditors' in the second half of 1842 and until January 1843. This records Craig's property being sold in lots, including land in Gordon which was auctioned by James Shiels.[45] What happened to the Leith Bank was far from uncommon. Craig himself had been involved on behalf of creditors in more than his share of sequestrations, relying on dividends being announced or compositions offered to satisfy the debts incurred. There is no reason to think that the bank's failure should affect any judgement about Craig's competence: it was a collective failure of management, probably over a number of years, in a very challenging trading environment over which he individually had limited influence.

Craig died in 1843 following a bout of bronchitis, according to Hall, at the age of fifty-nine. The sequestration brought with it financial ruin and had taken a heavy toll on his health and spirit, proving to be 'his death-blow'.[46] He had always been active, being away on his regular trips for several days at a time. He had taken the demands of fairs, long working hours and the 'bustle' of elections, in his stride.[47] He was rarely unwell. While he was confined to bed for ten days in January and February 1836, this was unusual.[48] Given his experience and reputation, financial failure must have weighed particularly heavily upon him.

Craig lies, beside Rev. Robert Douglas and Robert Fyshe, within the vault of the Scotts of Gala ('Gala Aisle') in the parish burial ground not far from his house.[49] His headstone is now unrecognisable. By contrast, grave markings of his predecessor, Bailie Paterson, and his successor, Bailie Hastie, can still be read today. In the case of William Hastie (1806–1849), testimony is given to his 'strict integrity, great ability, and unwearied attention to the interests of the community over which he presided'.[50] Less could hardly have been said of Craig.

Where Craig's house stood, an engraving commemorates the connection of the site to Sir Walter Scott, but Craig himself is not mentioned. Perhaps, like Scott, Craig worked tirelessly to recover his finances and his reputation, but we are unlikely to know. Bankruptcy for lawyers and bankers was a fact of life. In Craig's story, however, we see more than one man. His story is that not of one community but of the different communities with whom he interacted, from clothiers to schoolteachers, from lawyers to clergymen. It also represents the wider story of lawyers and bank agents across Scotland who lived similar lives in this era, men of great local reputation and influence whose lives combined their business with dedication to their community.

This book began by inviting the reader to consider whether a bridge is a fitting tribute to George Craig. It ends the same way.

[45] SBA/1303/9/717 (19 Nov. 1842); SBA/1303/9/718 (6 Dec. 1842).
[46] Hall, *History of Galashiels*, 483.
[47] SBA/1303/8/9, C&R/Robert Laidlaw SSC, 8 Aug. 1837.
[48] SBA/1303/7/154-5, Rutherford/Dr Monro, 2 Feb. 1836.
[49] *The Border Magazine* (Jan. 1900), 4–5. My thanks to John Gray for this reference.
[50] On Hastie see SBA, SBA/83/9; Sanderson, 'Old Galashiels', 26.

Bibliography

Books

Anderson, W. E. K., ed., *Journal of Sir Walter Scott* (Edinburgh, 1998)

Anon. [Alexander Somerville], *The Autobiography of a Working Man* (London, 1848)

Barclay, J. B., *The S.S.C. Story* (Edinburgh, 1984)

Barrie, D., *Police in the Age of Improvement* (Abbingdon, 2008)

Beard, G., *et al.*, ed., *Dictionary of English Furniture Makers 1660–1840* (Leeds, 1986)

Bell, G. J., *Principles of the Law of Scotland* (4th edn, 1839)

Bonnyman, B., *The Third Duke of Buccleuch and Adam Smith: Estate Management and Improvement in Enlightenment Scotland* (Edinburgh, 2014)

Brandeschi, E., *The Hidden History of the Royal Burgh of Lauder* (Selkirk, 2021)

Brown, Iain G., *Frolics in the Face of Europe* (Stroud, 2021)

Cage, R. A., *The Scottish Poor Law 1745–1845* (Edinburgh, 1981)

Cameron, A., *Bank of Scotland 1695–1995* (Edinburgh, 1995)

Campbell, R. H., *Scotland Since 1707* (2nd edn, Edinburgh, 1985)

Chambers, R., *The Picture of Scotland* (Edinburgh, 1827)

Checkland, S. G., *Scottish Banking: A History, 1695–1973* (Glasgow, 1975)

Chisholm, J., *Sir Walter Scott as a Judge* (Edinburgh, 1918)

Cockburn, Henry, *Circuit Journeys*, (Edinburgh, 1888)

Delle, J. A., *The Colonial Caribbean: Landscapes of Power in Jamaica's Plantation System* (Cambridge, 2014)

Dennison, E. P., *The Evolution of Scotland's Towns* (Edinburgh, 2018)

Devine, T. M., ed., *Farm Servants and Labour in Lowland Scotland 1770–1914* (Edinburgh, 1984)

Devine, T. M., ed., *Scottish Emigration and Scottish Society* (Edinburgh, 1992)

Devine, T. M., *Scottish Elites* (Edinburgh, 1994)

Devine, T. M., *The Scottish Nation* (London, 2012)

Devine, T. M., The Scottish Clearances (Milton Keynes, 2018)

Devine, T. M., & R. Mitchison, ed., *People and Society in Scotland*, vol. 1 (Edinburgh, 1988)

Dickson, P. G. M., *The Sun Insurance Office 1710–1960: The History of Two and a Half Centuries of British Insurance* (London, 1960)

Douglas, R., *General View of the Agriculture in the counties of Roxburgh and Selkirk with Observations on the Means of their Improvement* (Edinburgh, 1798)

Finlay, J., ed., *Admission Register of Notaries Public, 1700–1799* (Edinburgh, 2012)

Finlay, J., ed., *Admission Register of Notaries Public, 1800–1899* (Edinburgh, 2018)

Finlay, J., *The Community of the College of Justice* (Edinburgh, 2012)

Finlay, J., *Legal Practice in Eighteenth-century Scotland* (Leiden, 2015)

Fisher, D. R., ed., *The House of Commons 1820–1832* (7 vols, Cambridge: Cambridge University Press, 2009)

Garden, M. G., ed., *Memorials of James Hogg* (3rd edn, Paisley, 1903)

Gilbart, J. W., *A Practical Treatise on Banking* (London, 1927)

Grant, Sir F., *The Faculty of Advocates 1532–1943* (Edinburgh, 1944)

Grierson, H. J. C., ed., *Letters of Sir Walter Scott* (9 vols, London, 1932–1937)

Gulvin, C., *The Tweedmakers* (Newton Abbot, 1973)

Gunn, C. B., ed., *Records of the Baron Court of Stitchill 1655–1807* (Edinburgh, 1905)

Hall, D., and T. Barry, *Spottiswoode: Life and Labour on a Berwickshire Estate (1753–1793)* (East Linton: Tuckwell, 1997)

Hall, Robert, *History of Galashiels* (Galashiels, 1898)

Harper, M., *Adventurers and Exiles: The Great Scottish Exodus* (London, 2003)

Harris, B., & C. McKean, *The Scottish Town in the Age of the Enlightenment 1740–1820* (Edinburgh, 2014)

Higgins, J. P. P., and S. Pollard, *Aspects of Capital Investment in Great Britain, 1750–1850* (London, 1971)

Hughes, G., ed., *The Collected Letters of James Hogg* (Edinburgh University Press, 2004–8)

Jerdan, W., *Autobiography of William Jerdan* (London, 1852)

Kay, John, *A Series of Original Portraits and Caricature Etchings* (2 vols, Edinburgh, 1842)

Kerr, A. W., *History of Banking in Scotland* (London, 1918)

Lang, P. S., *The Langs of Selkirk* (Melbourne, 1910)

Lee., T. A., *Seekers of Truth: The Scottish Founders of Modern Public Accountancy* (Amsterdam, 2006)

Lenman, B., *An Economic History of Modern Scotland 1660–1976* (London, 1977)

Litchfield, H. E., ed., *Emma Darwin, Wife of Charles Darwin. A Century of Family Letters* (2 vols, Cambridge, 1904)

Lockhart, J. G., *Memoirs of the Life of Sir Walter Scott, Bart.* (Edinburgh, 1837)

Logan, W. J., *The Scottish Banker* (Edinburgh, 1839)

Macdougall, I., *All Men are Brethren: Prisoners of War in Scotland, 1803–1814* (Edinburgh, 2008)

Margarey, C., *Unbridling the Tongues of Women: A Biography of Catherine Helen Spence* (Adelaide, 2010)

Matthews, G. K., *Abbotsford and Sir Walter Scott* (London, 1854)

Michie, M., *An Enlightenment Tory in Victorian Scotland: The Career of Sir Archibald Alison* (East Lothian: Tuckwell, 1997)

Milroy, A. W., *Memorials of a Quiet Ministry, Being the Life and Letters of Rev. Andrew Milroy* (London, 1876)

Moffat, A., *Kelsae: A History of Kelso from Earliest Times* (Edinburgh, 2006)

Mitchison, R., *The Old Poor Law in Scotland* (Edinburgh, 2000)

Mitchison, R. & L. Leneman, *Girls in Trouble: Sexuality and Social Control in Rural Scotland 1660–1780* (Edinburgh, 1998)

Mortenson, Terry, *The Great Turning Point* (Arkansas, 2004)

Munn, C. W., *The Scottish Provincial Banking Companies 1747–1864* (Edinburgh, 1981)

Munro, N. *The History of the Royal Bank of Scotland 1727–1927* (Edinburgh, 1928)

Paton, G. C. H., ed., *Baron David Hume's Lectures, 1786–1822* (6 vols, Edinburgh, Stair Society, 1939–1958)

Phillips, M., *A History of Banks, Bankers and Banking in Northumberland, Durham and North Yorkshire* (London, 1894)

Prentis, M., *The Scots in Australia* (Sydney, 2008)

Pressnell, L. S., *Country Banking in the Industrial Revolution* (Oxford, 1956)

Pringle, Alexander, *The Records of the Pringles or Hoppringills of the Scottish Border* (Edinburgh, 1933)

Rankine, J., *A Treatise on the Law of Leases* (Edinburgh, 1916)

Reavely, G., *A Medley, History, Directory and Discovery of Galashiels* (Galashiels, 1875)

Robertson, C. J. A., *The Origins of the Scottish Railway System 1722–1844* (Edinburgh, 1983)

Romanes, R., *Lauder: A Series of Papers* (privately printed, 1903)

Ross, H. E., ed., *Letters from Rupert's Land 1826–1840: James Hargrave of the Hudson's Bay Company* (Montreal, 2009)

Russell, John, *The Story of Leith* (Edinburgh, 1922)

Rutherford, W., *Galashiels in History* (Galashiels, 1930)

Ryan, R., 'The Norwich Union and the British fire insurance market in the early nineteenth century' in O. M. Westall, ed., *The Historian and the Business of Insurance* (Manchester, 1984)

Spence, C. H., *Tenacious of the Past: The Recollections of Helen Brodie*, ed. J. King & G. Tulloch (Adelaide, 1994)

Urquhart, R. M., *The Burghs of Scotland and the Burgh Police (Scotland) Act 1833* (Motherwell, 1989)

Veitch, William, ed., *James Russell, Reminiscences of Yarrow by the Late James Russell D.D., Minister of Yarrow* (Selkirk: George Lewis & Son, 1894)

Whetstone, Ann E., *Scottish County Government in the Eighteenth and Nineteenth Centuries* (Edinburgh, 1981)

Whyte, I. D., *Scotland and the Abolition of Black Slavery* (Edinburgh, 2007)

Wilkie, B., *The Scots in Australia, 1788–1838* (Suffolk, 2017)

Young, J. F., ed., *J. F. Catherine Helen Spence: An Autobiography* (Adelaide, 1910)

Articles/book chapters

Bennet, R., 'An awful and impressive spectacle; crime scene execution in Scotland' 21 (2017) *Crime, History and Societies*, 101

Boot, H. M., 'Salaries and career earnings in the Bank of Scotland, 1730–1880' 44 (1991) *Economic History Review*, 629

Cairns, J. W., 'The definition of slavery in eighteenth-century thinking' in J. Allain, *The Legal Understanding of Slavery* (Oxford, 2012), 61–84

Cairns, J. W., 'After *Somerset*: the Scottish experience' 33 (2012) *Journal of Legal History*, 291–312

Cairns, J. W., 'Slavery without a *Code Noir*: Scotland 1700–1778' in F. M. Larkin & N. N. Dawson, ed., *Lawyers, the Law and History* (Dublin, 2013)

Cairns, J. W., 'Importing enslaved Africans into Eighteenth-Century Scotland', in *Deutsches, Europäisches und Vergleichendes Wirtschaftsrecht: Festschrift für Werner Ebke zum 70*, ed, B. Paal *et al.* (Munich, 2021)

Cameron, Ewen, A., 'Education in rural Scotland, 1696–1872' in R. Anderson *et al.*, *The Edinburgh History of Education in Scotland* (Edinburgh, 2015)

Cowan, E. J., Cowan, 'From the Southern Uplands from Southern Ontario', in T. M. Devine, ed., *Scottish Emigration and Scottish Society* (Edinburgh, 1992) 61–83

Devine, T. M., 'Did slavery make Scotia great?' 4 (2001) *Britain and the World*, 40–64.

Dodgshon, R.A., 'Land improvement in Scottish farming: marl and lime in Roxburghshire and Berwickshire in the eighteenth century' 26 (1978) *British Agricultural History Society*, 4

Ferguson, W., 'The Reform Act (Scotland) of 1832: intention and effect' 45 (1966) *Scottish Historical Review*, 105.

Finlay, J., 'The lower branch of the legal profession in early modern Scotland' 11 (2007) *Edinburgh Law Review*, 31–61.

Finlay, J., 'Scots lawyers and House of Lords appeals in Eighteenth-century Britain' 32 (2011) *Journal of Legal History*, 249–277

Finlay, J., '"Tax the attornies!" Stamp duty and the Scottish legal profession in the eighteenth century' 34 (2014) *Journal of Scottish Historical Studies*, 141–166

Garside, P., 'James Hogg's Fifty Pounds' 1 (1990) *Studies in Hogg and his World*, 128–32

Garside, P., 'Three Perils in Publishing' 2 (1991) *Studies in Hogg and his World*, 45–63.

Hall, C., '"The Most Unbending Conservative in Britain": Archibald Alison and Pro-Slavery Discourse' in T. M. Devine, ed., *Recovering Scotland's Slavery Past: The Caribbean Connection*, (Edinburgh, 2015)

Harris, B., 'Cultural change in Scottish towns' 54 (2011) *The Historical Journal*, 105

Hurl-Eamon, J. 'Did Soldiers Really Enlist to Desert Their Wives? Revisiting the Martial Character of Marital Desertion in Eighteenth-Century London' (2014) 53 *Journal of British Studies*, 356.

Hutchison, G. D., '"A distant and whiggish country": the Conservative party and Scottish elections, 1832–1837' 93 (2020) *Historical Research* 333

Jeffrey-Cook, John, 'William Pitt and his taxes' (2010) *British Tax Review*, 376–91

Levack, B. P., 'The prosecution of sexual crimes in early eighteenth century Scotland' 89 (2010) *Scottish Historical Review*, 172

Love, W. R. F., 'G.K.E. Fairholme, Gentleman, Scholar and Squatter' 12 (1984) *Journal of the Royal Historical Society of Queensland*

Macintyre, I., 'Alexander Monro tertius (1773–1859) 43 (2012) *Journal of the Royal College of Physicians of Edinburgh*, 282

Ritchie, J. N. G., 'James Curle (1862–1944) and Alexander Ormiston Curle (1866–1955): pillars of the establishment' 132 (2002) *Proc Soc Antiq Scot*, 19, 20.

Robson, M., 'The Border farm worker' in T. M. Devine, ed., *Farm Servants and Labour in Lowland Scotland 1770–1914* (Edinburgh, 1984) 71–96.

Rosner, L., 'Monro, Alexander, tertius (1773–1859) *Oxford Dictionary of National Biography* (Oxford, 2004)

Theses and unpublished material

Allfrey, P. D., 'Arms and the (tax)man: the use and taxation of armorial bearings in Britain, 1798–1944' (University of Dundee, D.Phil. Thesis, 2016)

Duncan, J. S., 'The Royal Burgh of Peebles in the nineteenth century: the impact of a locally organised railway on a moribund Scottish county town' (The Open University, Ph.D. Thesis, 2005)

Ferguson, W., 'Electoral law and Procedure in Eighteenth and Early Nineteenth Century Scotland' (University of Glasgow, Ph.D Thesis, 1957)

Krichtal, A., 'Liverpool and the Raw Cotton Trade: A study of the port and its merchant community 1790–1815' (University of Wellington, M.A. Thesis, 2013)

Leitch, A., 'Radicalism in Paisley 1830–1848 and its economic, political, cultural background' (M. University of Glasgow, M.Litt. Thesis, 1993)

Mullen, S., 'The Glasgow West India interest: integration, collaboration and exploitation in the British Atlantic World, 1776–1846' (University of Glasgow, Ph.D. Thesis, 1995)

Oliver, S. C., 'The administration of urban society in Scotland 1800–50, with reference to the Growth of Civil Government in Glasgow and its suburbs' (University of Glasgow, Ph.D. Thesis, 1995)

Sanderson, Elizabeth M. C., 'Old Galashiels 1793–1884: Its transition from village to industrial town' (1980) [SBA/83/9]

Index of names

Index of places

Index of subjects

EU representative:
Easy Access System Europe
Mustamäe tee 50, 10621 Tallinn, Estonia
Gpsr.requests@easproject.com

www.ingramcontent.com/pod-product-compliance
Lightning Source LLC
Chambersburg PA
CBHW061244220326
41599CB00028B/5532